Trading with the Enemy

Trading with the Enemy

A Yankee Travels through

Castro's Cuba

TOM MILLER

BasicBooks
A Division of HarperCollins Publishers

Grateful acknowledgment is made for permission to reprint material from the following:

Excerpt from "The New Woman," by Nicholás Guillén. Translation by Vera M. Kutzinski copyright © 1987 by Charles H. Rowell. Reprinted by permission.

GUANTANAMERA, original lyrics and music by José Fernández Diaz, music adaptation by Pete Seeger and Julian Orbon, Words by José Martí, lyric adaption by Julian Orbon.

Excerpt from "Bars," by Nicolás Guillén, taken from ¡Patria o Muerte! The Great Zoo & Other Poems, by Nicolás Guillén. Copyright © 1972 by Robert Márquez. Reprinted by permission of Monthly Review Foundation.

Excerpt from "Tropicollage" by Carlos Varela, translation by Luis Acosta. Copyright © 1988 by The Center for Cuban Studies. Reprinted by permission.

Excerpt from "Elegia de María Belén Chacón" by Emilio Ballagas. Copyright © 1965 Unión de Escritores y Artistas de Cuba.

Portions of this book originally appeared in The Washington Post, The Miami Herald, El Nuevo Herald, and Islands magazine.

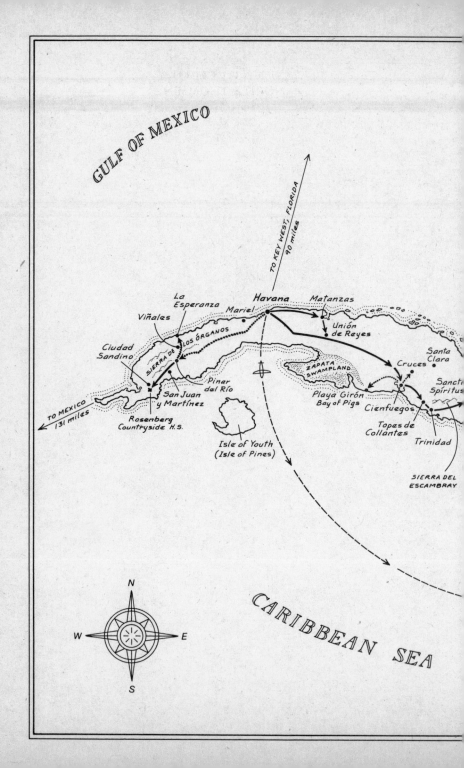

GULF OF MEXICO

TO KEY WEST, FLORIDA
90 miles

Havana · Matanzas
La Esperanza · Unión de Reyes
Viñales · Mariel
SIERRA DE LOS ÓRGANOS
Ciudad Sandino · Santa Clara · Cruces
Pinar del Río · ZAPATA SWAMPLAND · Sancti Spíritus
San Juan y Martínez · Playa Girón Bay of Pigs · Cienfuegos
TO MEXICO 131 miles · Rosenberg Countryside H.S. · Topes de Collantes · Trinidad
Isle of Youth (Isle of Pines) · SIERRA DEL ESCAMBRAY

N
W   E
S

CARIBBEAN SEA

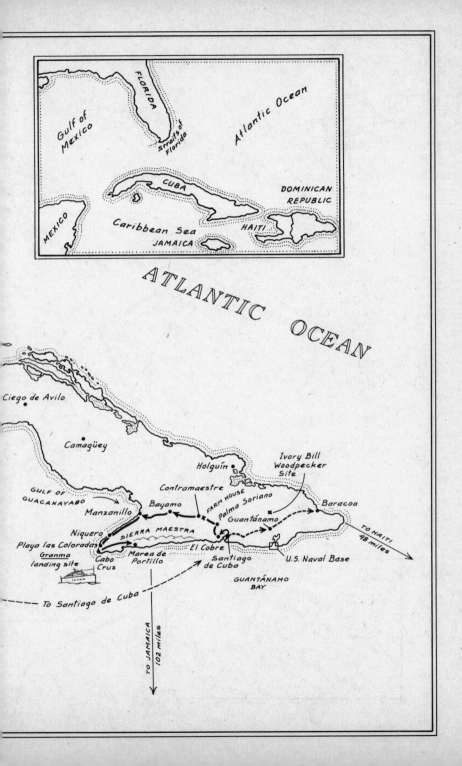

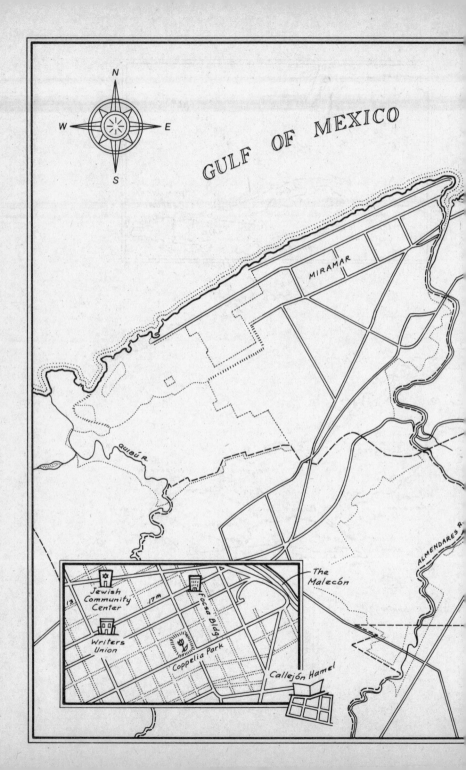

GULF OF MEXICO

MIRAMAR

QUIBÚ R.

ALMENDARES R.

The Malecón

Jewish Community Center

17th

Focsa Bldg

Writers Union

Coppelia Park

Callejón Hamel

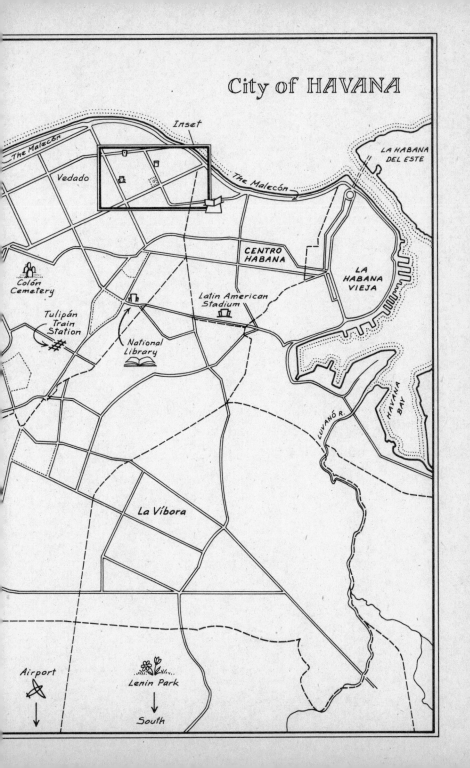

City of HAVANA

The Malecón

Vedado

Inset

The Malecón

LA HABANA DEL ESTE

CENTRO HABANA

Colón Cemetery

Tulipán Train Station

National Library

Latin American Stadium

LA HABANA VIEJA

LUYANÓ R.

HAVANA BAY

La Víbora

Airport

Lenin Park

South

Introduction to the
Paperback Edition

Bill Clinton, Boris Yeltsin, and Fidel Castro are having lunch one day with God at a fancy French restaurant. "God," Clinton asks, "will the United States ever be rid of discrimination and hatred?"

"Yes, it will," God responds with a nod to the President. "But not in your lifetime."

"Well," says Yeltsin, "will Russia ever be corruption free, with enough food on the table for everyone?"

"Yes, that will happen, Boris, but not in your lifetime."

Castro asks, "God, will the goals of the glorious Cuban revolution ever come to pass?"

"Yes, in fact they will," God tells the surprised Fidel. "But not in my lifetime."

Fidel Castro and his government, by crossbreeding nationalism with patriotism, by authoritarian wiles, and by masterfully manipulating their only enemy left in the world, have now held sway close to four full decades. Elizabeth Windsor had only been queen of England for seven years when the remarkable reign of Fidel Castro began. Hussein had been Jordan's monarch for a mere six years at the time. Most Cubans, regardless of age, background, or attitude, can recall a time when they were enthusiastic supporters of Castro. He wiped clean the slate and tried to begin his country's life anew, not just in the wealth of its land but in its people, their self-esteem, how they acquired goods, and how they apportioned their gains. Old values were smothered or outlawed, new ones were planted and nurtured—and imposed. The revolution changed the lives of everyone; it greatly improved the lot of many and overpowered the fortunes of others. In that first decade of frenzied activity, intellectual life went through convolutions, education and health became vigorous pursuits, and bold experiments played out in agriculture and industry. The bureaucracy bloated and its arteries hardened.

For its singular success, Castro's revolution immediately drew admirers impressed by Cuba's new wardrobe and those who fashioned it. Prime ministers, labor leaders, and leftist practitioners formed a steady stream of visitors in the opening years. Foreign writers, filmmakers, and artists found the atmosphere intoxicating. Entire sectors of the country's economy went topsy-turvy, while Che Guevara tested his theory of the New Man who valued collective well-being over personal gain. Cuba was indeed the place to be. In fact, if my reckoning is correct, there were a few weeks in that first year when the following all overlapped in Havana at the same time: Guevara (born in Argentina), Erroll Flynn (Australia), Graham Greene (Britain), Hemingway (U.S.), and Castro (Cuba). Could ever a city in heat boast such an assortment of international wild cards?

I talked about this with Jesús, a friend and literary *compañero,* as we walked through Havana's Parque Central in the summer of 1995. I had met Jesús while researching this book, and made a point of visiting him and his family with each successive trip. In recent years, Cubans had suffered mightily for their country's allegiance to Soviet assistance and Jesús had watched Havana's decay accelerate. "I hope something happens to save this city before it's too late," he said sadly as we passed a gaggle of baseball fanatics dissecting the humiliating defeat Cuba had suffered at the hands of the United States team the night before. As they reenacted key plays, the crowd concluded that Cuba lost because they had brought aging stars to the series and left their younger, sharper players home.

A bus given to Havana by the City of Montreal rolled by; Jesús noted its placard said "Metro Sud." Another bus, adoringly called "the little yellow school bus" as if it were a flop-eared cocker spaniel, became symbolic in the occasional tug-of-war between Cuba and its northern neighbor. It was a clunker used to haul kids, brought to the island from a Mexican port by Pastors for Peace, a U.S. organization that ships humanitarian goods to Cuba and other needy countries. When U.S. Customs refused it passage out of the States, attention focused on the whys and wherefores of a foreign policy so cruel as to deny Cuban children a ride to school. All this was too much for one leading Cuban intellectual. "People are raising funds to send us buses in cities all over Latin America, Europe, and even your country. They think they're doing us a favor, but they usually send these broken down, end of the line buses. The donors feel so heartwarm about it, then we end up spending all of our time and money repairing them. It'd be better if they just sent us the money so we could buy good new ones." U.S. Customs eventually relented, and the little yellow school bus soon rolled up to its new home at Havana's Martin Luther King Center.

* * *

The best place to probe the island's health is still the Malecón, Havana's lovely seaside boulevard. Sitting on the seawall one can imagine, without much difficulty, Key West, just beyond the horizon ninety miles and close to forty years away. Comfortable hotels on the Malecón with facilities for foreigners are nearby. Between them lie crowded apartments in such advanced states of decay that even the ghosts of their once-impressive character have moved on. The Young Communists League has opened a number of snack bars along the Malecón, and often stages open-air dances. A flea market has sprung up not far from the Riviera Hotel selling used books, pre-revolution major league baseball cards, folk art, leather crafts, and snacks. Independent taxi drivers, illegal but fairly public, gather nearby, ready to shepherd foreigners through town for dollars in their old Chevys.

At night, hopeful prostitutes line First Street next to the Riviera, looking for foreigners to take them nightclubbing at the Palacio de la Salsa. A *rubia tiñida*—bleached blonde—confused by my accent, which she couldn't identify, said, "Oh, you must be Mexican. Most of the other girls here don't like to go with them, but I just *love* Mexicans." The well-reputed appeal of *cubanas* once prompted Castro to declare, "The only thing we don't plan to export are our women. I want that to be clear."

Widespread prostitution in Cuba has kindled heated debate over its return. "It's good for the economy," a man explained. "These women come from homes that otherwise would have no access to dollars. A prostitute earning hard currency benefits as many as ten others Cubans who normally live only on pesos." Most simply say that the money earned from prostitution is a dire necessity and a damn shame.

A spit-and-polish new Fiat dealership shadows all the piecemeal developments along the Malecón. This brightly lit showroom resembles First World new car outlets. In the long-range plans for Havana, a city founded in 1519, surely Malecón storefront property plays a role. It is not unthinkable to imagine the restoration of the crumbled apartment houses with upscale retail outlets, sidewalk cafes, and ATM machines at street level and gentrified apartments above. Oceanfront footage along this splendid roadway will sell to the first and highest bidders. Yet in an economy unaccustomed to evaluating property solely for its commercial potential, the identity of this high-profile stretch of pavement will be determined by those who keep an eye on its character as well as its profit. In a decade, will the Malecón resemble

Barcelona's Ramblas, the boardwalk at Venice Beach (California), or Coney Island? The new Fiat showroom may lead the way.

Cuba's economy has become a patchwork of minor operations here, major surgery there, a cha-cha-cha in the distance, a swivel of the hips enticingly close. The street has led the state. When dollars were abundant but illegal, Castro reluctantly legalized them. When families ran clandestine living room restaurants, called *paladares,* and tradesmen plied their skills without permission, the government licensed them. So much produce from the countryside made its extralegal way into city kitchens that a more profit-motivated, direct system of distribution was put in place. Moonlighting government electricians installed clandestine rooftop satellite dishes for home television viewing; authorities scrambled the international signals, then offered to sell converter boxes. When Cubans saved a growing amount of foreign money from tourism and overseas relatives, their government allowed dollar bank accounts. When curbside money-changers dominated hard currency flow, the state established formal exchange houses at the free market rate. When hundreds, then thousands of young Cubans took off on rafts for the daring trip north, their government, ultimately, neither stopped nor chastised them. Some, near the U.S. Navy base at Guantánamo Bay, tried to swim from Cuban land to the base. The father of one successful swimmer handed me a letter to mail to his daughter in Florida. Why did she go? "You know. Youth. She's been talking about the United States for a long time. It was always, 'They do this there, they do that there.' It's clothes. Things like that. She knows a little English. Every day she'd say, 'Good morning, Father. How are you?' "

What's happened in Cuba is a tragedy; sadness lives under every palm tree. To the extent that the U.S. embargo is at fault for Cuba's tropical depression, blame lies squarely in Washington. Yet the embargo began in 1962, and except for tightening a couple of ratchets more than three decades later, it is the same embargo that Cuba endured during its high flying years. The sugar harvest ending in 1995 netted 3.3 million tons, the lowest yield in three decades. Ten years ago Cuba was a world leader in sugar exports; now it struggles just to get its crop to port.

Castro-bashing legislation such as Congress imposed after Cuba shot down interloping pilots in early 1996 emboldens embargo boosters. The new law has become a post-hole digger, emplanting animosity yet deeper in the ground. We have become accustomed to the spectacle of politicians promoting worse relations with a close neighbor. The terrible circumstances besieging Cuba in mid-decade have not been brought on by the omnipresent embargo but rather the rapid disintegration of Soviet communism. The hammer and sickle on the old Soviet flag, Fidel Castro has lamented, is now gone. "I've stopped looking at flags because I've seen so many people changing flags like they change their shirts that you can't keep up," he told a student group. "I prefer to wait until they put the hammer and sickle back on a lot of flags, that would be the best."

Families lay out their heirlooms, libraries, and anything that might have monetary value for reluctant sale to knowing foreigners. These downtown sidewalk bargains put rare dollars in peso pockets. Some sellers stick to one item and tend to group together. The used-book stalls at La Plaza de Armas have become a favorite haunt for me, tracking down obscure and rare tomes from Cuba's grand literary history. A year and a half after I casually named a title I was seeking to one antiquarian book dealer at La Plaza de Armas, he nonchalantly approached me with a copy of the book as if it had simply been the following weekend. I coveted most the complete works of José Martí, a twenty-seven-volume series published over an eight-year period. I had seen it selling for three hundred dollars new, and was prepared to pay well for a used set in good condition. Two days after Jesús put the word out, we got a bid: eighteen dollars for all twenty-seven volumes. "Does this fellow know what he's doing?" I asked incredulously. "José Martí's works lie at the heart of every home library in the country. This man is selling his literary patrimony for peanuts. Is he that desperate for dollars?"

He was.

Foreign columnists and overseas politicians still wait for the collapse of Cuba's economy. They are too late. Cuba's economy capsized in the middle of 1993, when a stiff Caribbean breeze could have knocked over the entire government. Fuel was doled out in eyedroppers and food could be measured in ounces and teaspoons. Dollars were legalized then, and the ills of capitalism set upon the scourge of communism. All of socialism's five-year plans, financial forecasts, production quotas, monetary manipulation, and state-driven economics went out to sea. With hard currency came entrepreneurs, farming cooperatives, foreign investments, and private employment. Castro has approved each of these steps with great public reticence. The high-profile accumulation of dollars by some makes the poverty of the rest all the more intolerable. For a society accustomed to reasonable equality, having some people

obviously with and others notably without creates a strain just beginning to be felt. You can already see some *mendigos*—homeless beg-
gars—sleep in the portals of churches. Magda, who for years taught
Spanish literature at a military school in the Havana suburbs, furtively
sold me black market bread on a street of otherwise licensed food
vendors. She lives with her son, a medical student. Most of her family
left the country in the 1970s. "Since they've gone I haven't heard one
word from them. Not one." She says of Fidel, "What can he do? He's
trying." Yet now, more Cubans are loyal to the U.S. dollar than to
their own president.

   Initiative and creativity, aggressiveness and inventiveness, these are
the long-dormant qualities that separate those who can plan their food
supply days ahead of time and those who scramble for their next meal.
One man makes furniture using scavenged wood, selling enough living
room sets to support an extended family. Nearby a woman despairs
that her household's monthly government ration won't keep them in
beans and rice more than two weeks, and her husband's monthly salary
of one hundred eighty pesos will buy them only another day, perhaps
two, of meals. Street scams and sophisticated hustles have become
steps on the stile from a socialist state to a market economy. Whether
along the Prado in Habana Vieja, in the Hotel Victoria lobby bar, or
behind closed doors in a government ministry, deals, bargains, and
compromises are the rule of the day. Financially, Cuba is going through
its Cambrian explosion, adapting skeletal architecture to its formless
anatomy. In today's Cuba, the high end is getting higher and the low
end lower. When diners at El Ajibe hear a soft, stuttering ring, half
the foreign businessmen and high-level Cuban functionaries reach for
their cellular phones. At stoplights near major hotels young boys rush
out to wipe windshields, begging for a pittance. Fire-breathers have
not yet arrived. Economically, Cuba has already entered the post-
Castro era.

Visit Cuba now because it will never again be the same. What has
happened there since 1959 is unprecedented. The lay of the land has
changed severely—its terrain, its rhythms, the flow of its money, and
its sense of identity. The Caribbean's largest island is changing radi-
cally, economically first and, inescapably, politically to follow. Castro's
Cuba has been a remarkable experiment whose achievements and suc-
cesses have overwhelmed and astounded, and whose gross miscalcula-
tions and colossal failures have disillusioned and inflamed. And because
it will never happen again, it's worth seeing before too much more

remodeling takes place. You will never regret a firsthand view of Cuba while Fidel Castro remains its leader.

The driver of a gypsy taxi swore he would never again use black market gasoline. "It used to be you knew who got it for you, but now everybody's doing it. Sometimes they dilute the gas with alcohol or other additives. I only trade on the black market when I have to. There are too many thieves out there now." Rationed gas, which comes to about a half-tank a month, has been superseded by a nationwide chain of brightly lit filling stations, infused with Panamanian money, selling gas to anyone with dollars.

The taxista dropped me off at a cultural center where I paid five pesos to see Los Bufomaniacos, a campy two-man comedy group, and Anacaona, a sexy twelve-woman band with bass guitar, two saxophones, a flute, lots of percussion, and a stunning six-foot mulatta trombone player who managed to hit every note while dancing a mean salsa. The following day I took Jesús to dinner in a private living room. For eight dollars total, this *paladar* served terrific pizza and a beer. The co-owner used her two words of English as she put our pies on the table: "Chicago style." The *paladares*—reasonably priced for tourists, not prohibitively pricey for Cubans—are now licensed, and crop up on every block. Across from the pizzeria were two more *paladares*; one run by a former Cubana airlines stewardess, and the other by a fading soap-opera actress.

Despite the law, some home restaurants remain without a license, which would require them to pick up supplies from government dispensaries. "If I were to get my ingredients from the state distributor," said one successful *paladar* owner, "they'd be overpriced, underweight, late in coming, and second-rate. Now I've got regular suppliers who come to my door from the countryside. I trust them." A former X-ray technician, lanky and clean-shaven, introduced me to the owner of another *paladar*. This one specialized in pork dishes. "We pay five hundred pesos a month for our government license," the proprietor said. "The inspector from the Department of Hygiene and Epidemiology makes surprise visits. If he finds something out of order we have to pay a one thousand five hundred peso fine." Has that ever happened? I asked. "No, no. We just give him a hundred pesos to look the other way."

The fellow who brought me to the *paladar* has followed the path of millions of Latin Americans migrating to their capital cities when their families in the provinces run out of money. He and his niece came from Santiago de Cuba and rented a one-and-a-half-room, twenty-dollar-a-month hovel that remains unfurnished save for a couple of mattresses, a television, and a refrigerator. Every time they climb the stairs to their second-floor flat, they must duck a web of live electrical wires that hang precariously low from the ceiling. They had been in the capital a year.

"The people of Havana, they think they're so superior. Fidel and Raúl are from the Oriente like us. That's where revolutions start, you know. Here, we sell cigars and *artisanía* like beaded necklaces and earrings. My niece peddles them on the street and at La Plaza de la Catedral. With the money we make, we can support our relatives and have enough to replenish our stock here. We fly back to Santiago every few weeks for one hundred pesos each way. We go standby, but if you slip the man three dollars you can always get on." He looked through the open-air window at the fifty other dwellings that open onto a common cement courtyard. "The officials have their cars, their fancy homes. Look, we have one light bulb in the entire place. We're the ones who are keeping this country going. We're the true communists."

Those who don't speak of bribing bureaucrats talk of spiritual corruption. "That's what's changed most," says a woman who has considered herself a revolutionary since the mid-1950s. "From the outside it looks great, this new foreign investment policy. Look at all the money pouring in! But to those of us who live here, we're saddened because they're selling our country from under us as fast as they can. And we can't even buy into it. We have no capital to invest in our own *patria*." How, I asked, does she see Cuba in the year 2000? "The end of the century? I don't even know how it will look the end of this week. *Mira,* I know I'm to see someone at his house in one hour. Beyond that, I cannot make plans. Tomorrow? Who knows. Everything could change by then. We could be out of gas. Or electricity. We may not be allowed on the streets. My friend may be called into the service. They have robbed more than our land. They have robbed our spirit."

A *muchacho* gets hold of some spray paint and begins to color a wall with the word *down*. He looks over his shoulder, sees no one, and paints *with*. Just as he starts the third word with an *F*, a state security man taps him on the shoulder. "Oh, am I glad to see you!" the youth says, turning around. "How do you spell that man's name? Is it Flinton or Clinton?"

* * *

Cuba, since the inception of the Farmers Markets and other street fairs, has given the illusion of progress. And for those who accumulate dollars that can be the case. But for the vast majority who fix flat bicycle tires for a living, grab rides on the backs of trucks, or have been let go during massive layoffs at work centers—and even those who weren't—the main currency is envy. Food comes from the countryside to outdoor markets at peso prices that would swallow a quarter of a month's salary for a family of four's dinner of ham, sweet potato, and avocados. "Before, there was money in the streets but no food," a housewife said sorrowfully as she fed her family their pitifully inadequate rations. "Now, there's food, but we have no money." Peek inside her pre-revolution Kelvinator and you'd think her family dines on ice cubes.

During a 1994 visit I rented an apartment on Concordia street in Centro Habana. The neighborhood was in the middle of a scheduled eight-hour blackout. Just blocks away in the next electrical grid life went at its normal, syncopated pace, but in my neighborhood, whole families sat in whispered silhouette on their front stoop. Candles shone through windows. A lone, independent vendor walked down Concordia with a wooden tray strapped around her neck yelling three indecipherable syllables. My ear is always cocked to pick up new phrases in Cuban street Spanish, but this woman's cries sounded like doo-wah-diddy to me. I nudged my companion and indicated the vendor. "Oh, her? She's selling homemade hamburgers. She's saying, 'McDonald's. McDonald's.'" Brand name identity will not be a problem when franchise food comes a-knockin'.

A more problematic import for Cuba remains American culture. The United States Information Service mounted an enormous photographic exhibit, underwritten by the Time Warner Corporation, of life in black America. The poster-size photographs, taken by Afro-Americans, were sharp and friendly. The theme was realistically handled, the message was entirely aboveboard: black America has severe problems, unquestionable joys, internal pleasures, and rough going. For non-blacks, it was a healthy look across the borderline, and for Cubans, whose black and mulatto citizenry far outnumbers its white population, it would have been a welcome and reasonably accurate look north.

The exhibit, destined for scores of countries throughout the world, was offered to Cuba for a month's public display. Casa de las Americas, the logical venue for such a show, turned it down. By happenstance one afternoon after a gallery opening at Casa de las Americas, its director, Roberto Fernández Retamar, met up with Catherine Moses, a functionary from the USIS office in Havana. For fifteen minutes they danced around the issue, she properly representing her government's point of view and he his. Her argument: This is a fantastic exhibit, one that Cubans could well understand, it's not at all propagandistic or belligerent, and it would speak well for both countries. It's free; all you have to do is unpack it and hang it. His retort: "Everything you say is true, but it comes with a string attached—you require us to say that it comes courtesy of the USIS." If it were a loan from the Smithsonian Institution, he said, or the Museum of Modern Art, he would have taken it in a Havana minute. But USIS's bureaucratic twin, the United States Information Agency, oversees Radio and Television Martí, two broadcast outlets whose goal has been to bring about the collapse of Cuba's government. To accept a generous gift from the left hand while the right hand tries to stab you would be untenable. "This we could not do."

The erudite Retamar, a former diplomat and relentless cultural emissary, danced a conga line of arguments around poor Catherine Moses. He was bright and sharp, caustic and witty. (He was also playing to his audience of a dozen onlookers.) Moses gamely countered with the USIS position, yet if Retamar danced circles around her, she refused to leave the dance floor. It was no contest; nevertheless, it was the first time in memory that officials from both countries carried on a public dialogue. Lightning struck neither of them down.

Talk about history repeating itself. What worries Cubans most these days is not an American invasion, either military or financial, but a Spanish takeover. A century after a protracted and gruesome war to rid the island of Spanish rule, a mix of shrewd and haute Spaniards are again riding herd, buying up hotels and investing in industries. Their displays of wealth in a country suspicious of ostentation coupled with their historical role as colonial masters makes them the current bad guys Cuba can't do without.

While vacationing Spaniards arrive by the planeful for sand and sex, American blockade-busters come in through the side door by way of Canada, Mexico, or the Caribbean. Some selflessly give their time and talent to artistic, scientific, or social efforts. Others bring Saturday night values with them: at José Martí International Airport in late 1995 I met a well-to-do Miami restaurateur who bragged that he had just pissed away some three thousand dollars within a few days on freelance guides, beautiful women, fancy clothes to dress them in, expensive rental cars, classy restaurants, and lavish tips. Everything he did, from entering Cuba through a third country to returning home with aged rum and fine cigars, violated the embargo. Could Cuba handle planefulls of similarly inclined American visitors—in short, are Cubans ready for Batista-era tourism? Probably not, but I suspect they're willing to try.

Tourists have virtually complete freedom to travel anywhere in the country, speak with whomever they want, and leave as much money behind as they care to. They take in the obvious destinations—the Hemingway Museum, the beaches of Varadero, the Tropicana Cabaret, and perhaps a ballet or play. Yet the greatest joys have always been on foot in neighborhoods and towns far from the international centers, where the pace slows from allegro to adagio. Rare is the visitor who does not return home with the address of newly made Cuban friends whom he or she will stay in touch with, perhaps send essentials to, or contemplate the fate of.

These snapshots remain from trips to the island's midsection: An old car that looked not much bigger than a go-cart sat on José Mendoza street in the colonial town of Trinidad. As I slowly took in its odd dimension, Nelson Borrell Martínez approached. "Do you like it? It's mine." He dashed inside his house to get its pedigree papers and a key. It was a 1923 King Midget, made in Athens, Ohio. Borrell unlocked the chain that tethered the Midget to a dormant power pole, literally cranked it up, and drove it down the street. "It uses as much fuel as a lighter," he said on his return. New, the car cost $770.

On a Sunday morning in Cienfuegos, a city not far away, a retired seventy-six-year-old dock worker and his wife walked home from picking up their ration of rice. His forty-year-old son had died of alcoholism a few months earlier. "I blame the current situation," he said. "Of course he was an alcoholic before and he was going to die a young death anyway, but in the last year he had taken to homemade rotgut. That's what did him in. Two more years like this and we'll all die of hunger." His wife quickly disagreed. "I fought in the revolution," he continued. "Things were worse before." He looked at his wife. "We'll see what happens."

Strauss waltzes rode the soft breezes of Palmira, a small town on a rural road north of Cienfuegos. The music came from a twenty-five-piece band, practicing for a concert the following Thursday in the town plaza. The musicians, all middle-aged or retired men except for a woman clarinet player, perform five times a year. In the midst of national hunger, these civic-minded musicians gathered weekly to blow life into woefully aged instruments and bring a measure of joy to their paisanos. "It's what we do," said Felipe, the sixty-four-year-old flutist and town barber, by way of explanation.

Modern Cuban transportation: a bicyclist holding on to the stirrup of a friend's horse as the latter clopped down a Sancti Spiritus street pulling the former.

Back in Havana, at a nightclub primarily for Cubans, the five-dollar midnight stage show featured transvestites enthusiastically simulating sex with a man randomly pulled from the crowd. As the country reached its statistical doldrums, its citizens hooted and howled at crossdressers in ribald splendor.

Some of the brouhaha about Cuba in Congress, the White House, and among media executives has centered around establishing news bureaus in Havana. Fortunately, coverage from Cuba has strengthened in recent years. For a long time, neither Castro's government nor visiting journalists were prepared to pass on impressions and information intelligently. "The average reporter is as well-equipped to discuss the complexities of Cuba and the nuances of Castro's personality," wrote Norman Mailer in pre-embargo 1962, "as a horse is equipped to teach syntax." Mailer suggested that Fidel let a passel of American writers roam the countryside and write their impressions. He recommended eighteen authors, among them Saul Bellow, James Baldwin, John Steinbeck, J. D. Salinger, and Truman Capote. No such delegation went, of course, but the results would have been intriguing. It might have helped demystify the country before the embargo set in, and given meat to bony reports that have filtered back since.

The best coverage of Cuba of late has appeared not under literary bylines or on network television. It has, instead, graced the comics page of American newspapers, where Zippy, a sort of Zen/dada clown, visited the island for a few weeks. Zippy and Griffy, the cartoonist Bill Griffith's alter ego, travel through the country, absorbing Cuba in mid-crisis. "I keep meeting Cubans who are extremely critical of their government," says Griffy, "but still remain idealistic about socialism—are they just kidding themselves? And why do I have this big lump in my throat?" With Zippy and Griffy as their guides, Americans saw a soft, sad, and friendly Cuba, one full of fierce sentiment and raw emotion. "If I think about it much longer I'm going to cry."

Both countries emphasize the harshness of the other in their public media. When the U.S. Congress considered the Helms-Burton bill, billboards in Havana shouted the legislators' names, linked by a swastika. In the United States, predicting the fall of Fidel has always been an op-ed page staple. It's also the fastest way to lose credibility, and in recent years headline writers have competed for this dubious status, even when the articles themselves haven't warranted funereal drumbeats: "Fidel Castro's Last Battle" (*U.S. News & World Report*), "The Last Days of Castro's Cuba" (*New York Times Magazine*), "Castro's Cuba—The End of the Dream" (*Time*), "Cuba's Living Death" (*Newsweek*), "Waiting for the End in Cuba" (*Life*), and the egregiously titled 1992 book, *Castro's Final Hour*.

When my book first circulated among magazine editors for excerpt consideration, one possibility was a Hearst publication. Hearst, which drummed up a frenzy for American intervention in Cuba in 1898, invented the phrase, "Remember the *Maine,* to hell with Spain." A Hearst editor sent me back a most curious note of regret: "I'm sorry that our house policy is hands-off where Cuba is concerned." Here was a media empire whose foreign policy had changed 180° in one century.

More disconcerting was a report from a fellow who wrote about his arrival in Havana carrying a copy of this book's hardcover edition. A customs agent questioned him. "I think the only words he understood were 'enemy,' 'Yankee,' 'Castro,' and 'Cuba,' " the traveler wrote to me. "He clearly didn't understand your intended irony. He took the book and disappeared into an office, then came back and motioned me to follow him. He put my bag and suitcase on a counter and rifled through their contents while a second agent came over and began questioning me about the book. He made me translate the title into Spanish, and I tried to explain to him that it was an ironic play on the wording of the U.S. embargo act. The guy wasn't impressed. He opened the book to the first page, and made me translate the first line: 'Havana knew me by my shoes.' That seemed to make him happy." And with that, the agent shut the visitor's book and put it back in his bag.

—Tom Miller
Spring 1996

Preface

In the summer of 1986 I had lunch with a friend in New York who was then an editor at a newsweekly. I told him I was casting about for a major project, and passed on some suggestions I'd received. Some of them amused me, others were too grandiose, too far afield, or too costly. Some subjects that piqued my interest had flash but no fire; I feared my curiosity would end long before the manuscript did.

"Cuba," he said. Everything you read about the country these days, he went on, deals with specifics like food distribution, human rights, medical care, politics, or Fidel Castro. Or else vicious attacks or uncritical tributes. "No one in this country has written a book about Cuba that simply listens to the people and describes their lives. Why not move there for a while, travel around, and write it up?"

The idea appealed to me; it seemed simple, it had a certain integrity, and it involved acceptable literary risks. Cuba had been a subject always lingering in the back of my mind. The legislation that forbids normal relations between Americans and Cubans, formally called the Trading with the Enemy Act, had become a de facto information blockade as well. Americans know a little about Cuba, but nothing about Cubans.

The idea also tantalized me because, while I had a fair amount of firsthand experience with Latin America, I'd had none with a Communist country. The combination, seemingly incongruous, was seductive.

Mrs. DeHority introduced me to Communism. She was my fifth-grade teacher in post–McCarthy Washington, D.C. One day in the Current Events Corner she told us, "In Russia, the government always lies to its people. But in the United States, we learn the truth." I have a distinct recollection of thinking at the time, wait a minute! Maybe we're the ones being lied to, and the Russians are getting the truth. How do we know? Just how *do* we know?

The United States, through the Trading with the Enemy Act, is the only country in the world that forbids its citizens to visit Cuba. Actually the law doesn't prohibit travel there; it simply bars Americans from spending U.S. currency in Cuba. There are, however, a few small loopholes. Among them: those with family in Cuba may spend dollars there, as well as researchers for scholarly or journalistic purposes. Even if you qualify for the latter, however, a visa from the Cuban government for an extended stay is not immediately forthcoming. During the months following my conversation with the magazine editor, I started nosing about, talking with people who had gone to Cuba, and reading travel accounts. I visited Havana looking for ways to establish residence there, once for two weeks in late 1987, and again for two more in the fall of 1989.

In the middle of 1990 I moved to Cuba, and returned to the States at the beginning of 1991 to begin writing. In the year following my extended stay the Eastern European socialist bloc went through its final convolutions, and when death throes settled on Soviet Communism, changes in Cuba accelerated. I returned for a few weeks in early 1992 to see how my family of friends was faring in a land for which, despite its frustrations and failings, I had come to feel great affection. In all, my time in Cuba covered almost eight months during four trips. This book tells of that odyssey.

A few words about identifying my sources: this name game has been a thorny problem for most foreign writers describing contemporary Cuba. The conventional wisdom holds that you use pseudonyms and slide a disclaimer in sideways. This, the reasoning goes, prevents any potential reprisal against the subject. But unless he or she asks for anonymity, that's always struck me as a cop-out, more a reflection of the insecurity of the writer than the security of the written about. It reinforces a distorted notion of the country, adding an unneeded shroud to an already veiled society. Except in extenuating circumstances, I've identified Cubans by name as much as possible, applying the same criteria I'd use in writing about people in any other country. My pledge: no fake names.

—Tom Miller
Spring 1992

Part One

H avana knew me by my shoes. This became obvious my first morning in Cuba's capital. I was staying at the Lido, a respectable small hotel on Consulado Street between Trocadero and Animas. That part of town, called Centro Habana, was crowded and lively, with kids playing on narrow sidewalks, and parked cars blocking one-way streets. Centro was in dire need of street sweepers and a paint job. I was anxious to get over to the Malecón, the seafront boulevard that separates the city from the water. On this sweltering midsummer day a stroll on the Malecón would be exhilarating. In two brief previous visits I had come to appreciate its around-the-clock procession of Havana society. You have not truly set foot in Cuba until you've paraded yourself along its wide sidewalk, felt the sea breeze stroke your cheeks, and traded friendly nods with passers-by. "The shortest line between two points," wrote Guillermo Cabrera Infante in *Three Trapped Tigers*, "is the curve of the Malecón." It is a no-man's-land between the devilish city and the bluest deep sea.

For generations the Malecón has been a meeting place for wholesome families and clandestine lovers. From its ledge, early-morning anglers cast for small fish, and late-night followers of Afro-Cuban religions toss oblations into the water. Exiles in Madrid, Miami, and Mexico City dream of it. From Havana's harbor the Malecón sweeps around to Paseo, on past the hotel district, ending at the tunnel that links the Vedado and Miramar neighborhoods. I took a cold-water shower—the only kind at the Lido—and pulled on a T-shirt, jeans, and a brand new pair of white Air Nikes. I tripped over some European backpackers in the lobby and turned left to the curve of the Malecón.

I passed a half dozen housewives filling buckets from a spigot on the side of a large blue water truck. Every few minutes young men would approach me and say something in thick Cuban Spanish that I couldn't quite comprehend. I flashed the simpleton's smile a foreigner wears when he doesn't understand what surrounds him, and kept on walking. After a few blocks a pattern emerged—young men would glance at my shoes and then, although I wore no watch, ask the time. On hearing a foreign accent they'd feign surprise and ask where I came from. Finally came the pitch: "*¿Cambio? Seis por uno.*" It was the money changer's mantra; they wanted to give me six Cuban pesos for one U.S. dollar. I shook my head and moved on. "*¿Siete?*" I must have looked like a naïf just off the boat.

"Look," I said, "six or seven, I'm not interested. This is my first day here. Give me a break." The ploy worked, but it had a shelf life of only twenty-four hours. I knew that officially one dollar was worth slightly more than eighty centavos. They were offering almost ten times that. The amiable black marketeers backed off, glancing from my face to my tennis shoes. Everyone looked at them as if they were laced with gold.

The sea breeze I had counted on must have stayed at sea that day. The rainy season was only a few weeks away, and the clouds had the dry heaves. I walked westward on the shadeless side of the street directly into the tropical afternoon sun; even my sweat sweated. Only a newcomer would brave such foolishness and only an intrepid *jinetero*, literally a jockey, but slang for street hustler, would venture over to try and change money. Soon a tall, thin fellow in shorts and thongs stopped me to trade six pesos for one dollar. Gustavo was his name. "Forget the money," I replied. "What is it with my sneakers?"

"They're Nikes, aren't they." He said this more as a statement than a question as he eyed my tennies, as Cubans call sneakers. "That's how we can spot you as a foreigner. The tennies we get here?" He exhaled a horse's neigh. "They're thin, they don't give you any support, and they fall apart in three months. They come from China and you have to wait a year to get another pair—*if* they have them in stock." My feet felt self-conscious as I walked away. "Seven for one?" he called over his shoulder as he returned to a game of dominoes on the shady side of the street.

A half hour later I reached the Focsa building, my T-shirt drenched with sweat. On the lobby phone I called Ron, an expatriate writer from the States whom I had met on a previous trip. He worked for a Cuban publishing house and lived alone in a roomy two-bedroom apartment on the twenty-sixth floor while he waited for his Scandinavian wife to come over. Focsa—the name is an acronym for a long-forgotten company—housed privileged Cubans and foreigners from the States, China, Ireland, the Soviet Union, and Eastern Europe.

Regimes were falling so fast in Eastern Europe that by the time my elevator got to twenty-six another country might have chipped off the old bloc. Ron and I talked about this over some cold Hatuey beer, and from the balcony watched twilight glide across Havana rooftops. Before us was a magnificent view of the city; we could see freighters churning to harbor, balcony laundry lines, children kicking a soccer ball, and the Malecón and the water beyond. Ron planned to be out of town often in the coming months; I could move in. On our way to clinch the deal at a Chinese restaurant, more money changers dogged us. The Mandarin was across the street from the Habana Libre hotel, ground zero for foreigners and *jineteros*. "*¿Cambio? ¿Cambio?*" they called out. Change? Change? Ron, accustomed to the hustler's annoying mantra, snapped back, "*Cambio tu fucking madre.*"

I went to Cuba because I was curious; because no one agrees on its strengths; because I'd read so much about it; because it is forbidden; because it's heartbreakingly lovely; because so many people have championed it while so many others have abandoned it; because Cubans make great music and aromatic cigars; because they've thumbed their noses at their former *patrón* for more than three decades; because I'd grown weary of writing about Latin American "democracies" where forlorn illiterate *campesinas* sit on city street corners selling combs, nail clippers, and undervalued handicrafts while their malnourished barefoot youngsters turn their palms up and say "gimme" instead of learning how to hold a pencil or read a sentence; because of its rich literary tradition; because my favorite players on the Washington Senators in the 1950s were Cuban; because I'm an incurable romantic; because we still have a navy base there; because Cuban women are astute and alluring; because in the last five hundred years of travel writing few cities in the world have been so effusively praised as Havana; because Teddy Roosevelt led the charge up San Juan Hill; because I liked *Our Man in Havana* and *The Old Man and the Sea*; because I got a kick out of Desi Arnaz; because I was distrustful of Cuba's bashers and its cheerleaders; because I liked the twinkle in Fidel's eyes; because I'd never been to a Communist country; because I wanted to learn to rumba; because Columbus landed there; because it has hundreds of miles of unspoiled beaches; because of its mystique.

Going to Cuba for a short stretch posed no problem; journalists and scholars are admitted for a couple of weeks with some frequency, loosely chaperoned, and sent on their way. If you want to stay longer, a Cuban government agency must authorize your visit. I had written to two such *organismos*, as they are called, the journalists union and the writers and artists union. The former said no and the latter, known by its acronym UNEAC—Unión de Escritores y Artistas de Cuba—said maybe. My intermediary suggested I establish strong interest and good faith by showing up in person, advice that led me to a plane filled with delegates to the 1987 Festival of New World Cinema in Havana.

Cuba's sophisticated film industry draws a thousand filmmakers and marketers to its festival each year. For two weeks in December, the mostly Latin American participants exhibit their wares, talk shop, strike deals, and give one another prizes. It is a film buff's dream. Theaters throughout the city screen hundreds of foreign films and documentaries for the public. I joined a group from the States that annually jumps through one of the loopholes in U.S. travel restrictions.

In Havana I met Miguel Barnet, a novelist, folklorist, and screenwriter, and UNEAC's vice president for international affairs. We connected in a restaurant at the Capri, the hotel where Ernie Kovacs, Alec Guinness, and Noël Coward stayed during the 1959 filming of *Our Man in Havana*. I explained that I wanted to move to Cuba and travel about to get a sense of daily life. My interest was not in Marxist health care or sugar harvest quotas, but rather people who get up every morning, drink coffee, go to work, take classes, come home, make dinner, make love, go dancing, sip rum, and strum guitars. "I'm not a blind supporter of the Revolution," I said, "but I am open-minded and fairly well disposed." I handed him a couple of books I'd written about Latin America as a bona fide. Barnet said there was no precedent for the writers union admitting someone from abroad like this.

No writer from the States had brought out a book of travel impressions of Cuba since the early 1960s. Earlier in the year the Argentine writer Jacobo Timerman had visited for a few weeks, but that was under the umbrella of MINREX, the foreign relations ministry. My idea appealed to Barnet enough, however, for him to invite me to lunch with some of the other writers union brass the next day.

We dined in a restaurant at the west end of the Malecón called 1830. It could have been an artsy watering hole in Manhattan: an important film director nodded and smiled from his table, an accomplished dancer stopped to shmooze, a promising composer waved from across the room, and a well-known playwright paused to slap some backs. Between *compañero* this and *compañera* that, Barnet fondly recalled his writing days in Greenwich Village, while the poet to my right, Pablo Armando Fernández, grumbled about a New York editor. "The fellow was all set to publish me," he complained, "but at the last minute he backed out." It was the sort of shop talk best avoided in the States, but over a leisurely meal among Cuba's cultural elite, I was intrigued. At the end of the meal it appeared they were, too, at least enough to ask that I type up a formal proposal.

The rest of the two weeks blurred by with movies, art galleries, ice cream, documentaries, music, short walks and long bus rides, and talk about cinema. A British director compared the lobby of the Hotel Nacional, the film festival's headquarters, with the Carlton at Cannes. "That's where all the business deals get done." A director from Uruguay complained about *Walker*, the movie about America's nineteenth-century plunder of Nicaragua. "Why," he asked the film's producer, "did you take such a flip approach to a subject so profoundly significant?" "Simple," came the reply. "We made it for a U.S. audience."

The doors opened to the main ballroom, and the crowd surged in to hear a steamy quintet fronted by Arturo Sandoval, the hottest horn south of Gillespie. In the middle of one long solo I swear I heard Sandoval wail the unmistakable sounds of an Iron Butterfly riff.

The next afternoon the Acapulco Theater screened an Argentine movie for the public. Near the film's beginning, an American tourist says of Buenos Aires, "It's a beautiful city, but there are long lines everywhere and the telephones never work." The Havana audience howled in recognition.

That night a group of us foreigners went to the Tropicana. Built in the 1940s as a playground for high-rollers who'd cruise over from Miami for a night on the town, the Tropicana is a wonderfully anachronistic holdover from Havana's more rambunctious days. During the Revolution Milly Wormold celebrated her sixteenth birthday there in *Our Man in Havana*, and her father's secretary shpritzed seltzer water on the chief of Batista's murderous secret police. The Vegas-style pizzazz and boisterous floor show seemed utterly incongruous in a country that prides itself on having done away with vulgar excess. It featured well-choreographed showgirls and guys prancing onstage, brassy, bouncy, and full of color backed up by a full band and large chorus.

The next day I ran into Barnet. His eyes were bleary, a condition explained by sitting through ten movies a day as a judge for the film festival awards. "What did you think of the show?" he asked of the Tropicana. I told him what a kick I thought it'd been. "I don't agree. I think it's sexist." We let the subject drop and instead talked about dominoes.

At Coppelia Park, the outdoor ice cream parlor the size of a city block, I got on a crowded bus with the remains of a cone dripping down my hand. An art gallery caught my eye and I *con permiso*'d my way to the rear exit of the bus and went to a showing of some energetic ceramic impressions of Cuban life. "We opened in 1960," the director of the Galería de la Habana proudly said, "in the second year of the Revolution."

A man in his late twenties kept glancing at me in the gallery's gift shop. Slight of build and hesitant in manner, he first noted what items I was looking at, then finally approached. "Hello," he said, "are you a foreigner?" I prepared myself to turn down a request to change money. But Calixto wanted to talk politics and travel, specifically Cuba's politics and his own travel. He wanted out. I left the gallery, Calixto alongside like a puppy, and we made arrangements to speak again the next day. "How about meeting at Coppelia for some ice cream?" I suggested. "No, no. Too many people are there." He preferred we meet outside the post office adjoining my hotel.

On the way back to my room I stopped to chat with a fellow on the street. His healthy-looking cocker spaniel tugged on his leash. I mentioned the maxim that you can judge the condition of a society by the appearance of its dogs, and that judging by his, things must be going well in Havana. "Well, yes," he replied. "but in some parts of the city the dogs aren't doing so well."

The next morning Calixto escorted me to his place. He spoke in a low voice, changing pitch and subject whenever someone walked close enough to hear. "My grandfather owned some land at the other end of the country. Every day the family had meat and vegetables. Now his land is no longer in the family. After the Revolution most of it was turned over to small farmers. My family's provisions no longer come from their own land."

We arrived at his home, one room adjoining the large Catholic church where he did odd jobs. On his dresser sat a 1937 *National Geographic*, photographs of Lebanon, and postcards of Mexico and Poland sent by tourists who had befriended him. He turned up the volume on his radio so no neighbors could hear us.

"I go to church," he said. "I'm not very Catholic, but I do have faith. When I apply for a job one question they always ask is if I'm a believer. As a result, I never find work. I took some classes in medicine, but I can't even do that anymore. I'm a nonperson." He described the events leading up to the 1980 Mariel boatlift. "When everyone occupied the Peruvian embassy grounds to get out, I came from Santiago at the other end of the country. I arrived too late to go. Prisoners were told that if they didn't agree to leave the country too, their sentences would be doubled.

"Socialism. Communism. In theory, they're great—far better than capitalism. But the reality is different. Here we have two classes, the government class and the rest of us. No system is perfect. I've been granted permission to go, but I need a sponsor in another country. It'll take forever. I don't want to go to the United States, though. The cultural difference would be too much. I'd rather go to Spain, or possibly to South America. I want to be my own man."

By day Havana wears Caribbean colors, a tropical rainbow reflected in smiles, flowers, and ice cream. At night the air turns misty, softly lighted by 1950s-era glass globes on metal streetlamps. It was under such black-and-white detective movie lighting one evening that another visitor and I stumbled upon a storefront art gallery around the corner from El Floridita, known in its Hemingway era as "one of the ten best bars in the world." We peered into the gallery. The two fellows inside motioned for us to enter. Paintings by Omar Godínez Lanzó, a thirty-four-year-old artist, hung on the walls. Godínez, said the pamphlet accompanying the show, grew up in Havana, studied art in Moscow, and has exhibited at home, and in Czechoslovakia and the Soviet Union. Thankfully, Cuba rejects social realism as its artistic line, and Godínez's oils were busy with modernistic sweeps through land and sea, with hints of Picasso shadowing his form.

"Where are you from?" "Really?" "What are you doing here?" I told them that the film festival had drawn me to Havana, that a restaurant had brought me to the neighborhood, and that art had pulled me inside their storefront gallery. They peppered me with questions. What did I think of Havana? Did I like Cuban movies? Would I have the chance to see the rest of the country? Was I impressed with Godínez's work? They seemed pleased that we had interrupted their night shift on the gallery watch.

That Sunday no Cubans made music, at least in public. The Cuban composer and musician Enrique Jorrín had died the previous day. Jorrín has left his mark on global culture. He invented the cha-cha, right at the corner of Prado and Neptuno in Habana Vieja.* In honor of his contribution to dance floors the world over, Cuba declared a day

---

*In English, two chas, in Spanish, three. "I can't explain why Americans dropped the last *cha* in *cha-cha-chá*," Omar Torres writes in *Fallen Angels Sing*. "It was either laziness or lack of rhythm."

of national mourning; pianists covered their keys, trumpeters muted their horns, and drummers stilled their sticks. I met some Canadians and we toasted Jorrín's memory. *"¡Qué viva el cha-cha-chá!"*

COMMIE PICS BOFFO IN CASTROVILLE. That was the headline I envisioned in *Variety*, but its reporter said he couldn't use it—Cuba won surprisingly few prizes at the film festival. For an audience groomed on the Academy Awards, Cuba earned high marks for doing away with acceptance speeches and commercial time-outs. Oliver Stone's *Salvador* won an award for "best film with a Latin American theme by a non-Latino." Best feature film was *A King and His Movie*, from Argentina, and the grand prize for the festival's best film went to a Brazilian documentary, *Land for Rosa*. Yet when it was all over, the movie with the most prizes, including best screenplay and the press critics' "best film of the festival" honors, was Cheech Marin's *Born in East L.A.*

At festival's end, film buff Fidel Castro had us all over to the Palacio de la Revolución for dinner and drinks. His date for the evening was fellow cinephile Gabriel García Márquez, spiffy in white from head to toe. Latin America's movie elite dined well in the company of two of the hemisphere's most extraordinary men. Admirers flocked around them while plainclothesmen, as obvious as 1930s-era movie gumshoes, checked who edged closest. The stand-up buffet in an enormous well-lighted reception hall included fresh seafood chased with aged rum. Sancho, the Communist ex-mayor in Graham Greene's *Monsignor Quixote*, would have felt at home. "The Party has never forbidden us to take advantage of bourgeois comfort so long as it lasts," Sancho said, defending his choice of a palatial hotel. "Communism is not against comfort, even what you might call luxury, so long as the worker benefits in the long run."

The writers union will call within a few months, I thought when I got back home. We had met, they had some of my writing and an outline of what I wanted to do, and they had my address. What more did they need to make a decision? Patience, I was cautioned, patience. These things take time.

Book people in New York had their own ideas. I was met with the same publishing industry aphorism I'd been hearing for years, each time pronounced as if it was being said for the first time. "You know," one editor after another told me with grandiloquence, "people are willing to do anything for Latin America except read about it." An editor at one major publishing house made it clear that he expected an anti-Cuba book. Another, the head of a highly regarded independent house, listened attentively as I described my conversations with the writers union. "That's what you told them," he said with a conspiratorial smirk, "but we know what you're really going to do."

Excuse me?

Later that week an editor at the *New York Times* introduced me to her boss. He and I exchanged pleasantries, but when he learned of my envisioned stay in Cuba he suddenly burst into a tirade—that's not putting it too strongly—about how it couldn't work. "They'll never let you do it," he blustered. "Once word filters back to the authorities that an American is making inquiries about the system, you'll be out on your ass right away. Or they'll restrict your travel and who you can meet." Then, realizing he was making a speech—his underlings had stopped and stared in astonishment—he quickly downshifted and stuck out his hand. "Well! Of course I wish you the best of luck and I hope you get in."

When two governments barely speak to each other, it's that much harder for their people to communicate, too. Hearing nothing from Havana, I started checking with the Cuban Interests Section, Cuba's office in Washington that handles visas, stays in touch with scholars and journalists, maintains low-level contacts with the State Department, and presents a face to the capital's diplomatic corps. (The Cuban Interests Section was then under the umbrella of the Czechoslovakian embassy, much as the U.S. Interests Section falls under the aegis of the Swiss embassy in Havana.) The problem, said others who had found themselves in similar circumstances, was that they never say no and only occasionally say yes. You are left in limbo, waiting for word that may never come. Years earlier I had been at Mexico's southern border with other journalists and human rights monitors trying to get into makeshift camps housing Guatemalans who had fled horrific military assaults in their own country. For permission to visit the refugee shelters we were told to write formal letters to authorities in Mexico City, then wait for authorization to arrive by return mail. We all had a good laugh at that, then managed to bribe, bamboozle, flirt, and otherwise wheedle our way past guards and into the camps—all except one painfully virtuous freelancer from Oregon who spent his time tethered to the hotel conscientiously waiting for his *permiso* from Mexico City. Waiting for word from Havana, I was beginning to feel like that reporter.

In the fall of 1989 word finally reached me that the writers union was favorably inclined to my plan. I could seal their approval by going to Havana once more. This time I latched on to a U.S. media group about to visit the island. The writers union meanwhile had gone through a housecleaning. Its members had voted out many of their previous officers, perceived as being a bit too vainglorious, and brought in new leadership. Miguel Barnet, however, had landed on his feet, more influential than ever. I met with him and Miriam Artamendi, the union's director of international relations, at UNEAC headquarters on a comfortable, tree-lined street in the Vedado section of town. The ornate white building, once the home of a Spanish banker, had high ceilings, marble walls and floors, a front veranda made for slow and easy conversation, and a cluster of tables shaded by tropical growth near a bar open to members late every afternoon.

I carried two books with me to the UNEAC building. I had found the U.S. edition of Barnet's *Autobiography of a Runaway Slave* in a second-hand bookstore a few weeks earlier, and gave it to him as a gift. He chuckled at the twenty-year-old author photo. I also carried a copy of the just-released photo book, *Walker Evans, Havana 1933*, compliments of the publisher. We chortled over the accompanying editor's note, which asked that I give it to Guillermo Cabrera Infante if I ran into him. Cabrera Infante had left Cuba in the mid-1960s; I had just missed him by twenty-five years. I donated his copy to the UNEAC library. (Guillermito—you can pick up your copy whenever you want. It's in the bookcase nearest the door, third shelf, left side.) We drank demitasses of strong coffee.

"So, what is it you need?" he finally asked.

"A visa that will allow me to stay for six months and travel anywhere and talk with anyone."

Turning to Miriam, he said, "I don't see any problem with that, do you?" She concurred; all she needed was a way to contact me by telephone or telex when all the paperwork was processed. Miriam seemed the model of the efficient bureaucrat, taking notes and shuffling papers. She was to be my main liaison with the writers union and other *organismos*. She told me that she came from Matanzas, a major city 100 kilometers east of Havana; from then on I called her La Plume de Matanzas.

La Plume led me to believe that I'd be hearing from her in a matter of weeks. We finished our coffee and departed in a glow of warm camaraderie.

* * *

La Plume's matter of weeks stretched into a matter of months. I sent a couple of telexes; no response. In the spring of 1990 I reviewed all my contacts with the Cubans and explained them point by point to a friend familiar with the machinations of travel between the two countries. He pounced upon my early disclaimer that I was neither a cheerleader for the Revolution nor one of its bashers. "*That* was your mistake" he exclaimed. "You should have said you were a cheerleader. You'd have been there long ago."

Ariel Ricardo, the press attaché at the Cuban Interests Section, enthusiastic in the early stages, seemed less and less optimistic. Once, when I was in Washington, he offered to send a fax to the Foreign Relations office in Havana on his special line and have a messenger hand-deliver it to UNEAC. I accepted eagerly, and the next day drove the one-page message down to the Interests Section. Quite by coincidence, just as I finished parking, Ricardo walked down the sidewalk alone on his way to the drugstore. Should I leave the letter for you at the front desk? I asked. No, don't bother, he replied. I'll take it here. He slipped the plain white envelope into an inside pocket while I got back in my rent-a-car and drove off. Total elapsed time, fifty seconds. How many intelligence agencies do you suppose witnessed that transaction?

I've posed that question to a number of people, and the median answer is two. Most mentioned a window in the apartment building across from Cuba's office on Sixteenth Street as the main U.S. lookout post. When I next saw Ricardo I told him about my survey. "Sometimes their surveillance helps," he said. "One of our men was in upstate New York when he was the victim of a hit-and-run. The surveillance man following him saw it and reported it to the local authorities. They picked up the hit-and-run driver."

In July 1990 a telex arrived from La Plume. My visa was ready. After two and a half years, countless informal inquiries, and two preliminary visits, authorization for the forty-minute Miami-to-Havana flight came through. As I moved my belongings to the twenty-sixth floor of the Focsa building in Havana, the interminable delay finally seemed worthwhile.

I prefer Pepsi to Coke and both to Tropicola. Unfortunately Tropicola is not just Cuba's soft drink of choice, it is the only choice. It's too strong on sweetness and too weak on flavor. To each his own, and this was Cuba's own. I had a Tropicola at a sidewalk café in Habana Vieja, the old section of town. Earlier I had stood in line a half hour for a slice of pizza. The line crawled along, then inexplicably stopped for five minutes, then almost imperceptibly started up again, then came to another halt. I would have to learn Zen patience to survive in this town.

During the interminable wait you can read, talk with the people around you, eavesdrop, watch Havana street rituals, or daydream. When you're last in line you feel the whole country is in front of you, a sensation that dissipates only when someone taps you on the shoulder and says, "*¿el último?*"—are you the last in line? After the third halt the pizza line moved somewhat more briskly, and I got my slice. Actually it was a slice-sized whole pizza with no choice of toppings. The dough was warm and spongy with a shmear of tomato paste on top. It had little taste, but its aftertaste begged for a soft drink, which led me to the sidewalk café in Habana Vieja.

Within minutes I was seated at a table along with three young blonde women from the Soviet Union. The *sovieticas* were as surprised to encounter a *norteamericano* as I was to meet them. They were in Cuba as escorts for "the children of Chernobyl," young victims of the nuclear disaster being treated at a Cuban medical facility. They lived at the José Martí Pioneer City youth complex just outside of town. One spoke Spanish. "Oh yes," she said, "everything about our stay in Pioneer City is wonderful"—her friend nudged her, said something in Russian, and made a face—"except the food. It's terrible. This is our one day off for the week so we thought we'd be tourists today."

A few blocks down Obispo Street, Sabado del Libro was scheduled to begin at Moderna Poesía, Havana's main bookstore. Every Saturday a new book gets launched, often with the author present to talk about it and field questions from the crowd. I got there late, but the author of the day's featured selection never made it at all—traffic problems, we were told. The host, from the Provincial Center for Books and Literature, apologized, and the crowd drifted away.

When I had flown in a few days earlier, a customs agent had gone through some items in my bags with extreme care, and ignored others. He examined virtually every page of *Cuba Update*, a magazine supportive of activities on the island, but he totally ignored Jacobo Timerman's very critical *Cuba: A Journey*. When he saw some sticks of cinnamon brought at the behest of a Cuban family in the States for a friend, he whistled for an inspector from the Ministry of Agriculture. I told her the sticks were for tea, and as she took them she politely said that I could buy cinnamon in Havana. I tried to keep up some innocuous chatter about each item the humorless inspector removed from my bags—beads for a necklace with religious symbolism, cassettes of Bruce Springsteen, Los Lobos, and Tracy Chapman—but his only smile came when he saw my baseball glove. Finally he got to four videotapes. "I'm sorry, but we'll have to hold on to these."

"But two of them are blank," I protested, "and the others—"

"It's routine," he interrupted. "We look at all unsealed tapes. We want to keep pornography out of the country. Take them over there." He nodded to a small nearby office. "The *compañera* will give you a receipt."

I did and she did. Scores of videotapes were stacked on shelves behind her, she added mine, which included a PBS series with Harry Belafonte about Cuban music, and *Family Portrait*, by Boston film-maker Enrique Oliver who had asked me to show it to relatives in a small provincial town. *Family Portrait* is a sly and witty pseudodocu-mentary about a working-class Cuban family assimilating into the U.S. mainstream. Oliver's film gently mocks both cultures; would Cuba's video police consider it politically pornographic? I hadn't a clue; the confiscator simply said, "Bring your receipt back Saturday."

On Saturday I caught a cab to José Martí Airport and handed my receipt across the counter. My apprehension was unwarranted; the tapes were returned, with a slip of paper attached to each one. The one on Enrique's movie simply said "family members."

I began a ritual of daily walks along the Malecón. Usually I'd go for an hour. Often this meant about four miles; other times I'd barely go two blocks, depending on who I met or what book I carried. I'd return through back streets to get a sense of what went on there, too.

If I walked westward I soon passed the immense and unmistakable U.S. Interests Section building. Like most of our embassies, it is as architectually unseemly as the foreign policy it represents. The Interests Section, which rests on a prime chunk of Havana waterfront, looks like it should anchor a Midwestern American office complex. Most foreign missions today are in Miramar, a section with broad avenues and formerly single-family mansions. The opulent homes have been converted to schools, embassies, government buildings, and residences for foreigners and privileged Cubans. (The enormous Russian embassy is also there, even more obnoxious than the U.S. offices, and the object of far more derision.) Virtually every embassy has a guard post out front and a DO NOT ENTER sign blocking the sidewalk, reading:

ZONA OFICIAL
NO PASE

In front of the U.S. Interests Section the sign says:

ZONA OF CIAL
NO PASE

which seemed a clever but poorly rendered bilingual warning that the CIA lives within. It turns out OF CIAL doesn't have an extra L on the end; it's missing an I. An enormous billboard with a cartoon Uncle Sam faces the U.S. building reading IMPERIALISTS, WE HAVE ABSOLUTELY NO FEAR OF YOU!

Alejandro was just a few blocks away at the office of ICAP (Instituto Cubano de Amistad con los Pueblos), a hands-across-the-sea *organismo* that acts as a friendly host to foreigners regardless of their home country. Early on I began occasional visits to Alejandro. He worked in the North American section, and often entertained small groups from the States. He was the most upbeat Cuban I met, enthusiastic about Fidel's every burp and cheerful about Cuba's future. Who could get disheartened at the country's persistent problems with Alejandro around? Whenever I needed a dose of optimism I went to see him. We had met in 1989 when I told him I hoped to return for a long stay, and he greeted my return in mid-1990 like a fraternity president welcoming a new brother to the fall semester. "So you made it! It's great to have you here. You'll love it. Drop by if I can be of any assistance."

Right away he could; I needed the bus route to the Biblioteca Nacional José Martí, the national library in the Plaza de la Revolución, where I hoped to find Tomás Fernández, whom I had met a year earlier. Alejandro pointed out the bus stop where a half dozen people waited. After fifteen minutes a double-bodied red Hungarian bus wheezed to a halt. I had ten centavos ready, but curiously, only two other passengers put coins in the till. The rest simply walked on as if a pass were pinned to their shirts. The bus, crowded with students holding books and housewives with bags of produce, wended its way through side streets and major thoroughfares dropping off and picking up riders every few blocks. Even with a constant turnover in passengers, I never found a seat, never came close. I felt utterly ignorant of Cuban bus etiquette—whether to pay, where to stand, when to pounce, and which door to exit. I did like the Cuban word for bus, though: *guagua* (wah-wah), like a baby's cry, or the sound of a claxon.

Tomás Fernández worked on the library's second floor. He introduced me to Fannie Rushing, a professor from Chicago researching the abolitionist movement in nineteenth-century Cuba. I asked where I might find Cuban literature about the U.S. navy base at Guantánamo Bay and about foreigners' impressions of Cuba over the centuries. Fernández suggested *Bahía Guantánamo* for the former, and *Women Travelers in the Caribbean* for the latter.

"The treaty expires soon, doesn't it," Fernández said of the accord that allowed the U.S. Navy to settle at Guantánamo.

"Well, no, it really doesn't," I replied. "Basically it's in perpetuity."

"Are you sure? They've told us it expires in 1999." He paused. "We've always thought it was a bit strange—the fact that it's still there." We agreed on that, and he, I, and Fannie made a date for my birthday on Saturday.

The next day I dropped by to see La Plume in her office across from the main UNEAC building. She assured me that the paperwork to extend my visa for the full six months I'd requested was in motion. I asked if she could arrange with MINFAR, the Ministry of the Revolutionary Armed Forces, for me to spend time with the Brigada Fronteriza, Cuba's border patrol whose domain surrounds the U.S. navy base at the other end of the island. La Plume was as sweet as the sugar harvest. "Of course, yes," she said, writing it all down, "I'll get to it. By the way, Barnet called; he can't make his appointment with you today. He's busy preparing for his trip to China." I walked across the street to relax on the UNEAC portico, where I found a distinguished white-haired man in a white *guayabera* and blue slacks reading the morning paper. He was Osvaldo Salas, a photographer famous for the 1960 picture of Castro and Hemingway together, the only time the two met.

"Look at this," he said, rapping the newspaper in disgust. "My wife came back from the Soviet Union three days ago. She said things are terrible there now. They have nothing to eat. They had a demonstration against the Cuban people!"

I introduced myself.

"I lived in New York and New Jersey before the Revolution, in the Bronx, Brooklyn, Port Elizabeth, and Hoboken. Do you know Lyle Stuart, the publisher? He has visited here a number of times. He's been a friend. He hasn't been here lately, though. He's mad at the Revolution these days."

"Well, everyone is some days," I responded, weakly.

"I've been to the Soviet Union fourteen times," he said, jabbing his paper. *"Do you know they tore down a statue of Lenin?"*

Cuba entered the "Special Period in a Time of Peace," a phrase Fidel broadcast to the whole country. It meant Cuba was sliding into a wartime economy without the war, and from then on life was going to be more difficult and increasingly uncomfortable. This was apparent even on the Malecón, where the going rate for money changers became a solid seven, quickly sinking to eight. My Nikes were a bit dirtier and my clothes somewhat less conspicuously foreign. Usually the *jineteros* were bothersome, but sometimes, once convinced I had no intention of changing money, they liked to talk, and usually I did, too.

One morning Jorge, a street hustler on the morning shift, approached as I sat on the seawall with my back to the city. After the obligatory peso-and-sneakers ritual, he was harmless and friendly. He asked if I'd pick up something at a dollar shop for him. Dollar shops, found at major hotels, carry products from abroad—everything from clothes, foodstuff, and shoes, to cigarettes, jewelry, and computers. Trading on the black market could land Jorge in jail; even handling dollars was illegal. Only foreigners and specially privileged Cubans who used government-issued scrip had access to the dollar stores. The stores' exteriors were heavily draped or painted dark so as not to emphasize the exotic items within or attract undue attention. Everyone knew where they were, though, and it was not uncommon to find nearby pedestrians or even cabbies asking foreigners to pick up something for them. They offered dollars miraculously produced from back pockets and purse bottoms.

In turning Jorge down I used the word *"jinetero,"* which got him started. "Everyone's a *jinetero*," he spit out. "Even countries. Everybody wants something from someone else and they'll do what they can to get it; people, nations, everyone."

From where we sat we could see the tourist cops in front of the Deauville Hotel, stationed there to keep some distance between foreigners and Cubans. Jorge's friend Víctor, who worked in a little refreshment stand nearby, strolled over and listened attentively. Finally he spoke up: "Do you know of the American writer William Kennedy? I just finished reading his book *Ironweed*," a best-seller in Cuba. "We're here every morning if you'd like to talk with us some more." A breeze blew smartly enough to offset the strong sun, and a little girl across the street started dancing to a radio I couldn't hear. Jorge pointed up a side street. "Yes, and I live in the neighborhood. If you need anything you can call on me anytime."

During a previous trip I was taken by the professionalism and popularity of Havana's classical music station on which I heard a Vivaldi oboe concerto. I get wistful when I hear an oboe. I played one through high school, never especially well, rather "like a dog's walking on his hind legs," as Boswell quoted Samuel Johnson about a woman preaching. "It is not done well; but you are surprised to find it done at all." The first oboist of Washington, D.C.'s National Symphony Orchestra gave me lessons and taught me how to make reeds. The high point of my short career was playing in the all-city junior high school orchestra; the low point came a few years later when, during a performance of a community light opera company, I soloed ten bars too soon, unnerving conductor, cast, and audience. The oboe, "an ill wind that nobody blows good," has become decreasingly important to me over time, yet I've never given it up entirely. I've made a ritual of taking my instrument out once a year, soaking a brittle reed, and tootling for ten or fifteen minutes. Could I find an oboe teacher in Havana? On that same visit Alejandro the optimist helped me locate the office of Cuba's Orquesta Sinfónica Nacional, where I explained myself to a woman seated at the front desk.

"Ah, the oboist, yes," the receptionist said as if she had been expecting me. "He's in the rehearsal room. He'll be out in about twenty minutes. Won't you have a seat?" I sat among dozens of busy musicians. The violin tuned, a flute whistled, a French horn bellowed scales, a clarinet touched his high notes, and a bass fiddle scraped the bottom of its barrel. Some musicians were assembling their instruments while others were packing theirs up. Typical backstage.

"Excuse me." The receptionist again. "Did you want *the* oboist or *an* oboist?" Delighted to learn that Havana had more than one, I said any oboe player would do. She pointed to a man a few seats away. His name was Jesús Avilés, and he was just putting his instrument away for the day. I introduced myself and explained that I'd like to take oboe lessons when I returned for a long stay. "Do you teach?" He stammered in bewilderment, then questions jumbled out of his mouth. Why did I want to take lessons? What level was I at? Did I have my own instrument? What brand? My own reeds? My own music? What oboe music was I familiar with? Under whom had I studied previously? When did I plan to return?

He overestimated my ability and agreed to be my teacher. On my city street map he pointed out the neighborhood in La Víbora where he lived. "You must come over for dinner when you return," he said. "My wife, Laura, is an environmental scientist, and she speaks some English." He walked me to the door out of earshot of the others. "There is one thing you could bring back for me, perhaps." This had become a familiar refrain from Cubans of all walks of life. Usually the requests were benign—a book, some spark plugs, and once a jar of gefilte fish—but Jesús's plea struck me as eminently just. He wanted some precut stalks of raw bamboo cane from which to whittle oboe reeds. The country's import shortages extended from wheat for bread to cane for reeds.

A few afternoons later the city's municipal band played for the public at the Plaza de la Catedral. There were two more oboe players; one, a pleasant-looking mulatto, and the other, very black with a face wider than it was long. My God, with everything Cuba is known for—sugar, coffee, seafood, Communism, baseball, climate, the rumba, literature, coastline, and a tumultuous history—who'd have thought it was also a hotbed of oboe players?

An invitation to dinner with Jesús and Laura came when I telephoned after settling into the Focsa building. "Take the number 174 bus from Seventeenth heading south on G Street. Get off near the Monaco Theater; we're only a few blocks from there."

Which imitated the other first, Miami or Havana? Over the years builders in one have mimicked the architecture of the other. La Víbora, which dates back to the mid-nineteenth century, is one of Havana's oldest suburbs. Jesús and Laura's neighborhood, in one of the mid-twentieth-century sections, resembles the nice, tidy, working-class family homes and well-cared-for lawns found in parts of Miami. A Lada, a small Soviet sedan, sat in the driveway. Jesús came to the door and took me to the back, where he introduced Laura, then Pedro, her fifteen-year-old nephew from Cienfuegos who lived with them. "We're on vacation now," Jesús said. "We go to the park every day or stay home or go to the beach east of town. Look at how red I'm getting!" He touched his forearm. "Would you like some fresh pineapple juice?"

The bamboo cane I had sent to him with some friends earlier in the year was enough to feed an orchestra for months, and Jesús had shared it with his colleagues. Normally, to get cane for reeds, Jesús and the other oboists turn in requisitions, which go in a stack of requests for equipment from the other professional musicians and artists throughout the country. These forms travel through an increasingly remote maze of bureaucrats in the Ministry of Culture and then the Ministry of Foreign Commerce. The cane must be bought overseas with dollars;

but oboe reeds are not a high priority for a country that can barely import cotton or petroleum. At each succeeding desk, officials shave a little more from the oboe players' requests. Months later, when the paperwork arrives at Cuba's embassy in France where an attaché actually purchases the cane, the combined order from all of the country's oboe players is thinner than a well-whittled reed. More than half a year after the original request, the cane arrives back in Havana. The state also supplies almost all of the instruments. "I got mine in East Germany," Jesús said, "when I studied at a conservatory there."

Laura, a well-spoken woman in her mid-forties, had been to Mexico a couple of times for science conferences. "I went to Guadalajara and to Guanajuato. I love Mexico—except for Mexico City, of course." Her work had also taken her to Czechoslovakia. "I liked Coke before the Revolution. I went for years without one, and then I had the chance to drink one in Prague. And you know? I didn't like the taste. I'd become so accustomed to Tropicola. Ah, well, it's true we have less in Cuba now, but at least we have education and health. But the Cubans in the States— when they talk about Cuba they speak of another Cuba. They don't know what it's really like here now. Of course I have relatives in your country. They live in Atlanta. They went in 1945."

Laura went into the kitchen, and I assembled my oboe for my first lesson. Jesús and I started at the beginning—embouchure, body posture, wind flow, finger position. He listened enough to recommend some simple scales and arpeggios until our next lesson.

Next we went into the library, a room with shelves full of good literature by Stefan Zweig, Mark Twain, José Martí, Alejo Carpentier, Waldo Frank, and others. Jesús pulled a copy of a recent book profiling baseball stars off the shelf and gave it to me.

Once a year Laura has an opportunity to scrub down the house top to bottom. It must have come within the previous twenty-four hours, for everything was spotless and dusted—plates, cabinets, porcelain, floors, walls. "I work from eight to five every day. Then on Saturday I do the housework. I don't have the opportunity to cook the way I'd like." But she was on vacation, and this evening's meal had been planned a few days in advance. That night she cooked the way she liked.

"The orchestra went on tour last March," Jesús said as Laura brought in bowls of peanuts and popcorn. "We went all over the country— to the sugar mills, small-town plazas, big-city concert halls, in the mountains, and even to a military base." During a previous symphony tour of the countryside, cane cutters at a sugar mill in Las Tunas province had presented each musician with a small sack of sugar in appreciation after the concert. This time the most unusual concert took place on a field in the mountains. "The surroundings provided a magnificent natural sound. The audience showed up on horseback with their children. They sat on their horses throughout the performance." Jesús leaned forward to pour us all rum. "These were *guajiros*," country people, "in the Sierra; they had never heard symphonic music before. They were stonefaced the whole time. We weren't sure if they were simply being polite or if they were bored." Laura set a fresh avocado and cucumber salad in the middle of the table. "At the end they applauded wildly and shouted for an encore. They wanted us to play the same symphony again. They didn't know that there was more than one piece of music written for musicians like us. We called them the virgin audience."

A big platter of delicious sliced fried pork arrived. The 1967 Cuban documentary, *For the First Time*, had a theme similar to the recent symphony tour. In it, some *guajiritos*—kids in the countryside—who had never seen a movie before were asked what they imagined a film to be. "It's a mirage," guessed one child. "There are pretty girls," said another. "And handsome boys." "They're about great things in the city." That evening the film crew set up a projector and folding chairs in the middle of Los Melos in northern Guantánamo province. The first film these Cubans ever saw was *Modern Times*, starring Charlie Chaplin. Kids stared wide-eyed at the screen, and laughed at Chaplin gnawing corn off a spinning machine. Mothers nursed their babies, and a little boy fell asleep on his big sister's lap. What is a movie? At the end, a child responded as if he had watched the first earthling walk on the moon. "Something very pretty of great importance."

"Yes, it was sort of like that," Jesús said of the symphony trip to rural outposts. "We went in a chartered bus, but in a few places that the bus couldn't reach we hired a truck to haul us and our equipment. We took our formal clothes with us, and also our *guayaberas*. Where it was simply too dusty and dirty, we played in tennies and jeans." Corn tamales came next, served on yet another porcelain platter. I feared Laura and Jesús had blown a month's food ration for the occasion, plus excess money at what remained of the open-market system. Their fine china and glasses sparkled, the cloth napkins were smooth from a recent ironing.

"We played for a brigade of city bus drivers working at a sugar mill. They are a notoriously tough bunch to please. They liked us a lot." Do symphony musicians form a *brigada* to cut cane like everyone else? "No—would you like some more salad?—because we're so inexperienced that if we missed the cane and sliced our hands instead"—he demonstrated with an imaginary machete, hitting his fingers instead of the imaginary cane—"our musical life would be over." By this time we were nibbling on fried plantains.

"We also played for the Brigada Fronteriza at Caimanera," Cuba's border patrol next to the U.S. navy base at Guantánamo Bay. And how did they respond? "Just like you'd expect military people to react." He imitated a solemn soldier sitting bolt upright. "When it was over they politely applauded."

Laura went into the kitchen. "She has time to make this dessert only once a year," Jesús whispered. "It's our favorite." The international environmental scientist walked out with a wonderful pineapple pie, warm, flaky, juicy, and filling.

Tomás Fernández had suffered terribly since we last spoke at the National Library. We met in the lobby of the Capri. In the previous three days he had endured the following: a car had run over his dog, and the house where he lives with his mother—he is close to fifty—had been burglarized in broad daylight. His best pants were missing, along with a pair of shoes and some shirts. He was saddest about the loss of a cassette recorder that he used for interviewing subjects for books, and some family valuables.

"Did you report it to the PNR?" I asked, referring to the Policía Nacional Revolucionaria.

"Yes, but they have so many robberies these days."

"Where was the CDR when you needed it?" That's the Comité de Defensa de la Revolución, the often-vigilant block organizations charged with, among other things, keeping an eye out for unusual neighborhood goings-on.

Tomasito had every reason to badmouth his CDR. Instead, he took a broader view. "Well, these are the little things we need to do better."

Fannie—the Chicago professor—and I took Tomásito to dinner at La Cecilia, a fancy restaurant at the west end of the Miramar district. We were seated under a canopy on a patio surrounded by bamboo shoots and tropical shrubbery. Diplomats and other well-dressed foreigners sat nearby. Earlier, the sound system in the Capri lobby had played a tape of ten different versions of the Cuban song "Guantanamera," including the famous one by folk singer Pete Seeger and another by Julio Iglesias. "It's a funny thing about 'Guantanamera,'" Fernández said. "Older Cubans associate it with Batista days when it was sung on the radio every afternoon as part of a show announcing tragedies, murders, and crimes of passion."

We spoke of literature, ice cream, religion, and sports. The conversation was animated and friendly, none of us reluctant to energetically disagree with the others. We were three citizens of the world ventilating its foibles over good food and dark rum. The talk drifted to travel and its pleasures. "Why," I asked, "does the Cuban government make it so difficult for its citizens to leave the country?" This was the main complaint I had heard so far. Most said they had no intention of abandoning their homeland; they simply wanted to visit abroad to soak in different lands. Up to this point Tomasito had been candid, loyal, and revolutionary, critical only in constructive and understanding ways. My question, however, drew a silent and sideways smile. It meant that the answer was so clearly fraught with the basic flaws in the system that any response would acknowledge the illusion. The sideways smile is a vital element in Cuba's facial vocabulary, a reply that by saying nothing says everything. Tomasito's face slowly returned to normal.

"It's not that the government doesn't allow the people to leave," he said, "it's that the finances are simply not available. Besides, everything Cubans need is here."

We took a cab back to Coppelia Park at Twenty-third and L, Havana's Saturday night party central. Thousands of people wandered through the park, dancing on the streets, giggling, singing, screaming, joking. Hoots of laughter erupted, cars honked as they cruised by, and a policeman's whistle nudged traffic along. Young kids raced around their cooing parents, stylishly dressed teenagers preened for each other, some moviegoers emerged from the Yara Theater while others watched another film projected on the wall of the Habana Libre. Everyone slurped ice cream.

"You know, you hear about human rights from all the foreign press," Tomasito suddenly said as we waited for his bus. "They say how bad we have it here. I'd just like to make a film of all this." He swept his arm over Coppelia Park. "You should have been here during Carnival. Thousands of people dancing all night, carrying on. It was wild! People enjoying themselves like crazy! *Do they think we have no human rights?*"

Human rights was just what David Evans had in mind. Evans, the U.S. State Department's public relations man in Cuba, worked at the U.S. Interests Section. We met in the office of his boss, Jay Taylor, whom I had just finished interviewing. Taylor, who would be leaving his post in a few weeks, interested me as much for his literary inclinations as for his role as the formal representative to a country with which we have no formal relations. He was a man with a portfolio, but nowhere to present it. His son is an author, and he himself had a book out about China and India. We talked about writings from and about Cuba, going back into the eighteenth century.

Taylor's fourth-floor wall-to-wall picture window afforded him an unobstructed view of the bay. He could see the Malecón and kids playing in inner tubes in the water. A spyglass perched on a tripod in the middle of his office pointed to the Straits of Florida. Through it Taylor could discern the size, nationality, and sometimes the cargo of vessels coming into the Port of Havana. He leaned over the viewfinder, peered intently into the lens, and tinkered a bit with the angle. "Look," he offered with a smile. "See that ship out there? That's a Russian freighter."

U.S. journalists on quick trips to Cuba call on Evans not only for the State Department line on Cuba, but also for any insight or shortcuts he can offer on the subtleties of the government and its people. When his information is off the record, he becomes "a Western diplomat." Reporters with short visas and demanding bosses need all the time-savers they can find; Evans points them to the quickest stories most beneficial to his government. Few stories are easier to write and intimate a more global understanding than ones with "human rights" in their lead sentence. Evans's previous post had been at the U.S. embassy in Moscow.

"I guess you know I'm the human rights man here," Evans volunteered after reciting his boilerplate backgrounder on U.S. policy and Cuba. I had failed to mention the subject and he didn't want me to leave without raising his most pressing issue. "I volunteered for it. I feel that strongly about it." He described the situation as he saw it, the progress and setbacks he detected, and what the future portended. Then he ticked off a list of human rights groups and their leaders and offered to steer me toward any of them for an interview. The names were all familiar from dozens of news stories I'd clipped during the preceding few years, and now I had a better idea why.

Evans was a forceful proponent of his cause and made a strong case for its priority. Yet the hypocrisy of the State Department's manipulation of the issue while simultaneously sabotaging the Cuban economy made Evans's suggestion too uncomfortable. I did, however, ask about one group he had failed to mention—Ecopacifista, also known as

Sendero Verde (Green Path). Its orientation seemed to be world disarmament and ecological awareness rather than freeing wrongly imprisoned men and women of principle. Ecopacifista's aims broadened the definition of human rights and gave more character to its cause. "That's a very interesting group," Evans said. Unlike many of the others, he added, its leader did not want to leave the country; he was content in Cuba.

At least two security cameras had focused on me when I entered the U.S. grounds; presumably they saw me leave, too. One, hidden right above the door to the Interests Section, allows the U.S. marine guard inside to see who wants in. The other, peeking from behind some permanently shut second-floor curtains in a Cuban security office across the street, provides the same information to Cuba's Ministry of the Interior.

I stopped at a small neighborhood bakery on my way home to pick up two loaves of bread at thirty centavos each. During my entire stay, Cuba baked only one type of bread: white, long, hard crust, and little flavor. At the Socialism or Death bakery, next door to a pizzeria, I only had to wait in line ten minutes. ¡SOCIALISMO O MUERTE! seemed to be bannered above every bakery and produce stand, as well as half the buildings in town. Until recently the slogan had been ¡PATRIA O MUERTE!, fatherland or death; Fidel had changed the stakes. In Havana bread was still on the free market; outside the capital it had gone on the ration list to assure equal distribution of a dwindling supply. Like everyone else, I tore off a bite-size chunk to munch on as I left.

I saw La Plume a few mornings later. I walked the five short blocks to the writers union office passing one newsstand, two schools, three medical clinics, four busts of José Martí, and five bus routes. I didn't see any *jineteros* or street urchins—the former, because they don't hang out on Seventeenth Street, and the latter, because there were virtually none anywhere. La Plume said that with severe restrictions on government services, transportation, electricity, and even paper, that she would need a page or two outlining my intentions, interests, resources needed, and where I planned to go. "Your stay may be adversely affected by this," she warned sweetly.

The only public photocopy machine I could find was in a basement photo studio across from the Habana Libre. It was open just a few hours a day; the line forming two hours before the door opened, and you had to leave your order overnight. A maximum of four copies per page was imposed.

I went to the photocopy and photo studio for some small mug shots for my visa. When I returned to pick them up the next day a man seated nearby said something incomprehensible to me except for the word "*menudo*." I knew he wasn't speaking of Puerto Rican Monkees or tripe and hominy soup. He kept motioning at the floor until it dawned on me that a couple of three peso notes had fallen from my pocket. *Menudo*, it turned out, means loose change in Caribbean Spanish, a distant cousin to any Spanish I had been exposed to previously. And in Cuba, it also meant spare chicken parts like necks and gizzards.

The vocabulary differs, and the pronunciation—*what* pronunciation? Cubans talk as if they have sweet potato in their mouth. This impression is nothing new; a visitor in the middle of the 1800s wrote that he didn't like Spanish "as spoken by the common people of Cuba, in the streets. Their voices and intonations are thin and eager, very rapid, too much in the lips, and, withal, giving an impression of the passionate and childish combined."

A few weeks after I arrived, Martín, who works for the Prensa Latina news service, and his wife, Sonia, an English teacher, took me to see a comedy troupe at the Karl Marx Theater. Five thousand Cubans laughed at the show's quick skits, blackouts, and monologues, but this foreigner missed a lot; it was full of in-country humor, *cubanismos*, and machine-gun Spanish. Fortunately my indulgent hosts helped me along. The revue lampooned the Communist way of running workplaces. Sonia said the material in the group's previous show, a parody of official distinctions between foreigners and Cubans at vacation spots, had been better. Cubans call the separation "tourism apartheid."

The entertainers at the Karl Marx enunciated clearly, but to my ear Cuba's alphabet sprinted from R to T; they dropped all Ss and half of the other letters. I didn't know if a redhead I met on the Malecón earlier that day bragged that her Dad was a *pescador* (fisherman) or a *pecador* (sinner), whether Elvis had *patillas* (sideburns) or *pastillas* (pills). Someone told me how beautiful La Cascada Niagara (Niagara Falls) looked in a picture, and I thought he said *la caca negra*. Everywhere Spanish words spewed forth much like the incomprehensible Portuguese described by Moritz Thomsen in *The Saddest Pleasure*, "like the suckings and gushings of water swirling into a drain . . . like the twitterings of sleeping birds, like an old black woman crooning, like an old fighter with his teeth knocked out." Cuban Spanish has neither vowels nor consonants. It makes you wonder how they'd do on *Wheel of Fortune*.

* * *

The Malecón redhead who had the sinner/fisherman father said she worked the night shift on a construction crew. She and I met at the Socialism or Death snack bar where we were both in line for an *empanada*, which we got, and a soft drink, which after a twenty minute wait, we didn't—they had run out. She came from Baracoa on the northeast coast. She was attractive in a sullen sort of way, and wore a loose blouse over a dry bathing suit. She took my notepad and coyly wrote "bay" and "marina" and "Hemingway." Isn't this cute, I thought, all these words have to do with *The Old Man and the Sea*, a book familiar to every Cuban. A wedding party drove past us. The lead cars, showroom clean '57 Chevys, were decked out in crepe paper, followed by a half dozen somber Ladas and one infirm early 1950s Packard. As the newlyweds partied by, an acquaintance of the redhead walked up, and she took off with him.

Later I thought about the encounter. You fool, I said to myself. B-a-y is pronounced *buy* in Spanish, and "marina" and "Hemingway" go together. Marina Hemingway was not, as I had previously thought, the author's granddaughter, but an expansive yacht club west of town for foreigners, with pricey boutiques, condos, fancy restaurants, and glittering nightclubs. She wanted me to *bay* her things at Marina Hemingway. She was a prostitute.

A family emergency brought me back to the States for two weeks, and by the time I cleared Cuban customs on my return at three A.M., all the cabs were gone. A middle-aged woman in a flower print dress furtively motioned me over; she and her husband could help if I needed a ride into town. Pesos or dollars? Silly question. I agreed to ten of the latter, a fair price given the circumstances, and she pointed to a street corner a block away. They knew this was illegal, a private car picking up a foreigner for dollars. Two minutes later a beautiful black '53 Cadillac Eldorado pulled up. I followed my luggage into the roomy backseat and we headed to town.

The previous morning the government had dropped a bomb: gasoline was being cut way back. An oil tanker due from the Soviet Union had failed to materialize and transportation throughout the country was at a standstill; just about every pump around town was dry. The situation was that precarious.

"I filled up two days ago," my freelance cabbie said, "so I've got enough to get to town." The Caddy needs a paint job, he said.

"All Havana needs one. Don't apologize. It's a terrific car." It was also about the only one on Havana's streets that night.

The couple ran a gypsy cab service corralling foreigners at the airport for dollar fares. Both had day jobs. A Ministry of the Interior report the previous spring assailed this "second economy," labeling it "underground capitalism." Black marketeers, such as my private taxistas, weren't just "individuals leading a life of crime," the report asserted, but "a spontaneous political movement of highly explosive counterrevolutionary force." Instead of pulling up to the Focsa's building's lighted entrance, the counterrevolutionary force parked across the street. They doused the car's ceiling light before taking my money.

I was beginning to get a sense of the hidden economy, this intricate flow of goods and dollars that brushed all of daily life. At a party one evening I saw a platter with a wide assortment of normally unobtainable fruit that bore an uncanny resemblance to the buffet tray at the Habana Libre. Money changers, prostitutes, wildcat taxis. Cuba was full of victimless crimes and crimeless victims. Comparison to the U.S. is invidious and senseless. In many ways Cuba was in far better shape than other Latin American countries.

The next morning the streets of Havana looked like a science fiction movie—the part right after everyone flees in terror. No cars whizzed by where heavy traffic had been the rule, no trucksful of city workers herded to the countryside to harvest potatoes. A family could picnic smack in the middle of the Malecón and not inhale any exhaust fumes. You'd think every tire in town was flat. The classical station played a symphonic version of "I've Got Plenty of Nothin'," and the weekly best-seller list showed that Cuba's most popular novel was a new translation of William Faulkner's 1936 *Absalom, Absalom!* The best-known writer on the nonfiction list was Che Guevara, whose *Guerrilla Warfare* had slipped a notch from the top spot.

That week I returned from my morning Malecón walks through some narrow back streets in the Centro and Vedado neighborhoods. Mothers were out early walking their children to the first day of the fall semester. Housewives clutching plastic bags lined up to fill empty bottles at the Socialism or Death milk dispensary. Each held her ration book going in, and some fresh milk going out. I asked the man in charge if his milk was strictly rationed or whether I could buy some as a free-market product. To complicate matters, I had no empties to trade in, and no bag in which to carry full ones. I think he took pity

on me, for he sold me two bottles of fresh milk for two and a half
pesos, including the price of the bottles, and he found a bag for me.
I reminded myself always to carry a crumpled-up plastic bag in my
pocket; you never know when you'll run into milk, pineapple, or
bread.

The Bar-Cafetería Detroit, an open-air, Category IV restaurant, was
two blocks farther on. (There are seven categories of restaurants, one
being the fanciest.) A car dealership had once been across the street,
said the counterman, hence the establishment's name. For ten centavos
I got a thimbleful of morning coffee, the only item on the board at
that hour. The domestic blend in this poor land of rich *café* is cut with
chicory. Like many coffee-producing countries, Cuba exports its purest
grade. Regardless, the *cafecito* was a perfect pick-me-up. A table at
the Bar-Cafetería Detroit was perfect for watching Havana awaken.

Havana had prettied itself up for a big United Nations conference
on crime. Delegates had arrived from all UNESCO countries except
the United States and Oman. Evans at the Interests Section in Havana
thought the U.S. should have participated. When change comes to
Cuba, he said, "it will be hardliner against hardliner, and by taking
part in the conference we could start to open up the middle ground."
Anyone who wanted to come to the conference from the States had to
request permission from a bureaucrat in Washington called the Chief of
Licensing, Cuban Assets Control Regulations, Department of Treasury.
The travel blockade created its own officialdom.

Teenage Bulgarian girls roller-skated down my hall, a Czechoslovakian
woman joked with the elevator operator, and a Soviet boy wanted to
practice his English on me. His father worked for Tass. "What is the
right answer when I say 'How are you?' " he asked as we descended
from the twenty-sixth floor. "Is it 'Very good, thank you,' or 'Very
well, thank you'?" Fortunately some Chinese got on before I could
answer, and when we reached the lobby the *sovietico* darted out to play.
The Soviet embassy complex in Miramar included a school with 1,500
students. Buses met some of them in front of the Focsa building every
morning. Other foreign children went either to regular public schools
or to the English-language International School of Havana. ISH, also
in Miramar, schooled 120 students from twenty-seven countries in
two reconditioned mansions. (Hungary had the most, sixteen.) There
was one twelfth-grader, from Ecuador. The director is British, the
staff Cuban.

Unlike just about any other school in the country, the international school has a photocopy machine. When they need supplies, they fax or telex the States and the goods come down by U.S. diplomatic pouch. The IHS has a computer room, with Macintoshes donated by the U.S. Interests Section. The nineteen teachers get a base salary of 250 pesos monthly plus "responsibility allowances" for sitting guard duty, tutoring, or overseeing extracurricular activity, paid in *divisa*—hard currency—certificates. These highly prized *certificados* can be used in dollar shops. "There's also a formula for paying them dollars based on length of service," said Linda Daly, the school's director, "plus more dollars for teaching night school. In Cuba there is a complete and utter neurosis over the currency situation. Students pay in hard currency unless their parents' income is in pesos. Three fourths of the enrollment here pay in *divisa*. The tuition is $1,200 a term." Daly lit up a luxury length Rothman International. "I can't tell you how devastated I am that this is the last pack in town. The Diplotienda," a hard-currency department store, "appears to no longer stock it. This means more to me than the petrol crisis."

The curriculum at the International School of Havana is modeled after conventional U.S. schools. Ninth through twelfth grades are taken mail order from the High School Study Project at the University of Nebraska at Lincoln. The IHS has one other distinction: it is the only school in Cuba with no bust of José Martí.

Instead of going directly home I took a bus—two other passengers paid to board, four didn't—to San Lázaro Avenue, near where my map showed a little cul-de-sac called Hamel. A friend in the States spells his name similarly, and I thought I'd visit his street. To get to Hamel I passed another Socialism or Death bakery, a building with José Martí's likeness in the window, and a man on the next corner selling used records. His collection included Bobby Vinton, Mario Lanza, Stevie Wonder, and Sammy Kaye.

Hamel was hard to find at first; it's hidden in the backstreets of the Cayo Hueso neighborhood. A drizzle began to fall through the dusk, and I thought a quick walk-through would be more than sufficient for my purposes. I was already composing a postcard to my friend: "The street with your name is two blocks long, with the obligatory slogans championing the Revolution (rah-rah-rah) and a *bodeguita* selling rice and other staples. The houses are in severe need of a paint job, and they all have bright flowers on second-story balconies."

Instead I was confronted by a mural the length of a football field, overpowering in theme, presence, and execution. It was strong enough to physically stop me in my tracks, as if a lightning bolt had welded me to the ground. In a country where public art, especially on walls, looks as if it were almost all from the same brush, this mural on Hamel stood out for its intensity and intimacy.

Swirls of smoke, water, limbs, eyes, and roots swarm around feathers, goddesses, serpents, and sacrifices. Deities Yemayá and Ochun of the Yoruba sect entwine, others from the Abakuá dominate adjoining segments of the mural. The mural illustrates one man's interpretation of santería, the slippery and enormously popular religion intractably part of the country's daily life. Afro-Cuban beliefs, which came from what is now Nigeria, have evolved into a tradition firmly rooted throughout Cuba and surrounding lands. The mural on Hamel takes personal santería values and gives them public vitality. A note from the artist, in small letters on the mural's edge, said the work was painted from April 21 to July 24, 1990. He had wanted to complete it in time for the July 26 celebration of the 1953 guerrilla assault on the Moncada Barracks, the losing effort that nevertheless signaled the beginning of the Revolution.

A neighbor in a Miami Dolphins jersey came over as I stood admiring the wall. "You like it? It was done by a man on the street here. Originally it was a blank wall. The *muchachos* painted bad words up there. If you want, I can introduce you to the artist." Just then a man leaned out of a distant third-floor window above and behind the work. "That's him right there."

"I'll be right down," the man in the window yelled. And so began a warm friendship with Salvador González, who takes his influences from santería, Che Guevara, and contemporary art, whose frustrations with his country's shortcomings match his will to survive in it.

The work had been completed only a few months earlier, and Salvador González was interested in critiques. González, in his early forties, was ready to spend half the night explaining his art and its inspiration to anyone who would listen. "I started at ten o'clock every morning and sometimes I didn't stop until two or three the next morning. After a while, neighbors kept me going with coffee, snacks, even paint, and at night they shined a light to help me work after dark fell. I didn't have a blueprint or any paper. The bases of my work are the *cultos sincreticos*," the syncretic cults that make up santería. "I simply did it from my own feelings."

Feelings are part of the Hamel history. *Filin*, nothing more than a Spanish transliteration of "feeling," was a style of singing influenced by crooners such as Nat "King" Cole, and developed in the 1940s in the home of musician Tirso Díaz, who lived on the street. Hamel was named for a turn-of-the-century American in the rag trade.

I asked González if the city had subsidized his elaborate project but got no answer; he wanted to talk art. "I used an airbrush and a compressor. I've done other painting with the same theme. Sometimes I'm called on to paint bodies so they have a *santero* sense about them when they dance. This is my gift to humanity. I bet there isn't a mural dedicated to Afro-Cuban culture in the United States, is there? I want to show that Afro-Cuban is a living religion, even in a Communist society. I'm a member of the Cuban Association of Artisans and Artists."

By this time we were upstairs in his small apartment. His wife, Maritza, a leather worker, brought out some coffee, and we sat on padded wicker chairs next to the window overlooking Hamel. González wore silk socks and a silk windbreaker that said "Porsche" on it. He played a videotape of a Cubavisión documentary about religion in Cuba. A government-sponsored survey concluded that far more than half of all Cubans were *creyentes*, believers, the catch-all category encompassing Catholics, *santeros*, Protestants, Jews, Jehovah's Witnesses, and others. González was interviewed about the fluidity of Afro-Cuban beliefs. He had no use for the sideways smile.

"Remember, one of the first things you asked me was if the city underwrote this. No. I did it on my own. It's a noble calling. When you sell your book, you get paid for it. I get paid by the admiration of the people who pass by here. All these people who have talked with me about Afro-Cuban beliefs, I want to help them. They come from all over the world." He got out his address book with its calling cards from professors and journalists in Europe, the States, and Latin America. "But I have never heard from any of them. They film here, they take photographs. I understand there was an article in a German magazine about my work, but I never see these things.

"I know the mail system here is bad, but not once have I heard from these people. Is it asking too much that those who take from here should send back a copy of what they've done? Sometimes I feel like I live on another planet. I don't get paid for my work. The work others do using my help is my only curriculum vitae."

His poodle, Yaco, wet from the rain and almost too friendly, ran up to us. González climbed to the loft to get a shirt for me; mine was soaked from the rain and we made a temporary swap. Maritza went for more coffee. "I'd love to hear about new techniques among muralists in other countries. Someone told me about a new sort of paint for exterior walls; is it so? I want to continue to paint murals in Cuba."

Isabel Allende's *Of Love and Shadows* entered the best-seller list at number two that week, replacing a novel by Christine Nöstlinger, an Austrian writer. *Seeds of Fire*, an assortment of eyewitness accounts of the Revolution, fell from number one to number five on the nonfiction list. A collection of fiction by Anaïs Nin, who lived her young years in Cuba, had just been released. Would the book have been released had her opinions been fully ventilated? "Cubans are the most cynical, callous people in the world," she wrote in her diary after returning in the early 1920s. "As a rule [they] hold no respect for art, and still less for poetry."

With that in mind, I went over to the writers and artists union to see Barnet, who had just come back from his trip to China. We were to meet in time for the daily lunch hour, where UNEAC members can get a decent meal for about fifty centavos. Virtually every workplace in the country has a kitchen and dining hall for employees to eat together cheaply. I showed up fifteen minutes late, early by Cuban standards, for which Barnet gently berated me. He always gave the impression that he was late for his next appointment, that his wearisome life would finally fall into place if he could just make it through the day. He keeps twenty-five Chihuahuas in the hilly countryside and a temperate schedule in tropical Havana.

The food line had grown so long that instead of waiting in it we closeted ourselves in La Plume's office while she was at lunch. Barnet's English was impeccable, groomed in Cuba and perfected in the States. His novel *La Vida Real*, about a Cuban in New York, had been researched during the months he lived in Greenwich Village in the mid-1980s on a Guggenheim Fellowship. He speaks with a fair amount of American slang; when I told him I wanted to make a sweep through the country, he paused as if he hadn't heard "sweep" used in that context before. He absorbed it with a quick grin, and incorporated it into his vocabulary.

I repeated the warning La Plume had given me before, that the Ministry of Foreign Affairs wanted to know my plans to see to what extent they might impinge upon the country's resources. "Surely one person—"

Miguel cut me off. "I must give you a gentle warning. You may not be able to do some things. It is a terrible time here, and things will get worse. When people realize that they have nothing to eat, well, I don't know what will happen. I can travel around the world to China, but when I return I can't even get the gas to visit my dogs outside Havana. I don't know why I stay"—he threw up his arms—"but I love it. I love the craziness of it."

His trip to China at the invitation of that country's writers union had gone well. "It was wonderful," he said. "I saw an integrated economy work. They have goods from the West and quality homemade goods."

Barnet had once distinguished himself for his country by agreeing to debate Armando Valladares at a human rights conference in Geneva. Valladares, a prisoner in Cuban jails whose release after more than twenty years followed an international campaign, wrote *Against All Hope* when he got out and, by special Act of Congress, became a U.S. citizen and America's human rights delegate before the United Nations. His book, a powerful exposé of Cuba's internal security system and its prisons, has been attacked for its inventive accounts and severe distortions. It made its point forcefully, though, and became a best seller in many countries. "I made a fool of him," Barnet recalled of their confrontation. "I started talking in English, and he asked me to speak in Spanish. Why? I said. You're now an American citizen. You're the representative of the American people at this conference, you're their ambassador. I'm speaking your language. Valladares got so flustered he got up and left. All the reporters there laughed at him."

I asked Barnet about Jacobo Timerman's visit; he remembered Timerman as sensitive to subtleties in the government and very critical of Fidel. "I should be in his book. I gave him a copy of *La Vida Real* and he loved it."

Barnet wanted to know if I had been bothered by *jineteros* in the streets. Somewhat, I replied, but I tried to ignore them or turn their harassment into a conversation.

He was glad I had found a good place to live so quickly and easily. Originally I had naively told him I hoped to persuade a Cuban family with a spare bedroom to take me in as a lodger. He cautioned me that some families might be a bit suspicious of a U.S. writer. "Or their neighbors might. Not that the police would come—they don't do that anymore. But it would be unusual." As for the street hustlers, "Better watch it. I've only been robbed once. I was in Barcelona, and my passport was taken."

Cuba has three types of passports—regular citizens' passports, which are very difficult to come by; diplomatic ones, which go only to the foreign service; and red ones, used as a one-time only travel document when representing Cuba in some international event. "Red. Of all the stupid choices," Barnet said with great amusement. "That's like a magnet to immigration officials, to be from Cuba and have a red passport."

The conversation turned to artists. His voice lowered. "There is a new movement of Cuban artists, young ones, who are doing art that is highly critical of the system. They're becoming well known. It's not quite underground, and no one's critical of it, but it is gaining in notoriety, and," he repeated with an arch of the eyebrow, "it is highly critical of the system." He was too discreet to give me names.

A major campaign, urging thrift with all resources got underway. Signs in front of apartment houses exhorted us to SAVE TEN PERCENT MONTHLY of our electricity consumption. The Friar Andrade hospital, according to the daily *Tribuna*, "is one of the first centers in the health sector that has begun to apply energy-saving measures in response to the government's call during this special period in a time of peace." Savings were reported in gasoline and in the laundry, the kitchen, and offices, where unnecessary lighting and air-conditioning had been curtailed. A headline in another paper, accompanying a picture of a viewer nodding out in front of his television, urged, "If You're Not Going to Watch It, Turn It Off!" The article suggested cutting back on television viewing and making sure all lights in other rooms are off when it's on. "Use all your psychological resources to convince the youngsters not to use the television like a radio. A television uses ten times more electricity than a radio. . . . Remember, you don't need a lot of light to watch television. A conveniently located twenty-watt fluorescent lamp makes for an agreeable setting that won't hurt your vision." The article neglected to mention that twenty-watt fluorescent bulbs were almost impossible to find. Precipitating the entire crisis was the turmoil within the Soviet Union, the arrival of whose oil tankers were less and less reliable.

Veronica called that evening. She's a Russian translator who lives in the Focsa building. She often waters Ron's plants when he goes out of town. Her television was broken, she said; could her teenage son come up to watch *Roque Santeiro*, the captivating Brazilian soap opera, at 9:45? Ron had a lousy Soviet black-and-white TV, but it worked. I let Andre in and walked across the street to the Hotel Victoria to call the States and desperately try to salvage the cornerstone of a crumbling romance back home. I felt like a character in a Graham Greene story, the utterly out-of-place foreigner at the front desk of a fancy hotel in a third-world dictatorship, yelling in English over a bad overseas line while the bewildered native help in their starched uniforms stare, and the other foreigners in the lobby pretend they're not listening while I gesture wildly, tears welling. Well, it was not a pretty sight.

For solace, I indulged in some ice cream at Coppelia Park. The first line, in which you buy your ticket (fifty centavos a scoop), was only five minutes long. The second line, at the end of which you turn in your ticket for a cone, had an interminable delay while the hapless attendant waited for a new bucket of ice cream; swirl, this time. It was worth the wait, however, for never before had I seen someone dish out ice cream in public while wearing a Che button. I got another cone.

La Plume de Matanzas had my letter of introduction ready. In a country where your identification depends largely on your place of work, credentials aligning me with the writers union became an immeasurable help. Whenever I mentioned to acquaintances that I was in their country under the auspices of UNEAC, they'd nod respectfully and say, "Ah, la UNEAC." With La Plume's letter I could walk in unannounced on officials and get at least a cordial response. Without it, I might be entangled in a bureaucratic web in which one factotum miscommunicated on my behalf with another until one of us gave up.

The top of the UNEAC stationery, like all government letterhead, gave the date followed by "Año 32 de la Revolución," thirty-second year of the Revolution. This notion that the age of enlightenment commenced January 1, 1959, with the abdication of Fulgencio Batista has been institutionalized not just on paper but on billboards, in periodicals, and over the air. For some, that was indeed Genesis; many times, reflecting on the improvements in their lives since the Revolution, I heard Cubans say with biblical fervor, "In the beginning . . ."

The key words in La Plume's letter were, "Sr. Miller is preparing a series of magazine articles and also a book about Cuba. We would greatly appreciate your cooperation in helping him meet these objectives." When she handed over the letter, La Plume mentioned that she would be evaluating my outline of activities with the head of the North American section of the foreign ministry, and said I should come back the following week for the verdict. But from now on, she added, I could no longer buy my noontime meal at UNEAC; due to the countrywide austerity program, workplace lunchrooms could no longer feed outsiders.

I flashed the new letter from La Plume that evening at a Llamamiento. The Llamamiento, or "Calling," was a series of meetings sponsored by the Communist Party in order to gather proposals for discussion at its next Party Congress. Llamamientos took place at night for neighborhood people, during the day at community centers for retirees, and in workplaces for laborers at every level to make their feelings known. Everyone had an opportunity to attend at least one Llamamiento.

Grassroots democracy, as the Llamamientos were occasionally called, got off to a terrible start. Most people in this country of wide-ranging private views on everything from the designated hitter to the Soviet invasion of Afghanistan simply didn't feel comfortable speaking out in public. The Party acknowledged this, and reissued its call, urging Cubans to bitch away. The only taboo subjects were multiparty government and socialism itself. I showed up at a building run by the Ministry of Education for a neighborhood Llamamiento to see if a guest could sit in. A man at the front desk looked at the writers union letter and promised to pass my request on to the Party delegate when he showed up that evening.

I spent the afternoon at Colón Cemetery, one of the most colorful burial grounds in the Americas. I was looking for the tomb of José Raúl Capablanca, "the chess machine," Cuba's international grand master. A fictionalized biography of the world champion was to be published soon, and I wanted to get in touch with the man. Colón Cemetery extends for acres and acres with graves going back to the mid-1800s. Street names mark the footpaths. The mausoleums of the more wealthy deceased are overrun with abstract designs, curlicues, and heavy-handed religious symbolism. A gravedigger pointed me toward Eighth Street between A and B, where I found Capablanca in his usual resting place. Chiseled in front of the large aboveground tomb were his dates, name, and

CAMPEÓN MUNDIAL
1921 A 1927

A five-foot white marble rook stood on top of Capablanca's final home, daring anyone to go for his king. It was a fitting monument to the man who said, "There have been many times in my life when I came very near thinking that I could not lose even a single game."

Late-summer rains continued that afternoon. When clouds burst, rain poured in sheets throughout Havana. Pedestrians ran for shelter, parasols became umbrellas, and my bus was the only traffic moving on Twenty-third Street. Laundry hanging on balconies got drenched. Waves roared over the seawall onto the Malecón itself, inundating anyone walking or driving. Curbside gutters drowned under ravines. Cops rerouted traffic. Full-throated thunder snapped off power. Windows and doorways filled with *habaneros*—the people of Havana—watching the spectacle with Caribbean pride, as if the deluge was meant just for them. After dark a dreamy fragrance billowed through town.

Following an evening with Fidel in the mid-1960s, Graham Greene concluded that Castro was "an empirical Marxist, who plays Communism by ear and not by book." If that were still true, *el comandante* would get an earful at neighborhood coffee shops like the San Juan at Infanta and Twenty-fifth. The San Juan is L-shaped, one leg a bar that serves only rum, the other, a café. The latter was run by tall, thin, harried Florencio, who wore a white shirt stained by a full day behind the counter, and his wife, María, cheerful and chubby with well-coiffed red hair and dangling earrings. The first five minutes of our conversation duplicated the same give-and-take that I ran into everywhere; I was so accustomed to it I could have typed up the script beforehand. Sooner or later, however, natural inquisitiveness always gave way to individual personalities, and every chat took on its own contours. The contour at the San Juan went haywire when María laughed and said she wanted to marry me and move to Florida.

I looked over at Florencio. "Take her," he said as if shooing a cat off the counter, "take her!" He was enjoying this as much as she and more than I.

"But what if I like it here? Maybe I'd like us to settle in Cuba instead of the States." Carlos, the waiter, put my plate of white rice and a ground sardine sandwich down on the counter. Total cost: sixty-five centavos.

"Okay," said María, "we'll visit the U.S. and I'll stay there and you can come back here if you want."

Pedro, two stools down, found this especially funny. "Say, did you hear the one about the speech he gave in the plaza?" he asked, stroking a nonexistent beard. " 'God willing,' he said, 'we'll have enough bags of rice for everyone.'

"Younger brother Raúl leaned over and whispered: 'Pssst, Fidel—there is no God.'

" 'That's okay, *hermanito*. There're no bags of rice, either.' "

Florencio sneaked me a shot of rum past the barrier separating the café from the bar.

On the way over to the Llamamiento a dark blue '57 Chevrolet Bel Air hardtop splashed by, followed by an Olds 88 Golden Rocket from the same year. (Castro and his entourage traveled in a fleet of Oldsmobiles the first few years.) I had become inured to cars from the late 1950s. At first, of course, the pre-1959 cars cast an automotive time warp over the capital. Was this a movie set or a real city? Cars missing from American highways for decades lined every block. Often I'd go up close to inspect them, admire the dashboard, run my fingers along a tail fin and, if they had one, stand on the running board. If the owner was looking under the hood I'd join him, just for a glimpse of the last and greatest of that generation's high-horsepower cars.

The '57 Chevy, one of the most recognizable machines from that period, has Y-shaped chrome running the length of the car. Like rock 'n' roll songs from the same era, each car evoked smothered memories. A smiling Ozzie and Harriet came to mind, snapping their fingers in the back of the auditorium to Ricky's band. But surrounded by so many cars from those days, I began to hold out for stronger stuff—only early 1950s or even 1940s cars would satisfy me.

Seventy-five middle-aged people responded to the neighborhood Llamamiento. The meeting had been going on for more than an hour when an official saw me trying to slip in unnoticed behind a bust of José Martí. "This is the North American journalist we discussed," he announced to the gathering. "He will be joining us to observe our meeting." I flashed a half smile and a Queen Elizabeth wave and took a seat as a woman in light slacks stood up to state her gripe.

"Now, I'm a Communist and a revolutionary, but we have problems." She turned to face the audience. "These cutbacks in electricity are unfair. For years all the neighborhood children have come to my house and used my phonograph and watched my television. I've always welcomed them. But now I have to cut back ten percent of my electricity. Since I use the most I lose the most. That's not right."

"Do you have a resolution to propose?" the Party member running the show asked. She didn't.

Another lady spoke about the women's federation. "It should be restructured. The way it is now, it doesn't help us."

A man in a loose *guayabera* complained about the erratic and poorly maintained public transportation system. "We can't rely on it. You never know if a bus is coming or not."

At other Llamamientos workers complained about the food ration system, the quality of clothes, and imperious officials elected to community posts. Will the Party accept religious believers, end discrimination against Cubans at international tourist spots, and root out corruption? School facilities, workplace standards, and bureaucracies were attacked.

Whenever the woman in light slacks rose, silent groans said, "Here she goes again." A parliamentarian turned almost every issue raised into a resolution. By the time I left at 11:30 P.M., close to a dozen resolutions had passed, to be sent along with literally hundreds of thousands of others to Party headquarters.

Fabián Cisneros, a Party functionary, ran after me to explain the mechanics. "Each resolution is entered in a computer. The Party machinery weeds out the duplicates and determines patterns. They scientifically analyze public tendencies. This way every resolution is registered. This is a new process for us. We take it very seriously."

The juices of once forbidden fruit were still tasty but no longer startling. I was slowly growing accustomed to living in Havana; it ceased to be a taboo city. My bus etiquette improved. Not only were twisted street patterns emerging from the complex routes, but the protocol of riding became clearer, too. Passengers boarded through middle and rear doors as well as the front. Riders conscientious enough to pay simply handed their fares forward, trusting others along the way to give the money to the next *compañero* until it reached the driver. By taking part in this simple activity I felt slightly more integrated into the city's everyday hurly-burly.

Sidewalk second-hand book carts gave me an opening to talk with other browsers. Most carts carried text and history books, and one I frequented in Centro Habana also carried a wide range of literature, including works by Mark Twain, Langston Hughes, H. G. Wells, and Daniel Defoe. A fellow I chatted with there pointed out a Venezuelan book about Ecuador that I'd been looking for for years. In the upstairs gallery at Fototeca, the country's photography institute, an exhibit of turn-of-the-century pictures of Mexico by American photographer Charles B. Waite prompted conversations about the Aztec country, as Mexico was often called. Cuba began to feel less alien.

Yet Havana began to feel more stifling, and not just because of the heat and humidity. While the differences between it and other Latin

American cities were increasingly obvious, so too were the similarities. No one likes perpetually crowded streets, diesel fumes, long lines, overbearing slogans, and paperwork attached to everything bigger than a scoop of butterscotch ice cream. (Come to think of it, each cone required paperwork, too.) Everyone assured me that when I got to the countryside I'd see the real Cuba. Not that Havana wasn't real—it was all too real—but to know Havana was not the same as understanding Cuba. For that, I needed to go the provinces.

Cienfuegos was my first goal, and from there I could branch out to a dozen other places. "I am tired of loafing about Havana," wrote New Englander Edwin F. Atkins, a landowner from New England on his first trip to the island in 1869, "and will be glad to get over to Cienfuegos and have something to do." Exactly.

On my way over to see Salvador González, the muralist, to exchange shirts and fill him in on my travel plans, I stopped at a snack bar on Zanja Street. People were eating a delicious-looking cake called *tatienof*, a word whose origin no one could ascertain despite its suspiciously Russian sound. The open-air diner seated forty customers on malt shop stools. The menu, handwritten on paper, slid into place on a wooden placard. *Tatienof* was one of two items; the other was cold milk. *Tatienof*, when it finally arrived, proved to be a light chocolate cake, moist, almost creamy. I was sorry I had ordered just one. The menu at these places changes hour to hour.

A few days earlier in Habana Vieja I had stopped in a little restaurant whose offerings included something called *chu*—not cha or Che, but simply *chu*. I was game. "How many?" the waitress asked. "*Pues*," I hesitated, "*dame tres*." Whatever *chu* was, one person ordering three didn't raise an eyebrow. *Chu* turned out to be little bite-size puff pastries whose cheesy inside, halfway between meringue and cream cheese, was almost bitter. They cost thirty centavos apiece.

Tatienof also cost thirty centavos, and the milk, thick and rich, another nineteen centavos. I paid a harried-looking fellow who seemed to do everything slowly—take orders, fill them, pour milk, and wash dishes. Three other workers milled about, watching, not doing much. On occasion one would go into the back room and bring out another tray of *tatienof*, but just as often the harried slow-mover did that, too. Castro was aware of this phenomenon. "Cubans are the most hospitable, friendly, and attentive people in the world," he said at the dedication of a tourist facility. "But as soon as you put a waiter's uniform on them, they become terrible."

* * *

González could wait for his shirt. I was busy eyeballing an ageless Zephyr, a red compact British Ford. It looked like it was still dragging its original exhaust pipe. Farther down the block a red-and-white 1950 Chevy Deluxe squeezed next to the curb. Venetian blinds covered the rear window. Metal stars were soldered to the gas flap and fenders. The car, according to the rear chrome plate, came from Helms, a dealership in Grand Rapids, Michigan.

Then I met Raúl. He stood on Prado, the wide, tree-lined, European boulevard that stretches from the Malecón up past the Academy of Science—originally Cuba's capitol, modeled on the U.S. Capitol. Raúl was taking care of his immaculate gray four-door '48 Plymouth Deluxe when I walked up. He insisted I get in the driver's seat while he darted around to the passenger's seat. He showed me which dashboard features came from the factory and which he had improvised. He showed off the original hood latch and sideview mirror, and pressed the starter button. He had installed a fan on the floor that worked straight off the battery, and hid the radio in the glove compartment. "It's safer there."

The right side of the front window was somewhat shattered. "A few months ago some young thieves tried to break into the car. They didn't get anything. I saw them and came running before anything happened." We got back out and he continued the tour of the Plymouth's exterior. His car was a year younger than I, and in better condition. If Plymouth ever reopens a Havana showroom, Raúl would make a terrific salesman.

Raúl drove an interprovincial truck for a living. Had I seen the rest of the country yet? Not yet, and I'm anxious to, I replied. By this time his wife, Leonor, had joined the conversation. We were just three *habaneros* leaning against an old car on the Prado *pasando el rato*, chewing the fat. They had parked in front of the Arab League of Havana art gallery, cultural center, and restaurant. Would it be possible for me to hitch a ride to another part of the country? Leonor encouraged the idea, but Raúl downshifted a bit. Well, it would have been until a little while ago, but now with the massive gasoline cutbacks the authorities are tightening up on our trips, our cargo, everything. I mentioned that I wanted to go to Cienfuegos. "Oh! That's not so far away. Maybe we could do that." He asked for my number, but I never heard from him.

González had my shirt hanging, newly washed. He motioned me to take a seat while a journalist visiting from Buenos Aires interviewed him about art and Afro-Cuban religion. The talk drifted to Che Guevara, the Revolution's authentic guerrilla hero. Guevara was the Argentine doctor who made a house call on Cuba in late 1956 and didn't leave until the patient appeared healthy some ten years later. He was killed by Bolivian soldiers as he tried to get another guerrilla revolt under way. "When I was a youngster," González told the Argentine, "I was visiting my cousin out in the countryside once and he started yelling, 'Look! There's Che!' We all waved at him. He was in a car driving by. We could see his hair and his hat, but I'll never forget his smile. You know, the people who killed him failed to realize that by killing him he became that much brighter. He was the energy of this country, he was the electricity that charged us all. *Was* the electricity and *is*, too. I love him. The guerrilla Che meant so much for Cuba and for us all personally."

González took us into another room to show us his most recent painting, *Olokun*, the masked androgynous master of the seas. Highly sexual and intensely Afro-Cuban, it featured water, clouds, eyes, and smooth undulating body parts. González planned to donate it to a Cuban-Peruvian friendship group. "They're doing something honorable—they will sell it, and the proceeds will help people in the poor *barrios* of Lima."

The pencil and airbrush work looked like it had taken a week or more to complete. "Do you really think so?" He laughed in appreciation. "It took me one day. I started it first thing in the morning and by nightfall I was done."

La Plume never reported back on her conversation with the foreign ministry about my plans. Instead, after some weeks she handed me my passport, whose visa had been extended a few more months. Technically it had expired the previous day, but when I pointed this out to her she laughed at my anxiety. "Don't worry, no one will lock you up for having a visa overdue by one day." I didn't tell her, but that's exactly what happened to an American visitor I had heard about, a Communist Party member enthusiastic about the Revolution. He had overstayed his visa, and when authorities learned about it, *click*—jail.

Fortunately I had UNEAC and Fidel on my side; the writers union by authorizing my visa, and Fidel, by a front-page comment he made: "Now, in order to visit Cuba, you must be brave and have deep-rooted convictions." At the time he was speaking to the rector of the University of San Marcos in Peru, who was awarding him an honorary degree, but it applied to me, too.

To note, however, that a comment by Fidel made the front page is to overstate the obvious. In addition to all his other titles, Fidel Castro is also editor in chief of Cuba. His speeches, sojourns, and associations set the national media's agenda. When he clears his throat, it's news, and when he visits a school, clinic, factory, construction site, military camp, farm, or research laboratory, a front-page story invariably heralds the visit, leading to a center spread with pictures, text, and reports of normally calm Cubans squealing with delight. My files bulge with such stories, among them: a twelve-hour sweep through Villa Clara Province covered in two pages accompanied by nine photographs, eight featuring Fidel; a visit to a trade fair showing off the country's sophisticated medical equipment—good for two pages in which *el comandante* manages to appear in all nine photographs; and a story about a day trip to some farms that spills over three and a half of the newspaper's first five pages, in which Fidel shows up in a perfect fourteen of fourteen photographs. It's a record any politician would envy.

Buoyed by Fidel's endorsement, I dropped in on Alejandro at ICAP, the international friendship center. A group from Puerto Rico was due in a few days and he was ironing out details of their itinerary. I waited on the porch reading mail that La Plume had saved for me. My sister had sent a clipping about a "Predict the Fall of Fidel" contest, sponsored by a group in Washington. How long will Fidel last? Mail in your entry with the date you think he will abdicate/die/lose power/be overthrown. The winner gets a three-day trip to "free Havana," the runner-up a briefing in Washington on Cuba's transition from Communism.

This is just the sort of supercilious Cuba bashing that obstructs any reasonable effort to restore relations between the two countries. When I showed the clipping to Alejandro, whose job it is to encourage informal links between Cubans and Americans, he read it over and over in disbelief. I had been away from that sort of sniggering, imperial attitude long enough to be taken aback by the sheer contemptuousness of it, too. The contest made fun of Alejandro's country, its leader, and his hero.

He just stared at the item. "It's meant as a joke," he finally said, "but they're a little bit serious, aren't they."

"And somewhat arrogant and mocking as well," I added.

Alejandro shook his head and took the clipping back to his office so he could type out a copy to show others.

* * *

The government could act fast when it needed to. Within a few weeks' time, razor blades, newspapers, virtually anything that required combustibles for manufacture or distribution was added to the ration book or produced in diminishing numbers. The nighttime carnival near the Malecón, whose noise, muffled by my twenty-six floor altitude, often lulled me to sleep, now ended at one in the morning instead of four, to save electricity. Even Coppelia suffered reduction; less ice cream on hand, fewer flavors, shorter hours. Some major mines suspended operation. Virtually all nonessential activities were cut back. More electricity was saved by reducing the normal workweek. It became the only cutback everyone cheerfully accepted.

I practiced my oboe more than I had planned but less than diligently, and never before nine in the morning. The sound was odd enough to neighbors already awake; I didn't want to startle too many too early. I continued my postdawn walks along the Malecón. The sea never failed to startle me with its brilliance at that hour or its rich blueness late in the evening. Even on the darkest of nights, with no moon, it still shines a dazzling aqua. It has its own shimmer, much as the air in the country's mountains. When I looked away and then back, the subtle differences continually astounded me, yet the water always retained its Caribbean tint. Even at midnight the coast is clear.

The phone interrupted my oboe practice one morning. It was David Evans's assistant from the U.S. Interests Section. Mr. Evans and his wife were having a backyard gathering at their home in Miramar in a few nights he said. Some foreign press, some Cubans, a few diplomats from other countries; a mixer. Would I attend? "He has a satellite dish," the assistant added. "You can watch Tom Brokaw."

"What's second prize?" I asked. With some apprehension I accepted the invitation.

Matches were added to the ration book the next week. Lighting someone's cigarette became as much dialectical as friendly. A banner headline quoted Castro: THOSE WHO ARE WILLING TO STRUGGLE SHOULD FEEL FORTUNATE, BECAUSE THESE ARE VERY DIFFICULT TIMES THAT DEMAND GREAT VISION AND TALENT.

I planned to travel the 335 kilometers to Cienfuegos by train—see the countryside, chat with passengers, arrive refreshed. This met with approval whenever I mentioned it, though everyone agreed that the rail system was pretty terrible. Then I added that I hoped to take the *lechero*, the milk run that stops in every two-bit *pueblito* en route. I might just as well have told them I hoped to swim the English Channel in winter.

"Nobody rides the *lechero*." "It's even less reliable than the regular train." "Does it still run?" "It'll take all day, and it's unsafe." "They put the worst cars on the *lechero*." "Don't be a fool." "Can't you afford a few pesos more to take the regular train?" "Take the bus."

These common sense reactions only reinforced my determination. "Look," I said, "if I wanted swiftness and efficiency I'd take the train from Zurich to Geneva."

Once convinced of my intention, they offered advice: "Hold on to your bag the whole time, even when you're dozing." "Wear a money belt." "Don't forget to bring a bottle of water."

Havana has two train stations, the major one in Habana Vieja, and Tulipán, little used and largely ignored. No printed timetable existed; the schedule and ticket procedures changed periodically and unannounced. Telephoning the station was virtually impossible, and even had I gotten through, the information would be no more reliable than the opinion of a stranger in line at Coppelia Park. I set aside a morning to go to the station and book my seat in advance.

Jesús, my oboe teacher, was pleased that I had chosen Cienfuegos for my first trip. My apartment was not far from the Sinfónica Nacional rehearsal hall, nor from the conservatory where he taught, and he preferred the novelty of visiting the building with privileged foreigners to having me over to his house. All guests, foreign or Cuban, had to show identification at the front desk and get a *permiso*, which listed the caller's name and ID number. The slip, initialed by the resident, had to be turned in to the elevator operator on the way down. The penthouse floor, where Meyer Lansky lived in the 1950s and which now housed high-ranking security officers, has its own small, private automatic elevator. Those of us who lived within a few floors of the penthouse level often took the *chiquitica*, as the little elevator was called, when the others were too slow in coming or simply too crowded.

A two o'clock lesson meant Jesús showed up within a half hour either way, and after the oboe part we'd chat and sip rum for another hour. Very Latin, very classical. Alcohol improved my Spanish; would it also help my oboe?

Jesús asked me to play a scale in *si bemol*. I looked at him as if he had asked me to recite revelations from the Koran. He repeated himself.

Finally it dawned on him that I knew notes from A through G, with sharps and flats thrown in. Once we established that my musical vocabulary equaled my ability at the oboe, he wrote out:

A = *la*	F = *fa*
B = *si*	G = *sol*
Bb = *si bemol*	b = *bemol*
C = *do*	# = *sostenido*
D = *re*	*ejemplo:* C# = *do sostenido*
E = *mi*	Db = *re bemol*

This was, more or less, the standard do-re-mi. Having clarified that, I ran through some scales—*si bemol, fa sostenido, re,* and every beginner's favorite, *do.* "Relax," Jesús advised, "loosen up." I had a tendency to tense my arms. "You'll get better sound from a relaxed posture than from an intense one." He gave me some sheet music to practice, and a book of simple solos published in the Soviet Union. He suggested I prepare the first one for my next lesson.

Since I had last seen them, Jesús and Laura had vacationed at near-deserted beaches on the south coast and visited a former student's countryside home for a weekend pig roast. The symphony's first performance of the year was the following night; Jesús had an English horn solo in the last piece. "The concert won't be especially good because everyone's just returning from vacation." Still, he said he'd have a ticket waiting for me at the National Theater box office.

In front of me lay two photographs. One was part of a 1906 *National Geographic* article, "Cuba—Pearl of the Antilles." The other adjoined an article promoting this sort of transportation, and came from a newspaper the day after my music lesson. In both, oxen pull wagons full of provisions. I started hearing nervous jokes about the Chinese bicycles Cuba would soon be importing. Fewer buses were on the streets; a shortage of spare parts and fuel kept the rest garaged. Iraq had invaded Kuwait a couple of months earlier, and Desert Shield led the international news on television every night. Erratic and reduced oil deliveries from the Soviet Union coupled with upheavals in petroleum production and supply from the Middle East further threatened the country's already dwindling reserves. The new long-range program of island self-sufficiency encouraged beasts of burden and bicycles rather than internal combustion engines. A domestic factory was gearing up to make rum bottle plastic stoppers to replace cork ones, a hard currency import. Until the new plugs were ready, rum was hard to come by, and sold on the black market at a one-hundred percent markup. Day by day, Cubans were becoming increasingly aware of the situation their country foundered in.

Correspondence back to the States: "The Island is getting in a very critical condition; it brings out the real character of everybody and most of them have so little pluck that they are ready to lie down and have circumstances kill them. I do not wish to write too gloomy a letter nor have you think that I am losing courage, but want you to understand the real condition of things."

Fortunately that was not my letter. It was written in 1884 by Edwin Atkins, the Massachusetts man whose family owned a sugar plantation near Cienfuegos. A series of uprisings against Spain had taken place and more were brewing. Thirty-one-year-old Cuban José Martí, based in New York, had been traveling through the Americas encouraging Cuban independence and Pan-American literature. He was good at both.

Seldom would a day go by during my stay in Cuba that some writings of José "Pepe" Martí were not republished, or a statue of him erected in another country, or a reading of his poetry staged, or a symposium on his importance held. The Center for the Study of José Martí, his daughter-in-law's home until her death in the early 1980s, keeps busy reinterpreting his output, collected in seventy-six volumes. A point of view on almost any subject can be found in his prodigious and humanistic works. Radio Martí, the U.S. government radio station beamed exclusively at Cuba, has become part of the Caribbean's airscape. Informally, it goes under a variety of names, among them Radio Pepe, and Radio Casualidad ("Accidental Radio," explained to me once with a twist of an imaginary radio dial, and a look of surprise, as in, "Look what just popped up on my radio!"). So well known is the station that a child growing up in Cuba right now might think that Radio was the name of one of José's children. The station's credibility does not match its notoriety.

I went out to look for Calixto, the religious believer I had met three years earlier. He would be able to give me a different perspective on the country. A courteous young man answered my knock at the church door. A Catholic youth meeting was just breaking up and a dozen extremely polite and quiet teenagers milled about. Padre Pedro spoke with me. The youthful Dominican father wore newly polished tasseled loafers beneath a neatly hemmed white lightweight robe. Calixto had left the country in May 1988, six months after we met, he told me. He went to Spain, then Canada, Mexico, and, the padre thought, back to Canada. Someone had received a letter from him recently. If I came back in a few days he would have Calixto's address for me.

During my visit to Havana the previous year I had met a plastic surgeon who headed the city's Jewish community of one thousand. We'd met at a cocktail party for the media group I was traveling with, sponsored by ICAP, the government's international let's-all-be-friends agency. The doctor, gruff-appearing in his fifties with a perpetual stogie in his mouth, was quite friendly. His last name was Miller, his ancestors from Lithuania. Mine too. *Could we be——?* No, too farfetched. We compared family trees. His father came to the New World in 1924; my grandfather about thirty years earlier. He knew all his Western Hemisphere relatives. We compared Millers, Jews, and countries. Chanukah was only a couple of weeks away, and I had brought a box of Chanukah candles with me from the States. As we bid each other good night, I offered him the candles. "Here. These are from the North American Millers to the Caribbean Millers."

His hands trembled slightly as he took them, his face softened, and his eyes moistened. I had doubled the number of his synagogue's candles. "Thank you," he murmured.

Dr. Miller went to shul most evenings for a brief prayer service, and I hoped to find him there. I was late for prayer, but I found a theater at the far end of the building, the Brecht Theater. That night a small variety troupe called Los Amigos was performing. Two pesos later I took a seat in the basement playhouse, which could have been a dinner theater had there been dinner. Fifty small tables were set up, waiters took drink orders (a choice of rum or Tropicola), and the Amazing Rhythm Aces played over a good stereo system.

Another fellow was seated at my table. He had been educated to teach Cuban history, but with no openings he worked as a sports therapist. I had run into this often—bright people in their twenties and early thirties, well trained in a specialty for which few or no positions were available, working in unrelated fields until something opened up. Cuba must have the most overeducated, unsatisfied work force in Latin America. We sipped rum and ate peanuts from paper cones. I asked him about José Raúl Capablanca, the chess master. He wrote the names of the country's three top chess players on a napkin. The lights went down.

Two clean-cut white actors came out accompanied by a mulatto actress. The guys wore glasses, black pants, no shirts, and speckled jackets—one gold, the other red. The woman wore a shimmering gold pants suit. She had the pizzazz of a front-line Vegas show girl with teeth that could lead ships into Havana harbor under a new moon. She opened the set with a big band number backed by taped music. Sexy sweet banter between the men and another actress followed, but the riskiest topic they touched on was *Three Trapped Tigers*, the novel by the long self-exiled Guillermo Cabrera Infante. From a fade-out they went into a parody of a droning self-centered television ballet host who, after an interminable introduction with innumerable false endings, finally allowed two ballerinas to dance for a scant few seconds. It could have been Dan Aykroyd on *Saturday Night Live*.

Next, a quiz show. "What did the Spanish bring to our country?" gold-speckled jacket asked red-speckled jacket. "Wine. Sausage. The guitar."

"Very good. And what did the African bring?" "Music. Rhythm."

"Yes. And what do we have now?" *Drum roll*. The *mulata* walked out on gold stiletto heels in a tight, gold strapless minidress with a frilly white hem. Both speckled jackets looked drunk with pleasure.

"Okay, now we're going to talk about the land between Patagonia and the Rio Grande." The jackets bent down to her ankles. "Here we have Argentina." They crouched just below her knees. "And here, Uruguay." She looked slightly nervous as they inched toward her thighs. "Next come the Andean countries," said gold jacket with a smile. "*Rápido, compañeros*," minidress said with quick-witted concern. "Let's get to Central America."

The Sinfónica Nacional played in the thoroughly modern Covarrubias Hall at the National Theater, which faces the Plaza de la Revolución. When Fidel gives his orations in the plaza, the area is jammed for blocks around. When he isn't speaking, however, the plaza looks like a shopping mall parking lot on Sunday morning. The concert Jesús invited me to celebrated the orchestra's thirtieth anniversary, but appreciation of symphonic music, opera, and ballet is a strong tradition that goes back to Spanish colonial days. For sheer notoriety, Enrico Caruso's 1920 visit caused the biggest international stir in the history of formal concerts in Cuba. Tickets were priced well in excess of forty dollars each, and Caruso's fee—ten thousand dollars per performance—outraged press and public. During the second act of a performance of *Aida* on the star's last night in Havana, a bomb went off in the theater. Caruso, in costume, was in the office of the tour's promoter, who later wrote: "Total confusion reigned with cries of terror as some of the decorative figures adorning the proscenium arch of the stage began to fall in shattered hunks. . . . One of the balcony columns collapsed, injuring some of the audience. . . . The conductor had run out of the pit like a flash of lightning when the bomb exploded." Extras also ran out of the theater. Caruso and the promoter "hurried out onto the stage, dodging bits of scenery, to get the audience to remain calm. The first trumpet of the orchestra, a Spaniard named Rivero, had the good sense to start playing the Cuban national anthem, and the rest of the men who had left the orchestra pit gradually joined in with their instruments. Fortunately this seemed to hypnotize the audience and avoided any further misfortunes." Caruso went back to his hotel. In the States, he bitterly blamed the Cuban press for whipping up hysteria against him.

At Covarrubias Hall the orchestra tuned to the oboe's A, followed by the intricate and effortless cacophony of some seventy-five instruments all getting in their last licks before settling down. The Brahms violin concerto opened the concert. About two hundred people attended, half under twenty-five, it appeared. The low turnout, Jesús's wife Laura explained, was due to the start of the university semester that day, and the fact that most *habaneros* had just returned to work after four-week vacations. And then with the gas shortage in full crisis, fewer people were willing to use precious fuel to drive to the symphony; likewise fewer buses were running. Besides, Laura added, the night's program wasn't especially appealing.

A European woman visiting in 1913 wrote that Havana's orchestra "is good, and composed of blacks and whites, like the notes of a piano, mingled in harmonious confusion." Still true. About twenty percent of the orchestra was black, including the concertmaster, soloist Zenón Díaz Lauzurica. The conductor wore white tie and tails, the men black pants and white long-sleeved dress *guayaberas*, and the women, white long-sleeved blouses and, for the most part, full, calf-length black skirts. Thirty-five-year-old soloist Díaz wore a snappy dark brown suit. According to the program notes, he had studied not only in Cuba but later at a conservatory in Odessa, then at the Tchaikovsky conservatory in Moscow. He had made records in Kiev. He played wonderfully, interrupted only by a five-year-old who started crying and coughing. The child's outburst continued, the acoustics in the hall delivering his wails with clarity. His mother, a musician onstage, sat on the edge of her seat. Did blood flow thicker than music? Of course. Mamá put down her violin and dashed into the audience to collect her boy.

The next piece was a concerto for guitar by Leo Brouwer, the symphony's director and an acclaimed composer for classical guitar. The young soloist, Ileana Mateos, played strongly and gamely, but the piece itself was limp. The Ravel piano concerto in *sol* major rounded out the evening. Soloist Dagmar Muñiz was an activist, her torso twisting in rhythm with Ravel's adagios and prestos. Her fingers danced the rumba all over the keyboard. Jesús played his English horn solo.

Twenty people were lined up at Coppelia, but no one was selling ice cream tickets. "*¿El último?*" I asked the lady in front of me, knowing full well that she was the last in line. The kiosk was empty. More *últimos* came, and soon the line stretched past the bus stop halfway to the corner of Twenty-third and L. Still no one in the booth. A half dozen people finally drifted away. More time passed. I was getting closer to—to what? The booth had been abandoned, yet paradoxically I was nearer the goal. This was pure performance art. Should I leave? Damn if I was going to walk away from my spot in line after twenty minutes, even with nothing at the end. The line was the ultimate *último*. Instead of a fore it had an increasingly lengthy aft. It was quintessentially Cuban. People clung to their place in a line with no reward in sight. That week a new edition of Lenin's *On Art and Revolution* was released.

Video machines in Cuba use Beta rather than VHS. To play the tapes I carried with me I had to transfer them from one system to the other. I wanted my muralist friend González to see the PBS special on Cuban music; the other tape, *Family Portrait*, I planned to show to the filmmaker's relatives, most of whom lived near Cienfuegos. The only conversion machines were at the government film institute, ICAIC (Instituto Cubano del Arte e Industria Cinematográficos). To transfer the tapes by the book, La Plume would have had to call the Director of International Relations at ICAIC, who would then authorize another department to requisition blank tapes, and other offices to arrange equipment, time, and staff for the transfer. Enrique Oliver, director of *Family Portrait*, had given me the name of a colleague at ICAIC just in case.

Tracking down the colleague only took one morning, but now she had to find blank tapes and book equipment time. With the energy crisis, ICAIC had tightened up on extracurricular use of its hardware and electricity. She would have to slip it in during time assigned to her crew. Blank tapes for personal use were extremely difficult to come by, even for workers in the broadcast and film industries. As a foreigner, though, I could purchase as many blanks as I wanted at the hard-currency electronics and liquor store on the ground floor of my building. I picked out the videotapes and some other items and brought them to one window to be written up, then to another to pay; total bill, twenty-nine dollars. The cashier asked to see my passport to make sure I had the right to carry dollars, then she took my money. I took the blank Betas and original tapes over to the film institute and left them on my contact's desk. Ten days later she dropped off the goods at my building. I was one step closer to leaving for Cienfuegos.

The book launching for *Capablanca*, the fictionalized biography of chess champion José Raúl Capablanca, took place at the Plaza de Armas. A dozen chessboards—actually, squared-off plastic sheets—were set up for anyone to play on, and copies of the newly released book were sold at two pesos each. Although Capablanca's international success brought chess to new prominence in Cuba, the game had achieved a comfortable role in daily life long before him. Carlos Manuel de Céspedes, a nineteenth-century leader in the struggle for independence, once organized a chess match as a cover for plotting against Spanish domination.

Capablanca, whose youth was spent in a Cuba ruled by Spain and the United States, was sent off to Columbia University in 1906 to study chemical engineering after having already proven himself Cuba's best chess player. His sponsor was an industrialist who soon cut off his aid because José Raúl spent far more time at the Manhattan Chess Club than at his studies.

For the next few years Capablanca played throughout the U.S., victorious in tournament after tournament. Europe and South America followed; finally his government awarded him a job in the foreign service as an inspector of consulates. Not so coincidentally, his tours of duty corresponded with overseas chess tournaments. Capablanca was an ambassador of goodwill; one biography describes him as "dark-haired, blue-eyed, with the ability to turn on the charm . . . a chess-playing Rudolph Valentino." He could "attract mass adulation. Even women turned up to watch when Capablanca played."

In 1921 Capablanca beat Emanuel Lasker, a German who had held the world championship for more than a quarter century. The Cuban chess machine held the top rung until 1927 when Alexander Alekhine defeated him in Buenos Aires. The foreign ministry demoted him from Minister Plenipotentiary and Envoy Extraordinary at Large to Commercial Attaché.

Capablanca's impact came not from his reign, which was relatively short, but from his personal and professional style. A strong ego, a graceful and powerful middle game, and skill at tennis and billiards kept him enormously popular at home and abroad before and after his championship years. A stroke at the Manhattan Chess Club felled him in 1942, and he died the next day. Today, every crossroads in Cuba has a Capablanca chess club.

"I like chess although I don't play it very well," Fidel Castro once told an interviewer. "I play it very casually, but it seems to me more entertaining than dominoes." Bobby Fischer inscribed a copy of his chess book to Fidel when the two egos met in Havana in 1966: "I sincerely hope that my book will help you play better chess."

Cuba was far more hospitable to the American chess wizard than the U.S. was in 1988 to Guillermo García González, a Cuban grand master who won ten thousand dollars in a New York competition. The Treasury Department stalemated his prize money under the Trading with the Enemy Act. García could only claim his purse if he abandoned Cuba for any other country in the world (except Libya, Vietnam, North Korea, or Cambodia).

For the Trading with the Enemy Act to take effect, the U.S. must be at war with the "target" nation, or at least be under a presidentially declared "state of emergency." When John Kennedy signed the embargo papers against Cuba, neither was true; he relied instead, on Harry Truman's 1950 state of emergency over "the threat of world communism." Congress, drawing on the legal authority of the act, passed the Cuban Assets Control Regulations in 1963. One provision allows the Treasury Department to freeze any money in which a Cuban national has "an interest." Guillermo García, your crime is not that you play chess too well, but that you come from a land too wicked.

I bought a copy of *Capablanca* and asked to meet the author. "He just left," the saleslady said. "There he is, over there. That's his father pushing him around the corner, see?" She was pointing to a thin, white-haired man guiding a wheelchair down a street in Habana Vieja. The author, Jorge Daubar, was in his late forties. I caught up with him and we stopped to chat at a crowded snack bar. I told him of my interest in the legacy of Capablanca and how delighted I was to learn of his book. Daubar belittled it, promoting instead his detective and spy thrillers, *policiacos* as they are called. He had one *policiaco* already contracted and another pending. He had grand ideas for the theater, television, film, the works. He wanted to talk about Ludlum, John D. MacDonald, and Stephen King. We made a date for morning coffee at his place.

Havana is for walking, no matter what neighborhood you're in. The sidewalks are seldom wide enough for people to freely pass each other, but common promenading etiquette allows spilling out into the street. The country wears its history in the streets, from plaques commemorating sixteenth-century structures to busts of Martí to today's unimaginative architecture.

No cardboard encampments ringed the city. Crowded neighborhoods such as Centro Habana, in serious need of replastering, replumbing, repainting, rewiring, and rebuilding, stood out for their ills, yet the utter absence of people so destitute they had to sleep on sidewalks was continuously impressive. The few scavengers knew to dig in dumpsters near buildings like mine, where foreigners lived.

One night at two o'clock I saw a couple of middle-aged women sitting half asleep against a store window on Galiano Street. Could they, I wondered, have been the first indicators of the economy bottoming out? It turned out they lived around the corner. They wanted to be first in line for goods at a women's apparel shop that they hoped would stock skirts their size when it opened eight hours later. Both women had ration books that corresponded to the category this store would sell to that day. Nothing guaranteed that the skirts would be in, or that there'd be a selection of size or color or style—nonetheless, they'd be the first to know.

The complex ration procedure and the declining availability of merchandise reflected poorly on the system. People had little, but everyone had access to about the same amount of little. This system, unlike those of any neighboring countries, had found a roof to cover everyone at night, but still couldn't assure city folk that country food would arrive on time—or at all. Fidel, said a joke making the rounds, goes to Santiago de Cuba on the southeast end of the island to make a speech. "I've got some good news and some bad news," he tells the throng. "Which do you want first?"

"*¡La buena!*" they yell back. The good news!

"All right, *compañeros*. The good news is that for the next six months you'll have to eat stones."

A hubbub rises through the crowd. "That's good news?" "Has he finally flipped?" "Stones?" *El líder máximo* held his arms out for silence.

"The bad news is that there aren't enough stones to go around, so you'll all have to share."

Anaïs Nin thought *habaneros* walked with a "peculiar indolence" when she described them in her diary in 1922. "It is a slow, dragging step, a deliberate, swinging movement, a gliding serpentlike motion, something speaking indefinably of that characteristic laziness of the tropics and . . . a state of mental apathy, a universal malady of Havana."

I knew just what Nin meant about slow-dragging steps and mental apathy. That's just how I felt as I pulled myself from barbershop to barbershop in Habana Vieja, the section I called O-town because within a few blocks you could find Obispo, Obrapía, O'Reilly, and Oficios streets. The first barber shop was closed in the middle of the day. Another had a sign out front announcing that its staff was on vacation and wouldn't return for another week. A third required appointments until the afternoon hours. On its wall hung a reprint of a 1552 document licensing Juan Gómez, Cuba's first barber. Evidently this barbershop on Obispo Street was a direct descendant of Gómez's shop.

Finally I found one open on O'Reilly Street, Salón Soroa, named for an area in Pinar del Río province. Inside were three chairs, three fans, mirrors the length and width of the shop, and clumps of hair on the floor. A stocky man in white shoes was cutting a youngster's hair while the other barber was out to lunch. When he was done Roberto Hechavarría nodded at me to sit in his chair. The other cutter returned, and soon both barbers had customers. Roberto, in his sixties, gave me a good, basic working man's scissors and comb job. He used a straight razor to shape the back and sideburns.

Earlier in the year Roberto had visited relatives in New Jersey, he told one of the waiting customers. "Those people, they work all day for eight dollars an hour, and they get double time on weekends. I spent a day in New York." He stopped cutting and focused on the Big Apple. "I loved it, the buildings, all that traffic, big crowds, and the stores! One day, that was enough. After that, no more." He was the resident expert on crossing the Hudson. "You can get there through a tunnel, take a ferry or a bus, or you can take a train. Of course you can drive if you want, across the George Washington Bridge."

A list of twenty-five different services and their prices was posted on the wall, from a shave (sixty centavos) and a "*champú simple*" (simple shampoo: eighty centavos) to a blow-dry (six pesos). "We can't do a lot of those now." He looked over at his equipment and nodded at the unused wall socket. "Electricity."

Have prices changed much over the years? "Why change the prices? Everything costs about the same. *I was there that day in August 1951 when the barbers union set the rates.* They're almost the same today." Hechavarría now must meet a daily customer quota set by the state. My haircut, presentable in every respect, cost eighty centavos. A friend suggested the appropriate tip would be one peso. I got home in time to tune in channel 6 and watch reruns of *Benny Hill.*

The barbershop had been relaxing. Everyone was sociable, and their Spanish posed no problem, all except a worker who dropped in from the kitchen stove repair shop across the street. There'd been no comments about the government, no complaints about food availability, no woeful tales of the current crisis—unlike the story about the time Fidel went to a barber he'd patronized since early 1959 for a trim. "I've been reading about this perestroika and glasnost," the hair cutter begins, "and I was wondering—"

Fidel cuts him off. "That's not for us," and he goes back to reading the morning paper.

A few minutes later the barber again says, "You know, about this perestroika and glasnost—"

Fidel glares at him. "We are at a different stage of revolution. I don't want to hear about it." He returns to his newspaper.

Five minutes later the barber ventures, "I just can't help wondering about this perestroika and glasnost—"

Fidel puts the paper down, turns around and wags his finger. "If you mention those two words again, I'll have you locked up for ten years."

"Okay, have it your way, *comandante*, but it makes my job much easier."

"Makes your job easier? How?"

"Well, every time I say perestroika and glasnost your hair stands on end."

I finally tracked down Raúl Riesgo. That's the pen name of a contributor to the foreign language weekly newspaper put out by *Granma*, the country's daily. English, French, Spanish, and Portuguese editions of the weekly are distributed at international hotels in Cuba, and at newsstands and consulates abroad. Riesgo stands out because he writes not only about U.S.-Cuba relations, but also about U.S. domestic affairs. He is as reasonably informed as a columnist, native or foreign, can be expected to be.

He can also be funny, a quality seldom found in the Cuban press. He calls Jorge Más Canosa of the Cuban American National Foundation, an anti-Castro lobbying group, Jorge More American than Cuban Foundation. That appeared in his piece making fun of television Martí, the stillborn child of Radio Martí. (Television Martí was to be a U.S. government–sponsored television station aimed solely at Cuba, broadcast from a balloon off the Florida coast. Beset by technical, political, and even espionage complications, the project has never managed to broadcast much beyond test patterns.) Riesgo suggested that TV Martí use Star Wars technology to orbit millions of tiny broadcast balloons. Or distribute *TV Guide*–like booklets with color pictures that, when flashing by at twenty-four images a second, replicate television shows. He got mail on that one from a TV Martí contractor who wrote that if Riesgo was having difficulty receiving the signal, the station would gladly send him videotapes of its programming.

Another piece made fun of a projected constitution for a post-Castro Cuba written by exiles in Florida. Riesgo's parody highlighted the difference between the initial exiles entrenched in the commercial and decision-making world and the more unpredictable Cubans who followed, especially in the 1980 Mariel boatlift. "All exiles are equal," states Riesgo's constitution but "some are more equal than others." "Although representative democracy is the best system, its exaggerated use can cause irreversible damage." The mock constitution calls for the new country to include Florida, which will have "the industrious and hardworking Cubans and the businessmen," while Cuba itself will have those "less endowed and thus destined for physical labor."

Riesgo picked me up in his Lada and we drove through a downpour to the bar at 1830, the restaurant at the west end of the Malecón. The bar had not yet opened for the afternoon so we tried a few more with equally bad luck. Finally we drove back to his home, a nicely furnished third-floor Vedado apartment. When he opened the balcony doors after the cloudburst, we could see green treetops suffused with sun-sparkled droplets of rain. Riesgo is a retired military officer, thin, with a small mustache.

Riesgo got his start writing little pieces about Cuban social customs for *Opina*, a now-suspended publication. "They were satirical, but they made their point." When a friend became editor of the international *Granma Weekly Review* he began writing for it, too. "I have a vigorous daily regimen," Riesgo said as he poured the obligatory and welcome shot of rum. "I listen on my shortwave to the Voice of America, the BBC, and the Dutch, German, and French stations," all of which broadcast in Spanish. "I prefer the VOA for news and the BBC for analysis. The others give me a wider perspective." And Radio Martí? From the face he made I might just as well have spiked his drink with horseradish. "I tune in rarely, and only then to learn Más Canosa's latest invectives."

Through friends at the University of Havana, the Ministry of Foreign Commerce, and other offices around town, Riesgo sees newspapers and magazines from the States, Great Britain, and Spain. "To me, *El País* from Madrid is the best Spanish-language newspaper. I like *Newsweek* of all the periodicals from the U.S., but the best magazine in the world must be *The Economist*."

On occasion he sees *El Nuevo Herald*, the Spanish daily published by the *Miami Herald*. I had just shown him an article from the *Herald* about a guidebook to land that had been seized by the Castro government. "Do they really think they will be able to march in and reclaim their property? The Cubans in Miami, they engage in surrealism. They're stuck in H. G. Wells's time machine. Their traditional Cuba thrives in Miami but it's all but disappeared here. They have great influence on U.S. politics but almost none in Havana. The Cuban American Foundation is for U.S. domestic consumption, not Cuban. You notice that the State Department spokeswoman, Margaret Tutwiler, always distances herself from their comments." When he dropped me off back at the Focsa building I offered to save him copies of any U.S. or British publications I came across. He gladly accepted.

Anyone would accept, actually. No matter how outdated or frivolous the magazine, whomever I offered one to practically inhaled it. I gave *Rolling Stone* to a disc jockey whose nationally broadcast show highlighted hits from the English-speaking world. She used the magazine's gossip to pad her program with insider dope on the international rock scene. Literary journals from Mexico, fashion publications from Europe, book reviews from London and New York, an alternative weekly from Miami, newsweeklies from world capitals, sports magazines from anywhere—all of these were gratefully received, thoroughly digested, and quickly passed on. A poet saw me reading Walker Percy's *The Moviegoer* and begged me to loan it to him when I was done. My copy of Isabel Allende's *The Stories of Eva Luna* in Spanish raced through an average of three readers a week.

The overwhelming majority of Cubans saw no printed matter except state publications. Some of it was good—*Juventud Rebelde* (*Rebel Youth*, then a daily) ran lively personality profiles of factory workers, musicians and artists, cane cutters, and other real people, detailed pieces exposing corruption, and accounts of alcoholism, rowdy youth, and broken marriage.

One reason for the dearth of foreign publications is simple: importing them takes dollars, a currency harder to come by than caviar. The international long-distance telephone desk at the Havana Libre carried a half dozen copies of the *International Herald Tribune* and often a few of the *New York Times*. They arrived just after noon a day past the cover date. Three copies of the Sunday *New York Times* were racked every Tuesday. Next to them was a curious and always changing selection of other publications—*PC World, Good Housekeeping*, and *Self* among them. Plus the international editions of *Time* and *Newsweek*. News junkies authorized to spend dollars could arrange home delivery of the *Times* or the *Miami Herald* or a fair assortment of magazines. Mailboxes in my building regularly bulged with foreign periodicals. Beyond the international hotels, foreign publications were generally available only at ministry or academic offices. A graduate student in Asian Studies at the University of Havana, for example, had access to a Tokyo daily. The other reason so few foreign publications were permitted to circulate widely was that their content ran counter to the Revolution.

Despite the scarcity of a wider range of material, Cubans at every level of society were comfortably conversant about literature, current events, cultural drifts, and scientific developments abroad. This quality has been variously explained as a national trait, the result of an extremely high literacy rate, the tendency of island inhabitants to constantly peer over the water, a thorough schooling, and excellent radio reception. AM stations from Mexico, the Dominican Republic, Puerto Rico, southern U.S. states, and Venezuela come in with little difficulty; shortwave stations, too. One lady who lived in Vedado confided that on some days, for about twenty minutes in the late afternoon when atmospheric conditions are right, she can watch television from West Palm Beach, Florida. "It was a novelty at first, but really, this war of the airwaves, I don't see what all the fuss is about." Another woman told me she listens to *Larry King Live* to practice her English and keep up with right-wing America.

All this media talk took on greater significance when *Granma* ran a special boldface front-page notice announcing that since pulp delivery from the USSR was becoming increasingly erratic, changes in Cuba's newspapers were in order. *Granma* would be smaller and come out five days a week instead of six; Havana would get an abbreviated Saturday edition. Other publications would come out less often, or disappear

altogether, all except *Bohemia*, the venerable general feature weekly.
This was done "to prevent the information sector from collapsing. We
also hope that the measures will be temporary." A short while later
the newsstand price of *Granma* doubled. "Half the news for twice the
price," people said.

La Plume asked about my first trip out of town. I told her I hoped to
see Cienfuegos, visit the relatives of a friend from Boston, and travel
to the Zapata Swampland and Playa Girón, and also get over to Trinidad and possibly up to Sancti Spíritus. "Have you found someone to
accompany you yet?" I hadn't. "Would you be interested in staying
at El Castillito?" a small hotel between Cienfuegos and Trinidad in
the Escambray Mountains run by the writers union. I would.

That evening I walked over to a friend's place across from the Center
for the Study of José Martí. A refreshing drizzle cooled the sticky air.
On the way back along Calzada Street I passed the Presidente, a
comfortable hotel whose entrance was guarded by an attractive tourist
cop. I watched as she walked over to the corner and began questioning
an equally pretty young Cuban. The teenager wore Cuban eyes, a
Caribbean smile, and a short, black, cocktail dress. Her demeanor,
location, and dress labeled her a prostitute. She had been slowly walking along the sidewalk, eyeing men in cars and tourist taxis. The cop's
interrogation was neither violent nor threatening, but it was insistent.
She stood face-to-face with the hooker, her flashlight focused on a
reluctantly produced identification card. When the cop leaned forward,
slightly aggressive, the prostitute leaned back. Then they reversed
roles; the streetwalker became emphatic and the cop arched back. From
across the street their movement seemed symbiotic, almost synchro-
nized. They wagged their fingers at each other, their voices low, not
quite quarreling. Neither wanted to cause a commotion. The drizzle
had turned to a fine mist, and the two were silhouetted against a wall
under a full moon. I framed the scene with my hands and called it
"The Revolution at Work and Play."

The next morning at the main railroad station I learned that the second-
class train for Cienfuegos leaves from Tulipán, the smaller station in
Nuevo Vedado. I stood in a cab line for a half hour to get to Tulipán.
The fellow in front of me kept light banter going the whole time, yet
when he reached the front, instead of getting into a taxi he went back
around to the rear of the line and started all over. He was waiting for
his mother and sister to arrive from Santiago de Cuba, and he wanted

to be in the cab line when their train finally showed up so they wouldn't have to wait too long. Until then, he would repeat the cycle, inching his way forward, then walking to the rear. The Santiago train was already an hour late.

At Tulipán I found out that the *lechero* to Cienfuegos takes no advance reservations; just show up a few hours before the train leaves.

I took a bus to the State Department soiree at David Evans's home in Miramar, and walked up his wide driveway. Inside, it could have been Any Suburb, U.S.A. As promised, his big-screen TV had the *NBC Nightly News* on, reporting the progress of Desert Shield. Thirty-five guests filled the back patio. The party was catered by Cubalse, the government agency that supplies staffers to foreign legations. Waiters in starched whites and black bow ties walked around with platters full of Swedish meatballs, toothpicks stabbed in rolled ham, and breaded shrimp (with dip). A bartender mixed *mojitos*, a rum-based drink. Pizza squares came next. Diplomats mingled with Cuban journalists and foreign correspondents. Guests included a Cuban who had started a religious newsletter a few years previous with the help of the Interests Section and Arnaldo Coro Antich, the news director of Radio Progreso and Cuba's expert on radio technology. Coro is his country's best-informed and most persuasive spokesman against Radio Martí. He knows U.S. communications law and all its arcane technical lingo better than most American experts.

Coro had been introduced to me by Evans's assistant, who himself had an interesting past. He had spent most of his youth in Havana, where his father, a well-established Portuguese Communist, had served in his country's diplomatic corps. The son, after working in the Havana bureaus of Reuters and IPA, an Italian news agency, helped establish the Portuguese edition of the weekly *Granma*. The day after quitting the Party newspaper job, he started working the other side of the street; he walked into the U.S. Interests Section and has been there ever since. Or so he tells the story. Part of his job involves shmoozing with Cuban reporters and writers during happy hour at the journalists' bar and on the UNEAC patio.

"I'm responsible for the TeleMartí policy," he boasted. "I chose channel 13 at the time because it wasn't used by the Cubans." He told me which hotel restaurants were bugged, where the Cuban security forces work, and how helpful he was to everybody. I asked him about CIA presence in Cuba. He replied, "I don't know anything about the CIA—perhaps I know something."

Ondřej Kašina, a young reporter for Czechoslovakia's state news agency, Československá Tisková Kancelář, introduced himself in Spanish at Evans's patio bar. He lived in my building. When he realized I was from the United States he quickly shifted languages. "I feel more comfortable in English." I asked what sorts of stories he was doing.

"These days we're more papal than the Pope. All my editor wants is slanderous attacks on Castro. There's an article I'm working on that I can't interest him in about the old American cars all over Havana. They don't understand back in Prague. The only place I could sell it would be in the States. I have a contact at the *National Enquirer*. They pay for different sorts of contributions—so much for just an idea, a certain sum for the outline and material, and more if you write the whole thing. Perhaps you'd like to collaborate on it?"

Jorge Daubar, the author of *Capablanca*, was sure his thriller could be popular outside Cuba. Sitting behind the desk in his workroom one morning he excitedly told me about *Ceremonial de difuntos*, which, if it were to be published in English, would probably wear the title *The Cuban Book of the Dead*. It's the story of two Batista men who managed to remain in the government, their allegiance unknown to Castro officials. "It also involves the CIA. It'd be a perfect movie." (What was this, a pitch meeting?) "It's almost a thousand manuscript pages." With the publishing cutbacks, though, Daubar was skeptical that the book would ever come out. He looked through his files for his contract for *Ceremonial* with Letras Cubanas. His mother served us demitasses of thick, strong coffee. His father sat in the living room in front of the television.

Daubar surrounded his typewriter with the writer's usual newspaper clippings, reference books, and distractions. To the side was a well-used radio next to a bookcaseful of great literature. It spanned a wide range of subjects, countries, and centuries. "A few years ago a friend was walking down the street and saw a man selling old books and magazines. It turned out the guy had a complete set of *Bohemia*, from the first issue in 1908." Daubar's friend called around to raise the money; he contributed. Daubar's personal magazine collection included a complete set of *Enigma*, the international detective writer's magazine published in Havana for three years before it folded in 1989.

The boilerplate Cuban book contract calls for an advance at a rate of about twelve pesos per *cuartilla*, a thirty-line manuscript page. The royalty rate decreases as sales go up (a practice best kept hidden from

New York publishers). The publisher has rights for twenty thousand copies; after that a new contract must be negotiated. The author gets sixty percent of his advance on acceptance of the manuscript, half of the rest when it goes into production, and the balance on publication. And it includes all the mumbo jumbo found in book contracts the world over that gives the publisher everything and the author anything left over. Editorial Científica-Técnica printed eleven thousand copies of *Capablanca*.

"Would you like a drink of cold water?" To get it, Daubar's mother had to go to a neighbor's refrigerator. "Ours has been broken for six months. We have the money to get it fixed, and our name is on the waiting list. Meanwhile, the neighbors let us keep things cold in theirs."

Christopher Columbus is one of the few travel writers to come to Cuba who never wrote about the lottery there. Established in 1812 during Spanish rule, the national lottery blossomed further through independence and through a succession of governments until the Castro government brought it to a close. Ticket vendors "infest every eating-house and public way, and vex you at dinner, in your walks and rides," wrote Richard Henry Dana, who visited in the 1850s. "All classes seem to embark in it. Its effect is especially bad on the slaves, who invest in it all they can earn, beg, or steal, allured by the glorious vision of possibly purchasing their freedom."

The lottery spawned its own community from street-smart kids hustling tickets at the bottom to high officials regularly skimming the pool off the top. It also benefited hospitals and orphanages. Lottery culture has flourished in jokes, novels, songs, and superstition. Although it was outlawed in the early 1960s, something so entrenched never fully disappears. Daubar allowed as how there are still a few illegal lottery games around town, though not many. "They listen to the radio and use the winning numbers from Venezuela or Mexico. Of course I could buy into it, but I don't. Anybody could. If you have the money, you can buy into anything you want here."

We were occasionally interrupted by phone calls from friends congratulating Daubar on his book. Others dropped in for a minute or two to have him autograph theirs. Capablanca's chess game, Daubar told one caller, had a weak opening, but grew stronger as the game progressed, and he had a smashing close. "He was a brilliant strategist."

* * *

I stood in a bread line at the Socialism or Death bakery for forty-five
minutes and bought a dozen rolls for six centavos each. Then I went
to the Yara to see the latest Cuban movie, *Mujer Transparente*, about
women coping in a society that's changing as fast as they are. One
scene takes place in the lobby of the luxurious Hotel Tritón, where
the staff tells a Cuban calling on her relative from the States that she
can't dine or have a drink on the premises or even use the front desk
phone. The audience hissed long and loud at this typical example of
tourism apartheid.

"Tropicollage," a popular song by Cuban singer Carlos Varela, deals
with the same theme:

> *If you go to a hotel*
> *And you're not a foreigner*
> *They treat you differently.*
> *That is already happening here,*
> *And I want to change it.*
> *And whoever denies this fact*
> *Carries Tropicollage in his head.*

A Czechoslovakian cartoon followed *Mujer Transparente*. A plumber
becomes greedier and richer as his work gets worse and worse. After
each house call he drives off in his sharp new car. When a leaky faucet
he'd just plugged up springs another leak right after he pulls away,
the man of the house, in frustration, fixes it himself. He does such a
good job that he happily helps a neighbor with his plumbing problem,
scorning payment with embarrassed pride. Never, he scoffs with modesty, I did it as neighbor to neighbor. Soon he becomes the block
plumber, helping everyone, always refusing money. One day, in need
of spare cash, he accepts token remuneration, a practice he repeats with
increasing frequency. As his workload increases, so does his avarice. He
gets progressively sloppier until one day after plugging up the leaky
faucet in a neighbor's sink, collecting payment, and driving off in his
sharp new car, the same leak springs again. The audience loved it.

That evening I visited Reynaldo González, an executive at ICAIC—
the country's film institute—at his roomy Vedado home. He was
anxious to see *Family Portrait*. González popped it in his VCR and
watched, stonefaced. He never cracked even the slightest of smiles at
the warm and sly images of Cuban culture, needles mainly pointed at
Cubans in the States who have brought their customs with them. He

took it very seriously, but it allowed him to discourse about Cubans in the States.

"It's a fabrication! They invent a Cuba," he said with exasperation. "The image they have of us is pure fantasy! They have these 'Cuban American' nights at schools. I saw one on *Qué Pasa?* That's on PBS. Their image of us is frozen, so they must invent. They use us mercilessly in their own propaganda but they have no idea of our reality. Why do they do this?" He was as much perplexed as upset.

To complete my visits to some of the country's intellectual elite, the next day I met with the editorial director of the José Martí publishing house. Iván Pérez Carrión and I sat down in a conference room whose walls were lined with books in Russian, English, and Portuguese. His secretary brought us rich coffee.

The José Martí house dealt exclusively in foreign-language books. Their best-selling author was Fidel himself, whose speeches have been translated and packaged for foreign consumption. "Does he get royalties on these?" I asked. "Who's his agent?" Pérez replied by simply saying that Castro reviews the galleys of anything that goes out under his name.

"I understand you're researching a book about Cuba. Tell me about it."

I gave him the same description I'd given his country's diplomats in Washington and the writers union and foreign ministry in Havana. "Surely you're not interested in publishing it here," I said. "Are you?"

"Perhaps. Things are changing. We need an outsider's perspective. I was thinking that we could sell it to the tourist trade."

"Maybe I haven't made myself clear. This won't be a turn-left-at-the-plaza-and-there's-a-lovely-colonial-church sort of book. It's more experiences and impressions that won't all necessarily reflect well on the state."

"Yes yes, I understand. But by the time we'd be ready to bring it out—well, like I said, things are changing."

Among the changes was a lack of paper and ink. Iván's publishing house, in fact, had brought out exactly one book in the previous twelve months, *May the World Know It*, an account by a Mexican journalist of the U.S. invasion of Panama. "Could you write out your book outline and bring it in? I'd like to show it around." On my way out he gave me a copy of *The Rectification Process Is Nothing New*—a speech by Fidel. My favorite book on José Martí's backlist is *The Last American*, about some North Americans who, lured by a promoter just after the turn of the century, settled on undeveloped Cuban land.

Books from Editorial José Martí are sold in dollars only, and available mainly at tourist hotels; because they are not in Spanish, they never make the best-seller list. That week's domestic list showed *The Dwarfs*, a science fiction book, at the top, followed by a collection of poetry by young Cubans, a collection of short pieces by a Polish writer, a Russian novel, *The Master and Margarita* by Mikhail Bulgakov, and a novel by Canadian Hugh MacLennan, *Two Mourners*.

The nonfiction list, from the top: *Cosmetics and Health* (described as "useful advice for preserving youth and beauty"), *Celia in the Clandestine Movement* (eyewitness accounts of the role of Celia Sánchez Manduley, a heroine of the Revolution and a confidante of Fidel's), *Nerves, Nerves . . . of Interest to Everyone* (a translation from Russian), *Basic Principles of Electronic Sound*, and *Dispatches from Nicaragua* (articles about the Sandinista revolution). Nonfiction books about contemporary Cuba are very hard to find.

Literary events took place every week: a seminar on Alejo Carpentier, another on José Lezama Lima, a third on Martí's *Our America*. A pavilion full of the latest books from Mexico. An exhibit of illustrations from children's books. A reading of José Martí's work for children, *The Age of Gold*. An excerpt from *Bonfire of the Vanities* published in *Bohemia*. Every weekend, ballet, exhibits, opera, recitals, musicals, plays, theater, cabaret, galleries, puppet shows. You'd think the town was culture crazy.

The Special Period affected culture, too. Museums lopped a day off their schedules. Movie theaters opened later and closed earlier, "with the aim of reducing electricity costs." Nonetheless, movies still dominated public nightlife, films from Argentina, Russia, Europe, Mexico, Brazil, and mainly from the States: *Mad Max, Cleopatra, A Star Is Born, The Blue Angel, Funny Girl, Chinatown*, and *Moonstruck*. Two plays by Tennessee Williams, *The Glass Menagerie* and *A Streetcar Named Desire* were in repertory at the National Theater. In the early 1960s Williams's plays were staged with great frequency.

Tennessee Williams had been a frequent visitor to Cuba under Batista, to enjoy what Graham Greene called Havana's "*louche* atmosphere." The Revolution did not cool Williams's enthusiasm, and during a 1959 visit, writer Kenneth Tynan invited him to meet Ernest Hemingway at El Floridita. Williams found Hemingway "a gentleman who seemed to have a very touchingly shy quality about him." As Williams recounted the conversation in his memoirs, Hemingway said, "You know that this revolution in Cuba is a good revolution." Williams agreed, and Hemingway wrote a letter of introduction for him to present to Castro. After an interminable wait, Williams and Tynan were ushered in to see the youthful leader. Castro, Tynan wrote later, "told Mr. Williams how much he admired his plays, especially the one about the cat that was upon the burning roof. He hoped Mr. Williams would return to Cuba, perhaps to live there."

Jacobo Timerman complains in *Cuba: A Journey*, that neither Williams nor William Faulkner nor Günter Grass are stocked in Havana bookstores. "Furthermore, under the island's impenetrable glass dome there are no Cubans of average education with the slightest notion of who these authors are."

By the fall of 1990 when *A Streetcar Named Desire* was produced, Timerman was being published in the States, and in Cuba, Faulkner had just slid off the best-seller list and Grass's *The Tin Drum* was about to be released.

Fidel Castro thinks he's Jewish. Or at least part Jewish, buried in his past. "Castro" is among the more common names of Marranos, Spanish Jews who took on Christian identity during the Inquisition to avoid certain death at the stake. Fidel mentioned his heritage in private to Ricardo Subirana y Lobo, a chemical engineer and financial backer of the Revolution to whom he gave a diplomatic post in Israel in 1960. Castro, historian Maurice Halperin has written, "apparently was convinced that some of his ancestors were Marranos."

If Castro is a Jew, he's not a very good one. He doesn't attend Rosh Hashanah services, nor does he shop at Abraham Berezniak's kosher meat market on Cuba Street in Habana Vieja, which has messages to the Jewish community on its walls.

Every Cuban is entitled to a certain amount of meat and fish every couple of weeks in the ration system. (Entitlement doesn't guarantee availability, of course.) Each household, theoretically, has one ration book, called a *libreta*, which lists every occupant by age, name, and sex. I can't imagine that the ration books of any three neighbors selected at random would be entirely accurate. Relatives come and go, friends move in and out, some keep their *libreta* residence at one house and drink their morning *cafecito* at another. One entry in the *libreta* allows for special diets for medical reasons, age, or other reasons; those who qualify are assigned to special markets. To be a practicing Jew is another reason. Instead of going to their local butcher, Jews may go to Abraham Berezniak's place on meat days. To spend the afternoon at Abe's is to watch a remarkable flow of black, mulatto and white Sephardim, Ashkenazim, and their descendents pass through the door with two metal Stars of David on it and chat about the state of the world.

On the wall:

> Dear patron, to conclude the kosher process for the meat you are getting here, you should observe the following rules: 1) soak the meat in water for a half an hour. 2) Salt it on an inclined board with holes for one hour to let the excess blood run off. 3) Rinse off the salt—the biblical prohibition of consuming blood requires that the meat be thoroughly rinsed.
>
> Kosher chickens will come the fifth of next month. After that date you will lose your right for that particular ration cycle.
>
> Attention children—the Organization of Young Cuban Jews invites you to watch an Israeli film in Spanish called *From Toledo to Jerusalem* with Yehoram Gaon, the best Israeli singer.

Berezniak, balding and stocky, with a slight limp, has the personality to work behind the counter at the Carnegie Deli in New York or Goldenberg's in Paris. He wears nice loafers. A black fellow walked in, exchanged some doo-wah-diddy with Abe, and picked up his meat as Abe carefully marked his *libreta*. (Whenever Cuban Spanish sounded like high-speed mashed potatoes, I wrote "doo-wah-diddy" in my notebook.) A fellow of eighteen came in next for his family's allotment, then an elderly woman. A couple who looked like modestly successful retirees from Miami were next. As his assistant whacked at a carcass, loudly punctuating our conversation, Abe introduced me to the patrons, each of whom would invariably mention an old friend or relative who had abandoned Cuba for the States.

"Tell me, is there anti-Semitism there?" Abe asked. I thought for a moment, then said, a little, yes. "We have none here. For years we were called *polacos*," Poles, "even the ones who came from Spain. The Catholics gave us the space for this butcher shop in the early 1940s." A character in *Passing Through Havana*, a novel by Felicia Rosshandler about one girl's coming of age in Havana's Jewish immigrant community during World War II, explains, "All Jews are called *polacos* here because Poles immigrated by the thousands after the turn of the century. Yiddish, believe it or not, is called *el idioma polaco*, the Polish language."

Berezniak is also the administrator of Adath Israel, a temple around the corner from the butcher shop. He toots the shofar, the ram's horn, on Rosh Hashanah. As he explained this, a young man in glasses walked by and waved. "That's Elpidio. He works in the church next door, but he's interested in Jewish things."

Elpidio came back in and took me to his church. "Two hundred people come here every day, more for Sunday mass. The first mass was said here in 1674. This is the oldest church in Havana. There are catacombs down below. We no longer use them." He ticked off the well-known people who have prayed at his church, "José Martí's sister, too."

Back at Abe's, a short, thin woman who appeared to be at least in her mid-sixties walked in. A damp stogie drooped from an ill-shaped smile on her gnarled face. She looked around the small store and walked over to me. Suddenly she grabbed my crotch and gave a forceful squeeze. Then with a loud cackle she threw her head back and walked out.

"She comes by now and then. She's meshugenuh!" Everybody else in the place laughed, me last. Brief and crude as it was, I wasn't entirely offended.

Abraham Berezniak's neighbors that afternoon included a bare-chested man tinkering under the hood of his dirty green '48 Dodge. I went across the street to inspect the car. "It's got its original six-cylinder engine," he bragged. Clean, it would be the pride of any collector, a comment that gladdened him. Then he shook his head and drew a line through the dirt on the hood. "Think of this as an imaginary line. That's what it's like here. It's impossible to transfer private property like a car from one side to the other, but people do it all the time. For example, if this were your car and I wanted to buy it, we could make the transaction. But the next morning you want it back, so you take me to the authorities. Well, you have the ownership papers, and there's nothing I can do." Old American cars can only legally be turned over to a state agency, which will give you a Soviet Lada or pesos in return. The agency then sells the car—for dollars— to foreign collectors. An enormous lot full of old U.S. machines waiting for buyers sits at the end of Fifth Avenue. Paradoxically, the cars cannot go back home; for an American to buy one would be Trading with the Enemy.

A poster on the wall behind the bare-chested Dodge owner promoted the Sistema Único de Exploración, a national program to watch for foreign invaders. A drawing showed a man looking out into the horizon, his hands cupped over his eyes. *When you see or hear parachutists jumping or landing*, the caption read, *or buildings collapsing, or anything that looks like aircraft carriers at sea, or suspicious airplane or helicopter activity, or counterrevolutionary proclamations or explosive devices, call this phone number of the People's Power Council.*

A few lots away kids romped in a playground with swings, seesaws, and slides. Abraham Berezniak's life revolved around this immediate neighborhood—his home, synagogue, and butcher shop were all within three blocks of one another.

I learned about Abe's kosher butcher shop from Adela Dworin and Maritza Corrales. The two are daily fixtures at the city's Jewish community center, the Patronato, on the ground floor of the synagogue in Vedado where I had looked for Dr. Miller. Adela is executive secretary of the Patronato. Maritza is writing a book about the history of Jews in Cuba. Is there discrimination against Jews here? I asked. "There is no anti-Semitism in Cuba," Adela stated flatly. "We all get along. Even the PLO has an embassy here. They send thousands of students to Cuba every year. We coexist. There wasn't discrimination against Jews even before the Revolution. I've never seen anyone throw an egg at a synagogue. Never."

The Central Committee of the Communist Party has an office of religious affairs, Adela told me, "headed by Dr. José Felipe Carneado. He was a member of the first Communist Party in Cuba. He was a mulatto lawyer, so he knows what discrimination is. Of course, if you are a member of a religion, you can't join the Communist Party, so we have people who come here but don't claim to be Jewish, and some who even give money, but with no record of it. They come on the traditional holidays, and they're interested in reading about Judaism. Fidel said that someday believers will be members of the Party."

Maritza said Marxism wouldn't allow religion.

"But," countered Adela, "at Llamamientos some people have brought up the question—why can't believers be Party members? Believers feel discriminated against."

The two spend their afternoons in the Patronato library, a room filled with works in Hebrew, Spanish, German, and English. A calendar from the Jewish National Fund of Canada hangs on the wall next to photographs of Jewish writers. A list of Jewish winners of the Lenin-Stalin prize hangs nearby. I wouldn't have been surprised if the books on the Einstein shelf had been autographed by the Nobel physicist himself during his brief stopover in Havana during Chanukah, 1930. The Jewish community celebrated his visit, an event sandwiched between a dozen stops, including the Academy of Science, the Yacht Club, and a mental asylum. The morning after Einstein visited the synagogue, he insisted on touring Havana's poor neighborhoods. An account in the Cuban Geographic Society magazine said he went to "the most wretched homes in the disordered yards of the tenements and the boarding houses." In his diary, Einstein recalled "luxurious clubs side by side with atrocious poverty, which mainly affects the people of color."

After the Revolution, Havana had a rabbi who commuted on weekends from Miami, an arrangement that ended when the U.S. severed relations with Cuba in 1961. Adela said, "Jews don't need a rabbi for services. Someone simply has to know how to read the Torah. We've had rabbis visit us from Mexico and Venezuela." And what if a graduate of a foreign rabbinical college wanted to come?

"He'd have to live like us. Would he be willing to do that? He'd probably have a different standard of living. He'd have to take a room in a Jewish house and eat what we eat. You can't find kosher pickles in a Communist country.

"We used to get Passover wine and products like matzo early. This year we didn't, so we sent a cable to a rabbi in New York. He shipped us the things we needed on the daily charter flight from Miami— wine, canned gefilte fish, matzo. The man at the Party said we could do the paperwork later. The people at the customs house know about Jews. So *after* Passover I went to see the customs officials and legalized it all."

A German gentile graduate student working on her doctorate about Jews in Cuba came into the Patronato library and took her regular seat. She lived in a room rented from the University of Havana in a house near the Soviet embassy. Despite all the problems, she said, she'd consider staying if she could only find a place that carried black bread.

Adela continued. "This building was originally a cultural center. We had Sunday school classes, Ping-Pong, everything. At the old synagogue we had a mikva—it's like a sauna. There used to be five Jewish schools in Havana. After the Revolution we were allowed one Jewish school. They permitted the children to take Hebrew classes. The government gave us a bus for that school. It was in Santos Suárez. Then they decided that it wasn't in the interest of the government for children to learn Hebrew, so we held the classes ourselves on Saturday afternoons. We had forty to fifty children. Well, one teacher died and the other went to Israel. The president of the Jewish Community was a widower. He taught his maid Hebrew, and also how to play the accordion. Eventually he went to Israel, and she followed shortly afterward. She knew Hebrew better than anyone in Havana. When she left in 1981, the school closed."

Moisés, twenty years old, walked in for a few minutes. Adela motioned toward him. "See? We have some young ones, too." "Three years ago we decided to open Sunday school for children. We had ten or twelve children. We have a few more now. The Jews in Venezuela have been very helpful. A rabbi from Caracas came three years ago and asked us what we needed. We told him, a small van—a microbus to pick up the children for Sunday school and take the elderly to services. Ten months later we got the van. But now we can't use it the same way because of the fuel problem.

"Well, that's not our only problem. Most marriages now are mixed marriages. There is practically no circumcision because not only do we not have a mohel, the hospitals won't perform them either."

Adela and Abraham the butcher insisted that I delay my trip to Cienfuegos long enough to attend Jewish New Year services. A foreign Jewish male was quite a catch for a Cuban synagogue, they admitted. I'm not very religious, I countered, in fact I can't even remember the last time—

That's all right, they said. We know. Then we can count on you?

"So I committed myself to New Year's services at one synagogue in the evening and at the other the following morning," I wrote a *shiksita* back in the States. "I don't think this is why I came here; still, it's a legitimate slice of Cuban life and they're really very nice people. I must admit I did laugh to myself a little when each, on the same day, implored me to come to their services. For one brief moment, I was the hottest Jew in Havana. ¡Feliz 5751!"

At the writers union office La Plume asked if I had found someone to accompany me to Cienfuegos. "Let me know a couple of days before you leave if you still don't have anyone. I'll have to find someone from the UNEAC membership. If you're planning on renting a car and driving around, well, you don't know the roads, and the Escambray Mountains are pretty treacherous. You'd be safer with someone along. You can't go by yourself."

Foreign journalists in Cuba on short assignments are usually assigned a liaison from the foreign ministry. These guides have explicit agendas, sometimes they're helpful, and usually they bend. They're there when you need them, and sometimes when you don't. Reporters call them minders, or baby-sitters. The minder and the journalist both know how to play the game, and relations between the two, while sometimes strained, seldom snap. Since I was not under the auspices of the foreign ministry I never had one of their chaperons; I only watched them from a distance. La Plume was the closest thing I had to a baby-sitter, and her insistence that someone accompany me to Cienfuegos was her first attempt to exercise this authority. Meanwhile, she confirmed my reservation for two nights at El Castillito, the writers union mountain retreat, and gave me the address of the UNEAC office in Cienfuegos along with the name of its *jefe*.

That evening I dropped in on Salvador the muralist, but he'd gone out to persuade an art gallery to show his works. A block away a street meeting had just begun between nearby residents and some officials. A bare light bulb hung on a string stretched from one side of the street to the other. Under the bulb sat neighborhood officials taking turns with a microphone hooked up to a boombox. A crowd of one hundred from the community stood listening to the petty authorities tell them about pending improvements to the neighborhood. Then the floor was open.

A lady in a print dress complained about the upkeep of her building. "Water drips into the lobby each time it rains." A woman at the head table wrote down the address, and a man next to her announced that the situation would be attended to as soon as supplies arrived.

A man in a porkpie hat wanted to know when paint would be available for homes on his street. "We've been waiting a long time for it." The head table lady wrote down his address, and the man at her side said that when the paint came, porkpie would be informed right away.

A woman in tight faded slacks said that the front door on her building didn't close right. "When will we ever get it fixed?" The same lady in front took notes, and the same man promised that when the tools were accessible the door would be repaired.

This went on for a half hour. At first I thought this was a meeting of the block Committee for the Defense of the Revolution. "No, no," the couple at my side said. "This is the local Poder Popular," the People's Power Council. "The city is divided into constituencies, and each Poder Popular is responsible for keeping the neighborhood in decent repair. They have regular street meetings like this. We call this grass-roots democracy."

Does anything result from these assurances?

They gave me the sideways smile.

The San Juan café and bar was nearby, and the usual gang was on the stools and behind the counter. The San Juan proved a valuable and comforting place to drop in—no officials, no other foreigners, no hustlers. *"I love those bars and taverns by the sea/where people chat and drink just to drink and chat,"* wrote Nicolás Guillén in his 1958 poem "Bars":

> *There the white wave foams in friendship,*
> *The friendship of the people, without rhetoric,*
> *A wave of "Hey there!" and "How ya doin'?"*

After a San Juan dinner of more-or-less chicken soup, I had a peso in change coming to me. "I think I'll use it to play the lottery," I said, joking. "Not here!" Florencio protested, as if I had accused him of running a numbers game. "No, no lottery here!" "You can't play it here!" the others echoed. Then just as quickly they spread my Havana street map out on the counter, and each of them pointed out the neighborhoods where I could play the lottery if I really wanted to. The odds were usually about thirty-five to one, the most knowledgeable "not here!" man claimed.

Fidel gave a speech to the Unión de Jovenes Comunistas, the Young Communists League, in which he said, "If they told me that ninety-eight percent of the people did not believe in the Revolution, I would carry on fighting. Because a revolutionary must be a man who, even if he is left alone, continues to fight for his ideals."

The Communist Party, in the thirty-two years since the fall of Batista, had held three Congresses, meetings at which delegates from Party cells all over the country came together to thrash out an updated version of themselves. The neighborhood and workplace Llamamientos, whose resolutions were to be on the Congress agenda, were finally proceeding apace, but the next Party Congress, originally scheduled for 1990, kept being postponed. Signs around Centro announced that the Casa de la Trova on San Lázaro Street, normally a center for soft and friendly music, would be the site for a neighborhood Llamamiento. I came early and asked the Communist in charge if I could sit in. He welcomed me. This was my second Llamamiento.

After enough neighbors had strolled in, the delegate called the meeting to order and began reading the formal Call itself. *"The Communist Party of Cuba addresses itself today to all its members, the working class, the peasants, all manual and intellectual workers, the men and women in the different social sectors, all the organizations and institutions, our young people and all patriots and revolutionaries . . ."*

When I worked on underground newspapers in the States during the war against Vietnam, some offices had a special place for articles that, in turgid Soviet puppet language, lauded the people's struggles throughout the world. We called this hallowed spot Kim's Korner in honor of one of its most polished practitioners, Kim Il Sung of North Korea. Kim, one of the two world leaders who has held office longer than Fidel (the other is King Hussein of Jordan), could always be counted on to extend solidarity to his comrades. As if to prove his durability, he did it again just a few weeks prior to the Llamamientos. A member of the Central Committee of Cuba's Communist Party who heads the Committee in Support of Korean Reunification came home from a trip to Pyongyang carrying Kim's "greetings" to Fidel. *Granma* said the meeting was a success, "a chat among brothers, comrades in arms in the struggle against imperialism and for the consolidation of socialism."

Meanwhile, back at the Casa de la Trova, the reading of the Call continued: *"No! We will not renounce the Revolution, socialism, Leninism, and internationalism. We will not renege on our work, which is the most just and humane ever undertaken on Cuban soil. We will never yield to the arrogance of U.S. imperialism . . ."*

Kim's Korner hit its apogee in 1970 with a speech in Cuba by Comrade Todor Zhikov, First Secretary of the Communist Party of Bulgaria and Chairman of the Council of Ministers of the People's Republic of Bulgaria: "Dear brothers and sisters, heroic sons and daughters of Cuba. We extend to you the warm greetings of the Bulgarian Communists, and of all the workers of the People's Republic of Bulgaria. . . . We stand beside you in the difficult noble struggle for the construction of a new life in this marvelous part of the world that bears the name of Cuba. You may always count on the fraternal support of the Bulgarian Communists, the peoples of Bulgaria, the countries of the socialist community, and all progressive humanity. The great Soviet Union, with its unbreakable power, is the beacon of freedom, democracy, socialism, the independence of the peoples, peace, and social progress." On and on it went, a stunning example of Communist oratory. Finally Zhikov moved in for a smashing close, worthy of José Raúl Capablanca at his peak: "Long live the friendship and fraternal collaboration between the People's Republic of Bulgaria and Cuba, and may they develop without interruption! May the socialist community be ever more consolidated and strengthened! Long live the

78 *Tom Miller*

---

unity of all the progressive forces in their struggle against imperialism
and for peace, national independence, freedom, democracy, socialism,
and communism!" When I first read those words more than twenty
years ago I named my dog after Comrade Zhikov.

The Party delegate at the Casa de la Trova had turned the reading
of the Call over to a sub-delegate, who continued: *"We must advance
in the elaboration of models of economic and social development for the coming
years . . . we can count on our heroic working class, the bastion par excellence
of the Revolution, which true to its traditions and its history is now the main
protagonist of the process of rectification . . ."*

Mao Zedong, back in the days when he was Mao Tse-tung, would
have been struck by the language, too. "Some of our comrades," he
said in 1942, "love to write long articles with no substance. Why
must they write such long and lengthy articles?" the good chairman
asked. "There can be only one explanation: They are determined the
masses will not read them."

The Party delegate took over from the faltering sub-delegate. *"The
Fourth Congress of the Communist Party will give continuity to the encouraging
results of the process of rectification in the economic and social fields and will
firmly link them to the new concrete steps aimed at improving the work of the
Party, the state, and all the other elements involved in the system of institutions
of the Revolution. Our Communist Party, the basis for the political organization
of society . . ."*

Everyone in the Llamamiento audience sat attentively. To keep
myself awake that blistering hot afternoon, I pulled out a book I
carried with me about Japanese culture. It described a cult among
monks in Japan a millennium ago who rewrote history in order to
give themselves higher stature.

The sub-delegate again took up the reading. She and her boss
accelerated. Finally the Party delegate arrived at the end: *"With calm
optimism we can advance toward our Congress. A people of Communists and
their vanguard Party, of a single mind, will always assure the lasting
desire to exist, win, and develop ourselves."* His voice rising, the delegate
concluded: *"¡Socialismo o Muerte!"*

"¡Venceremos!" the crowd roared back.

The delegate exhaled. "Now, what suggestions do you have for the
Party Congress?" Nobody said a word.

He looked around. "Any resolutions you think should be brought
up at the Party Congress?" He held his worksheet up in the air.

Silence.

"Well, what did you think of the Call?"

"Oh! Very good!" "Quite complete!" "Well done!" "We're in agreement!" And the audience erupted in somewhat spontaneous applause.

The Communist Party delegate looked at his audience, at his worksheet, and then at his sub-delegate. "Well, in that case our duties here today are over." And with that everybody put their chairs back in the next room and filed out. The reading of the Call had taken forty-five minutes, the meeting afterward almost one minute.

"What happened?" I asked the man from the Party. "The last Llamaniento I went to lasted hours with lots of resolutions. Is today's meeting really over? Is that it?"

"Well, you have to understand, these are retirees." His assistant added, "Yes, that and housewives." All my life I've been a mediocre capitalist, but as I listened to the Llamamiento, I knew that I'd make a lousy Communist, too.

On my way home I had to step into the street a few times to bypass lines leading up to food outlets. I didn't recall lines that numerous or that long even a couple of months earlier. The government was starting to crack down on "paid queue-standers and other antisocial individuals . . . who profit from the sweat of our people during these times of combat and revolutionary work." Some Cubans, especially retirees, picked up extra money by waiting in lines on behalf of others. I arrived back at the apartment just in time to watch *The Mary Tyler Moore Show*, which had replaced *Benny Hill* in the late-afternoon time slot on channel six.

We had a minyan. Barely. The ground floor at Adath Israel at Acosta and Picota in Habana Vieja, where Eastern Europeans gather for dominoes weekday mornings, had been spruced up for the New Year's service that October day. Upstairs, the old synagogue lay unused. When the neighborhood became the main *barrio* for refugees from Nazi Europe, Acosta was called the Jewish Appian Way. *Polacos* had their own shops and newspapers, food and factions. They ate at Moishe Pipik's restaurant.

More than forty years later custom still prevailed along the Appian Way. At Rosh Hashanah services, each of the men put on a yarmulke and sat on the right. The women, also with their heads covered, sat on the left. The president of Adath Israel chanted his biblical prayers up front while the congregation mumbled theirs from prayerbooks and memory. Occasionally the two coincided and everyone was in unison for a few seconds, then each slipped off in autonomous prayer, as if strands from a fragment of floating seaweed had momentarily entwined and then drifted off on their own.

This intricate tradition, preserved here in the basement of a once-majestic Havana synagogue, had been choreographed by centuries of custom down to the last amen. Abraham, the butcher, brought the Torah out for the reading, then he blew the shofar. In a half hour it was over and we sat down in the adjoining room to some Schapiro's kosher wine from Atlanta and a kosher rosé from Ontario. Each of us was served a plate of chicken salad, sweet preserves, and a piece of bread. Next to me sat Mauricio, a youngish doctor trained in dermatology who was biding his time working in a clinic. On the other side sat Noel, a ship's mechanic on two weeks' leave. Mauricio asked if, when I returned to the States, I could find him a Spanish language history of the Jews. "The entire six thousand years, from the tribes through World War II up to the present."

Ten worshippers had already begun New Year's services when I arrived at the shul in Vedado the next morning. I picked a yarmulke from the pile and tried to slip unobtrusively into one of the back rows. Services took place in a small chapel next to the main room. A member later told me, "This is the tip of the iceberg. The iceberg is next door. In the old days we had more than three thousand people on High Holy Days, with the women upstairs in the balcony. If you pulled back the curtains there was room for hundreds more."

An elderly man came up and asked in a stage whisper that cut through all the prayers, "Are you Jewish?" He spoke in a curious mix of Spanish, English, and Yiddish. "Have you been brissed?" He made snip-snip motions with his fingers. "What was your father's name?" Morris, which he took to be Moishe. "What was your mother's surname?" Levy. "So you're Jewish!" With that he fetched a prayer shawl and draped it over my shoulders. "You'll take part in the service at the Torah!"

"But I'm just a *judío secular*. I'm illiterate in Hebrew. I haven't looked at a word of it since—"

He brushed aside my protestation. "You'll take part in the service! Tell me, have you been to Israel?" No. "But you have it in your heart, eh?" He sat down next to me.

The Vedado service, slightly less jumbled than the one in Habana Vieja, continued, and I started to pull out my notepad. The snip-snip man admonished me. "Don't take notes. You can do that afterward when we gather downstairs to eat." He invoked the Fourth Commandment about resting on the Sabbath as his authority, then gravitated to the front where he got into a heated argument with the lay rabbi over Hebrew pronunciation. The quarrel ended as abruptly as it had begun. The man in front of me looked up from his newspaper.

Each worshipper was called to the front to read a brief portion of the Torah and hold it for the next reader. Snip-snip bellowed out from the front, "Tom, ben-Moishe, please come up to the Holy Scrolls."

Blessed relief: lying flat on top of the Torah at my excerpt, underlined with an elaborate metal marker, was a transliteration from the Hebrew so I could pronounce my portion. Afterward we wished each other a happy New Year with gefilte fish, bread, and cake. In our blessing we thanked God for Tropicola.

I decided to ignore La Plume's insistence that someone accompany me, and arrived at the train station two and a half hours before departure, as suggested. A half dozen people were already waiting in line. By seven two dozen more people had joined the line, and the window opened for the 335 kilometer trip. A one-way ticket cost 3.45 pesos. At the same time a second window opened at the opposite end of the ticket platform, this one for coffee at ten centavos a shot. The passengers, who had spent half of their lives in lines, displayed a dexterity truly amazing to a hapless foreigner: they managed to hold positions in both lines at once without forfeiting their space in either.

The cars had slightly padded plastic reclining seats, an overhead luggage rack onto which I tossed my bag, and windows so filthy they could only have been washed a few times since Fidel entered Havana. The aisles were clean. No conductor actually said "all aboard!" Passengers just drifted on, and at nine o'clock we lurched out of the Tulipán station.

The railroad yard had a sign that told workers DOING SOMETHING IS THE BEST WAY OF SAYING SOMETHING. City streets were full of such high school gym sort of messages, but as we chugged through the suburbs and entered the countryside, they mercifully thinned out. Only the occasional statue of José Martí announced which Caribbean nation we were traveling through.

I was in the last car, facing northwest as the train headed southeast. Shortly after we got underway a skinny man lugging an enormous bundle walked to the north end of the car and, one by one, passengers from all the other cars drifted into ours and queued up. I did likewise, having learned the custom of quickly joining the back end of a line—"¿el último?"—without knowing what waited at the front end. A supply of anything was worth the wait. The skinny man opened his bundle and pulled out a large basket of fresh cheese sandwiches that he sold for forty-five centavos each. The lady in front of me said that this was the only food to be sold the entire trip. Many people bought three or even four sandwiches at once. Even on a moving train, lines remained the rhythm machine to Cuban life.

Rain began to blow in the windows about an hour southeast of Havana, a reminder that hurricane season was approaching. Once we had passed the outer perimeter of metropolitan Havana, only four others remained in my car, all women in their fifties seated together in animated conversation across the aisle. One got up and reached across me to demonstrate the trick to shutting the window. Cubans used this train to travel a few stops from one small town to another; I was the only passenger going the full distance.

My notes read, "men working in fields . . . anemic '57 Chevy stalled at r.r. crossing . . . ducks and cows near streams . . . small town, two teenagers playing chess in a carport next to a spitpolish clean '55 Chevy . . . elderly couple in horsecart outside of Bejucal near furniture factory . . . pix of Lenin and Che on walls of r.r. stations . . . workers in seats in front of me for a few stops talking doo-wah-diddy . . . no autos visible from train down streets of San Felipe— only bicycles and horses . . . cheese sandwiches not bad . . . nobody crossed themselves as we passed Catholic churches."

At Güines, two uniformed police from the Ministry of the Interior got on. One pointed to my feet resting on the vacant seat across from me. My sneakers, which when white had attracted street hustlers, now when dirty attracted the police. I quickly put them on the floor. The other cop asked if the canvas bag on the luggage rack was mine. Assured that it was, the two walked on. Five minutes later two more cops slowly walked through. They stopped in front of me and asked for my identification card. I hadn't yet been given my Cuban ID, so I handed them my U.S. passport. They looked at it, showed no response, and handed it back.

(Once in Guatemala the *guardia civil* stopped a bus I rode and demanded identification of everyone. They were searching for revolutionaries. Here the police were looking for counterrevolutionaries. Couldn't we eliminate the middlemen and have the authorities simply check each other's ID?)

The police left for the next car. The instant the door closed behind them, the four ladies, who had sat as if blind and deaf during my exchange with the police, leaned over, fairly bubbling. "What did they want?" "You could pass for Cuban, you know." "Yes, we didn't know what nationality you were." "Wasn't that smart of you to bring your own water," a comment I assumed, correctly, to be a request for a cupful. "What are you doing here?"

The ladies said good-bye a few stops later. Three policemen got on and took the last set of seats in my car. Evidently that was their turf; every two or three stops one set of police would get off and another would get on, always using the same seats. Halfway to Cienfuegos, shortly after noon, a sign announced that we were in Pedro Betancourt, a name I recognized as the ancestral home of a friend back in the States. I wrote her a postcard mentioning everything I could see from the train during our ninety-second stop. The list included run-down buildings, a large library, horsecarts, a short line, a couple of cars, and, outside town, lush green countryside. A bit farther, carved out of hundreds of hectares of sugar growth, was an impressive, well-manicured baseball field with a large cow near the first base line.

The countryside rolled green, most of it in cultivation, much of it in production. Housing projects obviously built since the Revolution formed settlements with small schools and white two-story rural medical clinics. Tractors and oxen worked the fields, mules and big trucks hauled produce. I don't recall ever seeing a pickup truck in Cuba.

The fearful warnings about *lechero* travel proved entirely wrong. Not only was it relaxing, but it allowed a view of the countryside even a car trip would have missed. Now, having seen some of the rural outback, I agreed with Ludwig Bemelmans, best known for the children's book *Madeline*, who observed in a 1950s *Holiday* magazine, "Landscapes of great beauty are everywhere in Cuba, of soft Pissarro and Cézanne color, and the tropical intensity of Gauguin. The earth is a moist burnt sienna, the fields of sugar cane the richest green." The sugar harvest hadn't really started yet in this part of the country. When the cane reached its maturity, though, sugar settlements everywhere would spring into action, organized to attack the crop with a vigor that has outlasted every sort of governing system Cuba has yet endured.

We reached Cienfuegos on time, in just under eight hours. I could report, as Edwin Atkins did 106 years earlier, "I have arrived safely at this city without being captured by any rebels."

I checked into the Jagua, a first-class hotel mainly for foreigners. To reach it I walked from the train station over to the Prado, Cienfuegos's main drag, and took a bus to the Punta Gorda district at the end of the line. The difference between Havana and a provincial city proved immediately palpable. People were less hurried, smiled more, relaxed more on park benches, and stopped to chat with one another in a manner as languid as the late-afternoon breeze off Cienfuegos Bay. A Coppelia ice cream parlor on the Prado had lines less lengthy than those in Havana, and more upbeat.

The United States doesn't recognize Cuba, but Cuba recognizes an Arizona driver's license. I made this pleasant discovery in the lobby of the Jagua, where I rented a Volkswagen bug made in Mexico, and bought gasoline vouchers for dollars valid at select stations. I also used my Mexican credit card. Cards from Canada, Europe, and Latin America are accepted with little difficulty in Cuba, but credit cards issued in the U.S. are invalid, because no link exists between Cuba and financial institutions in the United States through which to exchange money for receipts. Yet, as American travelers have discovered, the embargo can be punctured.

My credit card, issued in Mexico, enabled me to stay within the letter of U.S. law by spending U.S. currency in Cuba, permissible for journalists, and paying via a third country. With the card I could charge my purchases at dollar stores for myself and Cuban friends, buying incidental luxuries such as AA batteries, Heineken beer, and Habano shaving cream (ad idea: "The shaving cream Fidel would use!"). On occasion I found myself fumbling to explain to curious friends the mechanics of plastic money, compound interest, and usury. From their silent bewilderment, I might just as well have been describing American Airlines's frequent-flier triple-mileage bonus program.

Cubans, of course, had no access to credit cards, the means to pay a bill, or the goods to purchase in the first place. Shorter lines didn't mean that Cienfuegos had more goods or a wider selection than Havana, only that the people didn't have to wait as long to find out. A sidewalk billboard reminded passersby, WE CAN DO MORE WITH LESS.

I located the uncle of filmmaker Enrique Oliver at the other end of town, and handed him a letter from his relatives in the States along with a snapshot of me sitting with them on their couch in Boston. Enrique thought that this would establish my bona fide. "He's not political," Enrique said of his uncle Francisco, "but his wife is very much with Fidel." Regardless of their individual allegiance, they took me into their orderly home. Soon we went out in the streets of Cienfuegos in search of a VCR on which to watch the film starring Enrique's family.

We found a willing household on our first try. Two teenage boys reluctantly took a rock video out of the machine, much to the satisfaction of their parents, and we put on *Family Portrait*. The uncle explained the tape and its foreign courier to our host. When it came on, Francisco sat mesmerized. He hadn't seen this branch of the family in twenty years. *El tío* simply stared at his relatives, oblivious to the soundtrack. Then he asked to see it again, this time actually following the story. Afterward, he said that if he had had any food or drink at home, he would have invited me in for something to eat. He confirmed the addresses of other relatives in Cruces, a small town twenty miles away where I hoped to show the tape the next day, and walked me to a bus stop. In response to recent strictures, street lights had been either dimmed or doused. It gave the city an eerie aura. For writers and others in Cienfuegos and throughout the country, there was no more midnight oil to burn.

That night I ate across the street from my hotel at La Covadonga, which serves great paella. First you enter the front room and ask, "*¿el último?*" Once you know who's in front of you, then you find a vacant table in the bar yourself, or join some strangers, or elbow up to the bar. A new lesson in line etiquette emerged at La Covadonga: in loose situations where no formal line exists, such as waiting while sitting at tables in a bar, always ask the people you follow who they're behind, and keep an eye on both parties. After every two or three groups were seated in the dining room, everyone got up, and in a somewhat jumbled version of musical chairs, relocated to tables closer to the dining room door. This periodic shuffle looked haphazard, but its execution was flawless. Other diners at this bayside restaurant were sailors, dock crews and their families, and workers from the nuclear power plant under construction not far away.

Cienfuegos means "hundred fires," but it was named for José Cienfuegos, Captain General of Cuba when the town first established itself in 1819. Orlando García, the writers union president for Cienfuegos, took me on a walking tour the next day. Orlando was a provincial example of the undercurrent of change in UNEAC nationwide. He was, as he put it, "run out of the Party" in 1984—for what, he never made clear—but he won the writers union local presidency as an independent four years later.

Talking with Orlando and others I found myself mimicking their Spanish, dropping last letters and even whole syllables at a time. Those Ss and Zs at the end of so many words, who needs them anyway? My mouth still worked at 33⅓ rpm, but my ears were adjusting to 45 rpm patter. 78 rpm, however, remained an impenetrable barrier.

Kitty-corner from the UNEAC office sat the handsome century-old Terry Theater. Its director showed me around the ornate three-tier structure, with its inlaid wood panels and fresco design. Emilio Terry, whose family built the theater, had been a poor Venezuelan. In the mid-1800s, according to Edwin Atkins, Terry would buy sick slaves "for a song, nurse them back to health, and sell them at prices ranging from eight hundred to a thousand dollars a head. Then he bought a sugar estate that he might have a market for his negroes." His sugar mills produced boatloads of molasses, the profits from which he invested in drugs, medicines, and other articles to sell at a handsome profit in Cienfuegos. This wealth he sunk into railroads and government securities from the U.S., France, and England. Traveling widely, his family found the best designers and material money could buy for the elegant theater. By the time he died, Emilio Terry was worth close to $30 million.

The refreshing drive north to Enrique's relatives in Cruces took me past a few small towns in the thick countryside, and dozens of billboards. Cuba's two-lane secondary highways were decently maintained. Two cows lolled in front of a sign with black lettering on a white background surrounded by red trim: WE MUST FULFILL THE ROLE THAT HISTORY ASSIGNS US—FIDEL. DEC., '89. Because the countryside had fewer motivational billboards, they appeared more prominent. A sign in a field near Palmira, a few kilometers farther along, showed a soldier in her militia uniform firing a submachine gun. Five red stars came out of its barrel. READY FOR DEFENSE, read the caption. At a gas station just past the sign, a '58 Oldsmobile 88 powered by a '54 Cadillac engine was filling up.

   A woman of twenty flagged me down for a ride. In the countryside, the city, and everywhere in between, a civilian car drew dozens of people excitedly waving for rides. Terrible bus service made routine daily travel oppressive and undependable. With less gas, fewer spare parts, and reduced maintenance, unpredictability was the only constant. My rider, who worked in a sugar refinery, had been waiting an hour and a half for a bus that used to pass by every half hour, and she was due at a cousin's birthday celebration that afternoon. And if you hadn't gotten a ride? "I would have waited. The bus would have come by nightfall."

   THE FIRST DUTY OF A REVOLUTIONARY IS WORK. These words accompanied a profile of Castro, in dress fatigues, speaking into a microphone. By this time I had dropped off the sugar worker and picked up a teenager in a flower print dress. (Flower print dresses were available yearly through the ration book.) She had been in Cienfuegos

shopping for new shoes. "Look at these," she said, tugging at a very
loose plastic sole. "And I just bought them. Last month!"

Silence. "Are your new ones better?"

"What new ones?" She held her palms up. "The stores had no shoes
today."

I stopped to write down another roadside slogan: IN CUBA, REVOLU-
TION, SOCIALISM, AND INDEPENDENCE ARE INDISSOLUBLY UNITED.
The shoe shopper gave me a perplexed look. I said, "I'm making a
list of *lemas*," slogans. "I collect them."

At the word "collect" she became animated. "I have a collection,
too. I'm always on the lookout for stamps from other countries. I have
some from Russia, Bulgaria, and Czechoslovakia."

I dropped her at her home and turned off the main road just past
a billboard showing busy construction workers: BUILDING SOCIALISM
WHATEVER HAPPENS. My first stop in Cruces was the home of Adolfina,
a relative of Enrique's. She lived in a bare house with wooden walls
and an outhouse in the back that she shared with others. She sat me
down, then read the letter from her relatives in the States.

"My son, you know." She spoke in a low tone.

"Excuse me?"

"My son, you know. He's not here." An elderly woman shuffled
through the room. "He's at the Combinado del Este prison near Havana. For a year, you see."

Actually I didn't see, but the mere mention of her son slowed us
down almost to a standstill. "He refused the service. The military."
She corresponded with him regularly. She had received a letter just
the previous week, and visited him not long before. "He has less than
three months to serve."

I had parked across the street in front of a clean and solid house,
apparently the only two-story home in this town of five thousand. At
the time of the Revolution the house belonged to a family that has
long since left the country. A baker lives there now. Adolfina walked
across the street to his home with the video of *Family Portrait*. She
doo-wah-diddied with the wife, who said of course, of course, and we
entered a nicely appointed middle-class home. The husband greeted
Adolfina expansively, as if he hadn't seen her in months. They left us
alone to watch the movie. Like Francisco the night before, Adolfina
sat entranced through the whole twenty minutes. Faces that for two
decades had been frozen in her mind moved about and spoke. Her
eyes moistened, her face brightened. Our hosts joined us for the second
viewing and recognized Enrique's parents. "There's Zoila! That's Sil-

vestre!" On the VCR, they saw their former neighbors on the streets of Boston, U.S.A.

A horsecart clopped by, its driver in lively conversation with a bicyclist whose right hand clung to the cart's side. I made it to the next home on the family tour, this one with about ten people from four generations meandering in and out of a busy house. The eldest was a man born in the nineteenth century, still alert, who had worked more than seventy years in the sugar mills. A diploma from the Ministry of Industry hung on the wall. It heralded his "efforts to increase production." The certificate celebrated him as "the most distinguished worker from January to June, 1962, during the Second People's Harvest." It was signed "Ernesto Che Guevara, Minister of Industry."

This family had been closest to Enrique and his parents, and they quizzed me at length about his Hollywood success. He still lives in the projects with his parents, I said, demoting him from Cecil B. DeMille to a mere Woody Allen. His films have not exactly played in theaters nationwide. This was all irrelevant, of course, and when I presented them with the videotape of *Family Portrait* I could have been elected mayor of Cruces. A youngster scurried out to find a Tropicola for me. We talked of sports, Cuba, flowers, and language. I completely lost track of who was who. The husband of one of the daughters had served with an army intelligence unit in the Angolan war. "We were in the bush country a lot. Each settlement had its own dialect. You really get to appreciate language in a situation like that. We had to be able to communicate with all of them."

They gave me directions to the *santero*'s home, the last stop on my tour of Enrique's extended family. In his eighties, this lively priest of santería lived in a semirural setting on the edge of town. Although black Cubans have kept santería somewhat under wraps over the generations, more and more non-blacks in recent decades have adopted it as their own, too. "People outside the country say that we have no religion here under the Revolution," the *santero* said, "but as you can see we have all types. Even Batista's brother Panchín was a *santero*."

This *santero* had ministered to Enrique's mother, Zoila, who had given me a yellow-and-green necklace and some herbs and spices to deliver; the cinnamon confiscated at the airport had been for him. Chickens and a pig roamed the yard between the sidewalk and the side door. In admirable physical health, the slim mulatto called for his heavy white wife, and offered me a home brew that included wine and fruit juice. "It will make you strong. That much I can tell you."

When he had fully digested the letter from Enrique's mother and safely stowed her gifts, the *santero* got a key and motioned me to follow him through the backyard to what appeared to be a large wooden storage shed. "Let me show you something." He unlocked the door and flipped on a switch, illuminating the room in a dusky glow.

When my eyes finally adjusted I was staring at a rustic and elaborate altar. Candles burned on the floor. Stacked upon the altar, and on shelves and small platforms throughout the room, were objects ranging from children's dolls to machetes used in the War of Independence against Spain. "Each of these things represents a different *santo*." There was twenty pesos here, another twenty there. "People come and put money on the *santos*. I don't want it." Porcelain saints, paper saints, papier-mâché saints, glass saints, statuettes to the Caridad de Cobre, to Santa Lucía, to his own saint San Roque, to the warrior Changó.

My host identified with the Palo Monte sect of santería and belonged to the Sociedad Spiritual, the Heart of Jesus. I showed him an article about santería from a Miami weekly. "The *santeros* in Miami, they tend to exploit the people who come to them. Money." He rubbed his fingers under his thumb. "Here it's more pure. The people come to me with their problems and their fears. They bring me chickens. Meat. It's voluntary. To me it's all the same. Fidel, he doesn't have a *santero*, but he respects us. What we do is offer medical and spiritual aid."

He lighted a candle in front of his altar. Talking about the state, even in the amber privacy of his backyard church, he would only mouth words, not speak them out loud: "I was a revolutionary. I support the government, but I don't like it." His voice returned. "Do you think there's a chance for relations with America?"

He got up to show me the dolls on his altar. "There are four levels of saints. This one here"—he indicated a typical child's doll—"represents Lucumí. You know, the gods communicate by temporarily possessing the bodies of *santeros*. That's all we do. We're conduits." He closed his eyes and rocked from side to side for a spell. Then he returned to the here and now.

The faithful rest on the couch while he listens and talks to them from a well-worn chair. "If they're sick they want to be cared for. Those herbs you brought, they will help. They're medicinal." He declined to elaborate on the more intense aspects of santería, those involving chicken sacrifices and the like. Small games and toys were an integral part of the room's clutter; a little plastic sewing machine balanced on one shelf near the altar. Back in the house, a Last Supper on the wall faced a doll with a television under it.

In Cienfuegos the next afternoon María Isabel, head of public relations at the Hotel Jagua, invited me for a drink at the bar just off the lobby. She brought along Fefi and Mariela, both of whom worked in tourism. They were all in their twenties, well spoken and full of smiles, nicely attired. Pretty. Giggly. Almost goofy. I liked them. Except for us and the bartender and a trucker delivering beer, the bar was empty. The three young women were full of questions. What had I liked most about their country? Least? What movies were popular in the States? Pop singers? Had I heard Paula Abdul's latest? How did the Jagua compare to hotels back home? Why had I taken the *lechero* from Havana? Wasn't Cienfuegos preferable to the capital? What sort of house did I live in? Could I send them a phrase book of English slang when I got home? Had I gotten tired of black beans and rice yet? The three told me about their various boyfriends, husbands, and children as a second round of drinks appeared.

María Isabel was a *militante*, a member of the Communist Party. "It means being a model citizen, being aware of our country and its accomplishments. We must strive to be exemplary in the workplace and at home, and encourage others by our example." It was a Girl Scout credo description, patter that I heard almost word-for-word from *militantes* throughout the country. Mariela, evidently also in the Young Communists League, nodded agreement. Fefi went along for the ride.

More than a half million Cubans were part of the Young Communists, whose members are between eighteen and thirty-five. Most of them join at their workplace. To be a member does not require active participation, however, and accusations that the Party pads its rolls with an inactive constituency surface with some frequency. One Party member in Havana told me that he had tried to quit several times, purposely missed meetings to get booted out, and was general in a slacker. "They still keep me on the books. At my workplace they have a quota to maintain." A thirty-year-old hitchhiker once told me, "I was thinking of joining the Party a few years ago. But they only address sweeping issues. They don't confront the day-to-day."

Under the leadership of Roberto Robaina, the Unión de Jovenes Comunistas"—the Young Communists League—has taken on the role of cheerleaders who would not seem out of place in a Bud Light commercial. Members deck themselves out in UJC fashions—sweatbands, soft scarfs, colorful blouses, short skirts, bathing suits, stylish dresses, paint-splash T-shirts, tricolored totebags. They stage rock concerts in the parks, pop music rallies along the Malecón, parties at the beach. Git down with the Young Commies! They paint walls with ¡SOCIALISMO O MUERTE! in colors so electrifying as to awaken the socialist dead. (Paint for houses, however, was as difficult to come by as ever.) I visited UJC headquarters across from the Museum of the Revolution in Havana one day in a futile attempt to arrange an interview with Robertico, as First Secretary Robaina is universally known. The clean-cut staff was relentlessly energetic, bubbly, dedicated, enthusiastic over the most insignificant accomplishment, their buoyant devotion reminiscent of Eugene McCarthy's 1968 presidential campaign volunteers. The UJC was the liveliest show in town, but even these cheerleaders voiced real complaints.

The national UJC criticized the government's stagnant bureaucracy. It spoke against tourism apartheid. In a report from one meeting, a UJC national committee member asked, "Why is it that some of the hottest, most important issues aren't covered in the press? Is it fear or censorship?" Another told of a retired Party member in Pinar del Río province who jotted down the names of churchgoers from his vantage point in a park across the street. "As a result," said the woman, "a UJC member was sanctioned, accused of 'maintaining relations with believers.' It's still painful to talk about. It's just wrong." Finally, Robertico, who then sat as an alternate member on the country's Politburo, spoke about the shortage of leisure time. "The first thing we have to do is make sure we *have* some free time. And if it's *my* free time it belongs to me, then I'll do what I want with it. . . . And on the issue of fun: even the younger kids are feeling the pinch. Why are the playgrounds only open from eight to twelve and two to six? That's nuts, and it has nothing to do with the U.S. blockade."

Yet another tray of drinks had arrived at our table in the Jagua bar, and it was María Isabel's turn to answer questions. "Who do I regard most highly?" A bashful grin crossed her face as she repeated my question. "Well, of course Fidel." She said his name dreamily, as if she were announcing her new lover. Her look cast him as matinee idol, national hero, and perpetual font of wisdom which for many he still was. COMANDANTE EN JEFE, ¡ORDENE! is a common billboard; loosely, "Whatever you say, boss!" Lacking hundreds of consumer goods that clamor for twenty-four-hour attention, the state, its leader, and his philosophy became the only products constantly available to everyone.

"And Meryl Streep," María Isabel gushed suddenly. Mariela nodded strenuously. Fefi laughed.

This Meryl Streep business had me puzzled. María Isabel wasn't the only *integrada*—someone integrated into society through work, Party, military, or volunteer activities—who listed La Streep among their most admired. I had heard her name mentioned with some frequency as a favorite throughout the country. Nothing in the actress's background indicates particular appeal to Caribbean moviegoers, yet the evidence was daunting: Meryl Streep ranks among the most popular figures in Cuba. What is it about the Streep oeuvre that has won her such overwhelming Cuban acclaim? On screens large and small, her films are well known: *Kramer vs. Kramer, Out of Africa, The Deer Hunter, Sophie's Choice, She-Devil, The French Lieutenant's Woman, Silkwood.*

Fefi wanted to know about Cher and Glenn Close. They all knew of John Lennon's fiftieth birthday earlier that month, and that the tenth anniversary of his death was approaching. María Isabel delighted in anything British, and spoke English well enough to try it out after a few drinks. "Oh," cooed the Communist Party member, "I would love to be colonized by the British."

You can plant anything in the country's rich, tropical soil, and eventually it will grow, boast Cubans. John Muir was struck by the profusion of growth during his visit to Cuba in 1868, when he was twenty-nine years old. Muir spent his days in the coastal countryside near Havana. "I zigzagged and gathered prizes among unnumbered plants and shells along the shore, stopping to press the plant specimens and to rest in the shade of vine-heaps and bushes until sundown," the founder of the Sierra Club wrote in his diary. "The trees shine with blossoms and with light reflected from the leaves. The individuality of the vines is lost in trackless, interlacing, twisting, overheaping union."

The wife of Orlando, the provincial UNEAC chief, insisted I have lunch at their home one afternoon. She worked at the Botanical Gardens fifteen kilometers east of Cienfuegos. Over fried eggs, with rice and bread on the side, she suggested I stop at the Botanical Gardens on my way to El Castillito, the writers union hideaway.

Cubans once knew the Jardines Botánicos as the Atkins Garden, named for the New England sugar baron whose mill, Soledad, had for generations been the source of much of the area's economy. In 1899 Atkins bought some adjoining land called Limones on which to experiment with strains of sugarcane. Immediately he brought in some botanists from Harvard. "We hoped to produce a hardier race of cane by crossing vigorous types with weaker canes of high sucrose content," he wrote. The result was the Harvard Botanical Station, an institution that not only developed sugarcane hybrids, but evolved into a research center for the study of tropical plants. In 1924, the year Gerardo Machado was elected president of Cuba, the name and scope of the gardens changed to the Harvard Biological Laboratory, and foreign scientists were encouraged to study and live there. Harvard never owned the land outright, but an endowment at the university administered it, and the land was theirs under a ninety-nine-year lease.

During the thick of the Revolution, the rural countryside was controlled by Batista by day and by the rebels, who had staked out the hills east and southeast of the Gardens, at night. The American in charge practiced coffee neutrality, serving *cafecitos* to both sides. Although no battles took place there, Batista troops assassinated at least one man connected to the Garden, a noncombatant, and left his naked, deformed body at a nearby crossroads. In late December 1958 one of the non-*fidelista* anti-Batista groups "came roaring through and 'liberated'" the land, recalls one observer.

Harvard's tenure came to a close at the beginning of the Castro years with as reasonably smooth a transfer as could be expected under the circumstances. Cuba's Academy of Sciences now runs the 232 acre grounds.

An enormous rock garden in the shape of Cuba highlights the enclosed displays. It is big enough for cactus to be planted in each major region of the country. In all, the park holds more than two thousand species of tropical and subtropical plants, from tiláncia, used for treating arthritis, to a Pacific tree, whose bark relieves asthma.

The Gardens' nature trail passes trees and bamboo and palms and cactus donated from countries the world over. Footbridges cross a sizable stream that winds through the land. The trees at the Garden are sturdy and soaring, home for comforting trills from invisible birds, belching tree frogs, and noisy whispers from unseen creatures dashing through the underbrush. With few people around, the lush, hardwood savannah is as comforting as a traveler meandering through south Cuba could ask.

Cristóbal Ríos Albuerne, the acting head of the Gardens, was pleased to hear my impression. "We try hard to keep up with global developments in plant sciences, but it is difficult from Cienfuegos, and with no money. We are now in touch with the Royal Botanical Gardens at Kew, and informally with Harvard University." He thought a bit more. "And the Louis Pasteur Institute in Strasbourg. And we've had a little help from the University of Kentucky. High school and college science students come out to study and work here, but with the country's economic problems"—his face said more than his words—"fewer and fewer groups can visit. We maintain a collection of great importance to Cubans." Some 230 "protected areas" have been established throughout the country to preserve plant and animal life.

Dr. Ríos took me to the lab, the large front room in Harvard House where scientists were busy cataloging slides, washing equipment, and writing reports. Dr. Ríos led me into the research room and library. "We have a computerized database of all the plants at the Gardens. There's a rich potential for developing a learning center here, but as you can see, our library is quite limited." On my way out, I passed a scientist peering into a long, thick microscope in front of a mounted poster of Che Guevara wearing a beret. During Guevara's short tenure as Minister of Industry, the Gardens fell under his domain. The scientist, her equipment, and the Che poster made another freeze frame of the Revolution at thirty-two.

The Escambray mountain range has been, throughout Cuban history, the home of ornery and stubborn people. When they get in the way of the government they're called bandits. The longest-standing resistance to *fidelismo* was ensconced there, fueled by recalcitrance and the CIA. Topes de Collantes, a town originally built around a Batista-era tuberculosis sanitorium, sits a half mile high in the Sierra del Escambray. Many Cubans had cautioned me about the winding roads through this part of the country. Oh, the hairpin curves! The steep roadways! Watch out for the dangerous mountainsides! *¡Cuidado con las barrancas!* Beware the sloping banks! They call this hilly terrain mountainous? Ha! "I could show you hills," the Red Queen said to Alice, "in comparison with which you'd call that a valley."

A frightful rainfall began on the final approach to El Castillito, and a drenched mother and her daughter waved me down for a ride. The girl wore a USA! T-shirt, her mother clutched flowers. They were on their way to a nearby cemetery to visit her husband's grave. A hundred meters later I stopped to pick up a middle-aged woman, also soaked. She was staying at El Castillito.

Despite assurances from La Plume de Matanzas, the office at the writers union hideaway had no record of my reservation. Nonetheless, they fixed me up with a room right away, strategically located between the bar and the dining area. The building was a handsome, white, solid two-story affair, with a red tile roof and smooth Spanish-style tile floors. A portico surrounded most of the ground floor, looking out into nimbus clouds over the Escambray. Two front rooms on the second floor had stately red wooden balconies.

Guillermo Cabrera Infante painted the sierra in *View of Dawn in the Tropics*: "The air becomes thin and sometimes the traveler is surrounded by clouds and when they're like a rug it's because there's a precipice below. . . . The ground is covered with a herbaceous green carpet; the trees, bushes, and jungle run the whole gamut of green. Tree trunks are covered with a lichen that is like green rust and wet to the touch. . . . Thousands of pearls of raindrops drip from the leaves, and as you step, the grass sinks with a crackling watery sound."

The rain ended even more suddenly than it began. The wet guest I had picked up was Elisabeth, vacationing from Havana for a few days with a friend, Tatiana. Elisabeth was a lifelong refugee; Tatiana, a semiexpatriate. When she was young, Elisabeth's family fled Nazi Europe, finally settling in Chile. After the fall of Allende she and her husband joined many other Chileans seeking harbor in Cuba. Tatiana, a Russian, had lived many years in Havana and married a Cuban musician. Both women worked as translators. They were the only other guests at El Castillito.

We became great chums, we three. We dined together, went on walks and drives, and drank together, and played dominoes under the porch light with mosquitoes on the night shift. Tatiana was full of dark and wicked Brezhnev-era humor, much of which required only slight reworking to fit Castro-era Cuba. I was envious of Elisabeth's fluency in a half dozen languages; she just waved it off. "It's only because I've been forced to leave so many countries. Would you want to be multilingual for that reason?"

The dining room, said to be the great reward of a stay at El Castillito, came under the supervision of Andrés, a short and brooding cook who wore a tall chef's cap and a grease-stained white uniform. Alas, his food was bland, but the room itself had a nice air of rural elegance slightly past due. Each meal, however, came with the Andrés Curse. The cook had evidently seen full-page advertisements in foreign magazines of chefs poised at parade rest next to diners about to begin a sumptuous repast. At the beginning of each meal the unsmiling Andrés anchored himself a meter from the table, feet spread apart and hands clasped behind him, glancing at us with nervous eyes. He looked up only once, when we toasted Octavio Paz, who had just won the Nobel prize in literature. He never left until we finished the meal.

Andrés's wife was far livelier. One day on the portico, looking into the afternoon rainfall, I told her my impressions of the Botanical Gardens. "I don't like cactus," she pronounced. "*Punto*. There was a time when it seemed everyone loved cactus. I didn't like cactus then and I still don't. I like pines. Don't you?" She liked Edgar Allan Poe and Alejo Carpentier, a famous Cuban writer who spent most of his life in Europe. "But I don't like José Martí." She hesitated. "His politics, of course, yes, but not his writing."

The next day, instead of subjecting ourselves once more to the Andrés Curse, we drove a few miles to Los Pinos, the resort hotel for armed forces officers and their families. Elisabeth and Tatiana had sweet-talked their way into the comfortable and airy dining room at Los Pinos a few days earlier, and found its menu wider, food better, and its staff less intrusive. "Keep your mouth shut, Miller," Elisabeth advised as we approached the captain. "They'll charge us in dollars if they hear your American accent." We ate goulash, pork, squash, and rice, and lingered over beer. Los Pinos had a swimming pool, a gift shop, and virtually all the requirements for a comfortable military family holiday.

At El Castillito, each room had a private bathroom and shower, as well as its own powerful shortwave radio and television. A UNEAC executive from Havana visiting the mountain resort, the story goes, had been bored silly with nothing to do and little contact with the outside world. Immediately upon his return to the capital he ordered the radios and televisions so future guests would be spared the indignity of solitude. The BBC World Service came in clear. After I turned it off, a hard, driving rain fell for a half hour, and finally the ducks stopped quacking outside my window. Late at night the Sierra del Escambray was so quiet you could almost hear a human write.

The road to Trinidad in the foothills of the Escambray swung through ranching country. Twice I had to pull over to let cowboys and their cattle hoof down the highway from open range to huge pens. High grass obscured a small billboard that said: TO CARE FOR WILDLIFE IS A SOCIAL OBLIGATION. A deer and a bird were painted in the corner.

Diego Velázquez, the Spanish conquistador, founded Trinidad in 1514. At least that's what all the history books say, but what does that really mean? It has the same clean sweep as "Abraham Lincoln was born in a log cabin and grew up to be president." Did Velázquez hammer in a cross, leave some of his men, round up some Indians, harvest wild crops, or set up a gold mining camp? Whatever he did, it attracted a fellow Spaniard, Hernán Cortés, who five years later stopped at Trinidad before sailing for Mexico. There, pitting European might against indigenous faith, Cortés brought down the Aztec empire.

Carlos Joaquín Zerquera Fernández grew up in Trinidad learning these building blocks of Latin American history, and went into banking. I met him at his home, an expansive colonial place near the middle of town. Trinidad has benefited by generations of benign neglect from Havana; much of it remains unchanged from colonial days. UNESCO has anointed it a Patrimony of Humanity, not to be tinkered with. In his detailed and far-ranging account of early nineteenth-century Cuba, Alexander Humboldt observed that "all the streets of Trinidad are very steep, and the inhabitants there complain, as they also do in the greater part of Spanish America, of the bad selection made by the conquerors of sites for the towns they founded." The Humboldt Museum of Natural Science was closed for repairs, but Zerquera, now Trinidad's historian, waltzed me in and out of all the other museums in town. The cobblestone streets, the thick-walled houses with red tile roofs, the brilliance of the flowers and smoothness of the marble floors and mahogany stairways in the museums, all combined to give a sense of well-preserved wealth.

Lovely vases and porcelain centerpieces adorned elegant dining rooms in a former sugar baron's home, now a museum. Swiss and Austrian utensils hung in the preserved kitchen, Portuguese paintings hung on the walls. "This museum was home to one of the oldest families in Trinidad. They lived here until 1930." A cast-iron bell four feet tall sat prominently on the first floor. It came from Meneely's of West Troy, New York.

We next went to the National Museum of the Struggle Against Banditry, which, like most of the other politically oriented museums in the country, displayed the personal effects of Cubans who died defending their government. One soldier left behind a Remington Roll-A-Matic shaver. Another, a song book. A CIA radio transmitter was on exhibit. So was a poster showing a boy hoisting a rifle. MY MOUNTAINS WILL NEVER BE TAKEN, it said. A booklet said to be financed by the CIA read, *We work as slaves to serve the Russians! Russians get out of Cuba!* A detailed map of the country showed the areas most affected by "*bandidismo*." The museum was sponsoring an essay contest on the theme, "the struggle against bandits." First prize was three hundred pesos—somewhat more than most Cubans earn in a month.

Carlos Joaquín took me out to sip some *canchánchara* at a long, narrow open-air place named for the locally popular drink. The icy drink is made from raw rum, lime juice, and honey. We talked about the differences between Spanish as spoken in Spain and the same language in Cuba. Musicians played for the sunny weekend crowd, mainly foreign tourists.

The climate was right for a question I occasionally asked Cubans over forty: "What did you do in the Revolution?" It was neither lightly asked nor easily answered. Responses usually came in two speeds: rapid claims of active but unspecific support, or slow-murmured acknowledgment of participation. The former lacked credibility; the latter often concealed dark and intricate activities. Carlos Joaquín's reply was refreshing. "Nothing. I wasn't active. I was an accountant at a bank. You must remember, I come from a very old and traditional family."

I went back to my hotel at Playa Ancón outside Trinidad to take a swim in the sea. On the way I passed a billboard trumpeting UNITY AND IDEOLOGY—TWO PILLARS OF OUR PARTY. Another, common throughout the country, proclaimed THIS LAND IS 100% CUBAN. A tour group from Germany downing Cuba libres monopolized the beachside bar. After a dip I walked west a few kilometers until the hotel was far out of sight. Eventually I came upon small groups of Cubans passing the time on the beach. They were involved in *campismo*, a somewhat supervised outdoorsy retreat for older teenagers. Jorge, the most talkative fellow in a small group I chatted with, asked my nationality.

"*Norteamericano. ¿Y tú?*"

"*Cubano.*"

"A hundred percent, right?" I said, joking about the ubiquitous slogan.

"No, actually I'm fifty percent Cuban. I'm also fifty percent African." Vladimir joined in: "Me too." They were a comfortable mix of Afro-Cubans, mulattos, and a few whites. Jorge said he was a coral craftsman. He pulled some smoothly polished earrings, necklaces, and bracelets from a bag. Coral, highly prized and easily available from freelance divers, made fashionable and desirable jewelry. So much so that to regulate the endangered supply along Cuba's coastline, independent coral mining was expressly prohibited. When I asked about this Jorge dismissed it out of hand. He sold directly to customers for dollars rather than through state middlemen for pesos.

"Ah, a *jinetero*," I said, catching Vladimir by surprise.

"How do you know what that is? Foreigners aren't supposed to know."

Jorge ignored our exchange. "I'm a sea merchant. That's what I do. I can sell you lobster, coral, fish; anything from the sea that you want. Also clothes. Just about whatever your needs are." I turned down his offer of a large, polished seashell for ten dollars. He hesitated. "Five dollars?"

"*No, gracias.*"

Jorge conferred with his confederates and walked over to the bench where I had taken a seat for one of the best sunset vistas in the Western world, a 180 degree sweep of the Caribbean at high tide. "Here." He held out the shell. "We want you to have this as a gift."

Vladimir invited me to a dance that evening. "That is, if the guard doesn't mind." Jorge asked about the letter I was using as a bookmark. I asked, "Do you really want to hear it?" They were a hundred percent certain. Evidently afternoon entertainment was at a premium at *campismo*.

"Okay, here goes. It's from a friend at a university." I began to read: " 'A fraternity had a party, and a couple of the invited girls brought along some high school crashers, one of whom was black. They were asked to leave, and I gather the word "nigger" got used by a fraternity kid who later explained that he was from the South and that's the way they do things there. The crasher went and got a pistol out of his car, cops were called, and one cop shot at the armed kid. The bullet went through the kid's arm and killed another cop. Who fired the gun was withheld from the press for two days. A university spokesman said it was not a racial incident.' "

The crowd, about the same age as the partiers, grew to eight or ten. They listened with rapt attention, dead silent even after I finished. Then they flooded me with questions.

"Can just anyone have a gun?"

"Why did the police shoot at him?"

"Why did the other guy call him 'nigger'?"

"You mean at the whole party there was only one black student?"

"Do the police come when the whites have a gun, too?"

"Of course it was a racial incident. Can a university lie like that?"

My interrogators had all grown up in a country where getting an education is far easier than getting a gun, and I was helpless to answer most of their questions. Or rather all of my answers reflected poorly on American society.

* * *

An end-run around the uncooperative guard at the dance was impossible, the gang told me when I drove by their campsite that evening.
"Let's go into town," one of them suggested, and two girls and a guy
from the afternoon crowd climbed into the VW and gave me directions
to the Club Las Cuevas.

Las Cuevas was closed for repairs. I wanted to see Trinidad's Casa
de la Trova, the center for local musicians. "I don't want to go there,"
my youngest passenger whined. "Young people don't go to the Casa.
We like to go dancing instead." She sulked all the way to the Casa,
but her friends seemed happy to go there, or maybe just happy to go
anywhere. When we arrived, Los Trovadores de Trinidad, a four-man
band, was starting a set of traditional romantic ballads, playing for
an appreciative and well-dressed audience of two hundred. The sulker
to the contrary, lots of young people had shown up. The crowd had
arrived on foot and bicycle; mine was the only car there. A shot of
rum at the bar cost fifty centavos. Curiously, cigarettes were sold only
for dollars, effectively preventing virtually everyone from buying them.
Some men sat and played dominoes. Photos of local musicians going
back to the 1930s hung on the walls. There was no admission charge.

We cruised Trinidad some more, just a restless carload prowling
for Saturday night kicks. "This book you're writing, it's about Cuba,
right?" The sulker again. "In English, right? Well, a lot of Cubans
read English." She said this more in fear than pride. She didn't want
her name used.

"Don't worry. In delicate situations I won't use names."

"Well this is a delicate situation. My father's a cop and he'd kill
me if he knew I was with a foreigner."

Oh.

The town was thick with cops, the sulker said; plainclothesmen
were out in force at the Casa de la Trova. "They were wearing white
guayaberas. They tried to follow us on bicycles." She glanced out the
rear window.

Great. This was just what I needed. Picked up on the back streets
of a provincial town with the teenage daughter of a local cop on a
Saturday night. I started to play "Write That Headline!" in my mind.
The two other passengers laughed at this low drama, enjoying the
sulker's fear. "Don't you see? Nothing would happen to you. But
me—" She patted her wrists together and let out a hyperventilated
moan. We headed back to the *campismo* site on the beach.

"My dad's a Communist. My mom has no use for the Party. And my grandmother, she's a gossip. She's got a long tongue." She pouted. "Fidel's a *comemierda*," a shiteater. The sulker was going down the list of people she despised. "I wish he were dead. I wish my father was, too. Why can't we leave this country? Why are we so isolated?"

The fellow in the backseat. "And why are the goods the lowest of the lowest quality?"

This squall blindsided me. "Is this a common view?"

Sulker. "Yes. Well, no. Among the kids it is. Remember that guy this afternoon?" She described a quiet youth who had watched the conversation about the fraternity party. "He said I was a counterrevolutionary because I was talking to a foreigner and that you must be with the CIA. I told him you weren't."

"*Muchísimas gracias.*"

"They keep telling us that foreigners carry infections with them, like AIDS and venereal disease."

"*No, gracias.*"

Back at the road paralleling the beach I pulled over to let my three passengers out. A young man wearing civilian clothes and a military armband walked up to the car. He was a friend of theirs. He had pulled the night shift for beach patrol. His most distinguishing characteristic was the bolt-action rifle he carried. "It's a Winchester," he said. We talked about beaches, stars, and seafood. They had plenty of the first and second and little of the third. "Here." He put his rifle in my hands. "It's heavy, but it hits its target from a great distance." I took aim at a faraway bush and gave it back to him. He was talking with my passengers about the fellow who had called me a CIA agent.

"No, no, no." The beach patrol to the sulker. "He didn't say you were a counterrevolutionary for talking with a foreigner. He said you were an antisocial *gusana*." Within Cuba a *gusano*—literally, a worm—is someone said to contemptuously discredit the government by public words or deeds. More generally, it is the name good revolutionaries slap on evil Cubans who have crawled away from their homeland. At its loosest and most generic, it's applied to everyone in the first tidal wave of exiles, and many in subsequent waves. Castro once defined *gusanos* as "disgruntled bourgeois elements with counterrevolutionary tendencies." (At the Miami airport, the dufflebags visiting Cubans arrive with are called *gusanos* by the baggage handlers.)

The beach patrol came over and motioned me aside. "*No te preocupes*," don't worry. "The *compañero* who said you were with the CIA? He used to be her boyfriend. He's just jealous." I bid good night to the beach patroller, *la gusanita*, and the other nightcrawlers, and drove back to my hotel.

The seventy kilometers from Trinidad to Sancti Spíritus "looked like Africa," wrote journalist Martha Gellhorn, Hemingway wife number three, when she motored the same stretch during a visit in the mid-1980s. "Hump-backed, bony cattle, like Masai cattle, palms and ceibas . . . jungle-green hills, brown plains." When I reached Sancti Spíritus I checked into the Zaza, a hotel whose name I liked far better than its amenities. It was named for the lake on whose west side it was built. The Zaza had a full house; I was its only foreigner. Groups vacationing from job sites in Havana and Cienfuegos filled the bar, swimming pool, and restaurant. The most interesting part of my stay, aside from an afternoon fistfight between two drunken *machos*, was watching a cooking show called *Cocina al minuto* on the television in my room.

Cocina al minuto was hosted by Nitza Villapol, a woman in her sixties erroneously called the Cuban Julia Child. She puttered about her small kitchen fixing a fruit concoction aided by a helper who was less than helpful. When Nitza was annoyed at her assistant she flashed anger; when she was pleased with the dish's progress she smiled; and when she was done she seemed relieved. Nitza Villapol had been on Cuban television before the Revolution, and prior to that, radio. With the possible exception of Vilma Espín, Raúl Castro's wife, who heads the Cuban Women's Federation and sits on the Central Committee and has her face on billboards, Nitza Villapol is Cuba's best-known woman. Three generations of Cubans, many of them abroad, swear by her advice and her cookbooks. When her fifteen-minute show ended, the poolside noise level rose, the lobby filled up again, and people went on with their day.

The center of Sancti Spíritus resembled Trinidad in its age, its cobbled streets, and its long, narrow grilled windows, yet it lacked Trinidad's confidence and vitality. Possibly it was the heat of day, or too much time on the road. Perhaps I was simply colonialed out. Whatever the reason, the enthusiasm I felt elsewhere was missing in Sancti Spíritus. I crisscrossed the town a few times looking for Calle El Llano, reputedly the quintessential colonial street. It lived up to its reputation, yet its most conspicuous feature was not architecture from the Spanish empire but an automobile from the heyday of Detroit: parked on Calle El Llano was a two-tone Plymouth Deluxe made in

1934. Just a few months before that car reached Cuba, Gerardo Machado had been overthrown and Fulgencio Batista began the puppeteer phase of his political career.

The blue-and-white car sat in front of a house, and when I slowly circled it, admiring its well-preserved condition, its owner came out in shorts and thongs to show it off. "It has its original running board. Look." He showed me Detroit's sturdy workmanship. To crank it up he raised half of the hood from the side and tinkered with a few wires, then got inside and finally got it humming. Purring. He took me for a spin around the block. The car would never make it far out of Sancti Spíritus, its owner acknowledged, but then he probably wouldn't either. A whitewall was affixed to the rear. Emblazoned in white paint it said

1934 — PLYMOUTH — 1934

A Packard was the first automobile ever to drive on Sancti Spíritus streets. Fifteen years before the blue-and-white Plymouth on Calle El Llano came to Cuba, the Packard Motor Car Company sent E. Ralph Estep and a couple of colleagues to Cuba with a brand-new convertible. Their mission: to drive the length of the country. "We had imagined that Cuba was a sort of national park with an immense system of boulevards," Estep wrote, but soon learned Cuba had only one highway, fifty miles long. Still, emboldened with equal parts bonhomie, determination, and ignorance, Estep and the others set out from Havana to Sancti Spíritus. They traveled through small towns and up and down hills where faint paths became their roads, and seemed to spend most of every day changing flat tires and chopping at tropical growth that blocked their way. "We were not prepared for camping because we had anticipated spending our nights in villages or towns."

The hardships Estep accepted with equanimity, and the surprises with pleasure: "We forded nine shallow rivers and rushed innumerable short steep climbs up their farther banks. Some of these grades seemed to stand the car on end, both going down and coming up. At many of them we were forced to stop and cut out notches in the hard clay or solid rock, to clear the fly wheel, when the car should go over the sharp crown of the hill."

Finally, 313 miles after they set out, the Packard-sponsored crew arrived in Sancti Spíritus. "The town received us boisterously. Each crooked street filled with noisy crowds of men, women, and children, who darted from their homes to chase after us to the hotel . . . Sancti Spíritus was innocent in automobiles."

Jorge Daubar had suggested I look up Carlos, a friend in Sancti Spíritus. Carlos lived on the third floor of an old house now home to four families. I introduced myself. He was home alone while his wife was off visiting relatives. He had plenty of time for a visit. I glanced up at an unlighted chandelier that hung forlornly in the foyer. "I only have one working bulb," he admitted, chuckling at the situation. "I've been waiting for bulbs to come to the market for months now."

Carlos's passion was playing chess by mail. He was involved in games with people in Asia, Europe, and Mexico. He was active in the international organization that promoted chess by mail and handed me its most recent newsletter. But he also kept plenty of enthusiasm for his hometown.

"Let's go outside. I want to show you something." We climbed some steep steps to the roof of his building where we had a full view of the city. "See that?" He pointed to a church a block away. "It's one of the oldest churches in continuous use in the country. It goes back to 1680. I was born and raised here and I'm still proud of it. Its bell still rings for Mass every Sunday morning. Over there"—he pointed across a narrow side street—"my neighbor once had an aviary in the backyard, but there are no birds now."

Carlos, a civil engineer by trade, ticked off the local industries—cattle, sugarcane by-products, tiles, construction, and produce. "This is a very calm city. We pay a guard to walk the streets, but we have no juvenile delinquency. I can't even remember the last time we had a robbery or a break-in."

I asked him his source of news. "Well, sometimes radio. I see newspapers at work, but nothing, really. If you don't get news at all, you don't get either good news or bad news, so what does it matter?"

Do you have a bookstore or library here?

"What do you take us for, savages? Of course we do."

By the time my impertinence showed, we were back downstairs. I mentioned that I hoped to interview Fidel before I left the country, and wondered if he had any questions he'd like me to ask. He paused.

"Yes. I want to know why we are always the only country voting one way at the United Nations while all the others are voting the other way. And even in Latin America, why are we always right and the other countries always wrong?"

"Are you a Communist?" I still got a kick out of casually asking the question. You just can't do that back home. Carlos shook his head and smiled. "We have a saying—'*Tú no eras ni Pionero.*' You weren't even a Pioneer—the mass organization of Cuban youth. Not to have been a Pioneer! You asked if I was a member of the Communist Party—well, it's one thing not to be a Communist, but *everyone* was a Pioneer in his youth." He laughed. "*Tú no eras ni Pionero.*"

We dropped in on some neighbors and sat around the kitchen table where they served thick coffee and talked rabid baseball. The interprovincial league—La Liga Nacional—wouldn't start for almost two months, but the sport held year-round fascination. The North American World Series was up for discussion, and of course José Canseco figured prominently. "Is he worth it?" the man of the house asked about Canseco's salary. "I can't understand that much money." I mentioned some of the Cubans who played for the Washington Senators in the 1950s—Pedro Ramos, Camilo Pascual, Julio Becquer, José Valdivielso. "They were always my favorite players."

"Mine, too," the neighbor said. "We used to follow them very closely."

"Then the Senators moved from Washington and I stopped following the majors."

"Tell me, I don't understand how a club could simply move from one city to another." I tried to explain franchises. He said, "Okay. Say I live in Jacksonville, Florida, and I have the money to buy a baseball club. What do I do?"

"Well, first you'd need to build a stadium to show good intention."

"Okay, I've got a stadium. Then what?"

"Then you have to prove that you can fill it. Finally you have to find a team available in the marketplace that's doing terrible elsewhere and demonstrate that you can make more money for the other team owners than any of the others who also want to buy that club. It takes a few years and costs a lot just to get that far."

"But why can't I simply field a team?"

His twenty-year-old son came in and listened. He asked about George Steinbrenner and the New York, pardon the expression, Yankees.

When Carlos and I were about to leave, the son gave me a book by historian Orlando Barrera Figueroa about Sancti Spíritus. It starts with Spanish conquerors in 1514 and crescendos to late 1958, "The Final Days of the 444 Years of Oppression, Dependency, and Vassalage." Three hundred forty-six years into this O.D.&V., William Walker, the American filibuster who five years earlier had commandeered Nicaragua and declared himself its president, sailed along Cuba's south coast. The freebooter was "leading a powerful expedition . . . in a mood to conquer Cuba." His presence, Barrera writes, made Spanish colonial forces in Sancti Spíritus very nervous. (In fact, though, Walker never docked in Cuba, but sailed past it to Honduras.)

In 1895 a youthful, vacationing British officer named Winston Churchill went to Cuba to write for the London *Daily Graphic* during the War of Independence. Spanish authorities suggested that if he wanted to see a battle that he should go to Sancti Spíritus. He found it to be "a godforsaken small town, very unhealthy, with a raging epidemic of yellow fever and small pox. . . ." But, adds biographer Robert Payne, "Churchill found that he enjoyed the Cuban cigars." He also liked Spanish officers in uniforms and the bearded, barefoot soldiers they commanded. As for the home team, he "found the guerrillas tiresome," even if they were fighting for their freedom. A few days later, in a small battle at Arroyo Blanco northeast of Sancti Spíritus, a rebel bullet passed within a foot of the future prime minister's head. "There is nothing more exhilarating than to be shot at without result," he wrote.

Barrera's book suggests that Churchill was more than a reporter, perhaps "a spy or here to distort Cuban reality and its just war." Churchill himself gave history little to go by; a staunch fence-straddler, he wrote, "I sympathize with the rebellion—not with the rebels." As historian William Manchester wrote of Churchill's attitude, "The very thought of Cuban independence was as absurd as, say, an independent India." Churchill, Orlando Barrera adds in his history of Sancti Spíritus, was "an enemy of the Soviet people and of Communism to his dying day."

"See?" We were back at Carlos's place. "I left the front door open the whole time we were gone. There's no crime here."

How to kill a crocodile, by Walter D. Wilcox, in a 1908 issue of the *National Geographic Magazine*: "An old hat is placed on the end of a short stick, which is held in the left hand and waved over the water. The crocodile rushes blindly at the hat and is struck a sharp blow behind the head with a machete." Wilcox, describing the fauna of some miserable swampland along Cuba's south coast, added that "sharks were originally attracted by the large numbers of dead and dying slaves thrown overboard." Wilcox grew to love the area with its cedar and mahogany trees, parrots, herons, and white egrets, and the poisonous apples, harmless snakes, and royal palms. He was describing the Bay of Pigs.

The Bay of Pigs is a sizable body of water to the people who live nearby, but to the rest of the world it signifies the failed 1961 invasion of a Cuban exile force backed by the U.S. government. It became the pivotal event in relations between the two countries. It sealed official animosity and directly led to bellicose policies that have long outlived their usefulness. To mention "Bay of Pigs" in conversation evokes bitterness or pride, depending on whom you talk with in which country. The goal of the invasion was to provoke civil and military chaos culminating in the overthrow of Fidel Castro. The invasion of about 1,400 men has become increasingly fascinating because so much of its covert planning and operation has since been released and revealed. Through it, attitudes, money, policies, patriotism, and betrayal can all be traced.

In Cuba, the sequence of events that Americans call the Bay of Pigs is referred to as Playa Girón. Whenever I mentioned to Cubans that I planned to visit Playa Girón, I looked in their eyes for the faintest flash of anger, pride, or smugness. Instead, I got, "You'll like it there. It's very pretty."

I liked it there. It was very pretty. To reach this international shrine to intransigence I had to drive along a major highway, through small towns, and finally into swampland thick with marshy reeds along a road paved with potholes. My riders included two twelve-year-olds in Pioneer uniforms on their way to school, a man in his thirties who didn't say a word, large ladies going from one little town to another who acknowledged me only when they squeezed in and out of the VW, and near the end, Alejandro, who looked every one of his seventy years and then some.

Alejandro was on his way home from work as a guard at a nearby settlement. He wore a slightly dirty loose shirt over somewhat dirtier pants, and a peak-billed cap. He carried a bucket of eggs. His words surrounded his tooth and came out the side of his mouth. Through his thick doo-wah-diddy I learned that he was a retired *carbonero*, a charcoal worker. He had lived in the Zapata Swampland all his life. He hadn't taken advantage of government programs over the years to train for a new job, achieve literacy, or move to better housing. I understood why this last offer had been made when I saw his home. He lived in a one-room wooden shack with thatched palms for a roof and earth for his floor. He cooked on a crude stove and slept on a blanket that lay on a raised plank. It looked like a "before" picture touting the benefits of the Revolution. "I could live better if I was willing to move." Chickens and goats meandered around his home.

He had lived there at the time of the invasion. His home was fifty feet from the main approach to the Bay of Pigs, beneath U.S. bombers disguised as Cuban aircraft, smack in the way of Cuban troops rolling toward the beach on what would have been the road north for the invaders.

"What was it like?"

He flailed his arms wildly over his head and to his side.

"What did you do?"

"I did what the soldiers told me to do."

"What did they tell you to do?"

"Stay inside."

Had I taken a wrong turn? Over the years I had so immersed myself in the literature and mythology of the Bay of Pigs that by the time I drove the last few miles, my head was swimming in background, strategy, images, and numbers—2506, 1,189, 114, $53 million (brigade number, invaders captured and killed, and value of food, medicine, and tractors the U.S. traded for prisoners the following year). Artful propaganda, still photographs, documentary footage, fictionalized accounts, belligerent veterans, interminable analyses, Sunday morning pundits, and Monday morning quarterbacks—their cumulative accounts inspired powerful preconceptions. Yet when I arrived at the Bay of Pigs I found . . . a nicely landscaped resort complex. Sidewalks weaving around comfortable *casitas*. A gift shop. Restaurant. Disco. Equipment for fishing, scuba diving, water sports. Swimming pool. Cabanas near the beach. Ramadas on the sand. Cubans and foreigners playing in the tide.

This was not the Bay of Pigs of my fantasies. It was contemporary reality. What had I expected, hourly reenactments? Life-sized papier-mâché battle replicas? Bay o' Pigs video games? If the invaders had won, by now there would be T-shirts saying:

MY FATHER FOUGHT AT THE BAY OF PIGS
AND ALL I GOT WAS THIS LOUSY T-SHIRT

To find my wistful Bay of Pigs I dashed to the shelter of the Playa Girón Museum, where I met Petra George Caro.

Petra was my guide, a twenty-seven-year-old Party member well versed in the thrill of the victory, the litany of defeat. She slowly walked me through the professionally displayed artifacts, maps, pictures, and captured arms. Photographs of the Zapata Swampland went back to the turn of the century (but none of Federico García Lorca, who hunted crocodiles there in 1930). Charcoal workers lived in hovels before 1959, one caption said. "They sold their products to intermediate exploiters. The people were generally illiterate. The only transportation was a train to Covadonga. They had no way of getting to *zonas civilizadas*. No medical workers served the area. At the time of the Revolution the CIA was trying to subvert Cuba."

Petra led me to the next exhibit. With the Revolution came agrarian reform. Large tracts were broken into small ones. "The Revolution built two new highways," a sign related, "also rural roads, schools, clinics, and tourist centers. Banks and the property of Yankee monopolies and Cuba's bourgeoisie were nationalized." Photos showed fourteen-year-olds in militia uniforms and teachers working in the region's largely successful literacy campaign.

"Fidel came and asked the *carboneros*, 'How many families live here?' " Petra speaking. "He was told seventy. So he asked for seventy houses to be built." Recent Cuban history is filled with parables of progress with Fidel at both ends and the people in the middle, an observation I kept to myself.

The next room showed a virtual hour-by-hour account of the days just before the attack, when a major department store burned down (the CIA) and airbases were bombed (likewise). A detailed organizational chart of the invading Brigade 2506 was part of the permanent exhibit.

We arrived at a set of elaborate maps with arrows and emblems, accurate down to individual buildings. "They disembarked here." Petra outlined troop movements with a pointer. "We advanced here. Their parachutists landed over here"—she indicated a marshy, unpopulated area—"but our forces came down here." She had a no-nonsense way of describing the clash. "Our navy was very weak. It had no chance of a defense at sea." She could have been a general teaching military history at the war college. "We asked the captured mercenaries why they came. None of them admitted they were part of the brigade." She wore an embroidered shift from Pinar del Río and stylish jewelry from Guantánamo. "One said, 'Me? I came as a cook.' Then Fidel asked some of them why they took part in the attack. They said, 'We wanted to reclaim *nuestra patria*.' The mothers of some of the mercenaries came to see their sons in captivity."

Captured hardware took up most of another room: a recoilless .75 millimeter antitank rifle, mounted machine guns, and outside, planes and boats shot down or abandoned by the visiting team.

Mug shots of all the Cubans killed in action hung on one wall. Petra was especially moved by Eduardo García Delgado. García, mortally wounded in Havana during a coordinated attack, wrote FIDEL in blood as he lay dying. In a country with a surfeit of martyrs, García's final act afforded him instant status. A photograph of his body, facedown, his hand on the L, hung next to the clothes he wore at the time.

"The museum opened in 1964, but it was redone in 1976. We get lots of visitors every year in April." Petra told me this in the guest room, where we met after lunch. Vladimir Lenin looked at us from every wall. A medallion carried aboard a joint Cuban-USSR space shot rested on one table.

The man who ran the Centro Cultural in the nearby town joined us. I was curious how the invasion had been absorbed into mainstream Cuban culture. "What music has been written about the invasion?" He seemed a bit confused.

"Have there been any songs about the invasion or poetry commemorating the invasion?" He began to stammer an answer. Petra tapped me on the shoulder and leaned over. "We don't call it the invasion," she whispered. "Here, we call it *la victoria*."

He brightened up when I corrected my question. He and Petra came up with "Preludio a Girón," by Silvio Rodríguez, "La Victoria," by Sara González, and "XX Aniversario," by Oswaldo González. "You can probably find them at the record store on Boulevard San Fernando in Cienfuegos."

Petra gave me a copy of a 1983 book *Bravery and Fraternity: Internationalism and Solidarity Between the Armed Forces of Cuba and the USSR*. I asked her to show me the invaders' initial landing site. I waited for her outside, where a shiny blue '48 Studebaker Commander sat parked next to the provincial bookmobile. We drove a short distance to a peaceful beach. Petra swept a hand through the air. "This is where they came ashore that first morning." A few royal palms grew from the smooth sand. Laughing vacationers trotted in ahead of the surf. I couldn't see any history. It was a lovely day at the shore.

Part Two

D rifting to sleep is easier in the tropics because the humidity seals your eyes shut. The first night after my return to Havana I dreamed a swirl of sights and sounds from my trip to the south, the contours of the land, and the people and their energy. The journey reinforced my notion that Cubans, even with their worsening crisis, carried out their lives to a familiar rhythm, Caribbean and syncopated. Before leaving for Cuba I shed as many conceptions as possible, pre-, mis-, and mal-. Now after two months, I was building up a new set of impressions.

Daylight had not quite arrived by six o'clock my first morning back. Still, I could make out the coastline from my balcony and hear some predawn traffic rumble through the streets. I put on some coffee and unpacked, then filed the names and addresses of my new acquaintances, including the driver with whom I had ridden back to Havana. He was an interprovincial chauffeur whose job was to carry government documents—what other type was there?—to and from Cienfuegos. He could also take passengers traveling on official business. My status with the writers union qualified me. After some paperwork and a fee, we were off.

With tighter restrictions on transportation and cutbacks in gasoline, we practically had the Carretera Central, six well-paved lanes, to ourselves. Billboards on that stretch of the Central Highway were notable for their lack of heavy-handed slogans; in fact, they were wordless. All were art, impressionistic paintings of pastoral scenes—sugarcane, waterways, grazing cattle, fields of corn. My driver spent most of the ride boasting about his five children and their four mothers. "My oldest son is a medical student. And the youngest, I just bought this for him." He reached for a children's picturebook. "He's three." He finally quieted down when he saw me hard at work, scribbling in my notebook. I was trying to work "Havana" into a palindrome.

I looked up as we neared the capital, where roadside art yielded to pervasive slogans. We entered Havana beneath this reminder spread across the length of a bridge: THE FLAG OF REVOLUTION AND SOCIALISM CANNOT WAVE WITHOUT COMBAT.

Prideful belligerence seemed restricted to the capital, or at least that was its home office. I walked from the Focsa building down to the seafront thoroughfare, then headed west. Someone had put a garland of flowers around a bust of José Martí. I felt at ease inhaling the dawn breeze, walking the familiar promenade, nodding to the same fishermen. Autumn's northeasters had blown away summer's stale air, and the Malecón seemed renewed, even more inviting and invigorating than two weeks earlier. Before it was opened to the public in the 1950s, this stretch of the Malecón had seemed an Autobahn-sized playground to kids who spent their afternoons racing their bikes along the grand paved roadway.

Havana's shoreline was always wild, with a few natural beaches among the lush foliage. Small wooden vacation cabins dotted the coast, but no east-west road connected them. In 1863, Francisco Albear y Lara, an engineer, planned a road with a raised embankment set back from the water. "Albear's seaside drive combined the three activities that the sea had historically motivated in Havana," wrote one historian, "trade, defense, and recreation."

I might have been walking the Boulevard Albear if the same Spanish government that called for the blueprints had funded their realization. Instead, Albear's plans languished until 1901, when Leonard Wood, who commanded the U.S. military occupation of Cuba, mobilized construction. The updated design was intended to resemble Riverside Drive in New York, though coastal conditions dictated something closer to Albear's original layout. Kilometer by kilometer, decade by decade, the road continued westward as time, money, urban growth, and dictators permitted. The aristocracy walks the Malecón on weekdays, a Cuban wrote in 1923, but on weekends it is a place "for widespread enjoyment. After nightfall the farthest *barrios* spill into the middle of Havana, and the multitude of families, humble in origin, rush the length of its lighted byways." José Lezama Lima used "the bend in the Malecón" as a constant point of arrival and departure in his classic 1966 *Paradiso*. From the original one-lane road above a rocky embankment near La Punta Castle to the Río Almendares separating the Vedado district from Miramar, the Malecón has grown with Havana, giving it cosmopolitan character, bulging metaphor, and international identity.

The Focsa building, a couple of blocks from the Malecón, manages to plunk its bulky and oddly shaped body into most pictures of the city's skyline. The building is shaped like a concrete goddess with a flat, rectangular head and a floor-length shawl draped over outstretched arms. Offices fill much of the street level—an entire city block—and a meatlocker-cold restaurant, La Torre, takes up the top floor. La Torre has its own private elevator, and windows somewhat cleaner than those on my train to Cienfuegos. Its air conditioner appeared to have been going full blast since Batista days. You need a winter wardrobe just to get a table. When the Focsa building was new in the early 1950s, *guajiros* arriving from the countryside craned their necks to take in its enormity. "*¡Coño!*" they'd say. "*¡Mira ése!*" Sheeyit, look at that! As a result, for years people jokingly called it the Coño Building. To Russians it was no joke, it was an architectural marvel. So impressed were Soviet apparatchiks that they took the blueprints back home and built ten of them. Muscovites soon gaped at Focsa clones along Kalinan Avenue, five on either side of the street.

The phone was ringing when I walked back into the apartment. It was Daubar, inviting me over to hear about my trip to the south coast. I told him I'd seen his novelized account of José Raúl Capablanca's life in a Cienfuegos bookstore.

Daubar had a visitor when I came by in the afternoon, José. Like Daubar, José wrote thrillers and was an avid reader of the genre. He was exasperated at UNEAC. "I'm supposed to go to a detective writers' conference in Mexico later this year. The writers union is covering the airfare and hotel, of course, but my expense money beyond that is five dollars. Five dollars, that's five Cokes! Let's say I meet you at the conference and want to buy you a drink. I can't do that."

Daubar had started the day with a phone call from a friend at the Instituto Cubano del Libro. "He said, 'You're on the list! You're number two on the nonfiction list!' I couldn't get too excited about it. The best-seller list here is a joke. Almost every book released gets on the list. Besides that, they put *Capablanca* on the wrong list. It's fiction." The book ahead of Daubar, then in its seventh week on the list, was *Cosmetics and Health*. Only one Cuban book made the five top-selling novels, Félix Luis Viera *In the Name of the Son*; the other authors were Polish, Canadian, Czech, and Russian.

José had only read one Frederick Forsyth book, *The Day of the Jackal*. "I read my first and only John Le Carré just last year. My first! And that was only because a friend brought it back from overseas. Travel gives us some sense of what's being published elsewhere. We're hungry to find out here. We don't even get to see literary news from other countries. We'd like to know about the detective genre in the States, not because it's the States but because the field is thriving there now. I'd love to see the *New York Times Book Review* to find out what's selling in the world of fiction."

Daubar said, "One reason we want to get printed abroad is that it gives us protection at home. Not only is it prestigious, but it makes us almost untouchable. And it gives us more of a chance to be published here, too."

Daubar was working on a teleplay about drug dealers in Miami. I mentioned that *Nobody Listened*, a documentary about human rights in Cuba, had been broadcast nationally in the United States a few months earlier. It was the sort of film that could never be circulated in Cuba, so I started to describe it. "For starters, it's excellently produced, fairly damning, and full of dramatic and manipulative fare. The testimonies are credible except for Valladares. If it ever showed up here, the government would denounce it as CIA propaganda. It—"

Daubar cut me off. "I've seen it," he said, almost matter-of-factly. "Eight months ago. A friend showed it on his video machine."

"*Really?*" I was dumbfounded that such a passionately anti-Castro documentary had slipped into the country. "And what did you think of it?"

I'd met Daubar's parents, petted his dogs, chatted with his friends; we had discussed literature, the Revolution, the sea. He was an expressive man of strong opinions, yet when asked what he thought of *Nobody Listened*, he gave me the sideways smile. I waited. Finally his grin melted. "Very objective," he said. Well, many things can be said about *Nobody Listened*, but "very objective" is not one of them.

Graham Greene knew the difference between decent and indecent, and in Cuba he reveled in both. His life held an intoxicating mix of literature, espionage, revolution, and sex, and his works invariably provoke generous tributes. Few of his admirers, however, speak of the erudite and libidinous spirit that characterizes *Our Man in Havana*, his dark and funny Batista-era intrigue about Britain's espionage service. "The President's regime was creaking dangerously towards its end," Greene wrote, and through Wormold, a vacuum cleaner salesman and imaginative intelligence recruit, he mocked villainous police states and civil spies.

I carried *Our Man in Havana* with me for a self-guided tour of Graham Greene's Havana, and walked along the Prado to the Sevilla-

Biltmore, now the Sevilla; it was roped off, under renovation. The Inglaterra, where Wormold's secretary, Beatrice, spent her first night in Havana, and where Winston Churchill stayed when he went to Cuba in 1895, looked as grand as ever, having recently emerged from a cellar-to-rooftop overhaul. Its ornate dining room with chandeliers hanging from high ceilings and gilded walls reminded me of hotels in San Francisco. That evening a jazz quartet played in the bar next to the dining room, and Ella, a tourist from Belgium, sat at a table alone. She was reading *OMH*. I flashed my copy and sat down for a drink. "This place has acceptable decadence," she said. "I like it."

"That's all very well and good," I replied, "but we really should leave. Ella, don't you see?" I said, waving my own *OMH* in the air. "This was Graham at his most verdant." We talked about Wormold, who routinely had drinks at the Wonder Bar with Dr. Hasselbacher, a German émigré killed by Batista's goons. "We must find the Wonder Bar!" Ella was game.

The Inglaterra bartender, who seemed of age, had never heard of the Wonder Bar, but Martínez, the percussion player in the house band, knew all about it. "There were prostitutes downstairs and drunks upstairs. You'd find drugs, the Mafia, bingo, and dogs. Strippers and music. You could buy lottery tickets, you could buy anything."

"Are you sure it was called the Wonder Bar?"

"Absolutely," Martínez said. "I used to go there."

Ella and I followed his directions to the corner of Prado and Virtudes and entered a dark cocktail lounge with loud pop music blaring from erratic speakers. Our waiter, who was old enough to know, said it had never been known as the Wonder Bar. And to make matters worse, 37 Lamparilla Street, where Wormold lived and sold his Atomic Pile Suction Vacuum Cleaners, doesn't exist. We toasted Wormold anyway, his daughter, Milly, and of course, Hasselbacher.

I had met an English couple, one of whom worked at the British embassy. They were having a garden party; would I attend? I would. The house, at the far end of Miramar, had a backyard pool below the patio. This had been Frank Sinatra's home whenever he came to Havana during Batista days, according to the couple. "We don't hear him singing, but we were a bit curious when we had the floor dug up to redo the kitchen."

The bartender mixed me a *mojito*—rum, lime juice, sugar, and water, stuffed with fresh mint. Another white jacket produced a platter of croquettes. A few embassy workers, mainly security from what I could gather, introduced themselves and their wives. They were talking about the Falklands War. A handsome, white-haired man in a designer tank top and a striped bathing suit came up. He looked like Jacko, the famous Australian personality in the Eveready battery commercial. Tattoos colored his arms. "Bring your swimmers?"

No, I hadn't brought my swimmers. The only preparation I had made was to reread everything Greene had ever written about the country in hopes of sparking a lively literary discussion about Greene, British travel writing, and Cuba. I'd watched and read enough British spy thrillers to know that English diplomats were a well-read, chatty lot. I squeezed into borrowed swimmers.

The Eveready man had no admirable qualities and I liked him immediately. His Zippo lighter said BRITISH EMBASSY CLUB OF ADDIS ABABA. This was his second assignment in Cuba, and his eighteenth and last country before retirement. He was perversely proud that he spoke no Spanish. I told him I liked the London daily *Independent* for its writing in general and its international coverage in particular. He sneered. He preferred the *Mail* and the *Telegraph* for their domestic news. He thought their coverage of then–Prime Minister Thatcher was right on the mark. "Maggie. She's the only man we've got." With more men like Eveready, "Rule Britannia" would be more than a song title. He dove into the pool.

A British fellow in his early twenties came in. He attended a Cuban arts school and played guitar. Today he would sing for his supper. Two other Americans were there, a woman and her husband, a Texan who said he worked in "Admin" at the U.S. Interests Section. On Fridays his job was to go out to Havana markets and make note of food availability, lines, and prices. His wife often accompanied him. "Sometimes we see people lining up overnight." His previous assignment had been in Bulgaria. "Admin" is a common cover for espionage, and his job of economic surveillance reeked of intelligence work. He had the oily mug of someone who had just crawled out of the La Brea tar pits. I thought of Graham Greene's comment that he would go "to almost any length to put my feeble twig in the spokes of American foreign policy."

The snoop recommended some New Orleans restaurants to an attaché who planned a vacation there, then turned to the British security men. "Tell me, have they given you any guidance on how to deal with former Eastern Bloc countries?"

"Yes, one minute they're Warsaw Pact and the next they're our allies in NATO. We don't know what to do. There's a man at the Czech embassy. Bloke plays golf. Fine fellow. We don't know whether to report contact with him or not."

"Well, we have a bit of guidance on that."

"I'll bring it up at our staff meeting Monday."

"We still have to file a memo if we have them over."

Eveready turned to me. "Tell me, what do you think of Cuba? I'd invade the bloody country, that's what I'd do." He nodded an exclamation point.

After a few drinks their English got thicker and thicker, and I couldn't quite understand a couple of the embassy staffers. Eveready leaned over to explain: "They're from the north of England. I'm from the south." The drinking at the next table got heavier, and the singing began. "Too-ra-loo-ra-loo-ra." Stingy Scot jokes followed. "There were these Scots tossing five pence into the coffin of a dear departed. Then a Jew came along and said, 'I can top that.' And he tossed in a blank check."

"By the way. Congratulations on your new post. Malawi is it?"

"Do they have a golf course there?"

"I know they have a bowling green."

"Yes, and there's another one in the old capital where the High Command used to bowl."

Many of the embassy staff pulled in American television with satellite dishes. "Their news! They call it world news, but it's strictly events from the perspective of their government, nothing about other countries."

"I like CNN. They do a good job."

Eveready rose to get a Rusty Nail. "True, but their coverage of Liberia was so biased."

"And they call those games the World Series. It's the U.S. Series."

I reminded them that there were two Canadian teams. We raised our glasses. "Cheers," I said, in a silly effort to bridge the Atlantic.

"Yes," said an embassy man, "cheers, beers, queers, and brigadiers."

The military men talked Senegal. More Falklands.

"The Gurkhas, it was difficult to hold them back."

"Always is."

"Yes, I should say so."

"Russia has the second-best security force in the world. Cuba learned from them. That's why Cuba's is so good." They debated which British service was the best—air force, navy, or army. "The RAF is the most professional."

"No, no, no. The RAF is the most cultured, not the most professional."

"I watched the American show *Jeopardy*, and one day the question was, 'Who killed Macbeth?' Well, no one knew who did it! Turns out it was Macduff. I looked it up and they were right. Of course, when they say world history on *Jeopardy* they mean U.S. history. I only watch *Jeopardy* because it comes on before *Wheel of Fortune*."

La Plume de Matanzas was happy to see me. "I have some mail for you. And I've made progress on one of your requests. I've spoken with FAR," the Revolutionary Armed Forces. "They'll let us know about Guantánamo soon." She was only too pleased to make an interagency request on my behalf. The television cook, Nitza Villapol, interested me. Could La Plume set up an interview? "Ah, Nitza! She lives right over there," she said, indicating a building across the street. She spoke her name as if she knew her. "No, I've never met her. But all Cubans feel like they know her."

I gave La Plume some general impressions of my solo trip south. She was all ears as I told her about a restaurant in Cienfuegos, trees at the Botanical Gardens, Trinidad museums, and Sancti Spíritus from a rooftop. I mentioned in passing that by the time I got to Playa Girón I could recognize Communist Party members by their language. La Plume's facial muscles tensed slightly. Party members were no less friendly, I quickly added, simply with an identifiable lingo. She sat upright, tapped out her cigarette, looked into my eyes, and spoke solemnly. *"El idioma del partido es el idioma del pueblo."* The language of the party is the language of the people.

I dropped in on Alejandro next. He was his radiant self, and too busy to chat long. A group from the States was due and he had to make last-minute scheduling arrangements. "I'd call around but, you know, it's easier to show up in person."

I headed for the Socialism or Death produce stand at Nineteenth and A. I'd heard through the grapevine that a shipment of pineapples had come to town. On my way to investigate this rumor I picked up a copy of *La Tribuna*, the city's daily. Big letters on the front page shouted:"Next Month—Two Pounds of Fish Per Person." The pineapple rumor was true, but at this particular market they were already sold out. They did, however, have garlic, onions, sweet potato, and some tubers I couldn't identify. A consumer information chart in front listed what minerals and vitamins are found in which vegetables, how long to boil different foods in a pressure cooker, and how to judge the quality of several items. The chart had far more vegetables than the bins. That afternoon at Coppelia, this foreboding sign alerted ice cream lovers: TAKE NOTE—THE ADMINISTRATION WILL PERMIT UP TO TEN TICKETS PER PERSON ONLY. Shortages were affecting Havana's essential frivolity.

Unlike the other shortages, housing did not get worse. It was already about as crowded as it could get. The need for homes grew faster than full-time volunteer construction brigades could build them. Still, no families lived in the streets, and opulent mansions were not squandered on single families. Buying and selling homes was illegal. A move to better quarters was a workplace perquisite. Beyond that, everyone else had to be content with their home, move in with family or friends, or trade. One day I saw a bunch of people milling about on the broad pedestrian walkway that runs down the middle of the Prado. Tacked to trees were notices from people wanting to barter or trade their homes for other homes. All very legal.

> To trade: home with water and telephone. Two bedrooms.
> Marianao neighborhood. Need one bedroom. Lawton
> neighborhood.

Often notices ended with implied personal drama:

> Large, modern single house; living room; 4 bedrooms, one with a
> separate street entrance; combination kitchen/dining room; bath,
> and flush toilet. City water and well water. Gas tanks. Sidewalk
> with garden. Granite floors and factory-installed glass windows.
> Need—two homes in Guanabacoa.

And:

> To trade—large and well-ventilated apartment with big dining
> room, two rooms with closets, flush toilet, kitchen, balcony. 24-
> hour water and electricity. Need: similar or smaller, small repairs
> OK, 2 bedrooms required, in any part of town except Boyeros.

Some placards were displayed in briefcases tied to trees. One had a schematic drawing of the available home, another displayed photographs of the home for trade and its occupants.

Bartering, *se permuta*, was the rule of the day. A Cuban movie called

Se Permuta makes fun of the trading process: a scheming mother juggles a half dozen people in Havana and Matanzas in an attempt to satisfy all of their housing, social, and romantic needs. She manipulates her daughter into living in the Vedado section of town. "In Vedado she'll meet boys of a better class."

People on the Prado drifted from one small knot to another to see if anyone had a place that met their requirements. A thin fellow about twenty asked if I wanted to change apartments. Actually I had started to think about housing—the twenty-sixth-floor apartment at the Focsa building would no longer be available the last four weeks of my stay. I'd be out on the street. When the man discovered I was a foreigner, however, he said he really couldn't help, much as he'd like to.

"Look, my grandmother has a big house and she could rent you a room. But the next day the CDR would be over asking who you were and what you were doing there. It would be impossible."

The thin man, learning my profession, told me his brother was also a writer.

"Really? I'd like to read some of his writing."

"Oh, it's never been published. Some of it's against the state and some of it's about nature. He's saving it." I said I'd still be interested in meeting him. A somewhat older, equally thin fellow had joined us. I asked where they worked.

"Oh, nowhere. We're just waiting for a friend of Fidel's to commit *traición*—"

"—or else we're just waiting, *punto*." Period.

Traición was a new one on me, and I looked it up in my back-pocket bible. *Treason*, it said. *Treachery*. Oh. The man agreed that I should read his brother's work, and swore that he'd call me to make a date. I never heard from him.

Speaking of people I never heard from, it was time to call Jesús Avilés and schedule another oboe lesson. We arranged to meet the following week at my place.

Crime was on the upswing. Not violent crime, rather, black-market crime. I sat down to the stack of newspapers that had accumulated in my absence and learned the following. From *Granma*: "National Revolutionary Police have arrested two hundred Havana delinquents, perpetual criminals injuring the economy, taking advantage of increased shortages and the 'special period.' . . . The crackdown will continue to weed out 'social parasites.' " Economic criminals are "those who steal mostly from stores and sell on the black market."

The newspaper for workers, *Trabajadores*, had a picture of flower vendors near Colón Cemetery who hid prices from customers. The Restaurante Italiano was short-weighting some of the meat it served diners. A man at Dulcería La Villa, a bakery in the Cerro section of town, was short-weighting slices of cake. A pizzeria in Centro, Casa Bella, was fined for short-weighting slices. 4,353 cases of beer and 203 of soft drinks had been diverted to private parties and state agencies for which they were not intended. Parts for Ladas and Moskoviches were found stashed in the home of an official responsible for distributing them. "The fiscal chief of Matanzas Province said the perpetrators were economic delinquents, but above all, these were violations of an ideological nature." And a television documentary said that according to a two-year audit of thirty supermarkets, "only two did not have thievery deficits. Corruption is rampant. . . . There are no, or only a few, sanctions. Nobody goes to jail. In one store, 4,400 pounds of rice disappear within a few weeks. Often the few administrators who are relieved of their posts for discrepancies end up administrators at other stores."

By now I had detected three overlapping economies in Cuba— socialist, capitalist, and underground. The State Pricing Committee said that since its new enforcement law went into effect six months earlier, "three hundred places have been inspected and ten percent of them showed evidence that they were out of control. These manifestations of lack of discipline, which occur in . . . the management of resources, always end up corrupting the people. They should be energetically combated by all revolutionaries."

I had told Daubar that I was interested in the legacy of Ernest Hemingway. I suspected that the country exploited his presence in its midst as a propagandistic conceit. Daubar started to explain the sincerity of the relationship between the man and the country, but thought instead to introduce me to a fellow who had known Hemingway well in the good old days. He suggested we meet for drinks at the Habana Libre's mezzanine bar.

The Habana Libre was one of the few public buildings in which Daubar could maneuver his wheelchair around with some ease. The bar, afternoon home to businessmen and journalists from abroad, adjoins the hotel swimming pool. Cubans often take foreign visitors there, and vice versa. The main floor is a constant flow of tourists, hustlers, conventioneers, privileged Cubans, plainclothesmen, and hookers. Beyond the lobby the international long-distance booths draw a steady stream of callers; nearby is a maze of stores with goods and food available for anyone with dollars.

Daubar sat at a table on the far side of the bar with Hemingway friend Fernando Campoamor and Raúl Rivero, a poet. As a foreigner I could buy them drinks with dollars but they couldn't buy me one with pesos. They asked my impressions of Cienfuegos, Trinidad, and Playa Girón. Fernando pulled out a copy of *A Biography of Cuban Rum: Sugarcane's Happy Child* and signed it for me. Page 103 shows a photograph of Hemingway and the author drinking at a bar. The 1947 photo is inscribed, *"From Ernesto Hemingway, (the ugly bastard) to Fernando Campoamor from his friend. EH."*

In his day, Campoamor was a champion bartender; he's still considered a walking encyclopedia of Cuban rum. Every few minutes one friend or another would come by the table to slap a back and chat, then move on. After each departure, Daubar, Raúl, or Fernando would say sotto voce, "That's one of our best journalists," or "There goes a reporter who knows his stuff," or "He's a well-regarded official in UPEC." (Unión de Periodistas de Cuba; the journalists union.)

Their comments were a concentrated dose of what I'd been hearing since I arrived; every couple of days someone was pointed out as a simply great journalist. Looking at the newspapers every day, I had come to believe the words of an Argentine journalist who worked in Havana for a French news agency: "The relationship in Cuba between reality and the press generally borders on the schizophrenic." I couldn't take it anymore. Daubar was a friend; while Raúl and Fernando chatted, I put it to him: "I keep hearing about all these great journalists. If this town is so full of terrific reporters, why is the general level of journalism here so abysmally low?"

Daubar absorbed the question, then repeated it for Fernando and Raúl. They struck a pose worth framing: three writers, well read, articulate, and knowledgeable, all wearing the sideways smile. They froze in the inert gap between my question and their answer. Finally seventy-one-year-old Campoamor spoke. "Well, those aren't journalists who work at the dailies. Those are functionaries."

"And they don't function," said Rivero, ever the poet, *"como monjas no monjan y obispos no obispan."* Like nuns don't nun and bishops don't bishop.

"The real writers don't write for the newspapers," Campoamor added. "No, no," echoed Rivero.

No, no, yes, yes. The newspapers have a narrow berth that sometimes widens. The quality of the journalist hardly matters. Airing dirty laundry doesn't bother authorities; rather, it's whose laundry gets aired and how it got dirty to begin with. The papers show impish humor one day and stilted history the next. Of the former: side-by-side photos of George Bush and Margaret Thatcher, each yawning during a meeting in Paris. Caption: "Bored? Or digestive problems? Only they could explain . . ." Of the latter, this late-breaking news: "North American Banks Are Agents of Imperialism." The article described the nationalization of U.S. banks in Cuba thirty years earlier.

U.S. bashing is *de rigueur* in the Cuban press and, because of the crippling blockade, understandable. One headline in *Granma* summed it up nicely: "Cynicism, Demagoguery, and Mediocrity Shape U.S. Policy Toward Cuba." Yet the country's press distinguishes between official Washington and the rest of the country. A few pages after *Granma* proclaimed "Bush Criticized for Indifference to National Problems," it ran a piece about efforts to preserve an endangered wolf in Yellowstone National Park. Another day, an article about the prototype of solar-powered stoves, "designed by U.S. scientists . . . for underdeveloped countries," adjoined a piece describing protests against Yankee aggression in Panama. When Atlanta was chosen for the 1996 Olympic games, Voice of America boasted that Atlanta had been the home of Martin Luther King and was still a center of civil rights activity. The Cuban press simply described Atlanta as having one of the highest crime rates in the United States. And on the death of Frank Capra at ninety-four, *Granma* ran a half-page tribute to the venerable Hollywood director.

Bohemia used to have a popular mix of swashbuckling journalism and jazzy features. This continued for a spell after Fidel came to power but before the Soviet Union became a force. One April 1959 issue reprinted an exposé from *Look* about a Russian spy ring.

Whenever I brought up the press in conversation people always had an opinion. A small group on the Malecón laughed when I asked about newspaper credibility. "We don't usually use those two words together," a middle-aged lady said. "What you must understand," a student at the University of Havana told me one afternoon at Coppelia Park, "is that the credibility of the government determines the credibility of the press. When people have little faith in the state, they don't believe the newspapers either. Or they don't bother reading them."

With a few notable exceptions, the Cuban press is uniformly obsequious. Revolutionary self-criticism has led nowhere. Every few years

UPEC calls for reforms in the press. The Castro brothers and culture
minister Armando Hart have all urged the press to reform itself and
criticize more strongly, but little happens and the process begins again.

The Sunday following drinks with Daubar, Fernando, and Raúl at
the Habana Libre, *Juventud Rebelde*, reduced to a weekly because of the
paper shortage, ran an extensive interview with the head of UPEC,
Julio García Luis. "Look," García said, "we've added up the numbers,
and there have been no fewer than four previous attempts to transform
the mass media. An awareness developed in the early 1970s that the
press model . . . had already exhausted its potential and was not
keeping up with the demands of economic and social development. . . . The kind of press that we could call officialist, apologetic,
or *unamista* has used up its possibilities. . . . The press model that
we've had under socialism cannot serve us, but neither are we going
to take on a capitalist one. We have to find our own, one which goes
with a one-party political policy. . . . The press in Cuba often presents
people . . . talking as if they all spoke the same way, and had the
same opinions, too, which is of course not true. Occasionally, ridicu-
lously, we have tried to make people talk artificially, with expressions
unlike those traditionally used by Cubans." As the White Queen said
to Alice, "Why, sometimes I've believed as many as six impossible
things before breakfast."

For the next few weeks I read the morning paper with García's
comments in mind. "Cuba Isn't a Closed Society; The People Are
Happy" assured one headline above an interview with a visiting Australian. "We Will Never Forget the Deaths Nor Bury the Principles"
said a piece about Cuba's fighting men from the nineteenth century
War for Independence on through the recent war in Angola. "The
People of Havana Will Not Fail Fidel or the Party" was the next
headline. "We Will Forge a Will for Working Under Conditions Even
More Difficult" another foretold. Fidel's words are public truths, and
run as headlines without bothering with quotation marks. WE WILL
DEFEND OUR ACHIEVEMENTS, CONQUESTS, DIGNITY, AND OUR INDE-
PENDENCE was typical of this.

The rhetoric in *Granma* reminded me of the story about Fidel using
his superhuman powers a few years ago to invite some of the military
leaders of history he admired most to see the hardware in Havana's
annual May Day parade. Next to Fidel on the reviewing stand sat
Alexander the Great, Hannibal, and Napoleon. Midway through the
parade Alexander leaned over to Fidel and said, "If I'd had trucks like
those I could have gone all the way to China." Fidel beamed.

Hannibal tapped Fidel on the shoulder. "Why, if I'd had tanks like yours I wouldn't have had to put up with those stinking elephants." Fidel laughed at the compliment.

His third guest, meanwhile, sat reading *Granma*, ignoring the parade. Fidel nudged him. "Eh, what do you think?"

Napoleon looked up from the front page. *"C'est magnifique Monsieur Fidel!"* He kissed his fingertips. "If I'd had a newspaper like this nobody would have ever heard of Waterloo!"

A year earlier I and a dozen other visitors from the States met with some top UPEC officials at their building on Twenty-third Street. Union vice president Lázaro Barredo Medina criticized the job he and his colleagues had been doing, and showed us the draft of a new statement of principles they planned to adopt. "It will destroy forever the old way," he assured us. He rattled off statistics: UPEC has 3,800 members, thirty percent of whom are members of the Communist Party. It has fifty-three radio stations, one television station beamed to hotels for tourists, two national stations, more in the provinces, and one unit that produces newsreels for movie theaters. "Freedom of the press is the same here as everywhere else," Barredo said. "In the U.S. it is really freedom of enterprise, and enterprise has its definite interests. In our case, we defend our national interests instead of private enterprise."

Who should tell Cubans about Cuba? "Native Cubans themselves cannot do this in a proper manner, because the press is not free," said one foreigner, "and the works published here on this subject cannot but betray the influence exerted on their authors, by a jealous and narrow minded governmental policy." That's from *Yankee Travels Through the Island of Cuba*, by Demoticus Philalethes, published in 1856.

We asked how Cuban journalists deal with the universal roadblock of government public relations handlers. "Reporters can complain to us at the union if they find that the ministries aren't helpful." Just recently, he said, UPEC officials met with ministerial flacks to work out some problems. To a question about censorship, he said, "If you have to have an editor or a censor, I'd rather have just a censor." Journalists in Cuba are highly regarded, Barredo went on, and the country has journalism schools in Havana and Santiago de Cuba. "To be a journalist here, you need printer's ink in your veins. To be an editor, you need seven years' experience and a university degree."

Nestor Stamena, a spokesman for the broadcast industry, told us about an exchange between Cuban television and CNN. "We got images from CNN of what just happened in El Salvador"—the killing of some priests—"because they have a reporter there. We cover South America and Europe in the same way. We show respect to the countries and we try to avoid sensationalism. We try to be absolutely accurate. We don't go flying off the handle. We showed East Germans tearing down the wall, the demonstrators, and people leaving."

Music videos and films from the States are routinely shown on Cuban television. Some are bought from Latin American syndicators, but most are pirated off satellites. A popular Hollywood movie on Saturday night television, which usually begins at 10:30, has been known to clear out the baseball stadium at 10:15 and deplete the Malecón of half its strollers.

Salvador González, the muralist, was excited. A possibility had arisen for him to make an extended trip out of the country, to mix with other artists, to smell new air and walk on foreign streets. He knew better than to get too excited, that travel visas go through a wash and spin cycle before they're valid, but still—Venezuela beckoned, and Salvador was prepared to answer the call.

Daubar, too, was readying himself to travel abroad. He was engaged, and his Peruvian fiancée was back in Lima making plans for a family wedding.

Miguel Barnet had just returned from a quick Latin American trip. He was in especially good cheer; a movie he co-wrote, *La Bella del Alhambra*, based on his book *Rachel's Song*, was playing triumphantly in Havana, Miami, and elsewhere in Latin America. His uncle, a Miami moviehouse owner in his seventies who had just married a woman in her twenties, reported it was playing to packed houses.

Copies of Jacobo Timerman's book on Cuba were slowly reaching the hands of Havana's intelligentsia, and Barnet had every reason to be pleased; Timerman called him "a charming, cultivated man . . . a Florentine spirit." But the book offended him. "He knew what he wanted before he came and nothing could have changed it. He is a man of intelligence, but he simply came here to talk bullshit about Fidel. He told me he didn't like Fidel. When he was a young man, of course he did. He is a wicked man." Tomás Gutiérrez Alea (director of *Death of a Bureaucrat,* 1966, and *Memories of Underdevelopment,* 1968) agreed. "He seemed most agreeable and friendly, but his book is despicable."

Luis, the fellow whose resignations from the Party had been ignored, wanted to keep one foot in the country and one foot out. He had traveled abroad negotiating contracts on behalf of Cuban artists, and valued his overseas jaunts. He likened the internal situation to a stovetop coffeepot that, when hot enough, boils over. Still, he maintained a gracious countenance and lived his life within bounds. When I asked where we could have lunch near his workplace, he said, "The Hotel Comodoro is the closest, but I must make this uncomfortable statement—much as I would like to be your host they will only accept dollars and I cannot take you there."

The Comodoro had a classy dining room overlooking the water. Luis's explanations of Cuban customs were always useful. On this particular occasion we talked about money. When I arrived in Cuba I had wanted to open an account at the Banco Internacional but lacked the proper visa to do so. I asked Luis how banks treated personal accounts. "It's the opposite of your system. The more you have in your account, the less interest the banks pay."

"That runs contrary to every fiber in capitalism's muscles," I said. "I don't understand."

"They want to keep money in circulation rather than in savings. For example—wait, I'll draw you a chart."

Pesos	Interest
0–2,000	1.5% or 2%
2,000–3,000	3%
3,000–4,000	2%
4,000+	1%

"Then why keep money in the bank?"

"Exactly."

A month before I left for my extended stay in Cuba, Arturo Sandoval, the preeminent trumpeter I had seen on a previous trip, had defected. Luis knew all about it. "He was on tour in Greece and about to join up with a United Nations tour with Dizzy Gillespie in Rome. Instead he went to the U.S. embassy and made arrangements to fly to the United States." His wife and son were in London, and joined him.

Unlike most Cuban musicians, El Mulo, as some call Sandoval, toured abroad where he could buy equipment with dollars, and he lived in a well-appointed house with his wife, his son, and a CD player. His was an enviable life dedicated solely to his music. By denying him permission to perform in the States—even in nonprofit situations, a privilege often granted lesser-known Cubans—the State

Department made defection the only way Sandoval could soak up American musical influences firsthand. "They played him beautifully," a promoter of Cuba and its artists lamented. In Miami, supporters gleefully chortled, *"El Mulo espantó la mula."* Freely, "The chicken flew the coop."

Fully one month after Sandoval renounced Cuba and virtually everyone already knew, through Radio Casualidad or *radiobemba*—street gossip—the Cuban Institute of Music issued a statement: "The treason of Cuban musician Arturo Sandoval has been confirmed. . . . This defection is condemnable because it was the Revolution that allowed him to train and develop his talent. . . . The nation that admired his artistic skills will now impose on him the worst punishment: scorn. Sandoval has chosen to lead the life of a renegade, and from now on his soul will always be for sale." His music was pulled from stores. When I asked for anything by Sandoval at a record shop in Habana Vieja, the clerk gave me the sideways smile.

Jesús, my oboe teacher, had known Sandoval for many years. "We went to music school together. When he left, we were shocked. We couldn't figure out why. He could play just about whenever and wherever he wanted. He had whatever he needed." Abraham Berezniak, the kosher butcher, shook his head. "He represented Cuba, then he denounced it." At the José Martí National Library, Tomasito wanted to know, "Why are Americans so interested in him?"

Simple. His jazz was heavily influenced by American music, vibrating with enough mainstream riffs to invite familiarity but Caribbean enough to always reveal something unexplored. Shortly after he arrived in the States, he formed a band and began recording a new album, *Flight to Freedom.*

Despite my protestations, La Plume insisted on escorting me to my afternoon appointment with Nitza Villapol, the television cook. She had arranged it and, by God, she was going to see it through. When Nitza finally answered the doorbell she looked as if we had awakened her. She wore a sack dress, slippers, and no jewelry or makeup. Her neck-length light-colored hair was slightly tousled. Now in her mid-sixties, she was somewhat heavy, not quite dowdy. La Plume formally introduced herself and me.

Nitza Villapol, the friend in every Cuban's kitchen, was no friend in her own living room. She sat erect and glowered at us. I made small talk. She spoke curtly. I talked smaller. She was more brusque. I tried every conceit in the journalist's bag to get a conversation going—flattery, provocation, the weather, good cop–bad cop, subtlety, bluntness, flippancy, profundity. She was as likely to converse with me as José Martí was to cut a deal with the Spanish. The windchill factor on that eighty-nine-degree day was below zero. I thanked La Plume for arranging the interview and suggested that she leave. Inefficient yes, dumb no. She left.

Nitza began slower than my train to Cienfuegos. The question that finally pulled the queen of Cuban kitchens out of the station was about the typical Cuban kitchen. "It has a two-burner stove, up high, not on the floor. Some of them are charcoal, but most cook with gas or electricity. Most households now have refrigerators."

She glared, daring another question, then suddenly softened. "Do you know what I had for lunch today?" asked the country's most prominent expert on food. "Canned clam chowder." Her voice startled me with its sudden mix of exasperation, vengefulness, pity, and sorrow. "Cubans ruin their eating. I don't give a damn. All they want is pork, fried bananas, and rice. You don't need meat to be well fed. What the hell do I care about rice. Wheat is as good for you as rice. I won't stand in line for any food."

She spoke with fury: anger at Cubans, anger at their habits, resentment at everything. "People won't change their food habits. They eat what they like, not for their health. It's very frustrating. I used to think I could change their eating habits. Now I give them information, and if they don't change it's their tough luck. They're too finicky about what they eat."

A curious thing happened. A couple of words in English slipped out of her mouth. I responded in English and she continued in kind. She said she hadn't carried on a conversation in English with a native speaker in years. She spent most of her youth in the States, and she speaks fluent, accentless English, with a rich vocabulary acquired from movies, radio, and books. Personal emotions rushed to the fore. "I'm a sourpuss. That's what I am, a sourpuss. My life is like a jar of cookies—everyone wants to take something but no one wants to put something in. I'm old. I don't get out much. I don't go to the beach like I used to. My mother is old." Her mother, then ninety, was propped up in the next room, unable to walk or talk. "I have no family or friends." She scowled at me.

"She took care of me when I was young and now I'm taking care of her when she is old. It is my only priority. I don't invite people to come and visit. I don't cook for anyone. I don't care what they think. I used to think it was very important to be popular. Now I don't give a damn. Ask any man what he wants. He wants to be fed and he wants sex. I used to have friends. It's very sad. My mom is in the house. I have to feed her or she dies."

Silent tears suddenly gushed down Nitza Villapol's cheeks. We sat across a low table from each other; I reached out, not knowing what to do or say. "You look like you need a hug," I stammered. She grabbed my hands and squeezed.

"Ten million people think they know me. But in my private life I'm not very happy. I'm so alone. I do housework. I clean the goddamn place and I wash the dishes. That's what I do. I *hate* to wash dishes. I don't like housework." She mimicked a happy persona: "I ought to be glad to cook for anyone who comes by. Well," she continued, sternly, "I don't even bring a glass of water to anyone." In fact, I had been there almost an hour and she hadn't even carried out this most rudimentary etiquette offered in the most humble homes. "I don't give a good goddamn." She walked over to the window. She had the only venetian blinds I saw in a Cuban home.

She switched to Spanish. "I've been to England, Scotland, Italy, France, and Mexico. San Francisco, Boston, New York, Miami, and Africa. People have different objectives, but they're the same everywhere. José Martí said that you should love and construct rather than hate and destroy." Tears returned. "I try to belong with the first of those. I try to help because it's human. Usually people don't appreciate what doesn't cost them a centavo. Man is not very far from the ape."

Back to English. "It's not easy to grow old. Young people think we're dead but still breathing. They think we have no right to have things. I like things around me. Hell, I'm old. Fortunately I live in a country where old people have a lot more than in other countries. We have food, clothing, housing, and most important, work. In Cuba when you're old you may be lonely but you're not hungry."

Tears came once more. "I can't even talk to my mother anymore. All I have is this island that I love so much." She blubbered uncontrollably. "I wouldn't change my nationality for any place in the world. I'm so proud to be Cuban. The only misgiving I have is that my work has helped people who left Cuba to survive. People have stolen my works. I haven't received a penny for my books. Fortunately I don't have to steal to live. I don't like people who leave Cuba. With a few exceptions here and there they are *mezquinos*," stingy people. "The petite bourgeoisie in the Miami community—they have my books and they follow my recipes. I resent that. I *hate* them."

Her cookbook, *Cocina al minuto*, originally published in the 1950s, has been reprinted a few times in Cuba. Abroad, it has been appropriated as if it were public domain, most insidiously in the States, where not only has no contract been signed nor royalties paid but even her name has been removed. Even more insulting, *Cocina al minuto* has been translated into English as *The Cuban Flavor*, also published in Miami, again with no credit. It duplicates most of the recipes in Nitza's original book word for word: same contents in the same order, same number of servings, same measurements, ingredient by ingredient, right down to the *boniato*. Her bitterness is well founded.

Yet no one is fooled. In conversations with innumerable Cubans who have left their homeland, I have been told time after time that *Cocina al minuto* was among the most treasured possessions they packed in the one suitcase they were allowed to take. It is the Cuban *Joy of Cooking*. In households in Cuba and throughout the Diaspora, Nitza Villapol's *Cocina al minuto* has become the First Testament.

Nitza collected herself and spoke of the national diet. She bristles at the notion that she is a cook; she is a nutritionist first, she will tell you, and she teaches dietary basics through cooking. "I've tried for thirty years to change the Cuban diet. Cuba has a sweet tooth. Every country does, I suppose. Sugar is a baby taste, and people who have babies can help them by not feeding them sweets all the time. Sugar has a place in the human diet, of course. But people use it to replace other nutrients.

"I'm a diabetic. I use a little sugar, but not every day. The harm isn't in sugar but in the way people use it. In underdeveloped countries people are starving. With sugar they're still undernourished but they're not starving. Photographers in the fashion industry here and all over the world insist that the style is to be slim. Rubens's models wouldn't earn a centavo in Cuba. I would like to lose weight. I can do it if I exercise. I used to swim at a pool at one of the big hotels. They gave me permission to swim there because most foreigners don't recognize me." She got me that glass of water.

"Obesity is a problem in Cuba. We are trying to keep children from getting fat. Fat cells developed in childhood are like sponges—they may not hold anything for a long time, but they can still absorb later in life. If a child is obese, it's a lifelong problem fighting obesity. That's the most important thing happening in Cuba right now, as far as nutrition goes. Now the adolescents try all those freak diets."

Nitza Villapol's career goes back to 1951 when Cuba, one of the first countries to have television, first went on the air with a regular schedule. Nitza was in the first year's line-up and has brought her studio kitchen into living rooms ever since. By all accounts she has the longest-running television program in the world. Her college background was in home economics and education, with courses in dietetics thrown in. "I felt the responsibility to learn more. I was already working in television. They used to call me Cuba's Betty Furness. I sold Leonard's products, RCA Victor products, Stokley's food. I sold Osterizer blenders and Sunbeam frying pans." Nitza smiled for the first time since I walked in.

Her program, *Cocina al minuto*, was broadcast daily in 1958. "I didn't have the slightest idea what the Revolution was. I had no personal connection to it except that three friends had signed some document calling for change. It was common to see grown men and women going through trash cans foraging for something to eat. When many people were hungry, the rich in Cienfuegos used to have lobster and jumbo shrimp and rich coffee. Now all that good stuff is exported. I would *love* to sit down to a steak dinner with potatoes and tomato salad, and cheesecake for dessert. If it's a porterhouse steak, so much the better. But instead of that we have schools and hospitals.

"Anyway, my friends all left Cuba when they realized it was Communist. I had a domestic worker, and she said, 'We'll see if you'll be so happy when they take away what you have!' I said, 'Lolita, they can't. I work with my head and my hands. I'm not exploiting anybody.' " Nitza got herself a glass of water.

"I like TV. I truly do. I like to communicate with the public. I'm a teacher. I like to teach. The ways to good nutrition are difficult. Many people think the Occidental way is the only way to eat. Animal protein and the like. I could eat rice every day of my life because I'm a Cuban, but I don't think a tourist could." She leaned back and spoke with animation for the first time since we began. "I enjoy precooked rice, but most Cubans don't. It's a little yellowish and nutty. I don't have as much trouble as most Cubans because my food habits are more international. I like fish, vegetables, and meat. I like food very simply prepared."

Gabriel García Márquez called her once. "I couldn't figure out why, but he wanted to interview me." She whispered conspiratorially: "I don't like his books. I couldn't even finish *One Hundred Years of Solitude*. I like to breathe while I read a book. I did like his book about Bolívar, but I don't like fiction very much. Well, it turned out he was doing some research about food and needed some advice."

Her office had a comfortable clutter to it. Bookshelves were full of cookbooks, books on nutrition, fine literature. She pointed out *Elena's Secrets of Mexican Cooking*, by Elena Zelayeta, as a favorite cookbook. Also, *Love and Knishes*, by Sara Kasdan. A Remington portable sat on her desk.

With the writers union next door, I said this block had some of the finest books to be found in the country. "UNEAC is shit," she retorted. She walked over to the window and looked down on it with contempt. "I have to look at that building every day of my life. For forty years I've been in radio, television, and film. I've written more than one book and countless articles. And when I applied for membership, they wouldn't admit me." She put on her cheerful, sarcastic voice: "They said, you're an entertainer, not a writer." Had the window been open, she would have spit on the UNEAC grounds.

In 1965 Nitza went to London and Africa as part of a United Nations survey team. "I lived in Queens Way in London for almost four months. The British Museum was near where I worked. English food—it's bad and tasteless. I usually ate lunch at an Italian restaurant." Low moans came from the next room, and Nitza excused herself to tend to her mother.

Her radio sits in the bedroom. "I listen to the BBC and shortwave from Canada and the English Caribbean so I can hear some English. The BBC is a good station."

Nitza's father, a Cuban, lived in New York in the 1920s, where he met her mother, an orphaned Cuban raised by Dominican nuns in Texas. He worked for Macy's in Latin American exports. "He lost his job after the stock market crash. Two of his brothers were closely linked to the dictator Machado. One was his private secretary, and the other was the majordomo of the *palacio*. My father had political inclinations to the left. That's why my name is Nitza—it's a Russian name. At least my dad thought it was. It was in honor of the October Revolution. After the Macy's job, my parents had to sell all they had to support the family, and my father sold Eskimo Pies on the streets. He would buy them in the morning, and if he didn't sell them we'd eat them at home that night. Many times that's all we had. This was during the Depression. I was very fat as a child." She smiled broadly.

"My father spoke English well but he had a foreign accent. In school they used to call me a Spanish onion. Once he came to school to pick me up and I ran up to him crying, 'Don't speak Spanish, Daddy, don't speak Spanish!' On weekends he'd take me to the Palisades or the Bronx Zoo. He used to think about Cuba so much. When he realized what society was doing to me, he'd take me to the Museum of Spanish Art near Riverside Drive every Sunday. I remember him saying, 'This is your culture. Never be ashamed of your heritage.'

"My father didn't want to come back to Cuba when Machado was president, but my mother said, 'If you want to stay you can, but I'm going back. No more New York winters for me. So we sold all of our winter clothes and booked third-class passage. This was in July 1933. The women and the children were in one part, and the men in another. We were *aplastados*," squished. Nitza sobbed gently at the memory.

The Villapols sailed for three days on the *Orizaba*, the same boat from which thirty-two-year-old writer Hart Crane had jumped to his death a year earlier. "My father cried as we entered the Harbor. We could see the little Negroes dive into the filthy bay for a penny from the tourists. The poor little children were almost naked, underfed, and without any shoes. We arrived in Cuba just a few days before the fall of Machado. I was nine."

Señor Villapol sold insurance and managed a press, where he printed a Communist Party newspaper. Among his customers was Carlos Rafael Rodríguez, now the country's vice president.

"He never asked me to give up my American citizenship or to be a Cuban, but when I became of age I did anyway. He was so happy.

"He wasn't fit for underground work, but if the Party needed someone as a front to rent a house for a resting place, or an office to work out of, he would do it. After Batista had staged his coup and then Fidel attacked the Moncada, I said, what are you going to do about it, join that crazy man? I meant Fidel, of course. Batista's coup pushed Cuba back many years."

She stood up abruptly. "Let me get you something. Come with me." She led me around the corner to the kitchen. "I'm a friendly person, but I know I can be crazy. Here." She pulled a grapefruit out of a bag. "We have the best grapefruit in the world. Our only competitor is Israel." She squeezed two glasses of grapefruit juice. Her sink overflowed with a week's dirty dishes. Every counter was crowded with unwashed pots and pans, opened containers, spilled food, unidentifiable leftovers, and drying liquid. The most envied kitchen in the Pearl of the Antilles was a godawful mess. "On weekends I clean up. I may have to hire someone. It's getting too much to handle the house and my mother. I used to clean my bathroom and kitchen with a toothpick. Now I've been told that after the first of the year we won't have detergent because so much of it is imported."

"What will you clean with?"

"Soap! I remember the days before detergent when everything was washed with soap." She reached into a bag and pulled out some crackers. "And without detergent, we'll wash our things with *hoja de maguey*. Its juice is like soapwater, and the fiber is like an *estropajo*," a lufa. "The only hardship I won't be able to endure is if we have to stop the elevators. Those four floors will be a burden. I had polio when I was twenty-two. It's hard for me to walk. It's hard to take care of my mother and the apartment. But the Cuban people are not going to surrender. We're not going to go back! We're going to survive. It may be hard, but it's possible."

She opened her Coldspot. "Sometimes we have a power outage for two or three days and everything in the refrigerator spoils." She pulled out a cake and sliced two pieces. She loaded the cake, some crackers, and the fresh grapefruit juice on a small tray and we went back into the living room.

"I've been back to New York once since we left. I was at the Cloisters, and took a cab downtown. I told the driver, when you pass 137th Street, please go slowly. He asked me why, and I told him that I used to live there. He said, 'Lady, you wouldn't want to walk the streets there in the daytime now.' "

A soft dusk poured through the windows giving the apartment a nice muted glow. Or, put another way, it was almost dark and Nitza hadn't turned on a light.

"I think if I went back now I'd spend all my time at theaters and museums, and window shopping on Fifth Avenue. There's not much else worth doing there, is there. If I didn't live in Cuba I'd want to live in San Francisco or Rome."

The fresh-squeezed grapefruit was delicious.

"Last week's show was about grapefruit. I never work from a script. I just go to the studio and talk. I may repeat a recipe but what I say is different. I read. I read a lot. That's all my preparation. I love reading."

Nitza has earned the praise of three generations of Cubans for adapting to market conditions. When a shortage of tomatoes or an abundance of mangoes hits the produce bins, she knows, and adjusts her show accordingly. Her household food comes from the neighborhood market and bakery rather than the well-stocked Diplomercado, where, if she sought the privilege, she could surely buy groceries. *Cocina al minuto*, then weekly on Sunday mornings, could be like *Granma*, pretending that disaster hadn't struck, but her audience knows she uses only ingredients available to all. When she demonstrated bread making once, she mentioned that Cuba must import its wheat, while an un-named country to the north actually pays its farmers *not* to grow wheat.

We finished our snack. "Whenever I make soup I put rum in it. Don't people put sherry in soup? Why not rum? One rainy night recently I put some rum into canned clam chowder. It was three-year-old rum. If it had been seven-year-old rum it would have been better. You can use seven-year-old rum in all recipes that call for sherry or brandy."

She finally turned a light on.

"You *must* see the prehistoric murals in Viñales." I had told Nitza that I was going to the province of Pinar del Río soon. "Before the Revolution, Pinar del Río was called La Cenicienta," Cinderella, "because it was so very poor. I was there once and I remember seeing a boy peeling sugarcane with his knife and a girl on a swing. An accident happened and she lost an eye. Her mother said, 'One eye is enough.' This was a very poor country. Before, the only hope was a lottery ticket. There was such a difference between the poor and the middle class. At the time of the Revolution you had to decide whether you were with the people or with those who exploit the people. It's relatively easy to overthrow a dictatorship, but it's hard to build a society. It's very unfortunate that the so-called American way of life has blinded so many people. Most of my 'friends' left the country. I couldn't because of the way I was brought up. I remember the day that Fidel said that this was to be a socialist society. I said, ah! This is what my father was talking about. He died two years before the Revolution."

The telephone rang, but the caller hung up before Nitza could reach the kitchen phone.

"We still have a hard time in front of us. We've done a lot, but we could've done more. What we have gained is not reversible. The only mistake Allende made in Chile was leaving the army with its old generals and its old people. I remember Fidel wouldn't come into Havana until the old guard had left. Stubborn men! *No se puede dejar la iglesia en manos de Lutero.*" You can't leave the church in Luther's hands.

"Fidel had an army of peasants. The people were illiterate, but they had fought the Revolution to be free. Lenin once said that no one escapes his time. I think that if you truly love something, you hang on. That's why a revolution has to be based on the people. I was a charter member of the Federación de Mujeres Cubanas," the Federation of Cuban Women, "and the Comités de Defensa de la Revolución. The first years of the Revolution were much harder than this. But with the help of the USSR we have survived. I'm not a member of the Communist Party but my feelings are Communist Party.

"I can understand that someone would not like it here if you didn't see this country before 1959. People used to dig in garbage cans for food. Whole families used to live on the streets. I had a teaching degree, and for five years I couldn't get a job because there simply weren't enough schools. And with so much illiteracy! To understand, you have to have lived it. It's not easy here. Between now and the end of the year we don't even know what will happen. It is a special period. Fidel has said it." She laughed.

"Lots of people think that this government will be overthrown. But a true revolution brings so much to so many people, people who never had schools or hospitals, or who were discriminated against because of the color of their skin."

Nitza had talked with me for five hours. "I wonder if you see me as a fanatic. Because I'm sure, in spite of its problems, that what this country is doing is right. I'm sure we're on the right track."

The next day I was exhausted from my marathon session with Nitza, barely able to absorb a newspaper or even a conversation. It was a day for mindless activity, running errands, walking the Malecón, reading a book, standing in lines. The last of these disciplines was as close as the S or D bakery, where the following handwritten sign had been posted:

NOTICE
AS A RESULT OF THE SPECIAL PERIOD,
STARTING TODAY WE CAN ONLY SELL TWO POUNDS OF
BREAD PER PERSON.
PRODUCTION OF SLICED BREAD WILL BE CUT BY 30%.
THANK YOU.

If I lined up at the *supermercado* right after the dairy delivery I could still buy a liter of milk on the free market. The clerk there knew my face by now, and sold me a bottle after turning away a stranger in front of me. Sometimes it pays to be *el último*.

Morning hours at the S or D *agromercado* were already over, and it wouldn't reopen until the middle of the afternoon. On my way back to the Malecón I stopped at the office of the Orquesta Sinfónica Nacional to leave a message for Jesús. The receptionist, who was halfway down the hall, asked who he was. "He's an *oboísta* with the symphony."

"What? A *comunista* with the symphony?"

"No, no, no. An *oboista*." I demonstrated with a few notes on the air oboe. "Not a *comunista*."

La Plume had no mail for me but she wouldn't let me leave the office without hearing all about my visit with Nitza. "I thought for sure you'd be out of there five minutes after me." She was all ears. "What's she like?" La Plume couldn't wait to get the lowdown. Nitza's tears and bitterness were still fresh in my mind.

"She's a very complex woman," I said, and left it at that.

La Plume had a stack of complimentary tickets for the premiere of *Hello, Hemingway*, a new movie opening that evening at the Cine Yara. "Would you like two?" I went home and invited Fernando Campoamor to go with me.

I began reading Oscar Hijuelos's *The Mambo Kings Play Songs of Love* sitting on the Malecón seawall. Reading a book *en su jus* appeals to me, and Cuba was the Mambo Kings' *jus*. A well-written novel inspires literary detective work. The possibilities multiply with every street name, every tree, every smell. What a grand book to have published in Cuba; the Castillo brothers were *puros cubanos* no matter what country they lived in. They carried their *cubanidad*, vulgar and lyrical, to the grave. Editors in Havana's publishing world were well acquainted with the book, but were vague about an edition in Cuba. A translation had appeared in Spain, and I hoped to find copies as gifts for friends.

I stopped reading when I got to the section about the Imperial Ballroom in Brooklyn, and walked east toward the Prado. Although I had covered this route regularly over the previous months, this was the first time I noticed a sign next to the underpass connecting the sea-side sidewalk with the city on the other side.

PROTECT YOUR LIFE
USE THE PEDESTRIAN PASSAGEWAY
2 DEATHS AND 13 INJURIES HAVE OCCURRED CROSSING
THE STREET

On a wall a couple of blocks away, the Young Communists League slogan brigade was carefully scripting the latest in its bouncy wordplay: CUBANOS COMO LAS PALMAS; more or less, "Cubans are as free as the palm trees."

I spotted Fernando Campoamor in the throng outside the theater and we linked up just as we got to the lobby. As we waited for *Hello,*

Hemingway to begin, he explained how he met Hemingway. The fall of Machado in 1933 did little to change a custom ingrained in Cuba's middle and upper classes—that of sending their children to the States for school. The Campoamors sent Fernando and his brother to high school in Lake Charles, Louisiana, for a semester. "In school there I wrote a small book about the tragedy of Cuba and its wars against Spain and U.S. imperialism. We didn't have anything to do in Lake Charles on weekends, and a teacher suggested that we take the bus to Oxford, Mississippi, one Sunday to meet William Faulkner." Campoamor waved to a few friends in the opening night crowd.

"We were shy about going up to the door of the house. With our awful English, Faulkner felt sorry for these two Cuban kids. When he learned we were going back to Havana after the term he wrote out a letter for Hemingway and John Dos Passos, who was also living in Havana then. Ernest and John. Imagine, a teenage Cuban kid. I had goose bumps. When we returned to Havana I went to the Ambos Mundos Hotel where they were both staying. My heart was pounding. I was very nervous. When we met I got an *abrazo*, "an embrace," from each of them. I had a beer with them, then a rum, then a scotch. I was just a kid! I called him mister, not *señor*. It wasn't until many years later that I called him Papa. That was reserved for special people." The movie began.

Hello, Hemingway was a smooth, mainstream Hollywood sort of picture. The story follows fifteen-year-old Larita, a working-class high school student in 1956 who lives near Hemingway's estate in San Francisco de Paula, a village just east of Havana. She comes across a copy of *The Old Man and the Sea*, falls in love with it, and identifies with its allegory of man against the odds. In school she excels in English and qualifies as a finalist for a scholarship to study in the States. She loses the last round of the competition when the snooty scholarship administrator looks down her nose at a mere public school finalist. Meanwhile her father, a cop, is fired, which wreaks havoc at home. Proud of her proximity to Finca la Vigía, the Hemingway spread, Larita gets the nerve to drop in on her renowned neighbor. And should she actually meet the man she idolizes, what would she say? "I don't know," she says with a nervous giggle. "Hello, Hemingway?" When she finally makes it to the door, Hemingway's valet shoos her away. Later, when she sees Ernesto pass her in his chauffeur-driven car, the shy fifteen-year-old Cuban student and her fifty-seven-year-old Nobel laureate neighbor make eye contact.

Larita, played by Laura de la Uz, has a typical teenager's room lined with pictures of Elvis, James Dean, Fabian, and Frankie Avalon. She sees Hemingway in *Life* magazine and adds him to her wall. In the midst of her intellectual growth she gets confused by a nasty anti-Batista strike at her high school. The film ends on a bittersweet note with an emboldened Larita ready to face the future.

"Well, they used the right language from that era," Campoamor acknowledged as we left the theater. "School demonstrations really did happen like that. The man who answered the door at the finca? He was like a son to Papa. Hemingway trusted him completely. He was the majordomo. René Villareal. He would do his banking, and pay the gardener and the Chinese cook. He had seven or eight workers and some cows." René was the man on whom Mario, in Hemingway's *Islands in the Stream*, was based. "When you get back from Pinar del Río, won't you come over? I have some Hemingway memorabilia I'd like to show you."

What was this, Go Fly a Kite Day? I don't recall having read anything by José, Vladimir, or Fidel about kites, but scores of kids were sailing them above La Lisa, a western suburb of Havana that I drove through on my way to Pinar del Río 160 kilometers away. Weekday lines in La Lisa filled sidewalks much as they did in other parts of town, perhaps slightly longer. A department store line stretched at least half a block, a line outside a public library almost as long, and a lunchtime crowd queued up to the end of the block for pizza from El Globo.

A couple, both students at the University of Pinar del Río, flagged me down as I got on the *autopista*. "What do you think of Cuba?" the girlfriend asked.

This question invariably followed the initial where-are-you-from? exchange, and I had my shorthand reply ready. "It's a marvelous and deeply troubled country," I said, a response that not only covered both poles from the middle, but one I believed, too. I asked them what they thought of my country.

The boyfriend answered. "We both have relatives in the United States, but we've never been there so we have no real basis for comparison. Still, from what we know it is okay."

The highway had six well-paved lanes and lots of roadside slogans. REVOLUTION BEGINS IN THE HEART said one. A billboard showed a doctor and, in her arms, a small boy. CARE FOR LIFE! said the caption. A few kilometers farther, a smiling cartoon boy held a bank savings passbook. HIS SAVINGS GROW. We drove past a man steering his bicycle with his right hand and holding his leather hat on with his left. A machete slapped his thigh. White birds took off and landed on backs of cows wallowing in muddy brown ponds. The next billboard said CHE LIVES. It showed him in the famous pose gazing slightly above the horizon as if he had a crick in his neck.

I checked into the Hotel Pinar del Río. Some anti-U.S. slogans were painted on the walls of the university across the street. I got directions to the Francisco Donatién Cigar Factory. The building is an old, once-elegant structure with columns and arches in front and museum-quality farm equipment displayed on the patio. It had one large room with space for some eighty workers and a few side rooms for leaf selectors, quality controllers, and storage. A showroom adjoined the main room, with samples on the wall of different grades of tobacco and descriptions of their breed and availability. The posters looked like science fair exhibits. Each worker handled a *chaveta*, a rounded, all-purpose knife for cutting leaves, smoothing the wrapping, tamping loose tobacco, and holding the near-finished cigar in place while the wrapper is sealed. The workbenches, called *galeras*, held all the worldly tools needed to craft these noble handmade habits. Two workers sat side by side at each *galera*, with a small pile of loose tobacco leaves at their sides and, stacked nearby, larger leaves, called *capas*, for wrapping the cigars. The *galeras* were, in turn, arranged in two sets of about fifteen rows each. An intoxicating aroma of farm-fresh tobacco permeated the workroom. There I met Alberto Zubizarreta Fernández, who was to be my guide.

"May I have your attention," he called over the loudspeaker from the front of the room. Some workers looked up; most kept their eyes on their cigars. *"We have the honor of a visitor who is interested in our work. He is a North American writer. Let us demonstrate our skills and make him welcome."* When Zubizarreta was through, the room erupted in the cigar roller's cheer: each worker takes his or her *chaveta* and rapidly bangs it against the *galera*, creating a percussive din like a rackful of aluminum baseball bats pulled along a picket fence. The longer the racket, the more they like you.

Zubizarreta—in my notes I called him Zubin Z. Mehta—said that the building had been a jail since 1868, "but immediately after the triumph, the Revolution turned it into a cigar factory. It is a national monument. We roll more than three million cigars a year at this factory alone. A good roller can complete more than a dozen cigars an hour. We work from 7:30 until noon and then from one to 4:30, with two fifteen-minute breaks. We also work until noon on Saturdays. The workers get bread and hot chocolate in the morning. They can buy lunch here for less than fifty centavos. We make six grades of cigars, all for domestic consumption." His spiel complete, I wandered among the *torcedores*, the rollers, and watched them at work.

Christopher Columbus found Indians on the island smoking tobacco, which, according to historian Hugh Thomas, the Italian navigator brought back to Europe along with syphilis. Cigars have given Cuba identity, pride, and hard currency. Debates swing wildly about whether the quality of a Communist cigar is as good as one made under capitalism, but no one goes so far as to belittle the best that Cuba still offers. The highest-grade, most delicate tobacco that Cuba produces grows in San Juan y Martínez, just down the road from the city of Pinar del Río.

Well-known cigar smokers have always boosted the image of a good Havana. Arthur Rubinstein, after a visit to Havana, wrote, "No lover of cigars can imagine the voluptuous pleasure of sitting in a café sipping slowly a strong magnificent coffee and smoking rhythmically these divine leaves of Cuba." In the 1920s, the king of Spain reputedly had his own personal cigar roller in Havana. As a youth Federico García Lorca was said to fantasize about Cuba by gazing at the intriguing labels on his father's cigar boxes. In the 1950s comedian Ernie Kovacs would fly to Cuba for a weekend just to refill his humidor. John Kennedy and his press secretary, Pierre Salinger, both smoked Petit Uppmans, and one afternoon, as relations between the U.S. and Cuba grew increasingly acrid, the President asked his aide to get as many Uppmans as he could. The next day the President asked Salinger how many he had come up with. Twelve hundred, came the reply. As Salinger relates it, JFK smiled and said, " 'Fine.' And with that he pulled out the decree establishing the trade embargo with Cuba and signed it."

Cuban cigars have also spawned two excellent books, one witty, the other wise; Guillermo Cabrera Infante's *Holy Smoke*, and *Cuban Counterpoint* by Fernando Ortíz. Cabrera Infante writes that he was watching John Ford's *Wagonmaster* on television at a cattle ranch once when Fidel, who started smoking cigars in high school, came into the room and asked, "Who has a cigar?" The author, who had four in his pocket, offered one to the premier. "As he got involved in the yarn . . . Castro asked for a second cigar. Then for a third. Fortunately I knew that *Wagonmaster* was Ford's shortest Western, barely ninety minutes long. It was soon over. Castro stood up, all uniformed and pistoled six feet of him, and commented: 'Too many songs and not enough Indians.' . . . Before leaving he turned to me and said: 'I see we have one Indian left.' . . . He meant my last cigar. He referred to it as if it were one more Apache. 'Do you mind if I borrow it?' What could I say? Don't mind if you do, *comandante*? I surrendered my last cigar." The three other cigars lay on the floor, "all but barely smoked. Obviously Prime Ministers make lousy smokers."

Castro, who gave up smoking in the mid-1980s, told Jacques Cousteau in a television interview that a good cigar burns well, evenly, and softly. Why did he quit? "It was good for the economy, but not so good for my health."

Fernando Ortíz's rich historical work contrasts the real and metaphoric roles of tobacco and sugar in the Cuban character. "Sugar is made by man and power. Tobacco is the voluntary offering of nature," he wrote in 1940, the year Fulgencio Batista won a relatively fair presidential election. "In the production of tobacco intelligence is the prime factor . . . tobacco is liberal, not to say revolutionary. In the production of sugar it is a question of power; sugar is conservative, if not reactionary. . . . The production of sugar was always a capitalist venture because of its great territorial and industrial scope. . . . Tobacco, child of the savage Indian and the virgin earth, is a free being, bowing its neck to no mechanical yoke."

The liberationist identity ascribed to tobacco goes back to the nineteenth century when the independence movement supplied assembly room readers with literature encouraging freedom from Spanish rule. The tradition of a reader daily addressing the workers, according to Ortíz, has its origins in nineteenth-century convent and prison dining halls. It was done "with a definite plan of social propaganda." José Martí, during the 1880s and 1890s, used the reader's platform to agitate for liberty among the Cuban cigar rollers in Florida. He called tobacco a "gracious plant," adding that workers handled it "as though each plant were a delicate lady." Workers in exile soon tithed ten percent of their income to support the rebellion. In the twentieth century, readers survived the threat of replacement by radio. For many years readers were paid by worker contributions. Now they're salaried like everyone else.

"Readers were very important in the growth of Cuba from a colony to an emerging country." Segundo Pérez Carrillo told me that. He's the reader at the Francisco Donatién factory. "I read two times in the morning and twice in the afternoons. The morning reading comes from the newspapers. I divide it between international and national news. Right now the Gulf conflict is dominant. I read from a book in the afternoon." Pérez, born in 1920 when the U.S. military occupied part of the country, began as a reader in 1941. "When I began we didn't use microphones. I also worked as a radio announcer on station CMAB."

Pérez's lead story came from Belgrade: " 'Yugoslavia Protests U.S. Meddling.' The Yugoslavian government complained today to the U.S. about its interventionist attitude in internal affairs. A spokesman for the U.S. Secretary of State last week threatened reprisals against authorities . . . if they did not follow Washington's electoral guidelines." Pérez stood behind a lectern on a platform with copies of the day's *Granma* and the provincial newspaper *Guerrillero* in front of him. The face of the lectern was covered with colorful decals from travel agencies and foreign cities.

The morning's second story came from Buenos Aires: "Overwhelming Majority of Brazilians, Chileans, and Argentines Complain About Salaries. A research consortium has released findings that seventy-six percent of the Brazilians questioned thought they received salaries below a decent standard of living, and that only six percent of Argentines and nine percent of Chileans earn enough to actually save money.

Pérez wore jeans, a striped sport shirt, and gold-rimmed glasses. He looked natty in a neatly trimmed mustache and a stylish felt cap he had picked up while visiting his brother in Florida the previous year. He wore a handsome old Soviet wristwatch. With his clear voice and a thin, erect body, Pérez seemed much younger than his seventy years. By appearance he could have just walked off the back nine at the local public links.

Pérez's next story came from Moscow, where, tobacco rollers learned, the president of the USSR's Supreme Soviet said that the Great Socialist Revolution of 1917 was the response to the need for permanent social justice. Next, he read a dispatch from Washington that George Bush had cut medical benefits for the elderly and froze other domestic programs. The article concluded, "The popularity of the President, who reneged on his campaign promise not to raise taxes, dropped from seventy-five percent to forty-eight percent in one month." As he read, workers walked up to the supply table to replenish their bags of tobacco. Then came news that Saudi Arabia would permit troops to be based there if the U.S. chooses "the military option," and another in which King Hussein of Jordan said there would be economic, ecological, and human devastation in the event of a Gulf war. In the middle of the next story, a short from Brazil about the prevalence of elephantiasis in Recife, Pérez stopped to ad lib an explanation of the disease. He read with sufficient drama to keep the news moving, but not enough to bury the reports beneath his style. "And that concludes the international news."

When Pérez returned after a break, his first national story came from the front page of *Granma* beneath an illustration of Lenin. The headline was in red: "Now, More Than Ever, We Need His Ideas." The piece began: "A day like today, seventy-three years ago, humanity began to emerge from prehistory." I found myself taken by Pérez's voice, following it through Marx and Engels, Russian history, Cuba's "fervent admiration" for the Soviet revolution ("the most just social concepts that humanity has ever known") and Cuba's role "in the trenches of the third world." Worker productivity neither increased nor fell while Pérez read the turgid paean to Lenin and the Russian Revolution. He alternately smoked cigarettes and cigars as he read. The workers at the Francisco Donatién Cigar Factory got their morning news.

That afternoon Pérez read a 1930s French romance, *Lil with Eyes the Color of Time*. Almost half of the workers were women, and every one I spoke with said they looked forward to the romance novels most of all. Rollers make a basic monthly salary of 160 pesos, augmented by production bonuses. "Most of them earn two hundred pesos a month or more," Zubizarreta told me. "We have a training course for new workers. The women especially, because we want to maintain a balance between the sexes. It never used to be like that."

Pérez gets 141 pesos a month for his four shifts at the microphone. "But he only works a few hours a day and he's done," a roller muttered to me as the reader concluded the day's installment of *Lil*.

Selectors worked with stacks of uncut leaves on their laps, picking and choosing which leaf should end up around what grade cigar. Ortíz: "The color of the different types of cigar, like that of women, cannot be simply reduced to blondes and brunettes. Just as a Cuban distinguishes among women every shade from jet-black to golden white, with a long intervening series of intermediary and mixed pigmentations, and classifies them according to color, attractiveness, and social position, so he knows the different types of tobacco: claros, colorado-claros, colorado-maduros, maduros, ligeros, secos, medios-tiempos, finos, amarillos, manchados, quebrados, sentidos, broncos, puntillas, and many others. . . . There are selectors who can distinguish seventy or eighty different shades of tobacco."

"They always appreciate Agatha Christie," Pérez said after his afternoon stint. "On deck I have Alexander Dumas, and perhaps I will read Hemingway's *For Whom the Bell Tolls*. Some books I bring from home, sometimes one of the workers will bring a book, and others I get from the library. I make a list of the selections and the workers choose in a secret ballot. It's a democratic vote." He paused to make sure that the last two words sunk in. "Sometimes I can finish a book in a few days, other times it takes a couple of weeks. It depends on the length and the interruptions." His reading of *Lil* had been disrupted by a busload of Swiss tourists who descended on the workroom, cameras blazing. They too had been formally introduced, followed by *chaveta* pounding.

The process of rolling proved fascinating, but I never got the sequence down pat. It roughly follows that of handrolling a cigarette, but far more elaborate and precise. Some rollers complete cigars entirely by hand, others, such as Félix Monterrey Chacón, use a desktop mechanical roller. First Félix put loose tobacco leaves in the roller. Then he picked up a large *capa* and rolled it into the device one complete cycle. The *capa* surrounded the loose tobacco, forming a long tightly packed cylinder, which he removed from the contraption. At this stage it was a creaseless, primitive cigar. To complete the procedure he carefully folded the excess of the *capa* around the ends with a fingertip of rice-based glue, circumcised the tips, and put the cigar in a rack with nine others to form a minyan of Havanas.

I felt at ease in Pinar del Río. It had the same aura of comparative freedom I'd felt in Cienfuegos, or maybe it was just getting away from Havana again. The little balcony on my third-floor room looked out on a large field, where a dozen teenagers had gathered to play pickup baseball at dusk. I ended up at the hotel restaurant seated across from a middle-aged Soviet woman. Two foreigners alone at nightfall in the soft Caribbean. Ah, the possibilities.

Wrong. Her Spanish was lost in the steppes. We tried writing instead of speaking; her letters were Cyrillic. From what I could gather she was a medical advisor to a family-planning project in Matanzas on holiday in western Cuba. That much took five minutes of infinitive verbs, genderless nouns, and a map. We simply couldn't understand each other and quickly lost what trifling empathy we had. You read that music is the international language, that humor bridges cultures and borders, that love conquers all. Maybe so, but she and I shared neither music nor humor nor love—didn't even come close—and we finished our meals looking at our plates in glum silence. I mention this dull encounter only because it was a situation far more prevalent than serendipitous meetings with scintillating people, but it's hard to convince anyone that traveling solo abroad can be full of dreary folk and dismal circumstance.

The man from the writers union came by after dinner. He was eager to take me to night English classes. A friend of his taught an advanced course, and we climbed the stairs of an old building. "During the Special Period we cannot have the hall lights on," a school administrator said as we tripped down a dark hall filled with construction equipment. "Only classroom lights."

Fifteen students sat at desks horseshoed around the blackboard watching a young scholar write the date and "Year 32 of the Revolution." I was introduced as a native speaker, a dessert they could indulge in after their main course. They spoke only English.

"Why is this date important?" the teacher asked.

Most students raised their hands. Said one, "Because it's the anniversary of the triumph of the Socialist Revolution, the beginning of progressive ideas throughout the world."

"And why is it important to Cuba?"

Another hand. "Because the great October Revolution started a new system called socialism." A third. "After the Second World War socialism was applied as a socialist system."

Teacher. "The best way to commemorate the Revolution is to participate in this class of English and work very hard, eh?" And with that they launched into the concept of trial by jury. Their textbook, published in Havana, had a dialogue on the subject that took readers through the trial of an accused thief. The jury found him not guilty.

The class met for two hours four nights a week. The students seemed between seventeen and thirty years old. The teacher asked them about films and actors. "What sort of movies do you like to see?"

"Love films," said a girl. The class giggled.

"Science fiction," replied a fellow.

"Do you like to go to the cinema alone or with a partner?"

Everyone. "With a partner! With a partner!"

"After the film, where do you go?"

"¡La Coppelia!"

"For—"

"For ice cream."

"Which actors do you like?"

"Robert Redford." "Robert De Niro." "Meryl Streep." This nationwide ability to speak well of Vladimir Lenin in one breath and Meryl Streep in the next continued to stump me. "Dustin Hoffman." They named a couple of his movies, including *Tootsie*, which had aired the previous weekend.

"What is Dustin Hoffman in *Tootsie*, a man or a woman?" They knew. "And how do you consider his performance in this film?"

"It's out of this world!"

During a break I visited the beginning English class. There were stick figures on the blackboard with the words MAN and WOMAN beneath them. One of the young workers from the tobacco factory, Rosa María Valdés, was in that class. Pérez the tobacco reader had stopped at a thrilling point in *Lil*, and Rosa María couldn't wait for the next afternoon when he would continue. She was taking English, she said, because it is international, it is used in science journals, it is the language of finance, and so many books are in English. "It is very helpful when traveling, I am sure."

Back in the advanced class a student asked me in English what I thought of Spanish. I said I was relieved that I was a native English speaker who learned Spanish rather than the other way around. "The more comfortable I feel in your language, the more I appreciate the complications and nuances of mine. English must be incredibly difficult to learn."

"Don't you like Spanish?" I hadn't made myself clear in my own tongue.

Of course, *bien sûr, claro que sí.* "My goodness, how can you not love a language that calls someone who plots a crime, like the accused thief in your lesson, *'el autor intelectual'?*," the intellectual author.

YANKEE, BACK OFF! NOBODY SURRENDERS HERE! That appeared in big red letters on the university wall facing the hotel lobby. A comic book fist punched through the wall between the two admonitions as if to say, *Eat knuckle sandwich, Yankee scum.* Nice artwork.

Pérez the reader had mentioned the local library downtown. It was named for Ramón "Mongo" González Coro, a fellow from Pinar del Río killed in the last month of the Revolution at age twenty-eight as he was rescuing another rebel. I wandered through Mongo's library, browsed the stacks, thumbed through the card catalog, and talked with the staff. What struck me most was that La Biblioteca Provincial Ramón González Coro was, in many ways, identical to a medium-sized library in the States. It held ninety thousand books, any of which could be borrowed by anyone with a library card, itself available virtually for the asking. It had a display highlighting new acquisitions, kids' artwork on the walls, phonograph records, books in braille, and old newspapers in a cluttered out-of-the-way room. Students nearing term paper deadlines pressed the reference librarian for help, and retirees relaxed at tables they shared with college students doing their homework. A bookbinding room had a large cast-iron press made early this century by Chandler & Price in Cleveland. "We call it the guillotine," a librarian said, laughing at its design. The Special Period had reduced Mongo's hours but not the lighting. A bookmobile traveled to small towns.

Books in braille were by José Martí and Fidel Castro. Martí's extensive works had been brought out so many times in so many editions over the last century that a Martí-of-the-Month Club could stay in business for years without once duplicating itself. Books by Anaïs Nin, Kim Il Sung, and Jorge Luis Borges filled the shelves. Recent arrivals from Mexico included Octavio Paz, Carlos Monsiváis, and the artist José Clemente Orozco; from South America came works by Eduardo Galeano. Carlos Fuentes's *The Old Gringo*, then the country's second-best-selling novel, had been recently checked out. Alice Walker, Daniel Defoe, and John Dos Passos were there. So were William Faulkner, Mario Puzo, and Theodore Dreiser's *Sister Carrie*, recently televised in a popular miniseries. Ana Luisa Alvaro Echevarría, a librarian, held up a copy of Gore Vidal's *Burr*. "This is a favorite of mine."

José Martí also showed up in the record section on an album of Pablo Milanés singing his poems. Other recorded writers included Ernesto Cardenal, Alejo Carpentier, and the lusty Nicolás Guillén. One record contained speeches by Salvador Allende. The most elaborate album was a three-record set of Fidel's orations. The cover design included his complete twenty-three-word title, lest any listener momentarily forget. Mongo also had some 250 classical music recordings. A print of Leonardo da Vinci's *Mona Lisa* hung on the wall above the record rack.

Posters trumpeting the October Revolution dominated another wall; all had Lenin in the background. A biography of Robert Louis Stevenson was tacked to the children's room wall. A parents' essay contest invited compositions on "social and political organizations in the promotion of reading." The "Artwork of the Month" had been painted in oil; it was called *Temptation*, and showed a boy reaching out for forbidden fruit.

I had been hoping to find an article by Gabriel García Márquez about Graham Greene, said to have run in *Juventud Rebelde* in either late 1987 or early 1988. Could librarian María Blanca Morejón help me locate it? She took this as a challenge to Mongo's resources and escorted me to the musty periodical archives. "You start looking from that end and I'll begin here," she said when we found the right shelf. García Márquez's column had run every Sunday then, and while it proved interesting—one on his visa problems with the U.S., another on soap operas, a third on the CIA—none featured Graham Greene. I was about to give up when, from around the corner, I heard María Blanca. "I found it!" She sprinted over with page three of *Juventud Rebelde* from January 24, 1988: " 'Graham Greene's Twenty Hours in Havana,' by Gabriel García Márquez, an account of the British author's last visit to Cuba." After effusive appreciation for her efforts I asked in passing where I might copy the piece. María Blanca's voice lowered. "That is one way in which we are deficient. I wish it were otherwise, but the library has no photocopy machine. Leave your address in Havana with me and we will see to it that you get a copy."

The week before I left Havana for Pinar del Río I rode by the corner of Paseo and Zapata on a crowded *guagua*. Out of the corner of my eye I saw a thin red slab planted in the middle of a vest-pocket park wedged between two streets. I had heard about this brick monument and quickly angled my way through a phalanx of straphangers to the middle exit. The driver opened only the front door at the next stop, so I executed an accepted rule of Havana bus etiquette—when your door stays shut, pound incessantly on the metal frame above it. The obnoxious racket cuts through the din of conversation, traffic, and the idling engine, and the driver either opens the door—or he doesn't. In this case he did, and I exited, followed by three others. (If only doors between countries could open as easily.)

The memorial was dedicated to Julius and Ethel Rosenberg, the American couple convicted in 1951 of conspiring to pass nuclear weapon secrets to the Soviet Union in 1944 and 1945. The pair were sentenced to die after a trial since shown to have been far less than fair. An extensive international campaign to commute their sentences failed, and the two were killed in the electric chair in 1953. Among the foreign groups asking for clemency was the Democratic Federation of Cuban Women.

The Rosenberg monument stands out as much for its design as its subject. In a city where powder white statues of revolutionary heroes and their horses appear to have all been cast from the same mold, the slim Rosenberg memorial has actual color, few words, and originality. It is a simple stack of bricks one deep, ten across, and about sixty-

five high. Nine cement doves flutter near the top, above the words
Julius Rosenberg wrote the day before he died:

FOR PEACE, BREAD, AND ROSES, WE FACE THE EXECUTIONER

A cement head-and-shoulders sculpture of the couple highlights the
design, above the inscription MURDERED JUNE 19, 1953. Four brick
spotlight casings at ground-level point toward the monument, their
bulbs all long gone. A tree next to the slab shades Ethel and Julius,
and small plants grow in front of their memorial. Benches line the
little park's sidewalks. A bus stop at the edge ensures constant foot
traffic. A three-man city work crew relaxed on the ground, leaning
against the back of the monument. Passers-by paused to look at the
inscription, then walked on. The monument was made by José De-
larram in 1983. A Dodge manufactured the year of the Rosenberg
deaths was parked nearby.

Cubans know the Rosenberg case better than most people in the
United States. In the mid-1960s, letters between Julius and Ethel
were read nightly on national radio. A French series about the case
aired on Cuban television, and a stamp in memory of the couple was
issued as well. Vast publicity accompanied the visit of one of the
Rosenbergs' sons some years ago. Then, in 1987, Cuba brought out
For Peace and Roses, a short documentary about the case. It opens with
footage of demonstrations in the U.S. against the electrocution, and
includes an interview with Vice President Rodríguez, said to be quite
the expert on U.S. history. Shots of flowers left at the Havana monument and interviews with members of Cuba's Artists' Brigade for the
Rosenbergs are also in the film. The brigade included Pablo Milanés,
whose song "Heroes of Peace" celebrates the case.

I mention all this because in talking about the Rosenbergs in Havana
I learned that Cuba named a school in their memory, situated in the
countryside of Pinar del Río Province. After my visit to Pinar del
Río's public library, I drove southwest on the central highway past
tobacco growing beneath enormous spreads of cheesecloth, almost to
Sandino City, a planned city built in the early 1960s, and turned due
south along a lonely two-lane blacktop that stretched almost to the
coast. I pulled up at a large campus composed of two-and three-story
concrete buildings joined by open-air hallways. I asked the first man
I saw if the principal was available, and after a few minutes Rosa
Hernández, the director, about thirty years old, came over. She invited

me to her office, where she served coffee, carefully read my writers union letter of introduction, and sent a student to fetch another administrator and a teacher. "We were not prepared for a visitor today, you know. Classes end shortly, and I'm not sure what we can show you, but we will try."

This much I learned from Hernández and the two others: Julius and Ethel Rosenberg School in the Countryside has some 370 students aged fourteen to seventeen, who, in two shifts, spend half the day in classes and the other half working the fields. The countryside school program, begun in the late 1960s, fulfills José Martí's simple nineteenth-century words of wisdom: "In the morning, the pen—but, in the afternoon, the plow." The school year lasts almost ten months, ending in mid-June. Most of the students will go on to another school and a college degree program. Almost all of them come from the neighboring municipalities of San Juan y Martínez, Guane, and Sandino City, and they go home on weekends.

The lemon and orange harvest had just ended on campus, and the next day they were to start tilling a wide variety of vegetables. The fields were behind the school; I never got to them. From my distant vantage point they looked like typical farm acreage. "We sell the crops to pay for recreation equipment and supplies for the medical clinic." They grow beans, yucca, sweet potato, and tomatoes for themselves. "We try to be as self-sufficient as we can."

Jorge, a recent medical school graduate who worked at Rosenberg High, joined us. The school also has three nurses. "We have thirty-seven teachers, and almost all of them have their degrees." The curriculum at Rosenberg High includes math, physics, Spanish, English, biology, computers, geography, and physical education. I was shown the decently equipped chemistry and physics labs, and the computer lab, with about two dozen computers. The librarian was thrilled when I asked to see her domain and rushed to get the key. The collection included Ray Bradbury, Fidel Castro, William Faulkner, and José Martí. I was asked to sign the school's guest book.

We toured the buildings as students in Pioneer powder blue shirts and dark blue miniskirts and pants, went to afternoon recreation activities. I stopped to watch two boys at a hand-drawn chess board. The darker boy had the lighter pieces. He easily captured the black queen and rooks before mowing down his opponent's front-line pawns. Woefully outmaneuvered, the lighter boy conceded by tipping over his king.

A boy walked by clutching a guitar. "The students play in musical groups and afternoon sports," the director said. They can also practice marksmanship. "We serve them breakfast at seven o'clock every morning. They get bread and butter, hot chocolate, crackers, and coffee. Then a break at ten for crackers, a soft drink, and sometimes ice cream. At 12:30 they get a snack, and at three there's another break. Dinner is served at six, when they have meat. *Always.* At ten they have a little something before they go to bed. It's all free, of course. The *muchachos* grow fast at this age. They never lack for food."

Near the entrance was a not bad portrait of Ethel and Julius, and nearby a framed black-on-red sign: *Julius and Ethel Rosenberg, North Americans, lovers of peace, were victims of their country's fascism. Accused of being Soviet spies, they were tried without evidence and condemned to die in the electric chair, June 19, 1953. History will absolve them!* History teacher Martildo de Roque told me, "The students know about the Rosenberg case. It's in their textbooks, and we talk about it in class, too."

We toured the dormitories, nice, tidy rooms with well-made narrow bunk beds, neatly folded clothes, and on many of the girls' beds large black dolls often associated with santería. A functionary from the Sandino City Communist Party, Oscar Montelier, joined us. The bed-top dolls prompted me to ask about santería and its prevalence among teenagers. "They don't discuss that here." Rosa Hernández was firm.

"Not at all?"

"No. Not at all. In class they discuss materialism and through that they learn about religion. Seventy-one of our students are on their way to becoming Party members." Montelier nodded.

We passed a statue of José Martí and then a garden between two of the buildings where, according to the school doctor, they grow medicinal plants. "With these herbs we can treat inflammations, stomach pains, and some infections. We call it our *jardín botánico.*"

A few dozen boys and girls walked by on their way back to their dorms. They seemed as cheerful and giggly as any teenagers would be with the work day over. I corralled a couple of them to ask about their school, but the novelty of a foreign visitor lured a dozen more than I expected, and they asked all the questions—friendly, straightforward, curious, respectful. As I pulled out of the parking lot, twenty-five students with big grins waved good-bye from the second-floor breezeway.

The next morning I checked out of the conventional Hotel Pinar del Río in the provincial capital and into the rural Spanish-style Hotel Los Jazmines just south of Viñales. The four-level Los Jazmines looks into the Viñales Valley, a wide, lush expanse with enormous limestone outcroppings called *mogotes*. The drive followed the most serene stretch of Cuba I had yet encountered, tiny communities by the side of a gently winding two-lane road with a minimum of nation-thumping billboards and lots of tobacco field workers going about their business. It was a warm day with moist air hovering over rolling fields, as if the land, soft and inviting, was proclaiming its own sensuality. The people I gave rides to were as friendly as their surroundings, relaxed, restful, and patient. This last quality served them well, as I got estimates of bus service ranging from a few hours late to "I hope the route hasn't been discontinued."

My drive to Viñales, then to the north coast village of Puerto Esperanza, drew out a rare sentiment. It can take hold forty miles from home or in a newly explored country. I tell myself, "Boy, I *love* what I'm doing." What could be more pleasurable than driving at a leisurely pace through the misty Caribbean outback, surrounded by new sights, fresh smells, and a terrain that seemed to embrace itself? I was so happy I threw my head back and started to sing the final rousing chorus of "Oklahoma!"

I took the approach to Puerto Esperanza at five miles an hour, gawking at a family in a covered horsecart with a stately old wicker chair in the back. A man in rubber boots and a tattered felt hat was hitching up two oxen in front of his plain concrete home. The most curious form of locomotion I saw, a skid, involved two oxen connected by a yoke from which two ropes extended back to the hands of a man standing on two thin twenty-foot-long logs, as if they were skis. The logs were, in turn, chained to one of the oxen's hind legs. The man simply stood on the logs, one foot on each, leaning back slightly, holding the cords taut as if they were reins, while the oxen pulled him and the logs.

I crept down all the paved roads in the tiny community and parked next to a seaside snack bar. The patio looked out into the clear water through some stately palm trees, some of whose fronds had fallen to the ground. The snack bar served big bowls of delicious warm rice pudding for less than fifty centavos. I took mine over to a bench under a palm and watched seagulls swoop down into the water.

Had the slogan brigade simply forgotten Puerto Esperanza and Viñales? The latter is a favored vacation spot, well known throughout the country. After my drive back I parked on a Viñales side street and walked through most of the quiet town. I could have been in a small town in any Caribbean country; The didactic atmosphere that suffo-cated larger places was absent. I passed the children's chess center, a big room with ten boards available to the youngsters of Viñales. Homes had well-tended flower gardens in front. (Oops—I found a sign, well worn, by itself on a corner: WE LIVE FOR THE REVOLUTION AND WILL DIE DEFENDING IT.) Horses passed by hauling a cart with a couple perched on its front board. The sound of horseshoes hitting the pavement gave Viñales a sturdy soundtrack. Benches on Main Street offered a front-row view of small-town Latin America. I pulled out *The Mambo Kings* and started reading, hoping to be distracted by a soft Viñales afternoon. Two motorcycles with sidecars sputtered by. I had just come to the part where the nice man who works for Pepsodent molests Delores, then living in the Bronx and working part-time at Woolworth's with dreams of teaching school. A rooster crowed—in Viñales, not the Bronx—and a bare-chested man galloped bareback down main street on a handsome gray horse. Two cigar smokers sat under straw hats with curled sidebrims. A two-tone '54 Oldsmobile parked in front of a house whose roof was soon to be covered by tiles stacked neatly at its side. Delores had met Nestor Castillo, one of the Mambo Kings, and the two were busy seducing each other but all Nestor could think of was María, who kept his soul in Cuba.

A thin young woman pedaled her bicycle through Viñales, followed by a thin old man in a hard hat, also on a bike. A barefoot bald man in jogging shorts and a tank top trotted by. Noisy students passed in a school bus, the day's classes over. Two mothers leisurely pushed baby-strollers down the street. A young couple walked by, glanced at me, and whispered to each other; the woman walked over and held out her bag of crackers for me to reach into. She wore a floppy red hat. The man in the jogging shorts passed again, this time on a bicycle.

I ate an early dinner at Las Brisas, a restaurant on Main Street with a bar lacking anything to drink. I was seated on a wobbly chair at a table with a glass vase of plastic flowers. Another single party was seated with me, Rigoberto Suárez Pérez, an accountant with the local agricultural co-op whose members tilled the Viñales Valley. After dinner he would go to his night classes. I ordered *aporreado de pescado*, a sort of fish stew. Not bad; 1.20 pesos. My dining companion was telling me about the cooperative, one of the first formed after the Revolution. Rigoberto was interested in *The Mambo Kings*, and knew people in Oriente, where the musical Castillo brothers started out. The bar at Las Brisas, despite its sorrowful condition, was full of Viñales folk buying packs of cigarettes and waiting for take-out meals. One man had ordered six such meals, and when they came, he mashed them all into one large plastic bowl.

After dinner I saw a note tacked to the municipal library's door announcing the new children's hours. A woman carefully wheelbarrowed her little girl onto a side street. Evening appointments were just beginning at the local medical clinic. Homes had tile roofs, patios, porticoes, and windows covered by shutters whose slats allowed air and a peek. One had a poster with pictures of revolutionary heroes Che Guevara and Camilo Cienfuegos next to an equally big picture of a tortured Jesus Christ. Some jeeps rolled by, followed by a horse pulling a couple of men sitting on a board mounted on two wheels. Two laughing boys played Ping-Pong using their palms as paddles and the sidewalk for a table. In the book, the Mambo Kings were now the fifth-most-popular band in New York, according to one poll. I must have been *buenas tardes*'d a hundred times.

Part Three

La Plume de Matanzas was gone! I strolled into her office expecting to see her puffing on a cigarette, shuffling papers, trying to patch up last week's crisis before this week's erupted. She'd ask me sweetly about my trip, then I'd ask for my mail. But in her throne sat a serious woman, articulate, black, no nonsense. I did a double take.

"Uh, isn't this Miriam's office?"

"Yes, may I help you?"

I introduced myself. The woman stood up and extended a hand. "I'm the director of International Relations now. Pleased to meet you. Victoria Peñalber. Won't you have a seat?"

"What happened to Miriam? I—"

"She now works at the Ministry of Culture. Just a routine job shuffle, nothing more. How may I help you?"

I gave her a quick rundown of my status in the country under the auspices of her department, and what help I hoped she could offer.

"These must be for you." She handed me a couple of letters mailed five weeks earlier from the States. Yet another side effect of the blockade—mail in both directions goes through Mexico or Canada or another third country to travel the ninety miles between the two. A delay of three to six weeks is common.

Victoria said she'd look into my Guantánamo request. Meanwhile, I felt familiar enough with the country that I now wanted to interview Fidel Castro. She asked me to write up a formal request outlining why I wanted to interview him, what I'm doing in Cuba, and a curriculum vitae.

I finally got through to Jesús, who agreed on the following afternoon for my next oboe lesson. When he arrived at my building the front-desk receptionist called to announce that he had another party with him. I gave my approval, and she sent them up to twenty-six. The second person was Pedro, another oboist. He had been a beneficiary of some of the bamboo I had sent down earlier in the year.

I had prepared for the lesson by practicing the first piece from the Soviet oboe book and by buying a bottle of rum at the hard-currency liquor store downstairs. Having two of the country's best oboists stare at my technique, one on either side, was slightly unnerving for a born-again beginner. Their critique was well taken, though—advice on breathing, posture, notes, slurs, staccatos, fingering, embouchure.

Pedro looked at my instrument with admiration and concern. He tootled a few scales and arpeggios and ran up and down the instrument in intricate rhythms, patterns, and variations from the lowest *si bemol* to the highest *do*. My God, that old hunk of metal and wood can do all that—and so effortlessly? He was able to approximate its year and place of birth by the wood and the metalwork. Early 1950s, possibly late 1940s; France. And he pointed out all sorts of minor problems needing repair—metalwork off-center, worn-out key pads, slightly cracked wood, leaky cork. He was a woodwind doctor. Could he work on mine? He'd have it back in my hands by the weekend.

Fine. How much will this cost? "No charge. I fix friends' instruments for nothing. As for the others"—he rubbed his thumb over his first two fingers and smiled—"they have to pay."

Having dispensed with the preliminaries, we got down to business. Jesús opened the bottle of rum while I got three glasses.

I had arranged an appointment with a publicist at the country's sports federation to talk about baseball, I told the oboe section. I wanted to go on a road trip with a team, and our meeting was to discuss that possibility.

"What team do you want to travel with?" Jesús asked.

"I really don't know. I don't know who's good and who stinks. I don't know how the league is organized, or when or even *if* I can go. I'll know more next Monday."

Jesús hunched over and started to explain the system. "Each province has its own team in the Liga Nacional," The National League. "The players are almost all from that province, except for the Havana teams, which are made up of players from all over. That's because it's rare to find a native *habanero*. My favorite is the Cienfuegos team, and I'd be honored if you chose them." We toasted the team from Cienfuegos.

"I brought my mitt with me from home, and—"

"You mean you have it here? In the apartment?" I went to get it, and as I walked back into the living room thumping my left fist into it, Jesús asked, "Rawlings?"

"Why, yes it is. How did you know?" It was signed by Larry Bowa, the shortstop who played for Philadelphia and the Chicago Cubs.

"Rawlings has a reputation for the best gloves." Pedro took it from me and tried it on. "It's a good glove, but it needs some oil. It's a little stiff."

The Orquesta Sinfónica was to play intramural baseball against Los Van Van, the hot nine-piece salsa band, in a month or two. Jesús asked if I'd play on the Orquesta team. "Well, I know the trombonist for Los Van Van. He'll know I'm a—" I couldn't figure the word for ringer. "He'll know I don't belong." Jesús brushed aside my concern. *"Bueno,"* I said. *"Juego el béisbol mejor que toco el oboe."* Fine. I play baseball better than I play the oboe. When we finished the last drop of rum, Jesús ceremoniously milked the bottle as if it were a cow's udder.

"As this issue went to press, the Cuban people and government were commemorating the seventy-third anniversary of the Great October Socialist Revolution and paying homage to its brilliant leader, Vladimir I. Lenin."

The same week that item appeared in a Cuban newspaper, the Soviet people and government were increasingly distancing themselves from the seventy-third anniversary of the Great October Socialist Revolution and questioning the brilliance of its leader, Vladimir I. Lenin. Posters and statues throughout the republics were coming down. Residents of Leningrad were beginning to feel more comfortable with its old name, St. Petersburg.

Domingo Rojo, Red Sunday—the annual celebration of the Russian Revolution of 1917—had arrived throughout Cuba. Work centers and mass organizations such as the Committees to Defend the Revolution and the National Association of Small Farmers had organized volunteer labor brigades to spruce up the cities and pick crops in the countryside. A side street next to my building was jammed with buses and trucks filling up with workers headed for a day in the fields. From my balcony I could see small groups all over Vedado picking up trash, clipping bushes, cutting grass, hacking at underbrush, washing windows.

I turned on the television. Regular shows had been preempted so we could watch construction crews spending Domingo Rojo working on the Pan American Stadium, hoping to get it done in time for the games. An interviewer in overalls asked workers why they were there.

"In tribute to Lenin!" they said with smiles. Viewers also learned that this was Soviet-Cuban Friendship Week in Holguín Province. The station returned to its normal broadcast schedule, finishing up the program *¡Hola, Mamá!*, about how to nurture independence in your two-year-old. *Cocina al minuto* came on next, and Nitza taught us how to make grapefruit marmalade.

I walked over to the newsstand at Presidente and Seventeenth hoping to get there during the critical forty-five minutes after the now-weekly *Juventud Rebelde* arrived and before it sold out. More happy Domingo Rojo activity: neighbors trimming their hedges and apartment dwellers sweeping their foyers. This was like a sunny Kiwanis Club beautification day masquerading as international solidarity. Havana was my city, too, for the nonce, and I felt guilty for not taking part.

I walked a few blocks farther to Nitza's place. Earlier in the morning Nitza had stood in line for chicken at Pío Pío, an outlet for—now Cubans, don't laugh at this—fast food. It took her from 9 to 11:30.

"I'm hoping to do a show about making empanadas with cornmeal and yucca, but this week there's no yucca at the produce markets."

I was going to offer to bring over the food and wine column from the London *Times* Sunday magazine, but thought better of it. The column was about restaurants in Rome. The writer's favorite meal, "mixed grill of sweetbreads, testicles, spinal cords, liver, duodenum— each item lightly and differently spiced," cost about seventy dollars a person. I described the article in general terms, and Nitza reassured me that she'd still like to see it. "It's true we can't eat like that here, but it gives me a better idea of what's going on elsewhere in the world. The only foreign publication I get regularly is from the Nutrition Institute of Jamaica."

Nitza had to carry her garbage out to the dumpster on Seventeenth Street—first out to the hall, then onto the elevator to the basement, next across the floor and up a driveway to street level, and finally into the trash bins. That's what I did on Domingo Rojo to commemorate the seventy-third anniversary of the Great October Socialist Revolution paying homage to its brilliant leader, Vladimir I. Lenin—I carried Nitza Villapol's garbage out to the street.

Two friends, Rolando and Rocío, had chosen Domingo Rojo to get married. Actually, I don't think Vladimir Lenin had much to do with their wedding. The tangled web of former marriages, children and parents in exile, as well as ensnared U.S. and Cuban immigration and emigration policies, compelled the betrothal. The only way to please everyone was for the two to wed and move to the States. Rolando looked upon the change of country with apprehension.

The late-afternoon wedding took place at the former home of a family that had left for the United States in the 1980 Mariel boatlift. The house, near the Sports City complex, had been appropriated by the state, turned into a Palacio de Matrimonio, and decorated so ostentatiously as to be high tack. The walls that weren't mirrored had motel room flower art, a sound system scratchily played old standards, and upstairs, a red-flecked velour bedspread covered an enormous double bed. Often the downstairs was rented for a reception to follow a ceremony.

Roland and Rocío presented their papers, and then we all went into a big room for the formal ceremony. A state official read the prescribed vows, after which the couple and their maid of honor and best man signed a large book. About twenty of us watched from the side, and when they were officially wed everyone clapped, patted backs, and kissed. Rolando coached a cycling team, and many of his cyclists showed up for the reception at his apartment, where we all ate sweets, croquettes, and empanadas cooked by Chilean friends. After Rocío cut the wedding cake we toasted the couple with champagne. The drink turned the guests' chatter to doo-wah-diddy, but it made my Spanish more fluent, so we came out even.

The next morning I made my regular stop at the Socialism or Death bakery after my walk along the Malecón. The city looked noticeably cleaner, thanks to Vladimir Lenin, with trees, storefronts, sidewalks, and hedges postcard pretty. I felt proud to be a *habanero*, and decided to drop in on Alejandro the Optimist at the hands-across-the-sea office. He had participated in Domingo Rojo, of course, and was feeling good, even confident about his country and his countrymen. "We're going to pull through!" he said, like an assistant coach at halftime. "Can't you just feel it? The determination is there!"

At that moment with true-believer juice pulsing through his veins, Alejandro's confidence was contagious and I wanted badly to believe him. But I saw that bananas were now rationed; it had been my pleasure on occasion to line up for a bunch at the S or D produce market, and now I couldn't. More to the point, Cubans could only buy a fixed amount, no more. Bananas rationed in the tropics? Is coal rationed in Newcastle?

A gas station on my street, one set aside for government cars, had to practically parcel out its reserves with an eyedropper. The line of cars waiting for gas along the curb extended for blocks. Some weekday nights government drivers would park in line around midnight or one o'clock to ensure their quota the next morning. Cuba's former European allies, their economies in ruin and their food distribution systems in chaos, received tanker-sized CARE packages from the West, a reward for abandoning Communism, but no one came to Cuba's rescue except Cubans. Domingo Rojo turned into Blue Monday.

I visited with Fernando Campoamor, the Hemingway buddy and rum expert I had met with Daubar at the bar of the Habana Libre. Campoamor was an impressive man, courtly, well spoken, and considerate. Many men of his age and class had either fled the country years earlier or had withdrawn from active life, but Fernando stayed, vital and curious. He is an old-fashioned *caballero* in a country where that species has become endangered. He is as gentle as his last name.

Campoamor lives in a comfortable two-bedroom apartment in Vedado. Books by Freud, Ortega y Gasset, Bolívar, Napoleon, and Alexander von Humboldt line the walls. Prominent on the shelf is a well-used six-volume encyclopedia of the sea. His wife is in terrible shape after more than thirty years of a progressively debilitating Parkinson's disease. She sat to the side, but Fernando included her in the conversation.

"I have a few things out to show you," my host said, indicating four large boxes marked "Hemingway." "The Biblioteca Nacional will mount an exhibit about him next year on the thirtieth anniversary of his death, and I am making these mementos available to them." He went to the kitchen to mix us each a shot of rum with a slice of grapefruit skin along the rim of the glass. "When Ernesto lived in Cuba, we used to have an informal society of bartenders," he said with a light laugh. "When I first met him after returning from Louisiana he was living off the advance from *For Whom the Bell Tolls*." As he talked I impolitely divided my attention between his words and the bookcase of great Spanish and Cuban literature. I pulled down an inscribed book of portraits by the Cuban artist Massaguer. The sketches were of the famous from the Hemingway era, among them the Windsors, Gandhi, Churchill, Chaplin, and Shaw. It included one of Eisenhower with a little black girl on his knee licking a lollipop and reading *Uncle Tom's Cabin*. "Do you like Massaguer's work? He was a wonderful artist, wasn't he."

At one end of the bookshelf was a trophy Campoamor had received for first prize in a 1934 Día de las Américas poster contest in Lake Charles, Louisiana. His winning entry showed Benito Juárez, José

Martí, Abraham Lincoln, and Simón Bolívar. A 1961 poster above the shelf advertised the Spencer Tracy movie of *The Old Man and the Sea*. A Quote from Fidel ran beneath the ad: *All the works of Hemingway are a defense of human rights.* "He said that during a trip to Uruguay."

Fernando pulled out a stack of photographs. The first one showed a smiling Hemingway and his wife Mary Welsh, the last of his four wives. He had a photo of the animal skin Hemingway stood on when he wrote, and another of his black Royal portable. "Two years after he died someone offered eighty thousand dollars for that typewriter. Eighty thousand dollars!" Campoamor had other shots of the household, of the bedroom, and one of a three-shelf bookcase in the bathroom. He had paper from a notepad that said "From the desk of Ernest Hemingway," and, in Hemingway's handwriting, "Finca la Vigía, San Francisco de Paula," the name and town of his estate. A close-up of him holding the Nobel medallion in 1954, when the sparkle was still in his eyes and his writing. Other photos show Mary and Ernest, in a smoking jacket, at El Restaurante Floridita, with the Duke and Duchess of Windsor. Another of him at a 1956 gala thrown by the University of Havana Student Association.

Campoamor had known Martha Gellhorn (Hemingway's wife from 1940–1945), who found Finca la Vigía in a classified ad. I described her entertaining and moving essay about her return trip to Cuba in the 1980s, and he asked me to send him a copy. "I need it for my archives."

Cuba clutches Hemingway to its coastline in genuine affection for a complex man. The universal verities at play in *The Old Man and the Sea* appeal mightily to the people off whose coast the novel is set. It is a book that reads as smoothly in Spanish translation as it does in its original English—in fact, when I reread it in English, parts seemed as if translated from the Spanish. One evening during an earlier trip to Cuba I attended a meeting of a neighborhood Committee for the Defense of the Revolution in Guanabacoa, a municipality next to Havana. With me were a dozen others from the States, including a white-haired man who bore a casual resemblance to Hemingway. On arrival we were met by the local Young Pioneers, in uniform, who greeted us with song, salutes, and applause. We were introduced to the local cop, the community doctor, and others who lived nearby. A CDR member looked at the man with white hair and said, "We like Hemingway because he was so supportive of the Cuban people. We think of him as a Cuban." As for Cuba's appeal to Hemingway, his friend John Rybovich, Jr., told an interviewer, "Ernest said he liked

Cuba because they had both fishing and fucking there. I believe they had him try out all the houses of prostitution. . . ."

Tourists today follow the Hemingway Trail by dining and drinking at El Floridita and La Bodeguita del Medio. "Right now they are rebuilding El Floridita." Campoamor. "It's like rebuilding Chartres. You simply can't do it. I wrote an article for *Opina* a few months ago about how scandalous it is that they're trying to duplicate the original. It's a falsehood. A pastiche."

A sign hangs above the bar at La Bodeguita del Medio. In large, handwritten letters, it reads,

> MY MOJITO IN LA BODEGUITA
> MY DAIQUIRI IN EL FLORIDITA
> XII/54

It is signed with the unmistakable signature, "Ernest Hemingway." This sign has worked its way into travel articles about Havana for years. It is prominent in guidebooks. It has become part of the accepted lore. Tourists get visceral contact with Hemingway. *He* drank mojitos here, *I'm* drinking mojitos here, ergo . . .

"You know about that, don't you?" Campoamor wore a sly grin. "You must understand the history of La Bodeguita. At first it was simply a *bodeguita*," a small neighborhood grocery store. "They sold rice and sugar and such. Mr. and Mrs. Martínez were the owners, and they had a little bar, too. They started seeing a few customers. Artists started coming. It was almost like a club for writers and painters and actors.

"After the Revolution they wanted to develop their business a bit and have tourists and a real dining room and serve pork and beef. We had a meeting in Miramar at the home of Leonardo Gómez, who was at that time the director of *Bohemia* magazine. Martínez was there, too. He was a *guajiro*, but he was intelligent and wanted to offer his customers more. We were trying to figure out how to help his business, and someone said, '*Mi mojito en La Bodeguita, mi daiquiri en El Floridita.*' It was a funny joke, nothing more.

"Gómez said, 'Let's write it out.' Like a true businessman, Martínez went for it, too. Well, I had all these things at home in Papa's handwriting, so they hired a graphic artist to imitate it. I protested this even though I enjoyed the humor at the beginning. This was merely a private joke among friends. But the little joke grew into a big lie.

"I wasn't confident about doing this, so I asked the director of INTUR," the government tourism institute, "if it was all right with him. He said, 'You know, it could help tourism. Just don't write about it in public.' I never have, but the legend that we created at that meeting snowballed out of control."

Campoamor talked more about Hemingway—Papa to some, Ernesto to others, and simply Mr. Way to still others. "I met Margaux Hemingway when she came in 1978." That trip, a fashion shoot for *Playboy* magazine, included stops along the Hemingway Trail and sites that she remembered visiting with "grandpapa" as a little girl.

Two restaurants, one in California and the other in Italy, have together sponsored an annual writing competition in honor of Ernesto, I said. This so impressed Campoamor that I didn't have the heart to add that it was called the "Bad Hemingway Contest," and it made fun of Papa's style.

"A lot of Cuban writers knew him and had drinks with him regularly at El Floridita," Campoamor said. One Sunday, I was told by another Cuban, Hemingway was having his customary drinks there with writer Luis Gómez Wangüemert. "He was pretty drunk. Enrique Serpa," another well-regarded writer, "walked in, and Hemingway said to him, 'It's a good thing you live in a third-rate country or else people could read your writing.' Hemingway liked Cubans in the abstract but not individually."

Poet Nicolás Guillén, who first met Ernesto in the 1930s in Madrid during the Spanish Civil War, told an interviewer, "Hemingway spoke Spanish badly, with a heavy accent. I told him: 'You should talk to more P&P.' 'Who's P&P?' he asked. 'Prostitutes and peasants.' . . . He really didn't know Cubans. I know this from experience."

Campoamor remembers Hemingway's Spanish somewhat differently. "He learned Spanish in Spain. He spoke it daily. He knew all the bad words. He used them all the time. He wasn't quite fluent, but it was no problem either."

"How did Hemingway view the Revolution?" I asked. Campoamor saw him frequently in the 1940s and 1950s, and his recollection would be more valid than two explanations that have Hemingway as a victim rather than a supporter of the Revolution. In one, Hunter S. Thompson wrote in the *National Observer* in 1964 that "Castro's educators taught the people that 'Mr. Way' had been exploiting them." This seems curious given that Hemingway is read in Cuban schools and that his books are among the country's all-time best-sellers. The other description, by Jacobo Timerman in his 1990 book about Cuba, said,

"The Hemingway cult is aimed more at tourism than anything else
. . . [it] is geared toward perpetuating the myth, toward creating a
sense that Hemingway belonged, toward convincing the people that
Hemingway is the North American of the Revolution."

Campoamor said, "In a public sense he was independent, but he
was always with the Revolution. It was obvious. Remember, he had
many friends in the Spanish Communist Party from the Civil War.
He hated dictators."

This attitude was evident when the government gave him an award.
"Although he said privately that he disliked living under the new
Batista dictatorship," Hemingway's biographer wrote, "he accepted a
Medal of Honor from the Cuban government 'in the name of the
professional marlin fishermen from Puerto Escondido to Bahía
Honda.' " Similarly, after he received Nobel status in 1954 he decided
to give the medallion to the people of Cuba. He turned it over to
Campoamor, in a public ceremony, entrusting him to display it at the
Sanctuary at El Cobre, a famous shrine in the countryside near Santiago
de Cuba.

Hemingway reportedly greeted a 1957 report in the international
press that Fidel had been killed by saying, "That is a lie! They say it
in order to discredit the Movement. Fidel cannot die! Fidel has to
make the Revolution." Shortly after that, when *New York Times* reporter
Herbert Matthews returned to Havana from the Sierra, where he had
clandestinely interviewed Castro, he was Hemingway's guest at Finca
la Vigía and told his host that Fidel was alive in the mountains.

Hemingway listened to the guerrillas' radio station, Radio Rebelde,
on occasion. His good friend and doctor, Herrera Sotolongo, said, "Hemingway was always on the side of the Cuban Revolution." *Hemingway
in Cuba*, by Norberto Fuentes, mentions that Papa bought a statue of
José Martí at a fund-raiser for "the *fidelista* organization." His fishing
buddy and the captain of his boat, the *Pilar*, Gregorio Fuentes, told
Norberto Fuentes, "From the beginning of the insurrection Hemingway
approved of the use of the *Pilar* to hide arms for the revolutionary
movement. He saw what I was doing, but never interfered."

When Batista fled Cuba, journalists called Hemingway, then in
Idaho, who released this statement: "I believe in the historical necessity
for the Cuban revolution and I believe in its long range goals. I do
not wish to discuss personalities or day to day problems." He told one
newspaper that got through to him that he was "delighted with the
news" of the Castro victory. "I felt instant disapproval of the word,"

his widow Mary Welsh later wrote. She convinced him to call the paper back. He changed "delighted" to "hopeful." The next day the couple heard from reporter Herbert Matthews that Finca la Vigía was safe.

Herbert Matthews last saw Hemingway in Cuba in March 1960, and observed that Papa was "still the great hero of the Cuban people. He is staying at his home working as a deliberate gesture to show his sympathy and support for the Castro Revolution." And why did Castro never seek out Hemingway? biographer Tad Szulc asked Fidel in an interview. "Castro said lamely that he never got to know Hemingway 'because those early days of the Revolution were very busy ones, and no one thought that he would die so quickly.'"

Ernesto felt in 1960 that the "Castro climate" had changed. "Not good at all," he told his friend, A. E. Hotchner. "I just hope to hell the United States doesn't cut the sugar quota. That would really tear it. It will make Cuba a gift to the Russians."

Castro said that Hemingway was "a writer whose presence here is of great satisfaction to us." Fidel competed in the 1960 International Marlin Tournament named in honor of Hemingway, and won the individual competition. As the two larger-than-life men met for the only time, the sixty-year-old writer-sportsman presented the trophy to the thirty-three-year-old revolutionary-fisherman. On the way home, Hemingway told his wife about their brief conversation. "He said he'd read *The Bell* in Spanish and used its ideas in the Sierra Maestra."

The novel *Papa and Fidel*, by Karl Alexander, considers a secret friendship between the two. The fictional Fidel takes time away from the revolution to go quail hunting with Papa, and Hemingway thinks of doing a piece for *Field and Stream*, commenting that "Castro's a pretty damned good shot for a commie." During Castro's famous trip to the United Nations in New York, the novel continues, he and Hemingway duck out to a Red Sox game at Yankee Stadium. He stands when Ted Williams socks a 3-0 pitch into the upper deck. "If they made Señor Ted Williams ambassador to Cuba, our countries would get along fine."

Hemingway in Cuba, the only Cuban book to dwell on Hemingway's residency there, pictures him far more supportive of the Revolution than any other account. Fernando Campoamor, among others, is featured in it. "Is the book accurate?" I asked. Campoamor made a face. "Let's save that for another day."

* * *

When I asked people whom to ask for clear reminiscences of Hemingway, Lisandro Otero's name often came up. When I asked the
same about Graham Greene, likewise. Here was a man who had befriended two of the most prominent English-language writers of the
twentieth century. Lisandro and his wife, Nara Araújo, a professor at
the University of Havana, live with their daughter in a very comfortable
home on a quiet tree-lined side street in Miramar.

The first part of Hemingway that Lisandro Otero met was his fist.
Otero had approached Hemingway because he revered him, and the
author responded with a jab. It missed his face, barely, but the message,
delivered at El Floridita, hit the mark: bug off, kid, you bother me.
Otero retreated to his table for a meal, only to learn on its completion
that his idol had paid the bill. On the way out Hemingway called
Otero over and invited him to stop by his home some afternoon. He
did, beginning a friendship that lasted until Hemingway's death.

Otero grew in importance in literary and government circles. In
the early 1960s he helped get the Committees for the Defense of the
Revolution and other mass organizations off the ground. He continued
writing, both journalism and fiction, and following the tradition of
literary luminaries taking diplomatic posts, Otero served in the Cuban
foreign service in the Soviet Union, Great Britain, and France. Back
home he rose to the highest levels of the writers union. He was voted
out of office by a membership that felt him elite, aloof, and too well
traveled. Rejected by UNEAC, he now rejects the union. "I hate
gatherings with intellectuals. I never go there anymore."

Whenever I'd mention to someone that I was interested in how the
nation's literary life intermingled with its history, they'd respond,
"Have you talked to the 'official writers' yet? You know, Otero, Barnet,
Fernández; them." The OWs could travel outside the country, they
were published abroad, they represented Cuba at overseas conferences,
they mixed in that glorious and tradition-laden world of Latin American literature. Through the years the OWs had learned how to jump
through hoops, even ones in motion, even ones on fire. They had
polished the sideways smile. They had paid their dues. Otero had the
qualities of the privileged.

That may be one reason he appealed to me. Also, he and he alone
sympathized with my search for a palindrome in Spanish. Sitting in
the back patio of his two-story Miramar home one evening we wasted
valuable time and paper in the noble quest for a palindrome with

HAVANA or, slightly more difficult, the city's name in Spanish, LA HABANA. I came up with a NAVAHO HAVANA. Otero wrote:

L'ABANA

ANABAL

GUANABANA EN LA HABANA

L'ABANABAL

LAB A NABAL

LA BANA BAL

"I've got one for you," he finally said. He carefully wrote it out, then passed it to me with the smug satisfaction of someone who had finished the Madrid Sunday *El País* crossword puzzle in fifteen minutes flat. In ink. DABALE ARROZ A LA ZORRA EL ABAD It is one of the few well-known palindromes in Spanish, a language whose word construction does not lend itself to mirrored phrases. It means *The abbot gives rice to the female fox*.

Just to make sure, I later looked up *zorra*, fox, in Larousse and found it also to be a vixen, or a sly person, or—seldom used—a prostitute. This last definition gives the palindrome more life and makes one wonder why the abbot gave the hooker some rice. Was it from guilt? Charity? For services rendered or imagined? Hidden in this seven-word palindrome is a dark tale, one fraught with soft shadows and ascetic desire that Graham Greene could have polished into a sterling short story.

Otero was better than the reference desk at the New York Public Library. His second-floor study has a personal computer and more books in more languages than any other Cuban home I had entered. Wall photos show him with Sartre, Greene, Igor Stravinsky, García Márquez, Carpentier, and Borges. He lacks a picture of himself with José Martí only because they missed each other by thirty-seven years. If I need help on prerevolutionary Cuba, call Enrique de la Osa. For matters ecological, contact Guillermo García, the Central Committee member in charge of environmental activity. García also knows about cockfighting, a sport once as common as a rooster; now that public wagering is *vedado*, however, the sport has lost most of its followers. For general resource information, see Zoila LaPique at the Biblioteca Nacional. For the lottery, ask him—Otero had published a novel, *El juego en Cuba*, "The Lottery in Cuba," which incorporates generations of lottery lore into its plot.

The word *"compañero,"* common throughout the country, intrigued me. Was it difficult for mainstream Cuba to accept it after the Revolution? "At first a lot of people tried *camarada*, but people resisted that a little. *Compañero* had been used among the Communists, but not many others. *Señor* and *señora* were seen as words from a bourgeois way of life, a bourgeois vocabulary. *Compañero* was adopted during the Renovation. It comes from *pan*—com*pañ*ero, a man who shares bread." People joked about the new word in the national vocabulary. A man got too close to a fancy lady in an elevator, and she said, "Do me a favor, eh? Please don't press against me." He replied, *"Compañera*, it's simply that the elevator is so crowded." *"Compañera*, my eye! My buttocks are *compañeras* and they don't press against each other!"

I told Otero I hoped to travel with a baseball team, expecting the rapid-fire devotion to the game I had run into everywhere else. "People get stupid about baseball here. I hate it."

¡Qué blasfemia! I proposed he write an essay about his distaste for the game, then reconsidered my suggestion. "Perhaps not. That would be treasonous, wouldn't it."

"No, not treasonous. Suicidal. In the early 1980s I was in the diplomatic corps in the Soviet Union. The situation was dreadful— long lines, shabby housing, no bread, little food. 'Yes,' they'd acknowledge. 'But we have the Bolshoi Ballet, the best in the world!' Well, now—'Yes, but we have the best amateur baseball team in the world!' "

A quiet rumor had spread among the city's diplomatic corps earlier in the year that Otero was considering a permanent move to another country, a euphemism for defecting. But Otero returned from every overseas trip on schedule and settled back into his home life. The scuttlebutt was scuttled, yet it showed the nature of gossip among foreign envoys. It also cast Otero in a light far different from his earlier profile when he was seen as a hard-liner who enforced the rigid half of Fidel's clever dictum on artistic freedom: "Within the Revolution, everything; outside the Revolution, nothing." Otero played a vital role on the government's side of the 1968–1971 Padilla case, in which the poet Heberto Padilla was chastised and condemned for insufficient revolutionary fervor in his writing. In historical accounts of the case Otero's role earns him the description "a Party hack," and "a powerful apparatchik." I only dimly knew about the Padilla case at the time I spoke with him, and did not connect him with it. I knew that he was well acquainted with Ernest Hemingway, Graham Greene, and palindromes, and that was enough for me.

* * *

Otero picked me up in his Lada at the Focsa building for a trip to Finca la Vigía, now the Hemingway Museum. Shortly after Hemingway's suicide in Idaho in July 1961, his widow returned to Cuba to sort out their affairs. Her late husband had willed the *Pilar* to Gregorio Fuentes and the fifteen-acre estate to the Cuban people, but there were some items around the house she wanted, and some manuscripts lodged in various Havana banks. Fidel came to visit. Mary Welsh wrote that Castro "headed for Ernest's chair and was seating himself when I murmured that it was my husband's favorite. The Prime Minister raised himself up, slightly abashed.

" 'No, no, señor, please be seated.' "

She served coffee, later to realize her own social gaffe—she should have poured whiskey. Castro "climbed to the top of the tower to look out over the hills toward Havana and the valleys with their groves of slim white-trunked royal palms. 'I imagine Señor Hemingway enjoyed this view,' he said.

" 'It's the truth. Every day.' "

That chair, the tower, and everything else have been preserved as if Mary and Ernest had gone on a long vacation and some friends had straightened the place up in anticipation of their return. Martha Gellhorn had spotted the place shortly after she and Ernest returned from the Spanish Civil War. She hoped that its size and setting would provide some refuge from downtown Havana. They bought the finca from its French owner in 1940 for $18,500.

The long driveway starts on a nondescript corner of San Francisco de Paula. We passed through a tunnel of tall, thick trees and emerged near the house itself. The house, built in the 1880s, is surrounded by well-tended tropical flowers and lush palms overhanging the roof. Most tourists had come by chartered bus; few private cars could be seen. Visitors cannot go inside the house itself and must content themselves with views through the numerous and large open windows. With tourists slowly walking around the house, sticking their heads in windows and shuffling on, it looked like a slew of friendly burglars casing the joint. The layout of the house and the surrounding patios and walkways allows a fairly full view of the interior, however, and the arrangement seems a reasonable compromise between preservation and access.

Privilege had its reward: the museum director assigned us a personal guide for a tour inside the home. What impressed me most that afternoon, aside from the lack of 5 MORE KILOMETERS TO HEM-

INGWAY'S HOUSE signs and BUY YOUR HEMINGWAY TRINKETS HERE shops and life-size cardboard cutouts of Papa with his arm around a headless body so tourists could step up for a photo, were his books and his mounted animal heads. Hemingway must have single-handedly kept Havana's booksellers and taxidermists in business.

Ernest and Mary each had a bedroom. Hers, a big airy salon, had a large double bed, and a painting by Dorothy (Mrs. Ezra to you) Pound on the wall, along with a deer head. A small pillow said "Skyline Drive" on it. I started to scribble down the names of books on the extensive shelves, but Otero suggested, "Wait till we get to the library." Admonished, I stopped, but I managed to note *How to Travel Incognito, A Date with a Dish*, and books by Carl Sandburg and Graham Greene, Homer and Walter Lippman. The January-February 1961 *Partisan Review* lay on the bedside table, as well as *Ellery Queen's Mystery Magazine* and *Better Homes and Gardens*. On the way out of Mary's bedroom we passed two miniature cannons that were fired on the arrival of honored guests.

Next to the 1950s living room phonograph was an LP collection that stretched from Louis Armstrong to Tchaikovsky. A pre-Columbian Peruvian ceramic rested on a table near the favored chair Fidel had accidentally occupied. A sizable collection of art books and magazines such as *Sports Illustrated* and *Bohemia* took up part of the room. A rug from the Philippines covered most of the floor. One time, sitting in his favorite chair, Hemingway put the butt of a Mannlicher .256 on the floor and leaned over so that the roof of his mouth practically swallowed the other end. "Look, this is how I'm going to do it," he said according to his friend Hererra Sotolongo. "Then, leaning forward, he would rest the mouth of the gun barrel against the roof of his mouth. He would press the trigger with his big toe and we would hear the click of the gun. He would then raise his head and smile."

John O'Hara, James Joyce, Goethe, J. D. Salinger, e. e. cummings, Barnaby Conrad, Dostoevsky, S. J. Perelman, the complete works of Balzac, Jean Cocteau, Mark Twain. I was in the library, another room with a high ceiling and tiled floor. It had an orderly, well-used feel. One shelf held Hemingway's own works in a dozen languages. A ceramic plate in the shape of a bull's head sculpted by Picasso sat in the library, as well as a leopard skin hanging from an upright stick, looking like it was about to pounce. At the far end of the library was a large wooden desk. "He would come in here in the afternoons to answer correspondence," our guide said. Looking out the windows behind the desk we could make out Havana's Plaza de la Revolución in the far distance.

Hemingway's room had his faithful Royal typewriter propped up on a 1954–1955 *Who's Who in America*, itself resting on top of a bookcase. Next to the typewriter lay a clipboard. "Hemingway would post his word count on the board whenever he was through for the day," the guide said. A stack of carbon paper was piled to the side. At the other end of the room were seven pairs of Hemingway shoes (size 10½). The bathroom was sizable, with a big scale and personal weight chart, a bidet, and a small bookshelf with *Houdini, The Art of Cockfighting*, and *Beloved Infidel*. Preserved in a small jar was a bat.

There were more rooms, more books, more mementos, paintings of mountains, bulls, and the sea from all over the world ; guns, photographs, tasteful gifts, plaques, everything to make a Nobel prize-winner and his guests comfortable. Russian dolls given him by Soviet diplomat Anastas Mikoyan stood on one table. The heads of very large animals Hemingway had killed in Africa were mounted on walls. You could not enter a room without a pair of spooky eyes following you around. "Don't know how a writer could write surrounded by so many dead animal heads," Graham Greene said when he toured the house.

The guide took us up the stairs to the top of a four-story tower Mary built for Ernest in 1947 as a retreat behind the house. His fishing and hunting gear remain. One floor, formerly reserved for the numerous cats on the grounds, is filled with press clippings, photographs, and publicity, including shots of the filming of *The Old Man and the Sea*. Nearby is the Hemingways' pool, where he swam a half mile daily and she twice as much. It is best known as the pool where Ava Gardner once swam naked.

I was pretty much Hemingway'd out by this time. He had a terrific house, he led a fascinating life, he had a way with words and had many fine possessions, and I was getting hungry.

Otero and I went to La Terraza, the seaside bar-restaurant in Cojímar, the village where Hemingway kept the *Pilar*. For such an inconsequential place it has gained international notoriety for having been in *The Old Man and the Sea* and *Islands in the Stream*. It's right on the water, with a roomful of tables looking out to the sea and a front area reserved for hard-currency diners. "You used to be able to dock your boat right at La Terraza and walk in from the Caribbean," Otero said. "It had a wooden roof and white walls." In the years following Hemingway's death La Terraza disintegrated into just another roadhouse "where great quantities of beer were sloshed down in paper cups," according to *Hemingway in Cuba*. Castro learned of its condition when he passed through the neighborhood in 1970, and commanded that La Terraza be restored "at least" to its Hemingway-era condition, "with the same menu."

Otero insisted on treating but, as in virtually all decent restaurants in Cuba, a foreigner at La Terraza must pay in dollars. As he got out of the car my host told me to wait while he got us a table. "And when we go in, only speak Spanish around the captain and the waiters—or better yet, just stay quiet." After he got a table Otero called over to me as if simply to another Cuban. He stuck up his hand and whistled. "*¡Oye*, Panchito! *¡Ven acá!*" Hey, Panchito! Com'ere!

As Panchito, I lowered my voice whenever the waiter approached. Fortunately we had a table near a corner far from the kitchen. We talked about Hemingway, literature, Europe. We didn't discuss baseball. Otero had read the edition of *The Mambo Kings* published in Spain. "Is it true the author grew up in the States?"

"Yes, but surrounded by Cuban relatives I understand."

"His descriptions of the culture in Havana and Santiago during that era are so precise. As if he had been there. Fantastic."

The waiter brought us a bottle of dry Albanian wine. Otero poured us each a glass. "When I go to Santiago I want to see if there really were two Castillo brothers who played music in the Oriente." Otero was a man of fiction and journalism; he understood my slightly daffy predilection for playing literary detective.

"It's such a warm book. *Muy cubano*. Could it be reprinted here? It'd be real popular."

"No." He shook his head. "No."

"Why not? There are only a few references to Castro. Of course they're negative but they're just in passing and hardly gratuitous."

"That's not it." Pause. "The book is about the exile community." *Punto*, period.

True, almost all Cubans permanently abroad were treated in print as traitorous, money-grubbing, scum-sucking, drug-pushing, villainous worms. While I generally admire literary absolutes, this blockade denied readers within Cuba some friendly writing. The argument against it was simply, why reward Cubans who have abandoned their homeland by publishing their works when there are many writers still here waiting to see print? The arguments on both sides were becoming increasingly abstract as publishers' lists kept dwindling because of the paper shortage. Otero paid in pesos.

A short distance away, in a small park called Plaza Hemingway, a bust of Papa sits surrounded by columns. It was dedicated one year after the author's death, *initiated by Fernando G. Campoamor*, according to a sign, *with the support of the Fishermen's Cooperative of Cojímar*. In the distance Hemingway can see the little beachfront fishing village from which the old man left for the sea. The fishermen contributed the bronze for the bust by melting down the propellers from their boats.

I spent the next morning writing out my request to interview Castro. Looking back, I might just as well have sat on the Malecón wall spitting in the ocean. It was a gesture made not because my petition might wend its way to his desk, but rather so I would have an answer to the question most commonly asked every time I returned from Cuba: did you interview Fidel? Now I could say no, but I tried.

I wrote that I wanted to chat with him about the places and personalities I had encountered during my stay, about baseball, about Cubans in exile, Caribbean music, Afro-Cuban culture, the Guantánamo navy base, literature from and about Cuba, and the aspirations of Cuban youth. I concluded by writing that in my travels through his country I had inquired of Cubans what they would want me to ask him, and that I hoped to·raise these questions as well. I didn't put it in my request, but I also was burning to know why Cuba, of all countries, had adopted the designated hitter, a decision I considered a metaphor for compromise and national disintegration.

Victoria, La Plume's replacement, turned my *solicitud* over to a bureaucrat in the Central Committee, who was supposed to pass it on to a functionary in the Council of Ministers, who was to shuffle it over to someone on Fidel's staff. Perhaps the Ministry of Foreign Relations was in the daisy chain, or maybe I have the order wrong, or possibly it blew out a car window and across the Malecón and ended up in the harbor. Regardless, I would have had better luck had I prayed at the Sanctuary at El Cobre. One thousand applications from foreign writers to interview Fidel are pending, I was told. Mine had the chance of a snowball in Cienfuegos. Is it any wonder I never heard boo?

The Malecón has sunny end points, but the origin of the word is clouded. Everyone has a theory, but not even the authority on Spanish word sources, *The Critical Etymological Dictionary of Castilian*, knows for sure. In a lengthy essay, the Madrid dictionary traces the roots of Malecón back to the thirteenth century. It speculates that Malecón came from pre-Roman Sardinia or Corsica. Malecón shows up in an

1831 maritime dictionary, but could it be Celtic or Basque? One thing is certain: "Inquiries into Cuban documents have yielded no results, despite Havana's famous Malecón."

I had become a regular on this thoroughfare with linguistic ancestors in the thirteenth century. The same fishermen with spools of line draped over the seawall greeted me at the same morning hour. If I Malecón'd later in the day—by this time it had become a verb with me—I'd often run into the same *jineteros*. My ear had sharpened, my vocabulary had expanded, my tongue had quickened, and my sneakers were still obviously foreign but at least they didn't look like they had just walked out of a mall.

The seawall promenade, wrote an essayist in *Bohemia* in the 1920s, "is full of grace and suggestion, rich with inspiration for the painter, for the poet, and for the philosopher." He describes a poor, late-afternoon pair "lovey-dovey smooching." It's a scene still prevalent, fading deep into night with couples grinding farewells before sadly returning to separate quarters.

The Malecón is a free-trade zone when it comes to international exchange. Jokes zing in all directions, with unexpected targets from unlikely sources. Humberto, who lived in Centro Habana, laughed when I told him about my sneakers. "*Por mis zapatos me conoce el pueblo habanero*," I told him in friendly exasperation. Havana knows me by my shoes.

"Did you hear the one about Gorbachev?" he responded with a glint in his eye. "He sent for Fidel to talk about reforms. *El comandante* went, but he was pissed. To show his anger he scolded Gorbachev at the airport, 'Even from here I can see that the shoes on many Russians are falling apart at the seams.'

"Gorbachev was astonished at such slander and pulled out a pistol. 'Here, take this gun,' he said to Fidel, 'and any person that you see with torn shoes, I give you full authority to kill.' Well, Fidel went looking all over Moscow, and after a few hours he was tired of walking. On his way back to the Kremlin he saw a man with torn tennies lying on a park bench under a blanket of newspapers. Castro shot him on the spot. The next day the headline in *Pravda* read, 'Maniacal Cuban Strongman Shoots Own Consul to the Soviet Union.' "

When I walked near the Habana Libre the money changers still attacked, most recently at nine pesos to the dollar. They had become more aggressive—not threatening, but more insistent, a palpable sign of a worsening economy. Victoria's efficiency at the writers union had produced a *carnet*—a state ID card—a document that made me slightly more integrated into mainstream society. Instead of producing my U.S. passport on demand, I could now show essentially the same little booklet everyone else had, with a terrible photo and the classification, *técnico extranjero (temporal)*, foreign technician (temporary). The *carnet* also became handy proof to *jineteros* that I wasn't just another foreigner, but someone who lived among them. It meant I had the right to spend pesos at dollar establishments. I had finally achieved second-class status.

I had made an afternoon appointment about baseball with Luis Salmerón Heres in the promotion department for INDER—the country's sports institute. I had been warned by others, foreigners and Cubans, that whatever you need from an agency, usually only one or two people can authorize it. The trick is to find the right person before weeks-long frustration swallowed you up. I kept thinking back to the movie *Death of a Bureaucrat*, the trenchant black comedy about Cuba's insufferable bureaucracy, which I now classified as a horror film. Rather than let a paper shuffler with no interest or clout string me along I was assured that Salmerón was my man.

Oh happy day, he was. He worked in Sports City, a mammoth complex encompassing playing fields, swimming pools, gymnasiums, offices, and a manufacturing plant for athletic equipment. I used my *carnet* at the security gate and went back to one of a series of two-story mustard yellow buildings that seemed precise duplicates of the temporary government offices built along the Mall in Washington during World War II. I waited the requisite thirty minutes for my appointment in a large room with poster-sized photographs of Fidel shooting baskets (wearing sneakers, no hat, a pullover), another of him playing Ping-Pong (a beret), and yet another of him kicking a soccer ball (bareheaded, T-shirt).

Salmerón's desk had a sportswriter's disarray; final results in one stack, press releases in another, a pile of league statistics spilling over a mound of team schedules. If I had asked for names of the top-ten base stealers in the Liga Nacional from two seasons past, he could have reached into the middle of the muddle and produced the list faster than you can say Saturnino Orestes Arrieta Armas ("Minnie") Miñoso. We chatted a bit—my allegiance to the 1950s Washington Senators continued to stand me in good stead—and talked around my specific request. Finally Salmerón leaned back in his chair, his unlighted cigar pointed to the ceiling, and said, "Now, what exactly is it you want to do?"

"I'd like to spend a week on the road with a team in the Liga

Nacional. It's as simple as that. Travel on the team bus. Eat in the same restaurants. Sleep in the same motels. Attend their workouts. Sit in the dugout." Salmerón gave me a quizzical look. "Oh, don't worry. I know all about the austerity program. I'll cover all my expenses—restaurants, hotel, any incidentals." His look turned to incredulity. "I don't want to be a burden. I'd just like to see how Cuban baseball operates from the inside." The look on his face—had he misunderstood me to ask if I could pitch the opening game for the Olympic team?

He called a colleague over to join us and exhaled a long pause. "You have no idea how we do things here, do you." It was more a statement than a question.

"I guess not. That's why I—"

He leaned forward, ignoring my response. "First of all, the teams do not eat in restaurants. Each stadium has two dining rooms, one for the visiting team, one for the home team." His colleague nodded. "Secondly, they don't stay in motels except in Havana. Every stadium has a dormitory on the ground level. They all stay together. It's less expensive and more efficient that way, and it builds the team's unity."

"Oh. In that case, I'd like to stay in the dorm with a team if at all possible."

"We couldn't allow that. It'd be like living with a family, then spilling the beans about their quarrels, their eating habits, even how they sleep." (Yes yes yes, exactly, I thought.) "They may be a perfectly normal family but of course they have their little problems. We all do." The colleague nodded emphatically. "That isn't the way sports journalism is conducted here."

He had a point. I had been reading the sports section for months and had yet to find anything but slathering praise for all teams. The sports page of *Granma* was a flack's dream.

"For example," said the colleague, "let's say you wanted to cover the Houston Astros. Would they give you total access like this?" "Of course not," his colleague added.

"Another thing you need to know," Salmerón said. "The last game of every three-game series is played in a small provincial town so everyone gets a chance to see a game, not just the fans in the cities." The colleague added, "Of course, you must go to Matanzas to see Cuba's first baseball stadium. It was built in 1874." I also wanted to see a series in Havana. Computing all this together, we came up with the Forestales, one of two teams from Pinar del Río. They would be finishing up a series in Cienfuegos and traveling by bus to Matanzas for a series with the Henequeneros, then on to the capital for a series with the Metropolitanos.

"I'll talk with the league directors about this, and I'll be seeing the Forestales officials this weekend. Call me on Monday and I'll let you know." Salmerón had been neutralized. I was no longer the dimwit Yankee.

Despite all the self-inflicted grumbling about what crazy drivers Cubans are, traffic in Havana moves far more orderly, and is safer and less frenzied than any other Latin American country I'd visited. Cars come to complete halts when lights turn red. They don't start up again until just before the green shines. Their speeds don't exceed far beyond the age of the Revolution in miles per hour or Fidel's age in kilometers per hour. One-way streets seldom have two-way traffic. No Parking areas are often free of parked cars. Habana Vieja and parts of Centro were planned and built for horses and carriages, and it's a wonder today's cars and trucks can pass through its streets at all. A few have been turned into pedestrian malls. You can usually inch your way down narrow streets without being forced to a full stop by abandoned vehicles. Traffic cops can be persuaded to issue warnings rather than tickets. Twice I was in taxis when we were pulled over by motorcycle cops; one time in Havana for an illegal right turn and the other, on the open road, by a highway patrolman, for driving too slowly in the left-hand passing lane.

A major reason for relatively safe streets is simply the absence of cars. Most families do not own cars and rely on friends who do, and buses and taxis. A majority of the vehicles on the street were government cars, whose drivers, in the Special Period, suddenly had to account for their time and gas instead of running personal errands half the day. More and more bicycles appeared around town through the fall, and the newspapers were full of stories about a new bike factory in one city, imports from China destined for another city, bicycle etiquette, impending cycling rules, planned bike paths, safety tips, and centers for bicycle distribution. Middle-aged men on bikes wobbling down the streets for the first time in years provoked laughter. The number of women cyclists, disproportionately small, increased noticeably. It was said jokingly that Havana would soon look like Ho Chi Minh City in those newsreels where bicycles far outnumber pedestrians and cars. Lots of people were looking forward to bikes for their efficiency, and the environmental advantage was trumpeted as well. But beneath it all was their necessity; contracted Soviet shipments of oil were simply not arriving and likely never would.

Buses continually lost on fares. About half of all bus riders didn't bother to pay. _Bohemia_ asked a few scofflaws why. " 'I'll pay when they improve the service!' screamed one annoyed passenger. 'Ten centavos won't get the country moving,' another said. 'See if anyone really passes the fare forward,' whispered a man in a jacket and tie. 'Nobody has a conscience,' added a little old lady." And finally, a high school boy replied to the _Bohemia_ reporter, "What's it to you?"

The most dangerous bus-riding practice had little to do with mismanagement or freeloaders or poor maintenance. It owed itself instead to brash youth, cheap thrills, audacious behavior: on buses so jam-packed they fairly bulged with passengers, teenage boys hung precariously outside the middle or rear door platforms. Buses often pulled away from the major stop in front of Coppelia Park listing dangerously to the right. One paper reported ten accidents a day resulted from boys hanging out the doors. "Every week someone dies or develops a serious injury from this behavior."

REVOLUTIONARIES IN THIS TOWN WILL NEVER BOW TO THE IMPERIAL-ISTS. That one was a golden oldie. It had a generic, almost timeless air, a slogan for all seasons. It was righteous enough to agree with, bland enough to ignore, and patriotic enough not to quibble with. In Cuba, one-size-fits-all applies to slogans as well as clothes. When I had mentioned to Nitza that the sheer preponderance of revolutionary slogans on walls, billboards, trucks, buildings, buses, bulletin boards, construction sites, playgrounds, homes, and every other flat surface in the country stunned me, she smiled and said, "Really? I guess I don't notice them. To me they're like the palms."

Yet every time a lugubriously nationalistic billboard came into view, I'd wonder, who makes up these . . . these . . . these faux maxims? Is there a room somewhere with a row of chimpanzees pecking away at typewriters? Do these stultifying dictums grow on bushes, and if so, who are the gardeners and would they please get to work? Is there a real office that generates these insipid slogans?

Actually yes, there is. It's called the Department of Revolutionary Orientation. It's guardian of the straightest line this side of the equator. It lives in a building at the far end of the Plaza de la Revolución. Hegemonies "R" Us.

* * *

"I spoke with the league officials this weekend." Salmerón answered on the third try. "Your trip has been approved. Instead of joining the Forestales in Cienfuegos, it'd make more sense for you to meet them in Matanzas." I was about to leave for a swing through the eastern end of the island, and Salmerón was off for Mexico with Cuba's national team for a series in "the Aztec country." He asked that I call him for details when I got back.

Salvador González was home, something increasingly rare for the muralist these days. His artwork was being recognized more and more, meaning he had to go out and talk about it with people with some frequency. The previous week I had quietly walked by his mural and put myself within its reach. I had not gone up to see him, nor had I talked with his neighbors. That night the mural pulsated into my subconscious, and I dreamed of being in a very hot place with fire all around me. I started to tumble, free-falling through darkness to another equally hot place, where, this being a dream, I landed safely on my feet. Flames engulfed me but I felt secure, even protected, as if in familiar surroundings.

I described the dream to Salvador. He was quiet, then he said, "You got this from my mural?" I nodded. "Then you understand." His smile cut through religion, geography, language, and isms. He nodded. "You understand."

I told Salvador I was flying to Santiago de Cuba the next day, then overland to other towns at the far end of the country. Salvador had some news, too. A gaggle of German musicians who play Cuban music and had an interest in Afro-Cuban culture would be touring the country and had agreed to play in front of Salvador's mural. Bring friends, musicians, anyone; the muralside jam session will take place in late December.

"German musicians who play rumbas and salsa? Salvador, I'm all for intercultural exchange, but you're going to have to prove this one."

"I know, I felt the same way. But one of them came by here and played a tape of theirs."

"Ah, yes," I deadpanned. "The Afro-Alemanes," the Afro-Germans. "Of course."

"Right! Right! The Afro-Alemanes!" Salvador interrupted his wife and mother in the kitchen. "We're calling them the Afro-Alemanes!" He asked for my itinerary, then rattled off a list of people and places to visit. In Santiago, this museum, in Guantánamo, that one. If you go to Baracoa, be sure and see Dr. Hartman. "He'll show you the cross that Columbus left there." Luis, a friend of Salvador's, seated nearby the whole time, broke his silence. "Don't forget the Casa del Caribe in Santiago." We unfolded my map to refresh their memories. They rattled off a half dozen more rivers and beaches that I must see.

"You'll have a wonderful time in Santiago," said Salvador. "People in Havana are so snobbish when it comes to Santiago de Cuba, but it's a great city. It's a black city, you know." Luis, the friend, walked me halfway home, talking up my impending journey, then, as we neared the Hotel Vedado, he asked if I would go in and buy him a pack of cigarettes while he waited across the street.

The flight to Santiago on Cubana airline took about ninety minutes. A flight attendant served us Tropicola. I went straight to the Hotel Casagranda, mainly for its location, but also for its literary history. Wormold stayed at the Casagranda in *Our Man in Havana* on a business cum espionage trip. "The night was hot and humid" when Wormold arrived, "and the greenery hung dark and heavy in the pallid light of half-strength lamps."

The expansive front patio of the hotel looks upon Céspedes Park, through which walk all manner of man, most manner of women, and kids by the cartful. A small black goat appeared in the park harnessed to a baby-sized carriage in which rode three small children. Their father followed, pushing the back of the carriage. No one took notice.

The desk clerk gave me a room on the third floor for 9.5 pesos. Neither the elevator nor the stair lighting worked. The hotel was in pretty awful shape, a condition that drove most foreigners to either the Leningrado, where I later lodged, or Las Américas, where I stayed on my last swing through town.

Nowhere in *Our Man in Havana* does Greene mention the Casagranda by name, but his description of Wormold's lodging matches the place, and when Wormold checked in, "He felt like an impostor, for this was a hotel of real spies, real police-informers and real rebel agents." A little more than a year before the 1958 publication of the book, Greene had been in Cuba and, through a series of literary and underground intermediaries, two complementary goals were agreed upon: Greene wanted to interview Castro, then leading the guerrilla army in the Sierra Maestra; and the *lucha clandestina*, the urban clandestine movement, wanted to get clothing to the *fidelistas*. According to Nydia Sarabia, a Santiago woman who worked with the *lucha clandestina* in

Havana, Greene was asked if he would carry a suitcase on the plane to Santiago. The clothes inside it were destined for the guerrillas. Once in Santiago, Greene would be led to Fidel in the mountains.

"At the time, Batista's police were checking the airports for rebels." Sarabia told me. "Greene was perfect for the job. He was tall, light-skinned, obviously foreign, and he looked like he knew nothing of what was going on at the time. He agreed to take the suitcase with pullovers, socks, and leather jackets with him. In the Sierra it was very chilly at night, and these clothes would help the guerrillas. I was to be on the same plane." Sarabia used a pseudonym in all her dealings with Greene.

Greene confided in her his suspicions that a Havana acquaintance, a *Time* reporter, was with the FBI. "Greene arrived at the airport in a Jaguar. Suspiciously the *Time* reporter showed up for the same flight as well. Greene and I never made eye contact the whole trip."

In Santiago Sarabia discovered that the reporter was indeed not to be trusted. "I overheard him in the lobby of the Casagranda talking on the phone with the Servicio Inteligencia Militar. We learned that SIM had transmitted to the reporter a conversation between Greene and me.

"Greene took the suitcaseful of clothes by my aunt's house—that was our appointed rendezvous—but he didn't stop there because he thought he was being followed. At ten the next morning we were finally able to link up and get the suitcase." At that secret meeting on San Francisco Street Greene met Jacinto Pérez, the nom de guerre of Armando Hart Dávalos, now Cuba's minister of culture and a member of the Communist Party Central Committee. Hart had, within the previous week, escaped police guard in Havana as he was being led into court. When Greene walked in, a barber was coloring his hair, changing him from Armando to Jacinto, from Hart to Pérez.

Left to his own devices in the streets of mid-revolution Santiago, Greene learned of three young sisters whom Batista soldiers had kidnapped from their home in the middle of the night. Their father was with Fidel in the Sierra, "so they were taken in their nightclothes to the military barracks as hostages," Greene recollected in *Ways of Escape*. The next morning, as word spread, students took to the streets in protest. "The shops began to put up their shutters in expectation of the worst. The army gave way and released the three little girls. They could not turn fire hoses on the children in the streets as they had turned them on their mothers, or hang them from lamp posts as they would have hanged their fathers."

Meanwhile, Sarabia told me, "The city was surrounded with Batista's army, and we didn't know if we could get Greene into the Sierra to see Fidel. We also told him about the British planes Batista was buying to bomb the rebels and civilians in the Oriente."

The interview with Fidel was off. Greene checked out of the Casagranda and returned to Havana. He told Sarabia that he was leaving for Africa. "He said he was going to interview the Mau-Mau guerrillas. He never knew my real name."

Years later, reflecting on the Santiago episode, Greene wrote that the U.S. could say he had been "used," but "I have never hesitated to be 'used' in a cause I believe in, even if my choice might be only for a lesser evil." Although he left town without interviewing Fidel, the brief trip had its literary value: details of his Santiago stay are sprinkled throughout *Our Man in Havana*.

When mealtime came, the Casagranda had a policy of putting local diners on the patio in front and its guests in a room out back with no windows, poor lighting, little ventilation, and drab decor. The air-conditioning was on full-blast, which, although it clattered and necessitated a sweater, at least kept me awake. The patio, on the other hand, a luxurious and broad affair, had a 180 degree outdoor view, a breeze, natural light, and a friendly atmosphere. I was perplexed when told one morning at the patio that I couldn't enjoy coffee and bread there. Perhaps I was misunderstood? Why else would they banish me to the rear dungeon? "No, no." I pulled out my key. "See, I'm a guest at this hotel." That sealed my exile to the freezer.

Two middle-aged women who had stopped at the patio restaurant for a *cafecito* on their way to work saw my predicament and called the manager over. He returned and led me back to their table. "Please, join us. There's no reason you shouldn't wake up to Parque Céspedes as well." After I sat down they ignored me as they talked about work, husbands, and households. I politely ignored them, too, and wrote a few picture postcards to friends back in the States. Wormold did the same while dining at the Casagranda. "A picture postcard is a symptom of loneliness," he observed.

I spent part of the morning walking through downtown Santiago. What had been a warm discovery in Cienfuegos had become nicely repetitive—travel outside Havana meant more pleasures, fewer anxious people on the streets, and a more-anchored populace. A British writer in the 1870s put it this way: "The traveler who wishes to be on good terms with Cuba should make his best haste to get out of Havannah. The smells and noises of that pestilential town had nearly killed me.

The quiet and fragrance of the country revived me." I wished to be on good terms with Cuba, and this was to be my longest out of town revival.

Unfortunately most of the hustlers clustered on Heredia Street, and as a new and solo face I was easy to spot. I made my way through the throng of *jineteros* to the local writers union chapter, a large hall with a small bar in back, a baby grand piano in front, and television monitors for video workers. A schedule proclaimed at least one public event a day—a reading, a roundtable literary discussion, a theatrical performance, a film, a jam session, a lecture—and from what I saw these get-togethers attracted a wide and varied crowd.

A serious young man from the city of Holguín sat on a chair arranging his papers. He was part of a theater troupe touring the eastern end of the island putting on shows for children. Their current production, he explained, concerned a bird who rose from the center of the earth. "The bird is ugly, and no one likes it except one little boy. The two become friends, but soon the boy is ostracized by his buddies for having befriended such an unsightly creature." Two others joined me to listen to the theatrical summary. "Soon the bird sprouts a feather, then another, and another and another, until finally he is the most beautiful bird for kilometers around. The boy is suddenly popular again." The actor smiled. I smiled. The two others smiled. "It's a tale about the world, really," the earnest young actor said. "Or it could be about one country."

I had read that the daiquiri, named for a small beach town southeast of Santiago, had been originally christened at the bar of the Hotel Venus in Santiago, and I hoped to order one there. The Venus was on a side street behind my hotel. It was in worse shape than the Casagranda. If carbon 14 dating techniques could work on layers of dust, I could have determined how long ago the Venus bar had closed.

Later in the day I went back to UNEAC, hoping to find Ariel James, president of the Santiago chapter. The provincial writers union must have attracted serious young men. This time the somber fellow, a playwright, was speaking to twenty intent listeners on "The Determination to Create." He spoke of Molière, of ancient Greeks, of contemporary Spaniards. Afterward he took questions. One lasted five minutes. A powerful and unpleasant memory came to mind. I was speaking to a similar gathering about U.S.-Mexico border literature in Hermosillo, Mexico, once, and after my opening remarks the floor was open. The first question lasted almost as long as my comments, and I mumbled, "That's not a question, that's a speech." I said it under my breath but over a mike. My audience began to squirm, then one by one, drift away. I wanted to join them. Within fifteen minutes I was facing a room devoid of spectators. The only sound was my host emptying ashtrays. The Santiago meeting lasted longer, with a more gracious audience and a more mannerly speaker.

Ariel James's assistant assured me that the local UNEAC president would be right back. I pulled out *The Mambo Kings*. Desi Arnaz had just recorded the Castillo brothers' song, "Beautiful María of My Soul," followed by Nat "King" Cole and Xavier Cugat. I read past Nestor's death to where Cesar's body sags under the weight of whiskey and fried *chorizo* sandwiches, when a thin, lively middle-aged man walked over and introduced himself. It was James, the provincial *jefe*. He wanted to arrange my eastern swing, or at least its framework. I was interested in birds, words, soldiers, and history. The ivory-billed woodpecker, once prevalent in the American South, was said to now exist in Cuba and in Cuba only. It lived in this end of the island; was there a naturalist I could talk to about it? Of course I was interested in what the local writers union was doing, as well as the one in Guantánamo, the city near the U.S. navy base. At the last minute, Victoria at the Havana office had been able to arrange an appointment for me with Cuba's Brigada Fronteriza. The anniversary of Fidel's landing of the boat *Granma* on the Cuban coast in 1956 was at hand and I hoped to visit the arrival point. Finally, I wanted to drive to the north coast city of Baracoa, said to be dripping with history going back to Columbus and before.

James made some calls and announced that I had a late-afternoon appointment at the local Academy of Science office with its chief, Luis Milán. "They're located at the local *jardín botánico*. At the entrance to San Juan take the road headed toward Playa Siboney." He drew a little sketch of the back roads.

He pointed out the town of Banes on the map. "It has a lot of history for such a small place. A famous bandit, El Águila Negro," the Black Eagle, "comes from Banes. One of the most important sugar mills in the country was in Banes, and the United Fruit Company had a mammoth installation there; it was an American-run company town. Fidel's first wife came from Banes. So did Batista." James had written his thesis on Banes at the University of the Oriente, later published as a book. He reached into a closet and pulled out a copy that he inscribed "In hopes that this book will be useful." It begins in the nineteenth century when foreign capital underwrote the local mill and closes in October 1960 with its nationalization. From the book I learned that the major sugar plant was called Boston (since renamed Nicaragua), that the American Club had a polo field, a pool room, and a baseball team, and that Jamaicans were imported to work the fields. In the back of James's book are old pictures of the United Fruit Company's operation, including one of a little steam engine used in the yards to haul equipment and cane, called Panchito.

I had been scribbling notes during our conversation. By the time I left, one page in my notebook looked like this:

> 3 p.m. miércoles
> Luis Milán—jefe de planes
> jardín botánico
> la entrada de san juan
> road to playa siboney
> águila negro—famous bandit from Banes
> 1/wife Fidel—Banes

I would be in and out of Santiago a few times over the following ten days, and we agreed to get together away from the office.

I drove my rented '85 Nissan toward the Academy of Science compound. A billboard shouted

LONG LIVE FRIENDSHIP BETWEEN CUBA AND THE USSR!

After I got off the main road I became slightly confused, missed the last turnoff, and kept driving through a barren area until I passed through a clump of trees and up to a series of tall wire fences and a group of bellicose and militaristic signs. Four soldiers with rifles pounced on me.

"Who are you?"

"What are you doing here?"

I had accidentally driven up to a secret military base. The guards had been trained to deal with intruders, evidently didn't get too many, and now had a live one—a *norteamericano* to boot. I told them I was looking for the Jardín Botánico and that I had an appointment at three o'clock.

"Identification, please."

One of the guards trotted over to his booth to report the intrusion to his superior. I pulled out my *carnet*, which identified me as a U.S. citizen who lived in Cuba. I left my U.S. passport in my bag.

Two trucks pulled up and four more guards walked over. One with a clipboard took charge. "What kind of car is this?" This seemed an odd question given that the make was in bold letters in front and back. The license tags read TURISTA, plates found only on rentals by foreigners.

"Nissan," I replied. "N-i-s-s-a-n." He carefully wrote it down. "It's Japanese," I volunteered, hoping to reduce the stress level some—his, not mine; I was almost enjoying this. He wrote down "Japanese." "Actually," I said in mock conspiratorial tone, "it was manufactured in Mexico." He dutifully entered this, too, without changing his dour expression. Finally he wrote down a description of me, glancing between my face and his notepad. I had penetrated security.

The two trucks blocked the only space in which to make a U-turn and leave, something I figured to do now that the interrogation was over. They wouldn't budge. I played "Write That Headline!" again, and I didn't like what I saw.

Just as the officer in charge seemed ready to let me go, he saw my notebook lying face up on the seat. Proof of my appointment! "See?" I pointed out the key words. "*3 p.m. miércoles*, and *jardín botánico*."

"What's that?" he asked. "Why did you write his name?" He pointed to the line that read *1/wife Fidel—Banes.*

"Ah. Fidel's wife." Fortunately I have bad handwriting and had written that in English. "Fidel's life. *La vida de Fidel. Quiere decir, en todas partes está Fidel.* It means Fidel is everywhere." He looked long and hard at my notebook and then at me. Fortuitously, I had not written Batista's name. There was no silent smile, just silence. Then he ordered the truck drivers to pull away and let me make my U-turn.

I found the road I had missed earlier and drove up a hill to a group of low buildings where Luis Milán waited for me. He turned me over to two field scientists. "Is anything wrong?" one asked. I didn't realize it, but I was hyperventilating from my run-in with the soldiers. The two scientists listened with increasing amusement as I explained what had just happened. "And to have a *norteamericano* breach their security!" I said.

They laughed. "Well, if it's any consolation to you, they treat us the same way."

They took me on a tour of the facilities—laboratories with other scientists, a caseful of well-used reference books, a roomful of shelves with snails and other creatures, and finally the research desks where both of them, Luis and Gabriel, worked. I had brought with me a couple of recent articles from scientific journals about a type of snail prevalent on the coast not far from Santiago. The articles were based on research a paleontologist and others had done in the Bahamas.

Luis and Gabriel ignored me for a moment as they skimmed the articles. Like innumerable other scientists in non-English-speaking countries, the two were fluent readers of the most dense scientific jargon in English, but utterly incapable of pronouncing a word of it aloud. Luis popped up and took me into the room with shelvesful of specimens. He peered at the labels and triumphantly, as if the first scientist to classify it, pulled out a long, narrow drawer with the precise species of snail that the article spoke of.

The two were happy to talk about the ivory-billed woodpecker, a source of national pride among Cuban scientists, and among the largest woodpeckers in the world. John James Audubon wrote of spotting them along the Mississippi in 1820, but as logging increased—the bird lives on beetle larvae in bark—the ivory-bill became increasingly difficult to spot. The last confirmed U.S. sighting was in the 1940s.

The bird was thought to be extinct—certainly endangered—until Cuban scientists in the mid-1980s identified bark stripping and bird-calls that could only have come from the ivory-bill. They invited a team headed by the woodpecker specialist at the American Museum of Natural History in New York to join their search. In Cuba the bird was once common in the Zapata Swampland and Pinar del Río, but the new exploration was taking place south of Sagua de Tánamo in the woodland adjoining the Jaguaní and Yarey rivers in Guantánamo Province. "Well," I said, "I guess birds come to Cuba and *gusanos*," worms, "go to the United States."

The binational search for the ivory-bill "had all the excitement and romance of a quest for lost treasure," wrote team leader Lester L. Short and a colleague of the 1986 expedition. One treasure flew near him across the Yarey River. "My God, I've seen it!" he thought as he spotted a female *Campephilus principalis*. In all, eight sightings were made by the researchers. "Do you know when Short is coming next?" the two at the Jardín Botánico asked. "He hasn't been here in a couple of years."

When authorities learned of the sightings they established an eighty-five-square-mile ivory-bill protection area, and rerouted a highway that was slated to cut through the territory. The minister of agriculture banned logging.

Short describes the ivory-bill's call as a nasally *kyent kyent*. Others have transcribed it as *wucka wucka*, or *pent pent*, or *week week*, or *yamp*

yamp. Audubon wrote *pait pait*. We three agreed that a trip to ivory-bill turf was out of the question—we were four months away from prime spotting season, and, further, my interest was entirely casual and not at all scientific. Neither Luis nor Gabriel had actually spotted an ivory-bill, but both had been on search expeditions. It makes a bleating noise, Luis said. With some prodding, he gave me his impression of the sound of an ivory-billed woodpecker. *"Ah-errrrr"* he called out in a strong, wavering tremolo. It sounded like a muted trumpet. *"Ah-errrrr."*

Luis's woodpecker call had a universal ring to it. Less so his Santiago Spanish, an accent that people in Havana made fun of. "You think it's difficult to understand us?" a *habanero* said before I left. "Wait until you hear the *santiagueros*." His warning was part of the national rivalry between the two cities. True, the people of Santiago sounded more sing-songy, but they spoke a bit slower. In both places, though, the last syllables of words must have been sugar-coated, Cubans swallowed so many of them. If they had dropped any more syllables, they would be speechless.

Pity the poor S; a good letter, an upstanding letter, a letter whose mere appearance can change a verb form or increase a noun's frequency. But in Cuba it was an abused letter, ignored as if it lacked the alphabetical rights all the other letters enjoyed. Cuba has an abundance of unused Ss. Where do they all go?

The country's excess Ss are dispersed to diners in restaurants. This became clear in the meat locker room of the Casagranda where my sole entertainment was the sound of fellow diners. Far more than in Havana, whenever diners in Santiago want the waiter's attention they call out "s-s-s-s-s-st." The sound pierces through all other noises. S-s-s-s-s-st has the same function in other Latin American countries, but in those it is a matter of social class, only slightly more elegant than clanking your silverware against a glass. In Cuba, they hiss in the classiest restaurants and the lowliest cafés, at work and in the streets. A restaurant with bad service can sound like it's full of snakes. In 1859, Richard Henry Dana wrote of the sound in *To Cuba and Back*: "They make it clear and penetrating; yet it seems a poor, effeminate sibilation. . . . I have no doubt, if a fire were to break out at the next door, a Cuban would call 'P—s—t!' " Cabrera Infante calls it a "Cuban sucking sound" in *Three Trapped Tigers*, "exactly like an inverted kiss."

Whenever I was a little under the weather, or simply exhausted, language was the first mental tool to fade. My ability to translate would retreat to neutral, as if it was a hearing aid shut down. Other times I simply pretended dumbness, a ploy first described by W. M. L. Jay in 1871 "in order to escape from the weariness of being civil and sociable in a foreign tongue, and to be free to use my eyes and ears to the best advantage."

I know exactly what you mean, W.M.L. The cumulative civility and sociability of five months in a foreign tongue had worn me down. I combated this dispiriting drift on the open road. I was off to Guantá-namo, first to scout about the city whose cash flow from 1899 to 1959 began with the U.S. Navy, and then to learn about the Brigada Fronteriza, whose lookouts watch the navy base watch them. The song "Guantanamera" looped interminably through my mind as I drove east.

> *Guantanamera,*
> *Guajira guantanamera,*
> *Guantanamera,*
> *Guajira guantanamera.*
>
> *Yo soy un hombre sincero*
> *De donde crece la palma,*
> *Yo soy un hombre sincero*
> *De donde crece la palma,*
> *Y antes de morirme quiero*
> *Echar mis versos de alma.*
>
> (Girl from Guantánamo,
> Girl from the Guantánamo countryside.
> Girl from Guantánamo,
> Girl from the Guantánamo countryside.
>
> I am a truthful man
> From the land of the palm trees,
> And before dying I want
> To share these poems of my soul.)

The harder I tried to evict the incessant melody and its words adapted from José Martí, the more entrenched it became.

Trabajadores, the workers newspaper, had recently run a tribute to the song. Joseíto Fernández, who died at age seventy-one in 1979, had written many popular songs, "But of all of them, 'Guantanamera' is the most listened to and has become Cuba's signature song in every corner of the world!"

Fernández featured the song in the 1950s during a weekday-afternoon radio show when he would invent verses to accompany skits dramatizing violent news events. In 1962, Pete Seeger heard a camp counselor in the States sing "Guantanamera," with the poetry of José Martí. He popularized this more upbeat style using Martí's poetry to such an extent that even in Cuba the Seeger style runs side by side with the more traditional one. And to generations of his fans, Seeger's midsong translation became their first Spanish lesson.

According to *Trabajadores*, "Guantanamera" has been played in all rhythms and styles. "I have heard 'Guantanameras' happy and witty and disastrous and off-key, but all versions are heartfelt." But nobody can identify the *guajira guantanamera*, the woman from the Guantánamo countryside, who inspired "Guantanamera."

I retaliated with my own version.

> *One ton of mierda*
> *I hear the one ton of mierda*
> *One ton of mierda*
> *I hear the one ton of mierda.*
>
> *Yo soy un yankee perdido*
> *In flagrante delicto,*
> *Yo soy un yankee perdido*
> *In flagrante delicto,*
> *On Thursday more irme quiero*
> *On charming versos de balsa.*
>
> *(repeat chorus)*

The country's southeastern terrain had a nice lilt to it. The highway snaked through small towns where clusters of travelers waited cheerlessly outside bus stations. A teacher flagged me down and described her elementary school students and her own small child who lived with her parents in Holguín. We went through the usual where-are-you-from and what-do-you-do exchange, and when we got to our ages, she said coyly, "Cuban women have three ages. The first is what we say. The second is what we appear to be. And the third is our real age." She was twenty-five on at least the first two counts. I dropped her off at the home of some friends in Cuatro Caminos, where, on the edge of town, I picked up a boy and a girl clutching freshly picked flowers. They were on their way to the grave of the boy's grandfather.

In the city of Guantánamo I arrived at my coast-to-coast host, the provincial writers union, where Rebeca Ulloa greeted me with good cheer and bad news. The cheer was in anticipation of a documentary that evening about Frida Kahlo. She expected a big turnout. The bad news: when she had last spoken with the man from FAR, the Revolutionary Armed Forces, he knew nothing about my visit. "*No te preocupes*," she counseled with maternal equanimity. Don't worry. It was to be our private mantra for the next few days. The officer said he'd call first thing in the morning. *No te preocupes.*

The Guantánamo writers union is housed in a large building on Máximo Gómez Street, named for the Dominican-born commander of the Cuban forces in the War for Independence from Spain. It has a small wooden front porch that reaches the sidewalk and two wooden doors leading to huge rooms with high ceilings. Big windows with iron grillwork allow entry for the breeze and the glances of curious passers-by.

Some fifty people turned out for Rebeca's evening program, which also included a videotape about Kahlo's husband, Diego Rivera. A lively discussion about Kahlo, Rivera, and their art followed. In the crowd was a woman from the States who had been touring Cuba with a dance troupe shortly after the Revolution. Relations between the two countries were deteriorating and, taken by the possibilities in this new nation, she stayed. The appearance of another *norteamericano* virtually fresh off the boat, as I was, provoked names of favorites from Cubans. One fellow liked Stevie Winwood music; another followed the Oakland A's. I met a woman who had published a series of short stories set on the border of the U.S. navy base. In one, a man named José Manuel tries to snorkel his way into base waters, but a searchlight spots him before he gets there. When he scrambles ashore, still on the Cuba side of the boundary, guard dogs chase him and a sympathetic woman hides him in her bed while a pursuing officer combs her house. After the search party leaves she undresses and joins José Manuel. Eventually he leaves to try again.

The television, used for the documentaries, was tuned to the national news. A meteorologist who spoke as lifelessly as he looked gave the weather. He had no jazzy images to play with, no 3-D overlay maps or film of moving clouds shot from a satellite to aim his pointer at. He was no-nonsense, serious, almost somber. "And he's wrong so much of the time, too," the fellow sitting next to me said. "They say he's from the Instituto de Meteorología," the Institute of Meteorology, "but we say he's from the Instituto de Mentirología," the Institute of Lying. I gave Rebeca a lift home, and as she got out of the car, I reminded her that the FAR man was to call in the morning. *"No te preocupes."*

But I was worried. Just before leaving Havana I had learned that the request La Plume had made on my behalf months earlier had been fielded by a petty factotum in the FAR bureaucracy who had left to join another government agency a few weeks later. She had not passed on my request to anyone else; in effect, La Plume had been assuring me all along that we would hear from someone at FAR who no longer worked there. Victoria, on the other hand, had said everything was now arranged, but in Guantánamo no one knew this. *No te preocupes* indeed.

I turned on the television in my room at the Hotel Guantánamo and flipped through the channels. Was something wrong? Channel 8 was broadcasting CNN Headline News. A spokesman for Warner Records was explaining Madonna's new video. Bush was inching closer to a decision on the Gulf War. Townspeople in the middle of the United States were organizing a Christmas card drive for soldiers in Saudi Arabia. Sports scores. The national weather picture. A short piece about those eccentric Brits. Hollywood gossip. This was not Televisión Martí, the hobbled U.S. propaganda effort. I was getting instead an armed forces station from the U.S. navy base. Every television set in the area got it. It was one of the secret advantages of living near the base. They get the World Series. David Letterman. College basketball. And best of all, feature-length movies. No blockade, no jamming, simply over-the-air, normal, superficial U.S. television, as if Cuba paid a monthly cable fee. The base radio station came in on the AM dial. Listeners heard a rotation of different U.S. radio networks' hourly news summaries. "Some of us learn English this way," a *guantanamero* said.

The next morning I suggested to Rebeca that we call the Cuban armed forces office, or drive out to the installation. *"No te preocupes,"* she said with a wave of a hand. "Everything will work out." She took me on a tour of the city of Guantánamo, a healthy provincial town. We went to a craft shop where cloth and straw bags were made. We took a long stroll through the main park. A teenager walked by, wearing an American flag T-shirt. Rebeca's eleven-year-old son, Aron, joined us. We dropped in on an art gallery, a theater where rehearsals were soon to get under way, and the obligatory museum. A museum guide said, "Guantánamo was founded in 1819 by French exiles from Haiti. In this area, Jamaicans are known as Englishmen and Haitians as Frenchmen." Driving was a little more difficult than other cities. "In Guantánamo, the streets have potholes," Rebeca said with a laugh as we bounced through the city. "In Guantánamo," Aron popped up from the backseat, "the potholes have streets."

Rebeca joined me for lunch at the hotel dining room. "You know Macondo in *One Hundred Years of Solitude*? Well, Cuba is a lot like Macondo." Rebeca also worked at CMKS, a local radio station. This was her second term as provincial UNEAC president, a job she threw herself into. She was considered an expert on Regino Boti, a Cuban writer and poet who died in 1958. She had published widely on his work as well as her own poetry. She got to Havana a couple of times a year, and had once been to Czechoslovakia. As we talked a large diner sat down at a piano in the corner. He sang a couple of ballads, then "Guantanamera."

"Do you ever get tired of that song?" I asked Rebeca, herself a lifelong *guantanamera*.

Rebeca hummed along with the singer. I ordered two *cafecitos*. She pondered my question. The coffees arrived. "Well?" The singer went back to his table.

Finally Rebeca shook her head: "No. When a bunch of us are just sitting around drinking, we start to sing it. It never wears out."

We returned to the UNEAC building at three o'clock. No calls had come in from the Revolutionary Armed Forces. I was in increasing despair; I blamed La Plume, I blamed Fidel, I blamed Dan Quayle, I blamed third-world inefficiency, I blamed it on the bossa nova. I sat at a table in a funk. Rebeca walked by. "I know, I know," I said, nodding with a wan smile. *"No te preocupes."*

At four o'clock four military boots came clomping down the hall making a noise like a rumba solo. Two lieutenants from the Brigada Fronteriza walked in to the writers union office. Never have I been so happy to see men in uniform come after me. They had communicated with Havana the previous afternoon. In the middle of the night approval to give me the Cook's tour had been granted, and now they wanted to take me to headquarters to show me the museum. Rebeca got a kick out of having soldiers in the writers union building and

asked if she could visit the museum, too. "What'd I tell you?" she
said as we followed the lieutenants back to brigade headquarters. "*No
te preocupes.*"

The Frontier Brigade complex was on the edge of town. Guards
saluted as I approached the gate and waved me past security checkpoints
and onto the grounds. The main building housed offices on one side
and the museum on the other. The museum told of the social and
human toll the navy base has taken on the area. Grisly photos of three
Cubans who had been killed on the base in the early 1960s took up
one wall. A sign said, *The imperialist government in Washington used
Guantánamo to organize and direct all types of counterrevolutionary transgres-
sions, among them: detention, torture, and murder of workers. They violate
air and sea space; they infiltrate and exfiltrate saboteurs and bandits in the
service of the CIA. They organize criminal attacks against the Directorate of
the Revolution. . . . As our Commander in Chief Fidel Castro Ruz has said,
the base represents ". . . un puñal clavado en el corazón de la tierra cubana,"*
a dagger plunged into the heart of Cuban soil.

A series of photographs shows "enemy provocation and immaturity."
One caption reads, *An enemy soldier, knowing that he won't receive the
response he deserves for his insolent attitude, tries to provoke the border Cubans.*
A U.S. marine is pictured throwing rocks over the fence. *Pointing their
rifles at Cuban positions, then scattering, is one of the marines' favorite forms
of entertainment.* The next two pictures show a marine at the fence
ogling a *Playboy* centerfold, and a marine hugging a woman at his
lookout post. And, beneath the last picture, *Sticking to his side of the
fence, an enemy soldier lowers his pants and shows his behind.*

My guides brought in Angel Alaguer Fonseca, the only *brigadista*
who had been posted to the frontier unit continuously since its inception in the early 1960s. How have things changed over the years?
"Well, both sides have pulled back from the fence so there are far
fewer provocations." What did he see in the future? "When we take
over, we'll plant crops there."

Raúl Castro, Second Secretary of the Communist Party of Cuba,
General of the Army, First Vice President of the Council of State and
of Ministers, and Minister of the Revolutionary Armed Forces, first
visited the brigade in 1964. Alaguer knew the exact date. Raúl's words
were emblazoned on the wall: "This unit should be an example among
exemplars." José Solar Hernández, a colonel whose shoulders and chest
sported rows of colorful bars and stripes, came over and introduced
himself. "Can you be here at seven tomorrow morning? I'll take you
around then."

I had told Jorge Nuñez, a writer I had met at the Frida Kahlo show the previous evening, that I wanted to go to a nightclub. Enrique said he'd take me to the Club Nevada, then added, "It's a troublesome place filled with marginal people. It's a black club." We got there about 10:30. Jorge huddled with the doorman who qualified us for the posted COUPLES ONLY rule and sent us upstairs to the club. The only lights pointed at the stage, where four *guantanameras* danced the lambada to a tape. They wore silver leotards with delicate black lace miniskirts. When they finished their bump and grind we took a table in the middle of the room and ordered drinks. About fifty couples were in the audience. A plastic tablecloth covered each table. The walls were nightclub red. Jorge and I were the only non-blacks.

The master of ceremonies wore an Italian waiter's jacket, black pants, a well-trimmed mustache, and a Sal Maglie shadow. He introduced me from the stage as a reporter for the *New York Times. "So let's show him some Guantánamo and Cuban hospitality!"* I raised my rum collins in a three-quarters *salud* to some polite applause. A singer came out. The four silver-clad backup dancers performed as if they had just finished their first rehearsal shortly before showtime. For this act they were dolled up like the Dallas Cowgirls. They were backed up by a band with guitar, drum, keyboard, and trumpet.

The MC came over. "I didn't know if you were a reporter for the *New York Times* or the *Miami Herald* or what, but the people here have heard of the *New York Times* so I said that." I told him I didn't work for any newspaper, but that I hoped to write about the base situation from the Cuban side. As the singer coochie-cooed across stage the MC shifted from his suave patter to Marxism. He wanted to explain Cuba to me.

The song ended and the dialectical slicky hustled back on stage. He corrected his mistaken introduction. *"Let's give him a welcome from the tips of our shoes to the tops of our heads!"* he said, this time to less applause. I raised my glass less than halfway. He dedicated a song to me. My song was sung by a man who came out in a well-tailored conservative suit and tie, a TV blue shirt, well-shined brown lace shoes, and styled hair. He was a crooner, but I couldn't catch his crooning because a fellow with very large muscles came over to introduce himself and welcome me to Guantánamo. He showed me a card as evidence that he had boxed in competition in Mexico in 1977.

The first singer had done a quick change and now reappeared in gold pumps, a striped and speckled leotard, and fishnet stockings. Yellow ribbons hung strategically around her body. I began to explain to my host what yellow ribbons had come to symbolize in U.S. culture, but the suave Marxist came over again, this time to ask where I was born. Washington, D.C., I said, but my home is in Arizona. "Then I will say you were born in Arizona. The United States is the only country where the capital is also the worst city." He returned to the stage and welcomed me yet a third time, much to my boredom and the audience's. I touched my glass.

Earlier in 1990 I had visited the navy base itself, starting in the United States. Theoretically, to get to the base from Cuba should be simple; head south from the city of Guantánamo until you reach the northeast gate, knock three times, and enter. That's essentially the way it was done until relations broke down in the early 1960s. To travel now from Guantánamo, Cuba, to the U.S. navy base, one must drive seventy-five kilometers west to Santiago de Cuba, take Cubana Airlines 950 kilometers northwest to Havana, hop on the daily charter northwest 225 miles to Miami, fly north 970 miles to Norfolk, Virginia, get approval from the navy, and take one of its twice-weekly charters out of Norfolk 1,200 miles southeast to the base. U.S. military planes can't fly over Cuba proper, so pilots have to dog-leg sharply around the country's southeast coast and angle in for a tense, peacetime landing. After this 3,048 mile, $791 one-way trip, you are virtually face-to-face with where you were four days earlier. José Canseco can slug a home run farther than the distance between the beginning of your trip and its end.

Why are we in Guantánamo? The answer goes back to Columbus and up to this morning's U.S. foreign policy. One day in 1494, Christopher Columbus landed at Guantánamo Bay (he called it Puerto Grande), but he set sail before daybreak the next morning. The English occupied the area in 1741, by then peopled with other Caribbeans, Africans, and Creoles, all under Spanish domain. The British only stayed a short while. Six hundred U.S. marines landed there one 1898 June afternoon during the Spanish-American War. A makeshift marine band, so the legend goes, played "There'll Be a Hot Time in the Old Town Tonight." The marines haven't left yet. Over the years Guantánamo has become an epaulet proudly sewn to the shoulder of America's body politic.

Acquisition of the navy base was sealed with the Platt Amendment, a nifty document the U.S. compelled Cuba to insert in its constitution at the beginning of this century. The amendment confirmed Cuban independence as long as the island agreed to subjugate itself to U.S.

oversight. Between then and 1959 Guantánamo was a low-profile military installation known to sailors for its easy access to wine, women, and the eastern end of a hospitable and beautiful country. (The Platt Amendment was finally dissolved in 1934, but the base lease continued.) Since the gates between the two countries have been locked, minefields have sprouted on both sides.

The base covers forty-five square miles. It faces south to the Caribbean, but a wide and deep bay splits it in two. The bay's east and west coastlines are filled with navy harbors, beaches, docks, and military housing. The bay continues north beyond the limits of the base into Cuba proper, with the odd result that foreign freighters routinely pass through U.S. waters to and from Cuban ports farther inland.

The original agreement between the two countries called for an annual payment of the $2,000 in gold, which has been periodically bumped higher, most recently to $4,085. That's a rental fee of fourteen cents an acre. Cuba has "ultimate sovereignty" over the base, says the treaty, but the lease expires only when both parties agree to abrogate it or when the navy abandons the land. In plain language, the navy has the base as long as it wants. As a result, the United States is in the enviable position of an imperious tenant who establishes the rent, controls the lease, and ignores the landlord.

American occupying forces made their intentions clear. "Our mission," Brigadier General Leonard Wood explained just after the turn of the century, "has been to build an Anglo-Saxon republic in a Latin country where about seventy percent of the people are illiterate; in sum, to establish in a little more than three years a Latin military colony exactly like our great republic."

Five hundred marines guard the fence line surrounding the base. Close to 1,900 navy sailors and their officers train crews from visiting ships in the Atlantic fleet, give each vessel a thorough shakedown, and monitor the airspace over the eastern half of Cuba. Officially, that's the entire mission at Gitmo, as the base is known.

I went out to the fence line one evening. In a watchtower at post 31, a marine had an M-16 slung over his shoulder, and stood looking past the fence into Cuba beyond. "ILANCECORPORALHEDGES-REPORTPOST31ALLSECURENOTHINGUNUSUALTOREPORT," he said. "ALLGENERALORDERSANDSPECIALORDERSREMAIN-THESAME.MYLASTOBSERVATIONREPORTWAS19:45.VEHICLE HEADEDEASTONCASTROBARRIERROAD." At least that's what Lance Corporal Hedges's spiel to his superior officer sounded like. From his lookout platform Hedges could see lights glow in nearby Cuban towns. With night-vision goggles he could focus on detail. Earlier in his four-to-midnight shift he had reported a small Cuban army truck crawling down Castro Barrier Road, the name marines give the wide dirt road paralleling the fence on the Cuba side. "They'll turn their lights on and off," Hedges said. "There's no apparent pattern."

Hedges's partner pressed the binoculars to his eyes and pointed out the nearest Cuban post.

"What are you looking for out there?" I asked.

"Movement."

"Our orders are to shoot to kill Cuban soldiers who come over to the base," said Hedges's boss, Lieutenant Joseph Dennison, "and shoot to wound Americans crossing into Cuba." Platoon commander Orlando Ortiz added, "We're very confident that nobody's going to go over to their side."

"On nights with a full moon you can see the outlines of the mountain crests on the other side," a marine sentry told me. "It's very still. The Cubans sleep inside their posts over there. The junior officer leans on the rail, and you can see him dozing off. When they put their weapons on and start walking patrol you know their replacements are coming in twenty minutes. One Sunday every month they have the equivalent of war games. They're pretty good. They're getting professional," the marine said. "Almost as good as our army."

"They're not much different from us," Lieutenant Dennison said about the Cuban soldiers across the fence. "They just work for a different boss. We pose no threat to them. We're not here to make any trouble. I may be going out on a limb, but I don't think they want any trouble, either." Still, the navy has dug holes beneath the main road connecting the fence line and the main base and filled them with explosives in the event of a Cuban invasion.

Waves of heat lightning flashed through the tropical night. Lance Corporal Hedges radioed in his report as another marine brought him a meal of roast beef, corn, and coffee. He would have preferred a marine seven-course dinner: a pizza and a six-pack.

At first glance the navy base looks like any other military community. Within its boundary children go to school, adults drive along four hundred miles of paved road, girls attend Girl Scout camp, and everyone shops at the exchange and eats at the only McDonald's in Cuba. The high school's interscholastic sports teams play against others in the Defense Department league, teams from Iceland, Bermuda, and Newfoundland. Base housing can be comfortable for officers and their families, and the quarters for everyone else are adequate. A health club,

five outdoor movie theaters, scuba diving, and other distractions fill off-
duty time. Gitmo even has a golf course and horseback riding. For officer
families Gitmo is the navy's Club Med. For most sailors, a year on the
navy's tropical beachfront gets boring fast. The base chaplain told me,
"Because of the isolation, a good marriage will be strengthened here, and
a shaky one will crumble." The base library museum has sea shells,
old bottles (one from 1890, another—Orange Crush—from 1920), and
Spanish-American War photos. A rock monument stands at the spot
Columbus landed, now called Fisherman's Point.

Gitmo's commanding officer during my visit was John Boyd. He was
as much Gitmo's mayor as its military commander. In all, some nine
thousand people lived on his base, including civilian workers and their
families, and foreigners—Jamaicans and Haitians, primarily—who
have jobs there, too. We met in his office.

   Could Gitmo's job be done elsewhere? I asked Boyd. Could the
navy batten down its hatches and sail away? "Roosevelt Roads in Puerto
Rico would be a suitable alternative," he replied, "but that's more
expensive to maintain."

   Boyd talked about the international line of scrimmage. "If Castro
wanted to, he could tear down that fence in no time flat. At first we'd
be overpowered and outmaneuvered. The best we could do is try to
hold out until help came from up north. We have weapons that can
fire twenty-five miles into Cuba if need be."

   Military hardware sits on a hill named for writer Stephen Crane,
on assignment for the *New York Herald* during the Spanish-American-
Cuban war. The Anti-Air Warfare Center, a dozen antennae, satellite
dishes, and other sophisticated equipment monitor Cuban air traffic.
Twice a year marines go on elaborate defensive exercises as if Cuba
was about to invade.

   Before the gates were locked, the base was the area's dominant
industry. Thousands of Cubans worked at Gitmo. They lived in nearby
towns and came every morning by bus and ferry. They even had a
union. After relations broke, an informal agreement allowed the existing Cuban commuters to continue working on the U.S. base, with
no new hires. At the beginning of 1992, twenty-seven Cuban citizens
still worked at Gitmo, their numbers dropping as old age and illness
overcome them. At six o'clock every morning they change into their
work clothes at a striphouse hidden from the base, and walk the final
hundred feet down a cattle chute to the northeast gate. They are the
last unfrozen trickle in our icy relations.

Sixty-five-year-old Santiago Pérez, a sandblaster, was typical of the commuters. After forty-three years of traveling to work every day from his home in Caimanera by foot, boat, and bus, declining health persuaded him to call it quits. His navy co-workers took him to lunch and escorted him to the gate for his final farewell. The other commuters helped him drag metal sheets loaded with clothes, stereos, VCRs, and other goods he'd bought on base with his dollar salary. On his last day a worker can bring just about anything he wants back into Cuba. On all other days bringing anything back is forbidden by Cuban authorities.

The commuters have always been a touchy subject within Cuba. How do the people in Pérez's town of Caimanera take to the commuters? "First there were mistakes in the way people treated us, but they don't bother us now." As he prepared to leave the base, exiled Cuban co-workers who live on base grabbed his hand for the last time and held it tightly. *"Tranquilo,"* they said softly. *"Siempre tranquilo."* Peace be with you always.

The exiled Cuban co-workers who bade Pérez farewell were once commuters themselves who one day simply decided not to go home. Enough Cubans have stayed that they have their own rent-free housing and a restaurant and community center. While their husbands are at work, many Cuban wives turn on their television sets—not to cable stations the base offers, but to Spanish-language broadcasts from Cuba. They watch soap operas, news, and dramas. Just as the city of Guantánamo gets U.S. television from the base, the base receives Cuban television from Guantánamo. No blockade, no jamming, simply over-the-air, normal, superficial Cuban television. Cuban radio comes into the base on the AM dial. Listeners hear headlines on Radio Reloj, the country's twenty-four-hour news station.

Cubans risk their lives trying to swim through swarms of jellyfish or float to the base on old tires. With increasing frequency, they show up at Gitmo. Among many Cubans, it's a well-known method of escape. A young street hustler I met in Céspedes Park in Santiago contemplated the ordeal. "I feel I can do it at night by the deep blue sea." he had told me. "Even with the sharks."

The navy "can neither confirm nor deny" the existence of fence jumpers, as they are called. Instead, the newcomers are hustled off to Florida, where they are treated as if they had been picked up by the Coast Guard or floated ashore. Among marine sentries it's considered a good mark to bring in a fence jumper. Between 1964, when complete records were first kept, and the beginning of 1992, an average of 137 fence jumpers have made their way to the navy base every year.

Gitmo prides itself on the best of small-town qualities with little of the plagues rampant elsewhere. The worst the navy runs into these days is drunken sailors. Marine offenses are far more serious. One Saturday night in the summer of 1986, some marines were sitting around the barracks watching a videotape of *Animal House*. Down the hall, Private First Class Willie A. was asleep. Willie was roundly disliked by virtually every marine who knew him—they said he was a malingerer who habitually faked illness, disloyal, untrustworthy, gutless, slow to follow directions. One officer called him "one of the ten worst marines I've known in my life."

Leathernecks in the barracks said he'd snitched about a marine firing shots over the fence line into Cuba. They didn't want him around, and when they told marine commanding officer Colonel Sam Adams their feelings, he agreed that Willie should be moved to another platoon the following week. As for that weekend, Adams was quoted as saying, "Let him sweat." By the time his attitude about Willie made it to barracks level, a lieutenant had told a squad meeting, "Don't take him up to the third deck and throw him off and kill him, but if he falls down the stairs in the middle of the night, oh well."

About two o'clock Sunday morning, as Willie lay sleeping, ten marines charged his room, blindfolded him with tape, stuck some bedding in his mouth to keep him quiet, and gave him a severe haircut. "He took pride in his hair," one of his attackers later said, "and wore mousse in order to look, how would you say, *GQ*."

This would have been a typical blanket party or "code red," marine jargon for pummeling someone to teach him a lesson, except that the gag blocked Willie's air pipe and forced fluid to fill his lungs. He arrived at the Guantánamo base hospital emergency room short of breath, coughing up blood, complaining of blindness, near death. They MEDIVAC'd him to a Miami hospital, followed by treatment at four more hospitals, including Bethesda Naval.

Heads rolled. Colonel Adams, a well-liked former pro football player, was sent packing to Camp Lejeune, North Carolina. Court-martial charges were pressed against the attackers. Some accepted "other than honorable" discharges. At least one got thirty-eight days in the brig and thirty days' confinement. One had his case dropped for lack of a speedy trial. A three-star marine lieutenant general flew down from Washington and chewed out the entire marine contingent at Guantánamo. Speaking of blanket parties, the general said, according to a number of marines in the audience, "If you want to try one on me, you'll end up dead."

This whole sorry episode in marine history might merely have ended up a fuzzy legend in the corps except that Aaron Sorkin, a young playwright, got wind of it and fashioned it into a fiery courtroom drama. In November 1989, *A Few Good Men* opened at the Music Box on Broadway. It starred Tom Hulce, and ran a healthy fourteen months. The production played off the conflicting values of loyalty, law, honor, and morality. A movie based on the play taken from the Guantánamo events was filmed, starring Tom Cruise, Demi Moore, and Jack Nicholson.

I met a Cuban exile named Harry who worked at the CPO Club on base. He had lived in Caimanera in the 1950s when it was a wide-open town with prostitutes and sailors. "The Cuban government took care of the women in Caimanera and the navy took care of the men. The girls came from all over the country. It was a twenty-four-hour operation. I was a playboy. I partied like hell. I always had a dame. They wouldn't let me in the Bambú Club and the Casino Room because I was black." He tapped his skin. "It pissed me off."

At one point some six hundred workers from Banes commuted to the base. They adapted well to the U.S. military because they had grown up in a town run by an American multinational corporation. "Batista's father and my father were good friends. They were real poor. When Batista was thirteen"—this would have been 1914—"Emilio Galicia left his watch in a bathroom. Batista stole it and ran away from Banes, and that's how he became president. He got money and forgot the little people. I remember seeing Fidel riding in a red convertible in 1947 with his brother-in-law Rafael. They were going to a dance at the American Club."

In the summer of 1963 Harry slipped onto the base. "There was a black market in passes in Caimanera. I used a confiscated one. I waited tables my first job on base.

"I pray for the opening of the base. Fidel has done some nice things, but I'm not going back to Cuba. I don't believe in politicians. They come and they go, but Cuba's always been where I was born." The U.S. Immigration and Naturalization Service classifies Harry as a Permanent Resident Alien. He could have become a full U.S. citizen years ago but decided to keep his Cuban citizenship. Why hadn't he cut the umbilical cord? I was looking for an answer that implied some patriotism to the old country, a whiff of residual loyalty to *fidelismo*.

"Simple," Harry said. "It has to do with my job. If I'm a U.S. citizen, they can lay me off. As a PRA they can't let me go. Being Cuban, I'll never lose my job. I have one year left before I retire. I'll do it then." He laughed. "I've got it made."

From time to time the U.S. has meddled in Cuban affairs from the base. In 1912, during a black rebellion in the eastern end of the country, troops from the base and others who sailed in from the States occupied a few Cuban towns, ostensibly to protect U.S. investments, freeing up Cuban forces to go after the rebels. And Cuba has documented that U.S. arms, ammunition, and landing strips helped Batista in his losing campaign against rebels forty-five years later.

Olga Miranda, a high-ranking expert with the Ministry of Foreign Relations in Havana, is very familiar with this history. I met with Dr. Miranda to learn the official Cuban policy on the base. We met in the ornate sitting room of a well-maintained former mansion in the Vedado section of Havana. A secretary poured me a demitasse of strong coffee. Dr. Miranda carried a fat folder marked "Guantánamo." She said that Cuba's arm had been hammerlocked by the U.S. at the beginning of the century with the original treaty and again in 1934 with a duplicate one.

"We see it as an occupation," she explained. "Since the Revolution there has been violence and provocation along the border. Murders!" Her body shook with fright. "It's part of the continuing history. A popular referendum has rejected the treaty." She showed me copies of the 1901 Platt Amendment, U.S. legislation foisted on Cuba, cables to and from the U.S., and a report from a European conference that called for the return of the base.

"We want a proper solution to eliminate this major point of contention. It is an important item on the agenda between the two countries. Legally, it's ours. Since the Revolution, not one rent check has been cashed. To us, they're not valid."

"Excuse me, but I understand the 1959 check *was* cashed."

"Oh, well." She smiled. "We didn't have a clear idea in the first months of the Revolution. Fidel and Raúl have both advised us to have patience."

"How much patience can you have? The U.S. has held Guantánamo for almost a century."

"We have faith that one day all of our *patria* will be ours. It has caused us a great deal of pain."

If Cuba had invested and reinvested each rent check received since 1959 at a rate equal to the Dow Industrial average, the country would have been $372,310.68 richer by the beginning of 1992. To bank them, though, would have recognized the legitimacy of the base. Instead, Fidel, the master of the photo op, brings the checks out for show and tell. When Jacques Cousteau asked him about Guantánamo the premier opened a drawer in his office desk, reached for an envelope, and laid the U.S. Treasury checks out for all the world to see, as if he were playing solitaire.

Jack Neal, a civilian construction coordinator at the navy base, lived with his wife in Guantánamo, Cuba, before the Revolution. "I have found recollections of the towns on the other side," he said at his office on base. "They had the best people in the world. It was a beautiful country. But by 1958 there was sniping between the different factions. Fidel was in these mountains and Raúl was in those." He nodded west and north. That summer, in fact, Raúl Castro surprised twenty-nine Gitmo servicemen on liberty in Cuba and held them for three weeks. "I got shot at a couple of times and we moved back on base. A lot of the Cuban workers here collected money for the Revolution. Even some Americans gave. Everyone seemed to support Castro." Including three sailors who went AWOL and joined up with the guerrillas for a while.

After the Revolution prostitution was condemned, but during the rebellion it helped Castro and his guerrillas. Nydia Sarabia, the woman who helped engineer Graham Greene's trip to Santiago in 1957, told me, "The prostitutes who catered to the Guantánamo sailors would ask for payment in arms. They would get rifles, bullets, grenades. We got all those arms left over from World War II. The sailors had to pay twice, first with weapons, and then a lot of the prostitutes insisted on being paid in cash, too. They kept the money, of course. The bourgeois Cuban ladies also helped. They would be invited to the formal club on base and get what they could for the Revolution. We had the *red de mujeres*," the women's network, "supporting the guerrillas. We'd also buy things from sailors at the base, like grenades for five pesos each, and bullets for fifty centavos apiece. Brownings. Winchesters. Springfields. So many of our arms during the Revolution were from the United States navy base."

Colonel Solar was waiting for me at seven A.M. when I pulled up to the Brigada Fronteriza administration building. He served me coffee and, using one of the four phones on his desk, summoned a small truck and a driver from the motor pool. I told him that I had been given the dog and pony show at the navy base earlier that year. Now it was his turn to give me *un gran baile del mambo y la rumba*; a song and dance.

We drove east through the Guantánamo countryside toward the base, passing thirty cyclists in black spandex shorts leaning into a 100 K rally. "See that garden?" He pointed to a plot next to a guardhouse where a young soldier saluted and waved us on. "We're growing bananas and yucca. We're trying to be as self-sufficient as possible."

We chatted about Cuba's war vets who had served in Africa (he had put in two years in Angola himself), about the rivalry between Havana and Santiago de Cuba, and Guantánamo's chances in the upcoming baseball season. Solar was a career man with low-key pride in the military, its accomplishments, its professionalism. He was born in 1938, the year Cuba's Communist Party became legalized. Any country's army would be proud to have a soldier of his caliber, but he wouldn't be happy anywhere but in the Fuerzas Armadas Revolucionarias.

We took a right, then a left for a few more kilometers, and started up a slight incline. Finally we got out and walked up a rocky path. A crew of bare-chested civilian construction workers labored to music from a portable radio. Soon we stood under a leafy *ramada* behind a waist-high rock wall perched on the south side of a hill called Malones. The Caribbean glimmered in the distance. The U.S. navy base lay between us and the water. Marines at the base had shown me Malones through their binoculars. Cubans call it El Mirador. The navy calls it Castro's Bunker, believing that Fidel has been there peering into the base. (One U.S. marine lieutenant had performed an imitation of Fidel for me, cigar and all, in a rumored visit by *el comandante* to the lookout point.) Solar pointed out base landmarks, accurate down to specific location and even name. He was familiar with the Anti-Air Warfare Center, the marine barracks, and the elaborate docking facilities. I mentioned the USS *Nashville*, a ship almost two football fields in length that I had toured when I was on base. "Oh, yes," he said matter-of-factly. "We know that ship." We had as clear a view as an enemy could want.

I looked down at the gate where the commuters enter on their way to work each morning and at the U.S. lookout towers that dot the fence line from the gate west to Guantánamo Bay itself.

If you could sit down and talk with your counterparts, I asked the colonel, waving toward the navy base, what would you say?

"I don't want to talk with them," he answered in measured tones. "It's our property. Our land. It's not a real border. I would talk with them when they treat us with respect and in a harmonious manner. When the United States realizes that the land is ours, we'll welcome it back into our heart. We struggle with it daily, not militarily, but politically and diplomatically."

In an odd set of circumstances, so too did the government of Great Britain. I had recently learned of an English wife on the U.S. navy base who wanted to get a British birth certificate for her newborn baby. She contacted her embassy in Havana, which had a dilemma. Was the infant born in Cuba?—in which case the embassy of Great Britain in Cuba should issue the certificate; or on U.S. territory?—in which case a British consulate in the States should issue it. The embassy turned to London for guidance. The answer: issue the birth certificate in Cuba.

"It's very costly for the U.S. to maintain a base here," Solar continued. "It's like an island on an island. We are prepared, but defensively, not offensively. We are prepared to defend our land." He scanned the airspace above the base. "No one can invade our territory. It's a reality."

Solar walked me over to a large round hole in the ground behind the lookout perch where the construction crew worked. He said it was going to be an elevator shaft going deep into the hill we walked on. Partway down the hill, we turned off the main path to another rocky path past some trees. We stood at the concealed entrance to an enormous fortified concrete tunnel. Two soldiers guarded the opening. It was a Cuban military hideout and command center, buried deep in a mountain.

We went down a large tiled passageway reminiscent of the tunnel beneath the U.S. Capitol, only more secure. The electrical generator was out that day, so a soldier led the way with a hand torch. The effect was to make the military bunker seen even more clandestine. We followed another corridor lined with framed pictures of the countryside, the Brigada at work, and the Castro brothers.

At the end of the second hall we walked through some curtains and into a circular room. Propped on a low table was a bas relief topographical map of the U.S. navy base. It was so detailed that we could see streets in the family neighborhoods and outbuildings in security zones. The Cuban military knew the base better than most Americans living there. An underground conference room, capable of withstanding overhead bombardment, was down the hall. Solar offered a slight smile. "We use it for meetings, especially when Raúl comes."

We got back in the truck and drove to the barracks area. Air-conditioned dormitories, just beyond the soccer field, were white-glove clean, with forty double-decker bunk beds filling each room. A picture of Lenin hung on the wall. We ate in the mess—as decent as the one in the marine cafeteria on the other side—and walked outside to a garden where onions, tomatoes, and peppers grew.

Solar wouldn't reveal how many soldiers were attached to the Brigada Fronteriza, but a minimum of five hundred seems a reasonable estimate. They have a gym, pool, rec hall, bar, sauna, and squash and basketball courts. A chess tournament was scheduled for the Lenin-Martí room. Soldiers played Ping-Pong, dominoes, and browsed in the library. Available authors included Joseph Heller, Engels, Gore Vidal, Gorbachev, and Castro. That night's movie was *Robocop*.

While the U.S. and its allies held Desert Shield exercises, Cuba's armed forces were holding what they called Cuban Shield maneuvers in response to increased activity at the Guantánamo base. Castro said, "It is better for us to mobilize twenty times and have nothing happen, for us to mobilize a hundred times and have nothing happen, than for something to happen and find us demobilized."

Considerable acreage on the Brigada Fronteriza grounds was devoted to farming; Solar's self-sufficiency goal was played out here with extensive organic gardening, banana trees, and crop rotation. "We plant two hundred to 250 trees a year," he said.

"We're experimenting with a female all-volunteer force. This is one of the first units to get them. They're working out fine." The women's dorm resembled the men's quarters in most respects except that many beds had sizable dolls propped up on them. Four soldiers walked by, and Solar suggested I talk with them. They all wore earrings, flowers in their hair, and wide smiles. Cuba has a lovely army.

Solar had a military motorboat with a crew of two waiting for us at Guantánamo Bay so we could cross over to Caimanera, slightly more than a kilometer from the base. These are the waters through which float Cubans fleeing to the U.S. via the navy base, but the colonel belittled the phenomenon. "Only eight or ten people a year try that," he said, off by a factor of fifteen or so, according to the U.S. statistics. "Mainly they're people who have trouble with the law."

We docked and passed through a backyard where a game of dominoes was the center of attraction. We stayed long enough to watch the eldest player win the noontime game. These dockworkers in shorts and loose shirts never once looked up at the passing foreigner or the army colonel.

For a town known to navy lore as dedicated to debauchery, Caimanera had been cleaned up so much that only a couple of the old buildings that once housed brothels still stand. One has been converted into a crafts workshop, and the other into another of Cuba's ubiquitous museums. Down the street, a small sign quoted Raúl Castro: JOKES, HALF TRUTHS, AND LIES ARE DIVISIVE AND COUNTERREVOLUTIONARY.

The country has pumped money into Caimanera since the Revolution, built new housing projects, and trained former prostitutes for more respectable jobs. The town, whose economy is based on salt, has been virtually rebuilt. Everyone I met seemed to have a relative who had once worked at the navy base. Gitmo was like a birthmark, so enormous as to be almost unnoticeable. At the edge of town, a billboard called Caimanera

CUBA'S FIRST ANTI-IMPERIALIST BUNKER

The people in this anti-imperialist bunker were easy to approach and chat with. A woman told of the overflights and rumbles from navy war games. "Five years ago when they had maneuvers the vibrations were so strong you couldn't even put a glass of water on the table. We had to turn up the radio to drown them out." An artist at a storefront gallery talked about her paintings. Young boys in karate whites waved as they practiced their kicks. On his flower-lined front porch, a retired bus driver from the base said, "Before the revolution there was more to do, but there was no real work here. Now there is."

Retired commuters such as the bus driver are due U.S. government pensions for their service. The Trading with the Enemy Act, however, forbids paying them their due, estimated in 1991 at $4.5 million, unless they leave home and renounce their Cuban citizenship. Just before I left Caimanera a customer smiled as he left a sidewalk shooting gallery on whose walls was painted an admonition from Fidel: EVERY CUBAN SHOULD KNOW HOW TO SHOOT, AND SHOOT WELL.

We took the boat back across Guantánamo Bay and returned to brigade headquarters.

The highway from Guantánamo to Baracoa follows the Caribbean for a lovely stretch, then turns north onto the most treacherous road I had yet driven. This second half was also the last major link to be completed in the national transportation grid. Baracoa, on the far northeast coast, was shut off from conventional traffic until after the Revolution when a highway begun under Batista was completed. Until then, goods and people reached Baracoa by plane or boat, or by horse, motorcycle, or jeep over terrible unpaved roads. Baracoa's isolation became a source of pride to the townspeople, but practicality dictated a link between it and the rest of the country. The road had 180 degree switchbacks, sharp curves, steep hills, and random debris from a storm the previous evening. Tree branches and rocks were strewn on the Farola Highway, as the road is called, and work crews had yet to reach them. At a few places riders I'd pick up and I had to get out in a howling storm and move clods of dirt, tree limbs, and small chunks of boulders that had rolled across the highway. Then, within ten minutes, the sun shone, the roadway was clear, and *guajiros* milled about attending to their daily routine.

Despite the brooding, deep-set eyes of José Martí staring out from every building, this part of the country lacked billboards with the revolutionary ferocity found elsewhere. In fact, along the initial stretch of the drive, five billboards in a row, Burma Shave style, speak of the Revolution as gently as the sea on whose shoreline they're planted. In the first, the kindly face of Máximo Gómez looks out from a Cuban flag next to the words THE CUBAN REVOLUTION IS NOT JUST IN THE HEART, followed by one with BUT IN THE MINDS OF ITS CHILDREN, then IT'S IN THE WIND AND THE PALM TREES (accompanied by raised machetes), then IN ITS CREEKS AND CAVERNS (artwork of pastoral scene), and finally, IT LIVES IN ALL THE AMERICAS (with a map of every country from Mexico south to Argentina).

Baracoa was established twenty-two years after Columbus first arrived in Cuba. It was the island's first settlement. Its strategic location demanded towers and fortresses to protect against unfriendly ships at sea and troops on horseback. One of the forts was high on a hill with a commanding view of the Caribbean. Today it has become El Castillo, a comfortable hotel with a full dining room and an empty swimming pool. I checked in and drove over to the Matachín Museum, once Fort Matachín.

In Havana Salvador González had suggested that I see Alejandro Hartman Matos in Baracoa. So had Ariel James in Santiago and Rebeca Ulloa in Guantánamo. As director of the Matachín Museum, Dr. Hartman was the town's walking reference room. Baracoa stretches east to west along the coastline, no more than a few blocks north and south, with a comfortable seaside walk to complement it. Hartman's museum anchors the east end of Baracoa's Malecón.

Hartman was in his office. He thrives on out-of-town visitors, happy to drop his normal duties to show off his town and its history. My mind, though, was on the increasing shortages I had seen in recent weeks, along with longer lines, more grumbling, and louder complaints about distribution of food and clothing. Hartman and I are the same age, and we felt an immediate and easy kinship. The first Hartman in Cuba in fact, a German émigré in 1820, was named Felipe Hartman Miller. Hartman and I spoke of Marx and literature, the U.S. and history. He quoted Sartre and Carpentier, Martí and Castro. He had a solution for the food problem.

"If the small farmers each had a plot of land and the state set the price for agricultural produce, this country would be back on its feet within three months. We want to show the world that it can be done. There is no precedent for what we are trying to do. And now we have to do it alone. Marxism and Darwinism—for an organism to grow, it needs a host organism, or at least it has to live in relation to another. For us it was the Soviet Union. Now we have to attempt the same but without another organism. All the socialist countries we relied on for trade are experimenting with another system. Capitalism doesn't interest me. Are Marxism and Darwinism irreconcilable? They're wobbly, but they've got an ongoing compatibility. Capitalism isn't a problem, it's a solution—but only a short range one. This is a great concern to people all over the country. The city people, the factory workers, and others who volunteer to toil in the countryside, they make a valiant effort, but they simply aren't farmers. Times are very hard now. And they'll get worse."

Hartman told me about a man in Baracoa, typical of the economy. "He lives on the black market. He has to. He has a car and he gets gas that way. This fellow and his family aren't *jineteros* off the street. These are respectable people. Simply put, his family couldn't live without the *mercado negro*. They get meat on the table, gas in the car, even rum to drink."

We took a drive around town. There was hardly enough motor traffic for a two-car collision. A boy on a bicycle steered with his left hand while his right hand clutched the frets of a guitar whose neck was perched on his shoulder. So few passenger cars traveled the streets of Baracoa that people reacted to my five-year-old Japanese rental as if I had driven a brand new XKE straight from a Jaguar showroom. I saw a cluster of women in a straggly queue and asked Hartman why they were there. "They're in line to get a number so that when that store opens tomorrow there'll be some order." The Casa del Chocolate, the Chocolate House, tempted me, but it had closed a few months earlier with no reopening in sight. We passed the Hotel de La Rusa, established by a Russian lady who had fled to Cuba from the Revolution in her own country. Fidel and Che, Hartman said, stayed there.

"Hello, room service? Could you send up some black beans and rice as soon as possible? Listen, we're kind of in a hurry. Better throw in a bottle of rum. Room 236. Castro. Right. That's C-a-s-t-r-o." He cups a hand over the phone. "Jesus, Che—is my name that difficult? You know, if we ever win this harebrained revolution, I'm going to make sure everyone in this infernal country learns how to spell." And so was born the great literacy campaign.

As we got out of the car back at his office, we heard a band playing in the street behind the museum. It was part of a funeral procession. The whole town turned out for the event. "Funeral parades are part of the Spanish traditions we've maintained. You find that a lot around here."

This provincial little town captured me on sight. On my way over to meet Hartman at the museum the next morning, I passed schoolkids in their Pioneer blues, housewives throwing buckets of water into the gutter, shoppers hoping to find something to shop for, and factory buses picking up workers. Their pace was unhurried, for rushing would accomplish nothing. Not enough customers filled the local Socialism or Death bakery to form a line. A breeze blew in from the sea, brisk and warm. Baracoa's Malecón had few loafers; I was its only dawdler.

"Did you see the *National Geographic* article about Havana?" Hartman asked over coffee in his office. Hartman had schooled and worked in the capital and still traveled there often.

I had, adding, "It was a fair treatment of the city, don't you think?"

"That's what I heard, but I never saw it. I subscribe to the magazine; it takes a long time, but it always arrives. Except that issue. When I opened the envelope, *this* was inside." He handed me an agriculture journal from the Soviet Union.

State suppression? The Havana piece was prepared with the cooperation of city officials; it should have pleased them. Had this tame and friendly article been banned? A less sinister, more benign explanation holds that someone in the post office had heard about the article, took Hartman's home for his family, and replaced it with the handiest magazine that fit the envelope.

Hartman bragged of some fifty-six archaeological sites in the Baracoa

area. His museum showcased the local population from before Columbus to the present. "We've found bones of the Taino," pre-Columbian
Indians who had a well-developed agricultural system, "also ceramic
bowls from the tenth century. The Taino were short with smooth,
olive-colored skin. You can still see those qualities in Baracoans, even
though virtually all the Indians were killed by the conquistadors."

Hartman's museum was a few steps better than most civic treasuries
of past life. One could take a disdainful view of the instant museums
that have popped up all over Cuba trumpeting the Revolution, but
museums in all countries are laden with national chauvinism; Cuba's
simply wears its on its *guayabera*. Done well, as at the Matachín
Museum, the island's history takes on genuine continuity, giving a
feel for the country's dim past.

We reached a display that said, *The conquistadors not only massacred
and robbed Indian riches, but justified it by spreading hundreds of falsehoods
about Indian customs*. As we entered the next room, where piracy and
British warships figured, an unassuming man walked through the main
door. "Look at him. He's Indian," Hartman said loud enough for him
to hear. "See?" He spoke of the fellow as if he were a mannequin.
"He's got that light bronze skin. He's a friend. He took part in the
Revolution. ¡Chico! I'd like to introduce you to a foreign visitor."
Chico stopped combing his hair and walked over. "I told him you
fought in the Revolution."

All I could think to say was, "When? Where?"

His answers were as short as my questions. "Nineteen fifty-seven.
In these parts." His name was José Luis Rodríguez. He was forty-
eight years old.

"Chico, tell him about the rest of your military service."

"Oh, yes. Well, I was in Angola." The descendant of the Taino
Indians began to comb his hair again. "Ethiopia, too."

I learned about the French influence on coffee and sugar production,
and the United Fruit Company. I saw coronets, machetes, and a pen
used by the *mambís*—independence fighters—in the 1890s. A picture
of workers' strikes at mid-century on one wall followed another of the
house where the local *fidelista* movement was founded. Hartman's Indian friend Chico could have been an exhibit in this room, too, combing
his hair and giving terse answers to blunt questions. Next were pictures
of "infiltrators and counterrevolutionaries sent from Washington," and
of the five Baracoa men who died fighting them. Hartman turned to
me. "If the United States was so friendly with Cuba, why didn't it

help the people who needed it most rather than support the worst elements in Cuban society? Look at these statistics." He pointed to a chart on the wall:

ACHIEVEMENTS OF SOCIALISM IN BARACOA

	1959	1989
doctors	4	117
nurses	4	361
dentists	1	39
buses	0	103
cultural institutions	0	18
sports centers	1	26

My favorite picture in the museum showed Magdalena Monasse, the Russian who had run the boarding house. She wore a society hat, sunglasses, a Red Cross pin, and a *fidelista* flag.

I spent the late afternoon in the small town square, actually a large triangle formally called Plaza Cacique Hatuey, watching and talking. Two girls about ten played chess while a friend kibitzed from the side. Next to them two men in their early twenties played checkers. A young woman in a screened-in kiosk sold the provincial daily and *Granma*, which arrived from Havana by noon every day. Two teenagers played Ping-Pong. Four old men surrounded a table playing dominoes; they looked as if they had been sitting in the park since the days when Batista was an army sergeant. From the far end of the plaza, across from a beauty parlor, a twenty-five-piece municipal woodwind band entertained slowly passing onlookers.

The schoolgirls had been replaced at the chessboard by two athletic boys about fifteen. As each game ended the loser walked off and another opponent showed up to play the winner, as if on cue. Three winners later I approached as if part of the daily script of Baracoa's plaza. The last winner nodded. We took colors opposite to our skin. He checkmated me handily. The sun had set, and the park was getting dark. No one else showed up. "Another?" I said. It was the first word between us. He nodded. After five moves the recreation director came around picking up equipment from all the tables. "Until the Special Period, we played much later under the lights." The band had not yet finished its repertoire. I drifted over as they played a medley of Broadway show tunes, movie themes, and marching songs. I was envious of the oboe player, disarmed by his station in life as nothing more than an afternoon musician for a small-town Caribbean ensemble. I could think of no more noble calling than playing oboe in the Baracoa municipal band.

Hartman's home, a few blocks away, was a roomy place on a quiet main street near the Baptist church. His backyard grew avocados, lemons, bananas, and guanábanas. A drawing of Jesus hung on the wall. We took seats in the front room where his wife Nydia soon joined us. Hartman admired Che Guevara, expounding on his philosophy and optimism. To Hartman and many others, Guevara was a symbol whose best years benefited their own. Nydia said, "We'd love to invite you for dinner but all we could serve you would be fried eggs."

"Maybe some yucca," her husband added. He turned on the color television. "At one time we could have served you fish."

We watched a veteran Cuban journalist being interviewed about his life, which, in the 1950s, included some years in the United States. "I served in the U.S. Air Force," he told the interviewer, who seemed jolted by the revelation. "The service was inconsequential but I learned English and also some technical skills." His career included reporting for Cuba from England, Vietnam, and Spain. Nydia brought us each a large bowl of vanilla ice cream with rich chocolate syrup on top.

When the people of Maisí talk of a nearby bewildering country, they mean Haiti. I wanted to see Maisí, thirty-eight kilometers from Baracoa at Cuba's easternmost tip. Hartman and I set out along a couple of paved roads through small communities outside town, and finally a dirt road. The rainfall that had hampered my drive up the Farola Highway had also laid waste to the Maisí road. Foliage grew as thick as the mud we drove through. Between copses of palms and dense jungle shrubbery we could make out occasional *bohíos*, the thatched homes of the outback. Cuba's beauty had a soft integrity to it; comforting, almost caressing. The Nissan sloshed forward until the road proved impassable even for first gear. We abandoned the car and walked.

Soon we arrived at Abra de Yumurí, a settlement on the banks of the Yumurí River where it spills into the Atlantic. To reach Maisí we would have needed a jeep—first to cross a 250 foot wooden bridge spanning the Yumurí, then to climb up a slippery hill.

Still, Abra de Yumurí satisfied my search for the end of Cuba. Its one business was the open-air Cafetería Yumurí, a bare light bulb hanging over a refrigerator and a rustic stove. Four men played dominoes on the porch. Everyone knew Hartman; he was greeted as a benevolent *cacique*, the local political chieftain who inquires of your welfare and asks about crops. We walked across the bridge. "It's made of cedar. Its construction shows the French influence in the area." Canoes were tied to the bridge's girders. Hartman pointed to a spot just beyond the hill leading up from the river. "When bananas come from Maisí, they're hauled by mule to a spot over there. Then they're loaded onto a funicular to the bottom where they're loaded into boats." Hartman walked off to talk with someone. All I could hear was the faint clicking of dominoes over the sound of the Yumurí emptying into the Caribbean.

A short distance away, heavy dark women in loose dresses folded their bodies over to fill buckets with water from the mouth of the river, much as I suppose women on the shores of other islands throughout the West Indies were doing at that same moment. By the time we meandered back across the bridge, recreational activity had taken a more active turn. The four dominoes players had taken a break, but nearby, on marshland skirting the Caribbean, a dozen energetic boys under ten had started a baseball game. They played with a hard rubber ball and a stick for a bat. They had one glove among them, and an outfield that stretched to the Lesser Antilles. They all wore shorts, a couple had shirts, and one boy wore shoes. On this marvelous makeshift playing field, if you hit Haiti you should get a ground rule double. Once a foul ball popped into the mouth of the Yumurí, to be retrieved by a fully dressed woman up to her waist in the brackish backwater. These were the future stars of the Liga Nacional, and if they were good enough, the Liga Selectiva, and if they were among the best, the national team that plays other countries abroad.

A lefty whacked his first pitch to the edge of Cuba. A barefoot outfielder ran it down among the seashells and tiny rocks in the loamy Caribbean beachfront. The southpaw crossed a pile of shells that doubled as home plate as an outfielder heaved the ball in from the light blue sea. These kid stars were acting out passion plays with each pitch. Through all the claptrap of baseball diplomacy, defections, and amateur status versus state-sponsored athletics, the screams of these dozen happy kids jumping up and down alongside the sea stood out as the most potent, wholesome vision I could take with me. I've kept that image in my mind, both the romance and the reality of it, afraid that I'll never again encounter such unadulterated baseball in my life.

"A thousand tongues would not suffice to describe the things of novelty and beauty I saw, for it was all like a scene of enchantment." Columbus wrote this after seeing Baracoa in 1492. Those words, at least, have been ascribed to him. Of course not Baracoa proper, but the land he saw from his ship. Then again, much of Columbus's account of that journey has been reconstructed rather than taken directly from his own writing, so he may have been describing an entirely different place altogether.

Pre-Columbian Indians, Spanish conquest, French influence, independence from Spain, U.S. neocolonialism, the Revolution and its effect—all these Hartman spoke of with easy authority. But he was most proud of the Columbus visit. Dr. Hartman has gone to great lengths to prove that not only did Columbus sail into the cove at Baracoa, but that he left a cross as well. Hartman walked me over to Nuestra Señora de la Asunción, Baracoa's original name, a church built in 1805 to replace an older one. "Columbus describes the Yunque mountains visible from the inlet. It's in his words. He says they were gray and black. He called the area Porto Santo because it reminded him of a Portuguese saint. He called the whole island Juana after Spain's infant princess, Doña Juana. "You should read *Cuba Before Columbus*. The author, Mark Harrington, visited here in 1915. He wrote about the Indian culture and the archaeological sites." We got to the church and waited for Valentín Sanz, Baracoa's youthful *padre*.

The famous cross was planted by Columbus at the mouth of a cove "on some rough stones," according to the account of the first trip as reconstructed by Bartolomé de las Casas. What we know of the next few hundred years at that site can be attributed to fact, speculation, inference, oral accounts, likelihood, supposition, logic, or the sort of retro-history that has anointed the *mojito* at La Bodeguita del Medio as Hemingway's favorite. Regardless, accepted wisdom holds that the cross was found under a vine in 1510 by Diego Velázquez's expeditionaries and used "to Christianize the aborigines." Baracoa became the island's first Spanish settlement, and its capital. Later that decade the cross was rehidden so it wouldn't be moved to the new capital, Santiago de Cuba. In 1530 the cross was brought to the local church, which, over the centuries, survived occasional plunder by pirates. The cross was rescued during one eighteenth-century attack that otherwise destroyed the rest of the church. When the replacement church was finished, the one at whose entrance Hartman and I now stood, the cross was stored there for safekeeping.

It's still there. Father Valentín went to get it while Hartman and I waited near the pulpit. "The cross was discovered on the far side of the cove," Hartman said. "Originally, it stood about two and a third meters high. Over the years souvenir hunters have whittled away fragments of the Columbus cross. It hasn't been well protected."

The *padre* carried the cross out. It was made of dark wood, about a meter high and a little more than half a meter across, adorned with metal attached to it in the eighteenth and nineteenth centuries. We handled the valuable piece of history as if it were an ordinary family heirloom. As we held the five-hundred-year-old artifact, Valentín said that up to 250 worshippers come for weekend Masses at his church, and fifteen or so show up for weekday morning Mass. "Except Wednesdays. We have fifty people then."

I handed the cross back to Hartman. "You've touched wood that Columbus touched," he said.

Had I? Hartman said European scholars had confirmed that the cross had been left by Columbus in Baracoa on Saturday, December 1, 1492. In the mid-1980s an investigator at Cuba's Forestry Research Institute in Havana brought a Belgian specialist, R. Dechamps, to Baracoa to ascertain the cross's authenticity. Dechamps took a four-centimeter sliver of the cross back to the Royal Museum of Central Africa in Tervuren. The Cuban wood anatomy expert went, too. They compared the wood from the cross to samples from thousands of different trees from Europe, Africa, and the Americas, and reduced the options to a type of wood that has a hundred species, twenty-six of which grow in Cuba. Twenty of these were ruled out due to tree size. Of the remaining six, they concluded that the cross of Columbus was made from *Coccoloba diversifolia*—common name in Spanish *uvilla*—closely related to the seagrape tree that thrives in the area where the cross is said to have been found. Concluded the scientists in Belgium: "Columbus hadn't brought the cross from the Old World; it was as Cuban as Baracoa itself." If they are right, and Columbus did use native wood to make the cross, this would make him the first white man to deforest in the New World. Said Padre Valentín: "This is the continent's oldest relic."

The next spot on Hartman's Columbus tour of Baracoa was the sound where Columbus landed and left the cross. We traipsed through vines hugging the ground, stumbled over hidden roots, and made it to the beach that surrounds the cove. "Columbus spent eight days on his ship here." Above us, a construction crew was at work on a large building. "That's going to be a hotel. It will look out over the cove where Columbus came ashore and left the cross. It will have sixty rooms, a pool, a bar, a restaurant and a cabaret. Guests will come down here to a natural beach. It will be called Hotel Porto Santo, after Columbus's name for the surroundings." They hoped to have it ready in time for the quincentenary brouhaha.

Hartman's Columbus saga seemed convincing until I returned to Santiago, where Ariel James at the UNEAC office explained otherwise. "Columbus never landed there." We spread my map of Cuba on his desk. "If you read his diary it shows he landed *here*." He placed his finger at Guardalavaca on the north coast west of Baracoa.

"But according to Hartman—"

"That's a *theory*. It's only a theory. There has been extensive research done to show where Columbus landed. It is conclusive. Without a doubt it was not Baracoa."

"Does this controversy—"

"It's no controversy. There is simply nothing to prove that Columbus was ever there. The country's historical society has determined that he disembarked *here*. Experts from Spain and elsewhere have analyzed the sites and Columbus's journal. There is no possibility that Columbus landed there."

"And the cross? I thought it had been authenticated."

"Yes, it has been authenticated. As to date and type of wood. But not as to origin."

Thoroughly confused, I registered at the Motel Leningrado for a day before driving into the Sierra Maestra. I chose the Leningrado because it was at San Juan Hill, site of the famous battle between U.S. and Spanish troops in which Teddy Roosevelt starred, while Stephen Crane and a passel of other foreign journalists watched. Spain surrendered; the U.S. had freed Cuba.

That's the accepted lore. But Cuban independence fighters were already beating the Spanish, and had U.S. troops not intervened, Spain would have soon withdrawn from the country anyway. Further, a contingent of mambís—the Cuban liberationists—was on hand at San Juan Hill, too. Yet from the legend you'd think Cuba simply supplied the hill and took a backseat to watch the war play out. When Spain surrendered to U.S. troops, the stars and stripes replaced the Spanish flag, and mambís were barred from Santiago. Cuba, in its War of Independence, simply went from the Spanish column to the U.S. column as if the country were a prize in a game show.

With San Juan Hill emblazoned in every U.S. history book, I expected an almost impenetrable hill with jagged rocks and steep slopes. The doorman at the Leningrado pointed me to the top. "Follow that road over there and keep walking." The angle of the paved road was barely noticeable, and after ten minutes I was on a flat stretch with lots of plaques and monuments. A couple walked by on their way to a nearby amusement park. I asked them how to get to the top of San Juan Hill. They looked around, then back at me. "You're there. This is it." I looked around, then back at them. "I'm there? This is it?" After all my expectations from history class indoctrination, this hill seemed better suited for testing a carpenter's level. San Juan is a pissant hill.

Roosevelt and his Rough Riders followed hundreds of other troops in combat that day and absorbed substantial losses. If this was a great victory, the participants certainly didn't think so at the time. Roosevelt sent word to President McKinley afterward: "We are within measurable distance of a terrible military disaster."

The hilltop is nicely landscaped with palms and pines, and has a 360 degree view of the surrounding valleys. Closer in you can see a ferris wheel at the amusement park, an array of monuments, and the Tomb of the Unknown Mambí. A few lookout towers and cannons have been preserved. Of all the small war tributes on San Juan Hill, only two refer to foreign assistance, and then just as a reminder that U.S. forces did not act alone. The main memorial mentions the blood *of the brave and true Cuban insurgents and that of the generous American soldiers who sealed a covenant of liberty and fraternity between the two nations*. Nowhere on San Juan Hill are Teddy Roosevelt and his Rough Riders mentioned. Not once. One last sign read, *Show your interest in this site—care for the grounds and the works that grace it*.

I took a bus to Céspedes Park, next to the Hotel Casagranda where a man wearing a cap saying 100% WITH NORIEGA was singing to a bareheaded man on the bench next to him. Down the street was the Casa de la Trova, an open-air center for singers of traditional local music. I had finished *The Mambo Kings*, and now I wanted to see if any old-timers recalled the fictional Cesar or Nestor Castillo from fifty years ago. Gerardo Aldana Calzado offered to help. Gerardo worked at the Casa de la Trova and saw my search as a grand opportunity to meet some of the elder statesmen of the Santiago music scene. We agreed to get together a few days later when I returned from a brief trip.

The opening game of the baseball season took place that evening. The game was televised from Matanzas, where the captain of the home town Henequeneros spoke to a full house during pregame ceremonies.

He equated victory on the playing field with victory in the sugar fields. Both seasons were beginning. In the bleachers, Young Pioneers flashed large cards spelling out

¡MATANZAS! ¡PIONEROS! ¡SOCIALISMO!

Go team go.

Cuba has no traveling salesmen, consequently no traveling salesman jokes. Humor in Cuba needs no salesmen, however; it travels on its own, racing through neighborhoods, cane fields, on buses and in lines. The jokes are straight, double entendre, political, sexual, global, local. They target the Castro brothers, dimwitted neighbors, the bureaucracy, the food shortage, sexy women and macho men. Not a day went by when a hitchhiker didn't pass on some wit, be it flippant, intricate, dumb, or sophisticated. A lot of jokes I didn't understand—they involved jazzy Cuban idioms, inflections too subtle for foreign ears, implicit punch lines, or popular prejudices I was ignorant of.

One joke I heard from a woman I picked up as I set out for the site of the second most significant arrival in Cuba's history. There was no doubt where this landing took place—Playa las Coloradas, on the eastern shore of the Gulf of Guacanayabo along the south coast. Nor when—early December 1956. Nor why—to instigate a revolution overthrowing Fulgencio Batista. Nor who—Fidel Castro, Raúl Castro, Che Guevara, and seventy-nine others.

"Have you heard the one about Bush and Fidel at hell's gate?" It was my mention of the Brothers C that prompted the hitchhiker to open up. "Well, both Bush and Fidel recognize each other," she continued, "and when the devil lets them in, they both blurt out, 'I've got to call my office and let them know *he's* here.' The devil lets Bush use the phone first. After he calls Quayle the devil says, 'That'll be one hundred dollars.' Then Fidel rings up Raúl and tells him, 'Bush is here!' Afterward, the devil says, 'Okay, that costs five centavos.'

" 'Five centavos?' Bush complains. 'I had to pay a hundred dollars!'

" 'Well, yes,' the devil replies, 'but your call was long-distance. His is local.' "

Instead of getting on the Central Highway I detoured to the town of El Cobre, where Cuba's most famous church sits on a hill on the edge of town. I dropped off the joker at an intersection near a sign indicating a Baptist seminary and drove into a town thick with historical events for each century: a copper mine opens in the mid-1500s with slave labor; in the 1600s three boys find a wooden image of Mary, identified as the Virgin of Charity capable of miracles, with her baby Jesus; a slave revolt succeeds in the 1700s; the copper mine, forsaken long ago, is reopened in the 1800s—this time with free labor; finally in the 1900s the Virgin of Charity is named Cuba's patron by the Pope.

The Basilica had not yet opened up to the public for the day—morning mass was still in session—so I drove to the town plaza, where I parked in front of one of the two coffee shops. By going to both, I was able to get a thimbleful of coffee, a glass of milk, and a couple of fried items that can only be described as a cross between latkes and Dunkin' Donuts.

I was interested not so much in the church or the Virgin of Charity as I was in a side chapel where visitors, over the years, have left offerings to the Virgin. A busload of medical students toured the chapel with me. Crowded onto the walls were crutches, leg braces, military medals, banners from the Revolution, police patches, letters, a medallion from a Russian visitor, and another from the 1987 Pan American games in Indianapolis. Some people call El Cobre the Cuban Lourdes. I was hoping to find the Nobel Prize medal Hemingway had given to the Cuban people. It had been placed in the sanctuary.

The medal was missing. The only object left under glass was a *Life* magazine spread on Hemingway turning the medal over to his buddy, Fernando Campoamor.

Sister Lucía, who worked at the Basilica, told me the story. On May 6, 1988, two fellows in their twenties came to the church. They cut the telephone lines. They broke the glass protecting Ernest Hemingway's Nobel medallion, pocketed the prize, and made their getaway in a waiting taxi. It created a national scandal. Two days later a jeweler in Santiago said he found the medal under a rock near his house. Two days after that he confessed that he was a party to the theft. "The initial news reports were accurate," Sister Lucía said. "But when they dramatized it, well, that was not so good. It was very exciting around here for a while. The medal is now in the custody of the Archbishop of Santiago. It will be returned when we can arrange a secure place for it here."

At Bayamo, I stopped at a hotel restaurant for lunch and exercised my second-class privilege as a "foreign technician (temporary)." Evidently that didn't happen too often at this place, and two assistant managers and their boss got involved before they would grant me the status of a commoner to pay with pesos instead of dollars.

Clusters of hitchhikers along the Central Highway jumped up and down whenever passenger cars drove by, as if they wanted to be on *Let's Make a Deal*. In urban areas Cubans hoping for rides would lean into the streets if you rounded a corner or slowed to a few kilometers an hour. In the countryside, one person would stand by the road while his party stood back. West of Bayamo a billboard said:

IN THE MIDDLE OF EVERY PROBLEM IS THE SOLUTION

"What do you think of that?" I said to keep the conversation going with a man who, since he had gotten in, had praised Fidel with all his heart, then equivocated, championed the Revolution for its glorious achievements, then condemned it for its sorrowful condition, spoke of the horrific crime rate in the United States and the great movies made there. His home telephone hadn't worked in two months and he had adjusted to a home with no phone. He was on his way to visit an uncle who worked as an accountant at one of the sugar mills. He was pleased that a foreigner was visiting the landing site of Fidel's boat, a sizable second-hand yacht bought for fifteen thousand dollars from an American named Ericson who called it *Granma*; Ericson must have been an affectionate sort.

I recommend a leisurely weekday afternoon drive through eastern Cuba to everyone. South of the highway the Sierra Maestra, a deep blue shroud protecting its settlements and history, stretches more than eighty miles from the Gulf of Guacanayabo to the city of Santiago de Cuba. I took a secondary provincial highway that rolls through sugar country and small towns, passing new housing, general stores, and medical clinics. Men on horseback with machetes strapped to their hips and lariats tied to their saddles rode in clusters; curled sweat-stained straw hats rested on their heads. The road was in admirable shape.

The drive paralleling the Sierra has stayed with me not because it was especially dreamy but rather because it was ordinary. Hitchhikers were traveling no more than twenty kilometers each, to and from school, family, work. If the country's failings were leaking through irreparable cracks, its strengths were visible through incandescent air. The people of the Oriente had a tempo, steady and unyielding. They were part of their land, fluid enough to fill its contours, slow enough to accommodate its heat. A billboard showed an American eagle biting the dust, with the words

TODAY, AS YESTERDAY, WE WILL NEVER BACK DOWN

At Manzanillo the highway turned south. Miguel, a man of seventy, flagged me down with his machete. He carried sacks of grain that he spilled in the backseat. He doo-wah-diddied me for a while, but I was able to make out a tirade against Fulgencio Batista's tyranny and the need to overthrow it. He spoke in the present tense; he was slightly daft. Then he went back in time, describing things as they were in the early 1930s. I wanted to tell him that Gerardo Machado had been toppled, the Allies had been victorious in World War II, the Dodgers had left Brooklyn, and yes, Batista had fled the country.

The Caribbean was to the right, fertile fields to the left. An impressive sports complex in Campechuela, a coastal town, proclaimed on its fence: *We don't play sports just to produce champions who give a sense of our technical achievements. We play sports for the well-being of our youth, for the well-being of all the people.* The next town south, Media Luna, was suffused with bicyclists, more noticeable than anywhere else I had been in the country. Some of the first shipments of bikes from China must have been trucked there. A fresh billboard showed a profile of a happy family riding together. The same scene played out live on the town's streets.

The thick scent of the sugar harvest permeated Niquero, the next town south. Almost everyone I passed had something to do with it. The fragrance was not the refined sweetness of a familiar bag of commercial sugar, or the less sharp aroma coming from a sack of raw sugar. The smell that blanketed Niquero had a rich, earthy, rough quality to it, pungent and alive. It hung in the air for months. Despite mechanical sophistication, sugar still brings out the same "steam, fire, smoke, and a drive of labor" that a visitor wrote of in the mid-1800s. Photographs from the 1850s by New Yorker Charles DeForest Fredricks, hand-tinted postcards of the sugar process in the 1920s, and recent portraits of raw-boned sweaty workers by Sebastião Salgado all show laborers confronting strenuous tasks, from cutting stalks to stacking sacks of processed sugar for export. *Gan-Eden*, an 1854 book by William Henry Hurlbert, describes Cuba's slave-era procedure breathlessly: "Wild-looking, half-naked hordes of negroes, many of them roaring out jokes to each other in savage dialects of the African coast, tramp up and down the platform of the mill, thrusting armfuls of the canes between the ponderous rollers of the crushing machine. . . . [H]uge furnaces glow with the fiercely burning fuel of the dried canes-talks." The "milky stream of cane-juice . . . endures all manner of

transformations, simmering here, foaming there, here moody and slug-
gish, a brown and turbid pool, there tossing and bubbling, an uneasy
sea of liquid gold, sending up its wholesome vapors in dense white
wreaths. . . . Sugar is in the air, the ground is yellow with sugar, the
dogs lap up the sugar from the shallow pans, the little naked negroes
tumbling about the door-ways, are crusted over with sugar.''

The mill itself was north of Niquero, but the industry consumed
the whole town. Freight cars on railroad sidings, storage silos, cane
bouncing from the back of oxen-powered carts, dumpsters full of cane
fresh from the ground, tractors hauling as many as six bins of raw
sugar staffs, trucks full of straw-hatted women returning to their dorm
from a day in the cane fields passing another truck carrying their
replacements. Sugar makes up three fourths of Cuba's exports, and
Niquero was doing its twenty-four-hour-a-day best to contribute to
it.

Cane grows whether the land it springs from is owned by a multinational corporation or a state cooperative or a local family. It has been
part of Cuba's culture and economy since the late sixteenth century,
and it inspires more ground-level patriotism than governments do
from above. Often I would ask people who grumbled about their
system if they had ever taken part in the harvest. Their bodies would
relax, their cheeks would rise and their eyes would soften. Yes, they'd
say, I worked two weeks, or a month, or two months, or a whole
season, years ago. The backbreaking repetitive stoop and slash routine
brought them in touch with their national character, renewing their
identity. Their political allegiance may be sagging, but they've paid
homage to King Sugar.

Castro's group was called M-26, Movimiento 26—for the unsuccessful
July 26, 1953, attack Fidel led on Batista military barracks in Santiago.
The assault, one century after José Martí was born, has become abbreviated to its number, 26. Throughout Cuba, the number 26 by itself
symbolizes the opening round of the guerrilla war. Fidel was captured,
tried, imprisoned, and eventually exiled in Mexico, which set the stage
for his return on the *Granma* in late 1956. His two-hour presentencing
speech at his trial is acknowledged as one of the most remarkable
courtroom orations in Latin American history. In making the case for
the fall of Batista, he cited European history, the deplorable situation
in rural Cuba, theology, philosophers, and José Martí. He concluded:
"Condemn me, it does not matter. History will absolve me!"

* * *

"This wasn't a landing," Che Guevara later described the pitiful arrival of the *Granma* at Playa las Coloradas, "it was a shipwreck." Everything that could have gone wrong on the revolutionaries' seven-day crossing from Tuxpán, Mexico, did. A storm made them sick, off-course, and late. They moored in muddy swampland south of Niquero, their original goal, with no one to meet them. After two hours of predawn waist-deep wading through thickets of mangrove and coastal mosquitoes happy to dine on fresh rebel, the insurrectionists stood on *terra firma*. *Memory of Fire*, Eduardo Galeano's masterful sweep through Latin American history, describes the scene: "The survivors consult the sky for directions but get the stars all mixed up. The swamps swallow their backpacks and their arms. They have no food except sugarcane, and they leave its betraying refuse strewn along the trail. They lose their condensed milk by carrying the cans holes down. In a careless moment they mix their little remaining fresh water with sea water. They . . . have a total of seven rifles, a little damp ammunition, and uncounted sores and wounds." Fidel Castro fulfilled his promise to return to the land from which he had been exiled, and foment revolution. (In 1960 a Russian film director asked Castro to reenact the landing, wading through the swamp, according to *90 Miles from Home*, by Warren Miller. "But Fidel told him to get an actor to do it; Fidel said that he had done it once and that was enough.")

I landed at the same place just before the *Granma* debarkation museum was about to close. Raúl, the swing shift guard, showed me the museum, a squat building next to a grandstand used for rallies and shows. The *Granma* arrival site snack bar had already closed. The museum taught me the following: the Batista-era Cuban exile community in Miami had raised funds for the revolutionaries' expedition by selling five-dollar bonds cosigned by Fidel. Immediately after the *Granma* landed, Batista's military announced that the boat and its passengers had been captured. United Press sent the story across the wire that Castro was dead, then followed it up with confirmation: "Air and naval forces intercepted the yacht where it entered the waters resulting in the death of Fidel Castro and his brother as well as 38 more expeditionaries." A WANTED poster asked for information about "a rebel band attached to Fidel Castro, Raúl Castro, and . . . other ringleaders." The government offered a reward of $5,000 to $100,000 "for the head of Fidel Castro. Note: The informant's name will not be revealed."

The guard pointed the way down a nicely designed walkway through mangroves to the actual spot where the *Granma* mired itself off the coast. No one else was headed toward the sea. Every few minutes someone passed me walking back in. They were all holding their shoes, their trousers rolled up, their feet wet. To each tourist straggling in, I offered, "¡*Bienvenido, comandante!*" as if they were Castro just coming ashore. "Are the rest not far behind?" One man helpfully suggested that I hurry a bit because by the time I returned darkness would have already fallen. The surrounding thicket grew more and more dense, and swampwater covered the sidewalk up to my shins. Tiny lizards and other frightening small creatures were waiting for dusk. Knotty trees grew so thick their boughs formed a natural cover over the cement causeway. It was as if I were walking through a tunnel. Mosquitoes sang in million-part harmony.

I could see the Gulf of Guacanayabo at the far end of the tunnel as the sidewalk emerged from the swampwater. Someone had imprinted in the cement ABAJO EL IMPERIALISMO, Down with Imperialism. The sidewalk ended at a sturdy cement and wood pier looking out over the water. In this country where slogans have smothered meaning, the *Granma* landing site stood out for its singular lack of words.

I was glad I was by myself. The spot was moving, historically and personally. A few birds sang, something caused ripples in the water, the sun was going down. The landing site was the fulcrum between the necessity for the popular uprising and its eventual victory. From this locale Fidel Castro galvanized the already existing intellectual, worker, *campesino*, and student groups struggling toward Batista's overthrow. Way to the northwest a small boat drifted toward shore.

Within three months of the *Granma* landing, the Batista government hadn't yet figured out how to use its considerable military force to contain the guerrillas in the mountains. The secrecy they attached to their efforts collapsed on February 24, 1957, when the *New York Times* published the first of a three-part series on Fidel in the Sierra Maestra, reported by Herbert Matthews under the front-page headline, "Cuban Rebel Is Visited in Hideout." By sneaking Matthews into and out of the mountains, past army checkpoints, Castro had won his first public relations battle, as he would most subsequent ones until recently.

M-26 was not the only guerrilla group operating in the countryside, but Castro and his band, by force of personality and organization, came to symbolize the fight against a tired, corrupt, and increasingly despotic dictatorship.

By all accounts Cuba, in the critical years of 1957 and 1958, was a most active and convoluted place. Hollywood and organized crime breezed in and out of Havana. Frank Sinatra and other entertainers from the States headlined there. Steve Allen took his Sunday night variety show to the Hotel Riviera along the Malecón.

Vacationers, mostly from the United States, flocked to the capital not only for its beaches and sunshine, but for its unrepentant gambling, onstage sex, thriving prostitution, and available drugs. Fulgencio Batista was the smiling maître d' who kept a blackjack behind his back. Havana was America's biggest border town.

Most of the capital's residents, increasingly agitated with the maître d's ruthlessness, shied away from overt political activity, but an active underground kept up hit-and-run operations that, while often unsuccessful, alarmed the government with their sheer audacity. Clandestine support groups contributed to the efforts, as did some wealthy industrialists. In the countryside, where miserable conditions rivaled those in other Latin American nations, sheltering and feeding guerrilla soldiers was common.

A very quiet night had come to the *Granma* landing site, and just as I was about to get in my car, Raúl, the night watchman, came over to chat a spell and give me a newly fallen coconut.

I had heard that there was a nice hotel on the coast not too far from Playa las Coloradas, but beyond that descriptions were vague. I followed a road on my German map of Cuba that should have landed me at the right place, but I ended up at Cabo Cruz, the very tip of the peninsula at the west end of Granma Province. The map was wrong; the road I sought didn't exist. A man sitting on a bench in the village laughed when I explained how I had ended up there. I was not the first to have been steered wrong by the Germans. To reach the hotel I had to double back north past Niquero, the sugar town, then head southeast to the coast. The only hitchhiker I picked up was a school bus driver. Niquero at nine P.M. was noisy and active with sugar workers toiling into the night—more freight cars, ox carts, tractors, storage bins, processing, and piling; the mill belched out white steam against a clear, dark sky. I followed a truck burdened with cane, losing its load one stalk at a time.

The last road, about thirty potholed kilometers through the Sierra Maestra, had billboard-sized historical markers along lonely stretches with large illustrations of the original M-26ers trudging through the mountains. Each sign had an elaborate legend explaining who had crossed the road at that particular point and under what circumstances. One said that Raúl Castro had crossed that spot, while another re-

counted Che Guevara's trek through the Sierra. At eleven o'clock I
finally pulled up to a guardhouse at the entrance to the hotel.

The watchman sat in the sort of kiosk that protects foreign embassies, not Cuban hotels. Signs pointed to the beach, a disco, and horseback riding this way; to tennis, the pool, and bike rental that way.
The Marea de Portillo Hotel was, unfortunately, closed for the season,
to be reopened two weeks later. The nearest lodging was in Manzanillo,
about sixty kilometers back up the road. I've been driving since eight
this morning, I told the guard. Another hour through the Sierra would
be impossible. If it's all right with you, I'll just pull over and sleep
in the car. He left for a minute, and when he returned he said the
hotel manager was waiting for me at the front door.

The manager allowed me to register for one night. He had a skele-
ton crew preparing the place for the onslaught of Canadian snowbirds
who come by the planeful for package holidays beginning in mid-
December. Charter flights from Toronto landed nonstop at Manzanillo, where a bus met them for the rest of the trip to the hotel. Most
rooms had radios, telephones, televisions; radio stations from Jamaica
came in clearly. The beach had endless fine, dark sand. Do you want
to scuba dive? Rent a moped? Play volleyball? The Marea de Portillo
Hotel was open to everyone except Cubans. It was socialism's Club
Red.

The previous day one of my riders had invited me to meet her family
at their rural farmhouse. Now, on my way back to Santiago, I thought
to take her up on the offer. My first morning riders were two refrigerator
repairmen going to a crossroads called Sevilla. "The one in Spain?" I
asked. One found this mildly amusing, the other said yes.

Another morning hitchhiker carried small sacks of beans. He was
a plainclothes cop. At one point he suggested I slow down. "There's
a speed trap near here," he said with a grin. "I don't want to see you
at the office, too." He also worked in criminal rehabilitation for newly
released prisoners. I asked him a bit about his job. "The standards are
set by our commander in chief," he replied. When I dropped him off
in Manzanillo he insisted I take some beans. "My family had a very
good crop this year. These are gifts for my *compañeros* at work. Please,
take a bag."

I never did find the hitchhiker, her farmhouse, or her family. After
an hour inquiring in the area between the towns of Contramaestre and

Palma Soriano, I was about to press on when a man led me to the hitchhiker's uncle's home. The house was set back from an access road that paralleled the main highway. A one-lane secondary road went off in another direction. In front of the house some heavy farm machinery was anchored to the earth. "We're waiting for spare parts," the lady of the house said with no hint of irony. Her name was María, her husband was Manuel. Their house was the neighborhood community center. So many people dropped in, passed through, waved as they went by, or chatted a spell, that losing track of blood ties was fairly easy. María said that the family of the hitchhiker, her niece, lived a few kilometers away on the other side of the highway, but no one was home there now, and why don't I sit a spell on the front porch?

María and Manuel's front porch faced the Sierra Maestra. The mountains stretch as far as you can see in either direction. They reminded me of "purple mountains' majesty" from "America the Beautiful." I mentioned this to one of their daughters, and she told me that the sugar mill nearest their home was called Free America. Soon a second daughter showed up, also late teens or early twenties. María poured us each a shot of rum. Then another, along with snacks from the kitchen. I went to my car and got some rum I had stashed beneath the seat. The sisters were the picture of the classic *guajira*, the beautiful countryside, innocent, demur, considerate, pliant personalities with sparkling eyes. We sat on the front porch admiring the magnificent view of the Sierra. They wanted to know all about Nitza, the television cook. What is she really like; did she cook for you? They knew other countries from school, and from books and magazines, but mainly from television and movies. "I would like to visit Mexico," the younger said. "Spain for me," said the elder. A third sister—or perhaps a cousin or a friend—had joined us and insisted on France. She wore thin silver bracelets and rings on every finger.

They brought out a cassette player and I rummaged through the car trunk for my tapes. I put on Los Lobos and María insisted I dance with the girls on the front porch. They agreed. This was turning into a farmer's daughter story. With a little more to drink I would have told them I was a clown and asked if they wanted to join the circus.

The farmer's daughters' father came home. Manuel. A grizzly man of sixty-six. He had the hefty stoicism of subjects photographed by W. Eugene Smith, and the bearing of miners I've seen in the Southwestern United States and Mexico and the Andes. The boyfriend of the eldest daughter came by on his bicycle. Another fellow rode up on a horse.

A half hour later a horse-drawn cart pulled up with more friends. A polite, city-dressed man came by and entered the house. He sat in the corner of the living room and said nothing.

Manuel had washed up, combed his hair, and was changing into a nice white *guayabera*. We sat in the living room beneath a portrait of Fidel and talked. He has thirteen children in all, most of whom are grown and have left home. George Bush and the crisis in the Gulf, then heating to the boiling point, were linked in the press to the oil shortage that had brought on Cuba's Special Period. "Bush and his Desert Shield are responsible for the Special Period," Manuel said.

"But the Special Period began within a week or so of sending troops to the Gulf. Iraq invaded Kuwait even before that. Something as elaborate as the Special Period had been planned for months. Don't you think that the problem is more that Cuba's trading partners are leaving the socialist camp?"

Clouds rolled over the Sierra Maestra. Another daughter showed up, bottle-feeding her five-week-old baby. Manuel saw me looking at the portrait of Castro. "Why do you like him so much?" I asked.

"He will have a plan. He will confront the problem on behalf of the humble people of Cuba." Manuel was not only a member of his local Committee for the Defense of the Revolution, he was the zone coordinator for five local CDRs. "Tell me, can you write about anything you want in the United States?"

"Yes. Now, whether you can get it published is another matter. Mainly it depends on the marketplace. And here? Can anyone write about anything they want?"

"Not about counterrevolutionary activity. They'd cut your head off!" Manuel drew his forefinger across his throat. He was not a man who spoke in metaphor.

I glanced at his wristwatch. "Well, I really must be going. Your daughters told me there is a hotel in Palma Soriano, and if I leave now I'll be there before it gets dark." I made about-to-leave motions.

"Won't you stay for dinner?" He called to his wife in the kitchen: "He will stay for dinner." He looked back at me. "We're like most Cubans. We like our rice and beans."

María served us more than that. First came tamales, heated up on a small fire in the backyard. Then *guiso de maíz*, a corn potage with rice, beans, carrots, and a little tomato. Finally María served *picadillo de carne*. "We have meat at least once a month," Manuel said. They ate far better than city folk. Their kitchen stored more vegetables than I'd seen at many produce stands in Havana.

Manuel and I went back to the living room, separated from the kitchen–dining room by a bookcase. A pile of stickers proclaiming the National Day of Defense lay on one of the shelves. "I was born less than five hundred meters from here." Before the Revolution Manuel had worked on a coffee plantation.

Two horses trotted up to the door; their riders got off to chat for five minutes. The visitors tracked mud through the house, and as soon as they left one of the daughters quickly swept up. "During the Revolution I ran messages to the rebels' hideouts. I drove a horsecart. There was a battle just twenty kilometers from here. I took part in the sugar harvest right after the Revolution."

"Are there any counterrevolutionaries left in the area?"

"No! We cut their heads off! We have a people's government. You have millionaires in the United States and look, you have many homeless people, too. You have a black population that has the makings of a revolution itself. Fidel says about the U.S. that its people aren't the enemy of Cuba, and vice versa." Manuel kept a machete bound to his side as if it were part of his clothing.

"Here we had a workers' revolution. Before, everyone was poor. Now look. I have a son in college. Another son is an engineer in Havana. He's been to the USSR. All my children have been well educated as far as they wanted to go. What other country in the world can say that? Look at our infant mortality rate." Manuel was a beneficiary of the Agrarian Reform law, which had broken up large land holdings. "As long as this law is upheld," observed Amiri Baraka, then known as LeRoi Jones, after a visit in 1960, "the majority of the Cuban people will love Fidel Castro even if it were proven that he was Lucifer himself."

Manuel, in retirement, was the head of a production brigade on a nearby farm. At seven o'clock he promptly stood and turned on the front porch floodlight. He put on his straw hat and looked outside. "We play dominoes after dinner. Please join us." A woman who lived in a house across the road came by. She was expecting her mother back from a visit to relatives in the States the next day.

I asked Manuel about the Committee for the Defense of the Revolution. They have a high profile in the cities, but rural CDRs were less visible. "It's very simple. We engage in revolutionary vigilance. We know what's going on in our area twenty-four hours a day. In Zone Five we have 336 members fourteen years old or over. The CDR watches over the community, both the good and the bad. The CDRista knows everything that happens in his assigned area. He develops the ideological work of the *compañeros*."

The first of the dominoes players arrived. So did Dénices, a teacher in her late thirties who worked at the little schoolhouse twenty-five meters from Manuel and María's home. Manuel introduced us. She lived in a two-room building between his house and the school, and traveled weekly to Santiago, where she was taking graduate courses in education. She wore a plaid shirt over her dress and a mouthful of extremely healthy teeth. She was treated as part of the family.

"I've been in the Communist Party since 1960." Manuel again. "The orientation of the Party is to direct the masses. When there's trouble, sometimes the CDR handles it, sometimes the municipality. I'm between the municipality and the people. We don't want any more people in the Party."

"Why not?"

"Because when we had more members they were the bourgeoisie and not the workers. Today there is no bourgeoisie. In Cuba, the bourgeoisie is gone forever."

We went outside where the nightly dominoes players had gathered. One of the daughters went around back arm-in-arm with her *novio*, her intended. A neighbor boy of sixteen leaned on a railing in the yard staring into the dark Sierra. "I work in the fields during the sugar harvest," he said. "Over there." He nodded toward the southeast. He seemed less than enthusiastic about cutting cane and, as our conversation developed, his country.

Dominoes? A game of chance. No strategy. No real brains required. The luck of the draw. Arbitrary. Something to while away the time. No gambits as in chess.

Ha! The joke was on me. This nightly game had been going on for decades, possibly since before the Revolution. I watched at first. The four men played with cunning. Initially it looked like they were slapping their squares down at random, with little concern. But as their game progressed a pattern became clear, like silently counting cards in a poker game. The daughter and her *novio* came from around the corner, their eyes blinking at the sudden light. She was fastening the top buttons of her blouse. The *novio* came over and watched the game. One of the players got up to leave and Manuel signaled for me to take his place. The young couple strolled off behind the house again.

Dominoes came to Cuba from the Andalusian region of Spain with soldiers who fought against Cuba in the War of Independence at the end of the nineteenth century. Some of the soldiers stayed on in Cuba and the game took root, modified by a similar game the Chinese had brought with them when they began migrating to the island. The synthesis of the two, according to Modesto Vázquez González, became what we know today as Cuban dominoes. "With the enormous exodus of Cubans escaping the Castro dictatorship," Vázquez writes from Mexico in his stupendous 560 page book on the history, rules, tactics, and etiquette of the game, "Cuban dominoes has now propagated and awakened interest in the four corners of the world." It is "the most recent and most perfect evolution of dominoes in all of Latin America." Castro himself plays marathon domino sessions, according to photographer Lee Lockwood, who once witnessed the premier play for seventeen hours straight. Graham Greene wrote that when he accompanied Castro to one small town, "In a bar two men sat playing dominoes and he sat down with them and joined the game." Manuel's daughter and her *novio* rounded the corner once more. Once again, she was buttoning up her blouse.

I hadn't seen Vázquez's book before I sat down at Manuel's table, but even had I busily referred to it on the spot I doubt that it would have helped. Once, when the player to my right opened with one particular square, I followed by blocking it with a double square. "*¡No!*" Manuel berated me. "Don't kill the opening move!" I had no other squares to play, but Manuel's admonition ignored reality. His advice came fast and furious. And at the end of each game, "*¡Dale agua!*" Shuffle those dominoes!

Manuel violated a cardinal rule of José Ricardo O'Farrill, the country's premier dominoes player in the 1930s: do not demonstrate satisfaction or disgust with another player. (Other guidelines: do not intimidate; don't ask who played what; don't ask another player why he laid down a particular square; no counting out loud; no silent communication with eyes or hands; keep playing, do not discuss the game; no peeking; and don't insult, bother, worry, or interrupt another player.) Once when Manuel kibitzed me I felt the wrath of all five local CDRs. Of some fifteen games we played, I won two. The Communists whipped me at dominoes.

I made ready to leave, but Manuel would hear none of it. "Follow me." He led me into a small house next door, part of the rural complex.

In the living room a color television was surrounded by a half dozen viewers. A documentary about Chile was on, but the real reason everyone gathered around the television was to watch *Roque Santeiro*, the Brazilian soap opera. There on the edge of the Sierra Maestra six revolutionaries gathered in a semicircle three nights a week to catch the latest goings-on among the melodramatic a continent away.

Midway through, the man I replaced at the dominoes table walked in, swinging an empty bottle. "Nothing," he said, sadly. "I couldn't find rum anywhere."

Before I could prepare to depart, Manuel said, "We have arranged for a bed for you. Dénices will sleep in the house and you may take her room."

Dénices's place was tidy and crowded. The front room held clothes and books. We talked as she gathered some belongings. She was raised by Jehovah's Witnesses, who, she said, gave her a broad perspective on attitudes. "It's a religion with views at odds with the government. They don't salute the flag or wear the kerchief of the Pioneers, but they do participate."

I had heard that the Revolution had wider support in the countryside than the cities. Why? I asked her.

"Life has changed more demonstrably here. Look at Manuel's family and you can see. Imagine what they would be doing, think of the level of education they would have if the Revolution had not taken place. Rural education was practically nonexistent before. The school I teach at, it's a product of the Revolution. We don't teach by rote, but by real objects. And it's free to everyone. In the United States you have to pay for schooling."

"We do?"

"I understand that it costs to go to school."

"Well, indirectly, I suppose—taxes on property and income go to public schools, and private schools charge tuition. But no, there's no fee to attend public schools." Dénices nodded.

The minister of education had been sacked the previous week, and a replacement had already been appointed. What hopes were there for the new one? "Improvement!"

She showed me the bedroom. Mosquito netting covered the double bed. A shortwave radio sat on a table next to it, and beside that rested a pile of history books. "Feel free to look through the books. Or to use the radio." I asked if it picked up Radio Martí. Without directly answering, she said, "Radio Martí gives a bad impression of the United States. It makes it appear everyone there hates Cuba. We're not against the people of the United States. We understand they have problems, just as we do." We went back to the front room. "Will you be taking a shower tonight?"

"I'd like to, but if—"

"Fine. I'll go heat up the water. Here's a towel and some soap. In fifteen minutes it will be ready." She opened the door and walked me to the outhouse, where she filled a bucket and lit a Sterno under it. "Don't forget to put on thongs when you come back."

Dénices went off to the house just as Manuel came out to say good night. "Are you all set?" He wanted to tell me about the house I was staying in. It was reserved for the teacher, and the teacher almost always became integrated into his family. "When Dénices takes her next leave from work to study, she'll stay on full salary. She gets 232 pesos a month. Plus, dorm space and meals when she's in Santiago studying. Now tell me, does any other country offer this sort of opportunity?" We shook hands good night. "By the way," he said on his way out, "is the door to your car locked?"

I read the following in one of Dénices's history books: U.S. sabotage through the spring of 1961 included the bombing of two airfields in the Havana area and one in Santiago. *Immediately our commander in chief ordered the mobilization of the Rebel Army and the Revolutionary National Militia. At the funeral for those who died, Fidel proclaimed the socialist character of our Revolution. In the Colón Cemetery, before an enormous crowd, our commander in chief announced to the world that the most beautiful flower that could be offered the fallen heroes was the socialist Revolution. It was an emotional moment.* I fell asleep to the sound of pigs, crickets, and the sweet noises of the Cuban countryside.

The next morning I awoke early and unlatched a wooden square from the window. Tropical sunlight gushed in and drenched everything in its way. Outside a fellow was slopping the pigs in the schoolyard. Birds sang. Stalks of corn grew taller than Fidel. I wrote in my notes, "I've finally seen Cuba from the inside the way it would like to be seen from the outside."

"Excuse me. Is the Archbishop available?"

"Please wait here, won't you?"

This exchange took place at the office of the Roman Catholic Diocese of Santiago de Cuba. I had driven there straight from Manuel and María's farmhouse. The Archbishop had custody of Ernest Hemingway's Nobel medal, according to Sister Lucía at El Cobre. Mirta Zayas, the Archbishop's assistant, came to the lobby. "He's out of town until Tuesday. May I help you? I'm sure I could speak on his behalf."

I explained I wanted to see the Hemingway medal. "Is it here, or at a bank?"

"It's in the safe deposit vault at a bank."

"How fortunate that banks are open all day Saturdays. I'm leaving town tomorrow; could I arrange to see it today?"

"No. Only the Archbishop can authorize that."

"I understand. Tell me, which bank is it? Even knowing that would help."

"It's in Havana."

"That's wonderful. I'll be there next week. Perhaps I can get authorization to see it then."

"No one there is authorized to permit that."

"Oh. Then may I leave a note for the Archbishop explaining the circumstances?"

"There's no way he can authorize it."

"How about by phone or letter?"

"It will do you no good."

"It sounds very simple to me."

"I have worked very closely with the Archbishop for years. He doesn't work like that. He won't do it."

"What bank in Havana holds the Hemingway medal?"

"I couldn't tell you."

"But surely—"

"He won't do it. It will be returned next year to El Cobre."

The day I wrote that section I was reminded once again of Cuba's sexuality, this time by an article in *Condé Nast Traveler*. Journalist Enrique Fernández and a photographer had been in Santiago de Cuba and reported that on the veranda of the Hotel Casagranda, "two lovely black girls notice us, and one of them sticks out her rump provocatively when she notices we're taking photos." Accounts of Cuba, from within and foreign, invariably allude to Cuba's sexuality, yet no one had the vision of Waldo Frank. Frank, a writer from the States whose 1961 book, *Cuba: Prophetic Island*, supported the Revolution generously, looked at a map of Cuba. Like many others, the seventy-two-year-old author saw an alligator with its head the southeastern chunk and its tail wagging off to the west. Then he turned Cuba upside down so the bulge was in the Gulf of Mexico, and he drew a profound conclusion: "Cuba has the shape of a phallus. Its scrotum is Oriente (the former alligator's head). In erection it points northward and westward, penetrating the widely open vulva of Florida and Yucatán toward the immense womb of the Gulf, whose north shore represents Anglo-Saxondom, with Mexico—Amerindia—closing in upon the west and south. These are the mother organs. Cuba's thrust into them symbolizes the new impetus of revolution from the east—Cuba, Africa, Europe—upon the mother Americas." Frank's metaphor reaches its climax: "Florida and Yucatán, representing the two Americas, are vulva leading to the wombs of America's future, and they have been fertilized by Cuba."

Well!

In six sentences Waldo Frank has taken the often dull field of political cartography and fertilized it with psychiatry. For the student of Cuba, however, sexual allusion is more the rule than the exception. When I first began climbing the mountain of literature from and about the island, I was surprised by the frequent descriptions of *las nalgas cubanas*, the Cuban ass. After a while *el culo*, the butt, became a literary fixture; unusual was the work that didn't allude to *el trasero*, the behind. Was this my own private *vedado*, or had my literary obsession entwined with a genuine strain in Cuban culture? I asked a number of people far more familiar with such things than I. Jesús, in the writers union library, suggested a half dozen references to *nalgas cubanas*, including a 1940s song, "El Volumen de Carlota"—"The Enormity of Carlota"—about Carlota's ass: "*¡Pero qué volumen tiene Carlota!*" But how big she is! Others recommended various poems, songs, short stories, essays, and travelogues. A professor at Yale cautioned me to look beyond Cuba to the entire Caribbean, where "fascination with the *culo* comes to us from African cultures." The *culona*, he said, is a folklore figure. "She is a black woman with a raised ass, contrived by some apparatus under her skirt." The late Lydia Cabrera, an expert on Afro-Cuban tradition, wrote of one legend in which frogs bequeathed their asses to Cuban women.

I soon found enough material to keep a culophile busy for months. *El trasero* has become part of Cuba's national matrimony. Some of the literary selections I came across describe, others analyze, and still more rhapsodize. They are, in turns, lyrical, crude, loving, wondrous, dumb, and sensuous. Many of the excerpts simply show enchantment with Cuban women and the aura of sensuality the island evokes. (Except Anthony Trollope, who in 1859 wrote that Cuban women were quite moral but not particularly attractive.)

The first allusion to *el culo cubano* I could find appeared in 1854 when, in *History of Cuba, or, Notes of a Traveller in the Tropics*, Maturin M. Ballou wrote "The feet of the Havana ladies are made for ornament and for dancing, though with a roundness of figures that leaves nothing to be desired in symmetry of form. . . . There is a striking and endearing charm about the Cuban ladies, their very motion being replete with a native grace; every limb elastic and supple." "Elegy for María Belén Chacón" (1930), the poem that established Emilio Ballagas as a leading writer, tells the sad fate of a laundress:

> *María Belén Chacón, with your ass in sway*
> *From Camagüey to Santiago, from Santiago to Camagüey.*

The Cuban laureate Nicolás Guillén celebrated erotic nationalism in his works such as "The New Woman" in 1939: "*The circle of the equator wrapped around her waist like a little world . . ./Crowned with palm tree/ like a newly arrived goddess/She brings the unknown word/the strong rump/ the voice, the teeth, the morning and the leap.*" The inimitable Beny Moré, "El Bárbaro del Ritmo" ("The Outrageous Rhythm Man"), sang "Mulata con cola" against an exaggerated swaying rhythm. The lyrics hint at the movements of the lobster, especially its tail. "I like a woman who has an ass like that," Moré sang, "the big Cuban *mulata*, how tasty, how delicious." Ludwig Bemelmans was intrigued by a successful Havana dressmaker and wrote in the December 1957 *Holiday*: "This local Dior invented a kind of reverse brassière, a sewn-in device which makes the most of the derrière. It disciplines this part of the anatomy and the girls who wear it develop a new wiggle." Alejo Carpentier, in *War of Time* (1958), wrote of a small black woman "whose buttocks jutted out like choir stalls. . . ." During his visit in the first year of the Revolution, Kenneth Tynan wrote in *Holiday* that he was distressed to see the military patrolling formerly rambunctious nightclubs: "It is as if the Amish had taken over Las Vegas. . . . In the water-front bars girls still cackle, seeking new friends and flaunting—especially if they are Negroes—incredible promontories of rump" "It's a maddening game to stare fixedly at any part of the human body; ears, for example, or just bellies," wrote Edmundo Desnoes in his 1967 novel *Inconsolable Memories*. "To say nothing of the different shapes and sizes feminine asses take on here. Their S formed by the stomach and the ass reaches a certain point in certain Cuban women where it becomes independent, out of proportion with the rest of the body, even having its own personality." In *Paradiso* (1966), the Cuban writer José Lezama Lima described a Havana woman: "The neat outline of her back stretched down to the opening of her solid buttocks like a deep, dark river between two hills of caressing vegetation." Leroy Lucas, in Elizabeth Southerland's *The Youngest Revolution* (1969), reduces the feeling to one sentence: "When I walk down the street and all those Big Swinging Asses pass me by, I go sort of Loco." A man in the 1930s describes some prostitutes he met in *Rachel's Song* (Miguel Barnet, 1969): "Just arrived, so to speak, country bumpkins, with the mountain smell still in their armpits. But pretty, round, well made, with nice asses." In Matanzas, Andrew Salkey (*Havana Journal*, 1971) saw "women with wonderfully high-pitched backsides and a slow, groovy walking pace" Musician Cesar Castillo, in Oscar Hijuelos's 1989 *The Mambo Kings Play Songs of Love*, "wrote unrestrained lyrics that tended toward obscenities, the change of a word for a laugh ('*Bésame Mucho*' to '*Bésame Culo*')." Jacobo Timerman, in *Cuba* (1990), put his mind to work on *nalgas cubanas*: "Eros is amply gratified in Cuba and needs no stimulation. . . . The female backside in general, and that of the mulatto woman in particular, occupies a prominent position in daily life. Women display their backsides—the bigger the better—wag them freely and rhythmically, and welcome appreciative gazes with a smile. . . . Yes, people tell me, it's the Caribbean, the heat, Africa, music, the smell of vegetation, slavery, the mixture of cultures. The Revolution granted universal rights regardless of sex, but no revolution could be more potent than Cuban eroticism. . . . The sexes had been equalized in Cuba, but backsides had particular values and meanings, a distinction much more significant here than in other cultures." Writing in *Mirabella* for January 1991, Mark Kurlansky says his Havana cab driver "stared intently at a group of pedestrians and then turned to me and whispered something that I didn't quite hear. Clutching my notebook I asked him to repeat it. '*Las prietas son muy grandes atrás*,' he whispered. He just wanted to tell me that 'dark-skinned women have large behinds.'" In July 1991 *Allure* readers learned from Elizabeth Hanly about *sandunga*, the undulating bodily sway: "A silent song that begins with the ankle and continues just past the ass." From Havana she reported, "*Sandunga* would not be *sandunga* without that cornerstone of Cuban beauty, the ass. 'I wouldn't say the Cuban ass is always better, but it's always bigger,' says Oswaldo Salas," the photographer. "As we talk I notice that the marble swan next to us in the hotel lobby has a woman's buttocks. . . . National campaigns to diminish sexual stereotyping aside, Cuban women routinely take in the waists of their jeans and uniforms to further outline nature. Physical therapist Ana Fernández is convinced that 'without asses in motion, we would never achieve the degree of feeling that we have here.' " The next month *National Geographic* followed with a report on Cuba in which Santiago experienced a temporary power failure. "After twenty minutes the carnival lights are on again, more bands and beauties pass, onlookers spout uninhibited comments. 'These men are terrible,' " says the writer's translator, smiling. "Don't women mind?" Oh no, she says. "In Cuba the women love to hear that they've been noticed—'You mustn't be too thin, of course, especially in the back.' In such a case the men might say *está infumable*—'she's unsmokable.' " John Sayles captures raw male response in this hospital scene from *Los Gusanos* (also 1991): " 'Will you look at that.' Roosevelt stares at Luz's bottom as she rolls out of the day room. 'Cuban women, goodgawd!' " Felicia, in Critina Garcia's novel, *Dreaming in Cuba* (1992), was asked to walk naked when she applied for a job as an "international escort." "Felicia felt her ample, dimpled behind quake seductively as she moved. 'Your buttocks are too large for Europe,' Madame Thibaut told her. But for here they will do.' " Common street saying: *"Niña, si cocinas como caminas, me como hasta la raspa."* Girl, if you cook like you walk, I'll lick the pot down to the dregs.

I got to Santiago's Casa de la Trova early for my appointment with Gerardo Aldana, who was going to aid and abet my literary sleuthing for the Mambo Kings. To pass the time I drifted down to Céspedes Park, where Pedro, a *jinetero*, stopped me. I told him I didn't want to change dollars for pesos. "No, no. I just want to talk." Pedro worked part-time, and had four children.

He talked about his friends who have married foreigners. "I know men who have hitched themselves to women from Germany, Australia, the Philippines, Italy, and Finland to get out. And Spain, of course. When they settle in their new country, then they're through with their new wife. It's their ticket out. If they opened the doors I'd go in a minute. Give me your phone number. I'll be in your city within a year." Pedro then went into a tirade against state corruption, haughty officials, and government ministers out of touch with Cuba's reality. He cursed, he reviled, he maligned, he vilified more than anyone I'd yet heard; he expanded my vocabulary. He ended by saying, "But Fidel, he's okay. It's those under him that are horrible."

Gerardo had arrived at the Casa de la Trova while I was listening to Pedro. Fifteen musical groups were scheduled to play that day, all listed on a placard at the entrance. The stage was a simple raised platform with two dozen folding chairs in front. Most performers sat on the edge of the stage. The back opened up onto Heredia Street, making the Casa both cozy and within reach. The Cuarteto Santiaguero, The Santiago Quartet, had just finished, and the Cuarteto Patria was scheduled next. Still to come were two seven-piece bands, Sones de Oriente and Típico Oriental. The name of another one, Melodías de Ayer, Melodies from Yesterday, complemented the looks of bygone bands pictured prominently on the walls. There were also photos of two poets who had been to Santiago's Casa, Carlos Puebla and Nicolás Guillén.

A man wearing a blue pullover and slacks and a black mustache sang songs of love to the palm trees. His voice was haunting, but he strummed his guitar as if his hands were frostbitten. A large woman with stringy hair, blue earrings, and a shimmering rainbow dress backed him up. She kept time with claves, two sticks, hitting one against the other. Two young boys accompanied them strumming backup guitars. Finally a woman took the stage by herself. She had simply walked in from the street, and wore shoddy clothes and sandals. She clutched a book of lyrics in her left hand. Her clear alto voice had a wide range. She and the other musicians had an unmistakable air of authenticity. The ancient album covers and pictures on the wall complemented the plaintive boleros coming from the singers. Two European photographers raced around at speeds far exceeding the music.

Gerardo and I began our search for the Castillo brothers from *The Mambo Kings* with the head of the Casa de la Trova herself, Luisa Blanco Brito. "Try Pepín—you know Pepín, don't you, Gerardo? He has an encyclopedic mind. He remembers names and dates. He's old, and it's a little difficult for him to get around, but he comes here every day between eleven and one. Come to think of it, there was someone named Castillo years ago. He'd do boleros, he was always here. He won a gold medal in Mexico once." She clapped out the rhythm he used: /// ////. "He had claves, and sometimes he played in triplets, like this: / // / //."

Gerardo and I rode a bus for ten minutes to a section of Santiago with row houses. We sought out Pepín Martínez, whose neighbors pointed out his house. He was seventy-four years thin, in good health, and wore green sunglasses, a pullover, and muted plaid pants over bronze skin. His hair was thin and white. Gerardo, who knew him slightly, introduced me. "I know this sounds unusual, but I'm hoping to find out if in the 1930s or 1940s there was a musician, Cesar Castillo, who played in Santiago." The question intrigued Pepín. "He and his brother, Nestor, are the main characters in a novel I've just read. Of course it is fiction, but still—"

"Let me think."

His way of thinking was to tell the story of his life. Gerardo hung on every word of it. "On November 11, 1924, I began studying music in Manzanillo; first Cuban music, then Italian." Pepín went to the next room and retrieved a large envelope of photographs. "Here I am at ten, in Manzanillo. My name was José Francisco Estrada Mujica, but I was known as Francisquín. At fourteen I played trumpet in a children's band. We traveled through the countryside." This would have been 1930, the year Machado closed down the University of Havana after demonstrations there against his regime.

Nieces and nephews and grandnieces and grandnephews passed through the long, narrow living room, each one introduced to Gerardo and me. "I helped establish the first musicians union in 1937," a year of especially intense labor organizing in Cuba.

"Nineteen thirty-seven," I said. "In the book that was the year Cesar Castillo played in Santiago dance halls."

"I don't recall any Castillo. This author must have been using his imagination."

"Well, yes, of course. But I thought I'd inquire anyway."

Pepín had a quick smile and a fast memory, and he wasn't about to let his two visitors leave just yet. "Now, Chepín Chovén had a band—Orquesta de Sabor. He had a trumpet, bass, and trombone. Wait—there was a Castillo. Pepe. A clarinet player. He died here. His son Alcides played trumpet. He was the director of the provincial concert band. And also Alciviades Castillo. He played violin and trumpet with the National Symphony Orchestra."

Pepín pulled out some more photographs. "In Bayamo I was known as Horacio Mendoza. I had to change my name because I fought against Machado." He showed us pictures of himself in a band at age twelve in 1928, and another in Puerto Rico, in the 1940s.

"In 1943," under a Batista presidency, "I played for the Huatuéy brewery band. See?" The band wore spiffy outfits and white shoes. "Also, for the Bacardí rum band." The walls of Pepín's house were covered with photographs of family, pastoral scenes, and a poster-sized picture of Fidel. "I was a member of the Partido Socialista Popular then."

More pictures. "Ah, here's the one I was looking for. It's of the musicians union celebrating the triumph of the Revolution!" In it, men are standing around wearing straw *campesino* hats, hoisting beers, looking very happy. One man plays the flute. "Fifty-nine musicians from Santiago took part in the Revolution." The next picture showed Pepín in the back row with other workers in the sugar fields. They all have machetes.

"Here." He smiled broadly. "June 7, 1959. The first executive committee meeting of the provincial musicians union. I'm most proud of having been director of the first National Revolutionary Militia Band. That was in 1959, too."

Alejandrina, Pepín's wife, walked in. "She is Spanish," he said with affection as he made introductions. "But me? I'm a native!" He laughed at this, then looked at more pictures in silence.

"We play music." His voice changed timbre. "But it's the rifle over the shoulder that counts. Even cutting cane, a rifle is nearby. Look at Martin Luther King. He got shot in the head. A revolution is made with arms, not the Bible or musical instruments or machetes. Fidel Castro said the revolution is made through armed struggle."

On Mondays, Wednesdays, and Fridays, Pepín hosts other musicians at his home. "You know, clarinets, horns, percussion. A jam session. You can hear us on the back patio here."

Gerardo and I returned to the Casa de la Trova where a group called Guitarras y Trovadores, Guitars and Troubadours, was into its last number. They sang that the streets of Santiago are full of passion, and the countryside in eastern Cuba has more beauty than heaven. When I closed my eyes I could almost hear the Cesar and Nestor Castillo play songs of love.

Part Four

On the way in from the Havana airport my taxi passed a city park filled with young people. A few bands were playing at one end of the square and the crowd was decked out in peaceful, flowery attire. I asked the cabbie to pull over. Through a speaker system came "She loves you, yeah, yeah, yeah." Thousands of Havana youngsters were singing Beatles songs. The tenth anniversary of John Lennon's death was that weekend, and the city's youth was out to commemorate the occasion. When the Beatles were popular throughout the world the first time, in Cuba their music was *vedado*, forbidden, but now it was in Vedado, encouraged. Popular bands Síntesis and Gens played, well-known singers Pablo Menéndez and Carlos Varela joined them. A crew from Cubavisión taped the concert for a one-hour special later in the week. The musicians were "paying tribute to an artist whose contributions revolutionized the sound of the second half of the twentieth century," reported *Granma*. Many fans waved posters of Lennon.

I moved that afternoon from the venerable Focsa building to a small hotel a block away run by the Ministry of Higher Education, called the Hotelito del M.E.S., short for Ministerio de Educación Superior. Most of its tenants were teachers from the provinces in town for workshops, or foreigners in Cuba to meet with national educators. The hotel also took walk-in guests, and my *compañeros* at the writers union had arranged for me to rent quarters there. Each room had a private bathroom with shower, a color television set, and, connected to the front desk, a telephone that often worked. The ground floor had two dining rooms, one for Cubans and the other for foreigners. Attached to the front of the building was a mailbox that had no bottom. A half dozen bus routes passed within one block. The same ministry ran another hotel in Habana Vieja—the Ambos Mundos, where Ernest Hemingway lived when he first came to Havana, a fact noted on a plaque next to the entrance. At the Hotelito del M.E.S. I was a block closer to the Coppelia ice cream emporium, and still only a few short blocks from the Malecón.

A book of twenty-five vampire stories led the week's fiction best-seller list. Theodore Dreiser's *Sister Carrie* was number three. A biography of Cuban pianist Ernesto Lecuona topped the nonfiction list. It was followed by a book with eyewitness accounts from Bolivians about Che Guevara's fatal guerrilla movement there. Number five on the nonfiction list reminded me to visit Salvador—it was about "filin," the musical sentiment made popular on Hamel where Salvador's mural still intrigued passersby.

He had had lots of visitors. "They come almost every day. I'm honored that they appreciate my work. That's why I do it. But look." We were sitting next to the window, and out back on Hamel some foreigners were admiring his art. Escorting them was a street hustler. "The *jineteros* take tourists around town and point out things to them like my art, and the foreigners pay them in dollars. And what do I get? Nothing." He looked out with sad incredulity. "This has just started to happen recently. A piece of my art once sold outside the country for two thousand dollars. The government paid me for it in pesos. You know," he said after a long pause, "I was eligible to go on Mariel, but I'm a revolutionary. I want to die in the country I was born in. I didn't want to be part of anyone's political struggle. I love Cuba. This land, it's mother earth to me. Fidel, he has charisma, but it's the same old same old. He keeps telling us how educated and healthy we are. We know that." Salvador made me promise to be out on the street when the Afro-Alemanes played. "We'll have a fiesta up here afterward." We left his building together; I to my new room and Salvador to a party where a friend was to be initiated into santería.

Bless her heart! María Blanca Morejón, the librarian in Pinar del Río who helped me find the García Márquez piece about Graham Greene, was true to her word. I had mentioned to a number of people in Havana that I had located the column but, because the library didn't have a photocopier, they would have to send it to me later. I got indulgent smiles. "They just said that out of politeness." "You don't really expect to see it, do you?" Yet when I picked up my mail from Victoria at the writers union, there was an envelope from Pinar del Río, and inside, the article typed out using a red ribbon, filling four pages of long blue onionskin paper. Someone had sat down and copied the entire piece, word for word. Do librarians have a patron saint?

Pablo Armando Fernández was sitting on the writers union portico and I went over to tell him about the unexpected mail. Fernández, editor of *Unión*, the writers union literary magazine, was delighted. His sixty-year-old blue eyes lit up. "Sometimes these things work!" I had met Pablo Armando quite by accident on the main concourse of the Miami airport in 1987 as we both headed toward the gate for the charter to Havana. The poet and essayist was returning from a literary symposium. I saw him all over town during that trip and all subsequent ones; foreign visitors find him a genial host, literary and well spoken. His father was Spanish Catholic, his mother Spanish Sephardic. His broad insights come from a Cuban youth in a sugar town run by Americans, and from his teenage years to twenty-eight, in New York, where he attended Columbia University, worked in a bookstore, went into business, and made literary contributions to the Revolution. He has a movie-poster face with a full mane of white hair and a Rasputin-like goatee, like a more handsome Uncle Ben. Since his return shortly after the revolutionary victory he has been in and out of favor, then in again. Fernández has settled comfortably into a position of responsibility and respect. He is one of the OWs, the Official Writers.

He loves foreigners. He gloms on to them. Seldom did I ever see him more than an hour away from dropping off this overseas visitor, meeting that one, or entertaining a third. The former LeRoi Jones writes of Fernández greeting him at the Havana airport. During a 1960 visit the American poet Lawrence Ferlinghetti had dinner with him at a restaurant from whose kitchen Fidel Castro emerged. "We were surrounded by his energy and force," wrote journalist Warren Miller when he and his wife met Fernández in late 1960. Andrew Salkey, a Jamaican writer, dedicated his 1971 *Havana Journal* to "the people of Cuba and to Fidel," also "the memory of Che"—and to Fernández. Wrote Salkey: "He seemed the happiest and most apprehensive man I'd ever met. He was like his favorite word 'beautiful.' He was happy and sad. He was winning and losing. He wasn't a poet for nothing."

Ernesto Cardenal, the Nicaraguan Marxist-*padre*-poet-sometimes government minister, quotes Fernández at length in *In Cuba*. James Michener took an instant liking to Pablo Armando, and in *Six Days in Havana* published no fewer than four color pictures of the photogenic poet, including a two-page spread of the two writers face-to-face over a table at La Bodeguita del Medio. Fernández's attitude stays sufficiently close to the government position that the Ministry of Foreign Relations often lines him up for interviews with visiting writers, yet it strays sufficiently that the U.S. Interests Section in Havana has done likewise. As a result Fernández's modulated outspokenness has become among the most quoted points of view emanating from the island. Practically every book I pick up on Cuba by a foreigner, it seems, pays homage to Fernández. If a book doesn't mention him I suspect foul play. One Cuban writer told me that he considers a mention of Pablo Armando a good luck charm. Whether for Fernández or the writer he didn't say.

Fernández feels enmity toward only one foreign writer: Jacobo Timerman. "He's crazy. He's a Marxist Zionist. In his book he told lies! He said my curtains are old and dirty. *We've never had curtains at my house since I was born. Never!*"

I looked up the offending passage. Timerman has drinks with some of the OWs *chez* Fernández: "We met in an old, spacious clean house, although the curtains and more than one piece of furniture were in fairly urgent need of repair."

Fernández had me over to his house. His home in Miramar rests across the street from the embassy of Ghana. It is an old two-story affair, in gentle decline. The ground floor has a piano and a computer; his wife and son play the first, and he plays the second. The living room chairs are comfortable. He has no curtains in the living room. Pablo Armando closed the shutters to block out the midday light, and it seemed more like eight than two P.M. He then placed an electric fan on the floor to circulate the remaining heat. The previous month Jay Taylor, then head of the U.S. Interests Section, had come for dinner. The electricity had failed and they dined by candlelight. "Taylor is very literary. I like him. He's not bad for us. Of course, he's not like Wayne Smith," head of the Interests Section under Jimmy Carter, "but he's very interested in books." Pause. "Of course, he is the enemy, but he's a friend, too."

I mentioned what I'd perceived of State Department types everywhere: after four or five overseas tours they either throw themselves into their environment or else they're oblivious to the people and land around them and simply treat their desk job as a generic assignment. The former can be enjoyable to meet; the latter are less fun than a clerk in the county recorder's office.

"That's true of diplomats from every country." Fernández served as cultural attaché at the Cuban embassy in London from 1962 to 1965. "We had some people there who went to work, then went straight home and watched television. Some of them never even bothered to learn English. They never went out in London."

Cultural attaché—a flattering position to many. To Guillermo Cabrera Infante, once an OW himself, a Cuban cultural attaché "is a slightly more important post than a porter's." Cabrera Infante speaks from experience—in the mid-1960s he was Cuba's cultural attaché in Belgium (where they had no porter). Mention of the self-exiled Cabrera Infante brought Pablo Armando to his forte, the blend of politics and literature. "Look at the ones who leave. They never write as well as they did in Cuba. The ones who settle in Miami—they are the worst because their energy is spent against Cuba. Reinaldo Arenas"—who joined the Mariel flotilla to the United States in 1980 after suffering in Cuba for his counterrevolutionary homosexuality—"he was a brilliant writer. Now look at him. His last few books have been poorly done."* "Heberto Padilla hasn't written anything really new. He aims everything at Cuba. These people think Miami is the center of literature. Bah." (Fernández is the only person I know who actually says bah.) "The best Cuban writers have gone to Barcelona, Paris, London, or New York."

"Cabrera Infante lives in London," I said. "Do you include him?" At the beginning of the Castro years the two had been colleagues at a literary weekly.

"Yes, but his best work was done in Cuba." Fernández underscored this with a jab of the finger. "*Three Trapped Tigers* was a wonderful book, a marvelous book. Since then he has not produced anything worthwhile."

"How about *View of Dawn in the Tropics?*"

"Bah, that was nothing." I've never known Fernández to flash the sideways smile. "Now, I don't have anything against those who leave. Anyone should be allowed to leave if they want, for any reason, to go anywhere, and then return if they want."

I ran into Pablo Armando a few weeks later, again on the UNEAC porch, looking natty in a sea blue *guayabera*, loose white slacks, and sandals. I had a recent *Esquire* with me. He took it out of my hands and started flipping through its pages. "I had a subscription to this magazine in the 1960s. Helen Lawrenson was here in Cuba. Years ago she wrote a famous piece for them, 'Latins Make Lousy Lovers.' " He focused on the advertisements. "Look at the quality of the photography and the reproduction! Look at her." He pointed at Elizabeth Taylor in an advertisement. "She's older than I am. She looks wonderful!"

---

*Arenas, suffering from AIDS, died of suicide in his Manhattan apartment four months after I spoke with Fernández.

I mentioned that I had been to the U.S. navy base at Guantánamo a few months earlier. "Oh, I would *love* to go there. I want to compare a U.S. company town in Cuba with a U.S. military town in Cuba."

A man entered the UNEAC building. Pablo Armando waved a genial hello, then turned to me. "He is an important man here. He doesn't do anything and he doesn't authorize anything. He doesn't care. All he wants to do is take trips to other countries and fuck the women. It's incredibly Cuban. He doesn't care who they are. He wants to do it so he can brag: 'I fucked three women in Portugal.' 'I spent a whole week with a woman and fucked her four times a day.' They come back with diseases. They don't care about their jobs. They just want to fuck. It's very Cuban, this—this—this machismo. Bah."

I could use some of Alejandro's optimism, I thought. When I asked for him at ICAP, though, the receptionist said he was working in the countryside. More and more *habaneros* were doing that. Three-week cycles on state farms were frequent. Most workers went, some of them willingly. The remaining office workers were surprised that fewer bureaucrats meant higher efficiency. Some workers were asked to move from the capital to farms for six-month stretches, with promises of decent rural housing. I met one who was told that if he and his *compañeros* didn't accept the offer they would be fired.

On the way back to the *hotelito* I stopped at the Socialism or Death bakery where I could scarcely believe my eyes: the line was short and the bins were full. A lady I knew who worked in the neighborhood had just come out with her booty. Our conversations had always been superficial and pleasantly friendly. "How lucky for us," I said. "A line so short. I can go from *el último* to *el primero* in one minute flat."

She said, "No one was here five minutes ago when they brought all the bread up from the back. You arrived just in time. In ten minutes the line will stretch to the corner." We were about to make our farewells when she looked straight at me. "Do you know that people are using toothpaste in the countryside to wash their clothes and bodies? '*¡32 y P'alante!*' " she spit contemptuously, referring to colorful billboards hailing the thirty-second year of the Revolution—32 and Onward! "Hah!" she snorted. "More like *¡32 y P'atrás!*," 32 and in Reverse. "I can see rationing in the first few years of the Revolution. Even ten years. But we're in the thirty-third year of the Revolution and people simply take it for granted. *I gave my youth to the country, my most active years*. Now I'm in my fifties and we're still being asked to make sacrifices." She turned and walked off with her bag of bread. The line was already out to the sidewalk.

Both Havana television channels and all the radio stations spoke excitedly of the impending film festival, officially called the International Festival of New Latin American Cinema. Even CMBF, the FM classical music station, plugged it. Instead of jetting in and out, as I had for a previous film festival, this time I saw the invasion of filmmakers, reporters, and cineastes from dozens of countries from the home team's dugout. It meant that Havana, long a sophisticated town for movies, would have ten days of cinema gluttony in movie houses all over town. Even theaters in the provinces upgraded their fare. An Ecuadoran feature film, *The Tigress*, unexpectedly captured moviegoers—initially because it was one of the very first feature-length movies ever from that country, and then, for its lusty tale of sisters, *campesinos*, and rural law. Anyone in town could go to most films, and the lines were long and occasionally got out of hand.

The major event was the premiere of the movie *Havana*, starring Robert Redford and Lena Olin, the same week as its opening in New York and Los Angeles. Tickets were hard to come by for the gala event. The film's director, Sydney Pollack, flew in for the occasion. Police cordoned off adjacent streets, crowded with *habaneros* who had no chance to get in. This was Havana's cultural aristocracy; if Cuba still had black-tie affairs, this would have been one of them. The latest in Latin American fashions paraded by the ticket takers. Men wore their best dress *guayaberas*, and women donned sparkling clothes and glittering jewelry. *Le tout* Havana was at the Karl Marx Theater.

Pollack opened the proceedings. The film, set in the final week of the Batista regime, had been shot in the Dominican Republic because U.S. law forbade shooting in Cuba—that would be Trading with the Enemy. (This, I noticed, did not stop the U.S. Interests Section from taking a row of seats.) The crowd of five thousand gave Pollack and his interpreter a standing ovation. "I must be crazy to show *Havana* in Havana," he said. "I apologize to any of you for anything that isn't authentic. I have the utmost respect for you and your country." And with that, Pollack left the Karl Marx Theater and the wide screen filled with Hollywood images of Havana, late 1958.

Robert Redford, a mid-stakes gambler from the States, meets Lena Olin, the European wife of Raul Julia, a revolutionary, and impulsively helps her smuggle weapons into Cuba. Julia is evidently killed in action. After Redford and the widow hit it off, news comes that her husband has not died; he's merely been disappeared and tortured. In the midst of all this she toys with the notion of following Redford back to the States. From that point on the two chase each other and dodge evil against a backdrop of revolution, repression, wickedness, and desperation. It bears a passing resemblance to the better-forgotten 1979 Sean Connery movie *Cuba*, and a canny resemblance to *Casablanca*.

Pollack's diligent research paid off, at least for the sets. His Santo Domingo 1990 streets looked respectably Havana 1958, those over forty told me afterward, right down to stores and intersections. Had he shot in Havana itself he would have used the Malecón more, he said later. The audience laughed with fondness at the mention of musician Enrique Jorrín, it spit out more laughter at the descriptions of Communism and revolution. At the end, the crowd offered polite applause. A Cuban I took with me said, "No guerrilla would act the way Lena Olin did." On the way out I bumped into José, a friend in his late forties, and asked, "Was it historically accurate?"

"Yes, a lot more than most movies about the Revolution, including our own. But the way Pollack showed it, the night Batista flees, all of Havana is out in the streets looting and breaking windows and celebrating. But it didn't happen that way. The news of Batista's departure didn't circulate widely until the next morning. *That's* when we started looting and breaking windows and celebrating."

Close to a hundred journalists and others confronted Sydney Pollack at his press conference the next day. "The film was demeaning to women," stated a freelancer covering the affair for the BBC. Applause. "It is typical of American imperialist attitudes," said a delegate from South America. More applause. Pollack sat behind a table, shrinking with each new accusation hurled his way. Even if Pollack was a well-intentioned friend, the middle-aged white Hollywood director personified American mainstream culture, and the progressive press wasn't going to let him get away unscathed. "Your understanding of revolution is lacking." Applause. "Why didn't you make your revolutionary a *latina*?" More applause. "This wasn't the real Latin America you portrayed." The clapping continued. Had this been football, the press would have been penalized for piling on.

Pollack rebounded softly. "I prefer to talk about politics through a love story. Whenever there is a man and a woman in a bedroom there is politics. The best love stories occur in tempestuous times." One Cuban thanked Pollack for using "the Revolution as the setting for your movie." This was followed by the day's silliest comment, from a *Bohemia* representative: "It is not we who should thank you for using the Revolution as a setting, but you who should thank us for having a revolution that you could use as a setting."

Pollack would have had a more pleasant afternoon had he volunteered for cane cutting in Niquero. "I wanted to film a love story," he explained, "and the weeks leading up to the overthrow of Batista were filled with turmoil, stress, and explosive activity. I wanted that for my background." Finally in exasperation he said, "I made my film. I didn't make your film." Applause.

This invitation arrived the next day:

Casa de la comunidad hebrea le invita a la fiesta de
CHANUKAH

Chanukah in Chavana! I had been looking forward to seeing the entire Jewish community gathered for this joyous occasion. José Miller, the doctor to whom I had given a box of Chanukah candles the year before, welcomed the hundreds of celebrants at the front door, one by one, in his capacity as president of the Jewish community. The annual Chanukah party drew Jews, half Jews, Gentiles, resident foreigners, and curious tourists. A few visitors who had come to Cuba for the film festival opted for the Jewish community center rather than the closing-night festivities at which *Hello, Hemingway* won top prize, and where the U.S. rap group Paris thrilled as many as it befuddled. Luis Chanivecky, the sweet retiree who served as the community's treasurer, came up to me smiling, holding a baby. "You want to meet the youngest Jew in Havana? Here he is." Abraham Berezniak, the kosher butcher and administrator of one of the synagogues in Habana Vieja, came with his family. I asked him if any of the Ashkenazi dominoes champions were there. Not yet, he replied, but he hoped that French-born Roberto Levy, in his eighties, would come, and also Samuel Nisenbaum, a Pole now in his seventies who moved to Cuba in the late 1930s. "I don't know if they're the best at dominoes or if they're simply the luckiest. But they always seem to win." Abraham's wife is a Gentile, as is Dr. Miller's. The statistic most discouraging to Cuba's dwindling Jewish community had been arrived at only recently: ninety-two percent of married Jews in Cuba have non-Jewish spouses.

Dr. Miller took the microphone. "I'd like to welcome everyone to the annual celebration of the Festival of Lights." We were seated at long banquet tables with tablecloths and vases of roses. "We always hold our Chanukah fiesta on a Sunday, and this year it falls on the sixth night." Miller drew attention to the foreigners who had come. "We live in Cuba and we have the opportunity to have a synagogue and to welcome all of you." He introduced the audience to some of the *machers* in local Jewry and thanked the women for arranging the elaborate gathering. If this had been a larger community he would have thanked the Hadassah. Dr. Miller's opening comments was one of the few speeches in Cuba that didn't close with "*¡socialismo o muerte!*"

Four giggling girls took the stage for a song, closing with a solo sung so off-key that twenty years from now the singer will still recall the event with horror.

Julie Avram, a twenty-one-year-old student from Caracas, spoke next. "I am visiting your city for the film festival, but I felt it was more important for me to be here than at the awards ceremony." She sang a song in Hebrew and gave a speech about the Jewish Diaspora. "Wherever we Jews are, in Cuba, in Venezuela, Miami, or Ecuador, wherever—we celebrate together." José Martí was impressed with a Chanukah service he attended in New York, and wrote about it for a Venezuelan newspaper. "For Jews," he wrote, "religious indifference is not just a crime, it is traitorous." Julie handed out copies of *Rumbo a Tu Judaísmo* (*Pathway to Judaism*), a magazine from Venezuela's Jewish community.

Dr. Miller lit the *shammes* candle with a lighter, then asked some youngsters to light each of the six candles. Finally the kitchen door swung open and the happy meal began: grapefruit, lettuce, tomato, chicken salad, cheese, a roll; a piece of chocolate and cake for dessert. The most impressive course came after weeks of fretting about ingredients: potato latkes. If it was *un milagro*, a miracle, that the Jews of more than two thousand years ago had enough oil to provide light for eight nights, it could at least be called *un milagrito* that the Patronato was able to come up with enough potatoes and eggs for latkes to feed the *fiesta de* Chanukah.

Carlos Ruiz de la Tejera, a high-profile actor and comedian, took the stage for an after-dinner monologue about life in Cuba. He made fun of the Royal Academy of Spanish in Madrid, and talked about the crowded *guaguas*, the buses. "They sure are an unusual way to meet people!" Ruiz de la Tejera had so perfected his stand-up routine that by its rhythm and flavored humor he could have gone straight from the Patronato to the *Tonight Show*.

Afterward in the lobby I met a man who had been active in Havana's

Jewish community until he left for Miami in 1961. He had returned to visit out of nostalgia. "I moved to the States because I wanted freedoms I couldn't get here. You know, we Jews can smell it when our freedoms are vanishing. We've sensed it for centuries. We thought we were supporting a Cuban revolution. We didn't know we were supporting a Communist revolution. Two of my closest friends live here still. One of them is sitting over there with his wife." He gestured to a nearby couch. "If there was an election tomorrow she would vote against Fidel. Him, he's not sure how he'd vote. The other friend is at the top of his field. He's a full beneficiary of the system. He shops in stores where he doesn't have to stand in line. He is privileged. He would defend the country against anything and anyone." We walked out to the sidewalk.

"I went to Habana Vieja the other day to see the houses I was brought up in. It broke my heart to see them, they were in such a deteriorated state. I wouldn't even show them to my wife. This was a beautiful city. Why did he have to turn it upside down? Things look so bad now. The people who have benefited from the Revolution are in the countryside. This country didn't need that sort of a revolution. Mexico or Ecuador maybe, countries where there is widespread poverty, but not here. You have to be very idealistic and dedicated to like living here now."

A few days later, on my way back from a stroll along the Malecón, I passed the entrance to the U.S. Interests Section and saw a short man wearing a yarmulke. I said in English, "You don't see many yarmulkes around here." Startled, he replied, "Are you Jewish?" He was an extremely Orthodox Jew, in Havana for a few days staying at a tourist hotel. He invited me to drop by later that evening.

In his room I asked what he did for a living. "Let's just say I have a degree in electrical engineering." He looked up at the ceiling. "They have a very lively smoke detector in this room." He implied that he works under contract to the State Department conducting routine electronic sweeps of overseas embassies.

He assumed his room was bugged. "I went to my rabbi about that. You know, under Jewish law it's forbidden to use electrical equipment on the Sabbath. I've sometimes found myself in situations where I knew I was speaking into a microphone on the Sabbath." He glanced up at the smoke detector. "I was very concerned that I was violating Jewish law. My rabbi said it was all right, that God understood."

The debugger had a consuming interest in Cuba's Jewish community. "I've only seen official Havana. I'm not allowed to travel around

town unless I'm with another person from the States. Regulations."
He eats devoutly kosher, and packs not only his own food, but also
cooking utensils, silverware, and serving dishes. Also tapes of Israeli
music, Bibles, wine, a hot plate, soup mix, gefilte fish, salami, black
bread; the whole shmear.

"When I go to another country I always travel with a suitcaseful of
extra things to give to Jews who can use them." He practiced *tzedakah*,
the Jewish act of charity, a trait taught in the Torah. He spread his
traveling offerings out on the bed. "I'm leaving on the flight tomorrow.
Do you think the community here could use any of this?" he asked,
pointing to the treasure.

My jaw hung open and I slapped my cheek. "Could they use any
of it? This stuff would be more welcomed than the Messiah!" In five
minutes he loaded me down with enough chozzerai to stock a Hadassah
flea market. "Just don't tell them my name. I'd like it to be from an
anonymous foreigner."

Of the eight degrees of Jewish charity, the debugger ranked second
highest: when the giver and receiver are both unaware of the other's
identity. (The highest is to give charity to someone in anticipation of
the need—a significant gift, a loan, or employment, for example.)

The next day I dropped by the Patronato and Adath Israel with
bagsful of the exotic food and cooking equipment. At the former, the
recipient was astonished: "You're like Santa Claus!" At the shul in
Habana Vieja, the tone was almost prayerful: "This is truly a *milagro*."
The debugger's next stop was Haiti.

Right after Carlos Ruiz de la Tejera finished his monologue on stage
at the Chanukah party I approached him. I had read about him in the
press, heard him on radio, and seen him on television talk shows.
He was fifty-eight and looked fifteen years younger. Long curly hair
surrounded an elastic face. I was curious about stand-up comedy in
Cuba, where everybody knew more than their ration of jokes—mocking, bawdy, or political. He invited me to drop by his place a week
later.

Ruiz de la Tejera has lived in the same nicely decorated two-bedroom
Vedado apartment near the Hotel Riviera since before the Revolution.
The living room is full of souvenirs from a dozen countries where he
has performed. He has the facial lines of an actor who can glide
effortlessly from Shakespearean drama to Neil Simon comedy. It is the
sort of face caricaturists love to draw and, in fact, hanging from
Ruiz de la Tejera's living room walls are ten large illustrations and

photographs of himself. The man must keep his modesty elsewhere. He also has an excellent stereo system, a VCR, and a twenty-one-inch color television.

Ruiz de la Tejera studied engineering in college. "But my heart really wasn't in it. I spent a lot of time writing satire and poetry. My father hated that. He said, 'Be an engineer!' He wouldn't let me take music lessons. Finally I won a scholarship to go to Holland and study engineering and I had to decide between that and trying to be an actor. It was the Revolution that allowed me to develop as an actor. If Cuba hadn't had a revolution I'd now be a bad engineer."

Shortly after the Revolution he studied the Stanislavsky acting technique. "I got the seed of acting there. I'd learned how to be serious and how to make people laugh. We all develop our own masks. As a teenager I was very funny at parties. It was my mask. I still wear it." Ruiz de la Tejera acted with different theater companies in the initial years of the Revolution. "I studied under a French mime and a Czech director. Eventually I made the transition from legitimate theater to musical varieties. For a long time I did a Victor Borge sort of takeoff with phonetic pronunciation, like this." He made nonsense noises, then launched into a dramatic recitation with gibberish words. His longest-lasting show, performed with Jesús del Valle, is called *Songs of Life and Love*, which includes poems by José Martí and Nicolás Guillén.

"I study Charlie Chaplin's films. American movies have been a great influence on me. I've seen *Modern Times* and *The Great Dictator* and the others so many times I had to stop and analyze them: why is Chaplin so good? I realized that satire is the elder sister of acting. Chaplin came from the music halls of England. His secret was his fear of loneliness. He's with women during the movies, but rarely at the end. He communicates fear."

Ruiz de la Tejera has acted in a dozen movies; his best-known role was as the psychiatrist in *Death of a Bureaucrat*. "I also admire Jack Lemmon and Richard Pryor and Woody Allen. I loved *Zelig* and *Hannah and Her Sisters*," then playing at Havana theaters. "I don't try to copy them, but I do study their technique."

A telephone call from a radio station interrupted our conversation. It was a live interview plugging a show to debut the following week. While Carlos was on the phone his full-time housekeeper—she shops for him and prepares his diet of fruit, vegetables, and fat-free milk—served me a glass of rum.

When he returned I asked if he had been active in the Revolution.

"Not really. Oh, I bought some *bonos*"—bonds—"to support it, and some friends were student leaders, but I wasn't active in the way you're thinking. I did work on the student strike, though." As part of a national theater troupe he cut sugarcane during vacations two consecutive years. "I also worked on tobacco plantations." More recently he's planted pine trees in Pinar del Río. "I love to plant trees. We've lost so much forest here."

"Are you a member of the Party?"

Carlos Ruiz de la Tejera shuddered. "Not me. I value my freedom." He laughed. "They tell you how to be and I couldn't stand for that. I am for the Revolution in my country. Look, I earn 340 pesos a month. I play hospitals and other places that need entertainment. I could earn double that if I wanted. I played for the soldiers in Angola. I went there twice with other artists and professors and doctors. If our troops hadn't been there Angola wouldn't exist."

Posted next to the front door to Carlos's apartment house was a list with the guard duty schedule for the building. His shift was the following night. "We take care of one another's things, look down the street, watch the stores. You feel good, like you're giving to others. See that maternity store across the street? I know everyone who works there."

He is familiar with Guillermo Alvarez Guedes, the popular Miami-based Cuban comedian. "I last saw him in 1958. He's against the Revolution. He's funny. He's very good, but he does the same things now that he did then." I didn't tell Carlos, but the lack of fresh material was the same comment *habaneros* made about his own humor. "Alvarez Guedes hasn't developed as a performer. He has no culture. To develop culture in a real way, well, you know what José Martí said: 'To be cultured is to be free.'

"Latin America has many problems. There's lots of gold and silver in Latin America but it's almost always in foreign hands. To open those hands would be to make Latin America great. It's the source of some of my material."

Do you use the ration book in your routines?

"No. You cannot joke about problems independent of ideology. It'd be very superficial to do that. There are other things deeper. For example, when I was last in the United States in 1985 I was in Chicago. First I went to the Art Institute and then I passed the Federal Plaza, where people were demonstrating against the contra war in Nicaragua. They held up pictures of those who had died. They suggested that people write their congressmen to protest the war. I was terribly moved. It was a very touching expression. The United States is like a giant losing his hair to cancer. Here, we're taking care of the cancer."

At four P.M. on the last Saturday of every month Carlos Ruiz de la Tejera gives informal workshops at the Napoleonic Museum near the University of Havana. In the crowded intimacy of the main chamber, the actor-comedian explains acting techniques, and fields questions from a public charmed by his rubbery face and his dramatic interpretations of José Martí's poetry.

If the five hundredth anniversary of Columbus's first trip across the Atlantic has brought on controversy and widespread reinterpretation, the one hundredth anniversary of José Martí's death three years later should bring on another sort of assessment and understanding. The legacy of Martí's writings has become embroiled in a tug-of-war between those who live in Cuba and those who have left. Castro quotes him often, but so do Cubans in the Diaspora. His political philosophy and literary output are part of the national heritage, and his words are well known throughout Latin America.

Martí, born in 1853, was raised in Havana, the son of a Spanish father and a mother from the Canary Islands. He was taken by the cause of Cuban independence from Spain while attending a private school in Havana. When a fellow student marched in a parade with the Spanish, fifteen-year-old Martí was arrested for writing a letter accusing him of selling out. Martí was sentenced to work in a stone quarry, an ordeal that left him with a hernia and half blind. After six months of hard labor he was transferred to a prison, finally pardoned, and banished to Spain. He was not yet eighteen.

In Spain Martí enrolled in a university, continued writing, and traveled to France and England and finally Mexico, where he worked for almost two years as a writer and editor. In 1877 he returned to Cuba under a false identity—he used his middle name and his mother's last name—but stayed less than two months. His next stop of any length was Guatemala, where he taught languages and philosophy. Along the way he met and married a Cuban living in Mexico, traveled a bit more, and with his pregnant wife returned to Havana, where, in 1878, they had a son.

The unsuccessful Ten Years War for independence from Spain ended that year, and Martí denounced the treaty that brought it to a close. Spanish authorities wanted to lock him up again—the guy just couldn't keep his mouth shut—but a high-ranking official agreed to let him off if he pledged allegiance to Spain. "Tell the general that Martí is not the kind of man that can be bought," he replied, speaking of himself in the third person. That landed him in prison in Spain.

He escaped, crossed into France, then traveled to New York, Venezuela, and back to New York, where he settled. In 1881 he was twenty-eight years old, unemployed, broke, in exile, with a wife and child back in Cuba.

From then until just before his death in 1895 he lived in the United States, making brief trips to Latin American countries to organize Cuban independence movements. Those fourteen years were spent in a tireless effort to stitch together the financial and intellectual support for an all-out war against Spain. He spoke and wrote eloquently for his cause in New York, Florida, and anywhere else people would listen. He also immersed himself in the culture of his adopted country and wrote for the *New York Sun*. His essays about the literary scene in the United States were widely published in Latin America.

"I am at last in a country where each one seems to be his own master," he wrote when he first arrived in New York. "One can breathe freely. For here, freedom is the foundation, the shield, the essence of life." These words, which were chosen by Radio Martí to grace the lobby of its building in Washington to show kinship with its namesake, are indicative only of the exuberance he felt upon arrival. Martí grew increasingly wary of his adopted country. "It is my duty," he wrote in his final days, "to prevent, by the independence of Cuba, the United States from spreading over the West Indies and falling, with that added weight, upon other lands of our America. All I have done up to now, and shall do hereafter I do to that end. . . . I have lived inside the monster and know its entrails—and my weapon is only the slingshot of David." That explains the billboards I saw in towns from Pinar del Río to Santiago—I AM WITH DAVID.

José Julian Martí y Pérez had a high forehead, a receding hairline, bushy eyebrows and mustache, deep-set eyes, a gaunt face, and ears that stuck out. He was thin. In the only photograph showing him with a smile he is holding his infant son. Like Castro, he appears to have worn only one set of clothes through his adulthood—in his case, a black frock coat over a high-collared white shirt with a black tie, and baggy trousers. Illustrations of Martí rowing ashore as he returned to Cuba to take part in the military phase of the war against Spain, and again as he rode into his only combat, show him in the same coat and tie. The full impact gives his brooding countenance a funereal sobriety.

Martí is considered the first modernist in Latin American poetry. The breadth of his political acumen casts him as a descendant of Simón Bolívar. Shrines to him are commonplace, not only in Cuba, but throughout the Caribbean and all of Latin America. Port-au-Prince, Haiti, has a rue José Marty. Costa Rica has a school named for him as well as a street that runs by the National Park, and a lyceum in Puntarenas; the country club run by San José's Cuban colony bears his name. In Brazil, both Rio de Janeiro and São Paulo have José Martí streets. Uruguay, which employed Martí as its vice consul to the U.S., memorializes him with a statue in Plaza Cuba. Even Spain, the target of Martí's wrath for most of his life, has a statue of him and another of his mother in the Canary Islands. Martí can be found twice in Paris: in the seventeenth arrondissement at the Square de l'Amérique Latine, and in the sixteenth at Place José Marti, a cement triangle in front of a cemetery. Florida, where Martí's speeches galvanized Cuban exiles, is full of monuments, parks, and streets dedicated to the intellectual rabble-rouser's memory. (He is said to have been a very un-Cuban-like speaker, slow, with final Ss pronounced.) Three New Jersey towns have Martí busts: Elizabeth, West New York, and Newark. The sculpture of Martí at the Avenue of the Americas entrance to New York's Central Park shows him the instant a Spanish bullet struck him dead, his horse rearing. The statue was completed in 1959, but its dedication was delayed six years because the city feared a nasty confrontation between competing ideologies that each claimed Martí as their own. In Los Angeles, a bust of Martí can be found at the northwest corner of Echo Park, in a working-class Latino neighborhood.

Godlike qualities were attributed to Martí immediately upon his death, which, writer Cabrera Infante has said, "was transformed by Cuban politicians into an unbearably messianic and neo-Christian burden." Tributes over the years have compared him to Buddha and, more commonly, to Christ. A magazine in 1957 called him the "perpetual ratification of love and goodness" who represents "for all Cubans decorum, dignity, sacrifice, and honor. . . . Let us see him as an immense and sacred God; like a Cuban God." Even before his death Martí had been called "apostle" in Cuba, canonization that eventually took hold in everyday conversation. His works have been translated into many languages, including Yiddish, and in 1953, a Jewish group in Cuba initiated a José Martí Forest in Israel. "There is no Cuban personality closer to the ideals of the ancient Hebrews than the immortal José Martí," a Jewish leader wrote in a newspaper column headlined "Martí and the Jews." In the 1960s Cuban bus tickets had Martí's words on them. Locks of his hair were exhibited. Many referred to him as the Cuban Gandhi.

An attempt was made around 1980 to change his status from apostle, with its disturbing religious connotations. It failed. In Cuba, it is not uncommon to see two, or even three books by or about Martí published the same month. Every week another workshop or seminar on Martí, his politics and his writing, takes place. The Center for the Study of José Martí in collaboration with the country's Geographic and Cartographic Institute published an elaborate *Biographical and Historical Atlas of the Life of José Martí*, in which the poet's life becomes the center of the universe and all events between 1853 and 1895 swirl around him. Detailed street maps of the different cities he lived in pinpoint his homes; a map shows the route he followed across the Atlantic from Havana to Spain. We learn he once mailed a letter from Waycross, Georgia; that Arecibo, Puerto Rico, had supporters of Martí's Cuban Revolutionary Party; that a Venezuelan newspaper didn't print news of his death for more than two months. His dimensions and the size of his clothes are included as well: Martí stood five foot six, weighed 140 pounds, and had dark eyes. The force behind the Cuban independence movement wore a size 65 (centimeter) vest and had a svelte thirty-two-inch waistline. (Dimensions courtesy Ramón Antonio Almonte, a tailor in the Dominican Republic who measured the apostle in March 1895.) It does not mention that because of his drinking his friends were said to have called him *ginebrita*, gin-head. Nor does it refer to his ode to hashish, "the mysterious plant, fantastic poetry of the earth," which concludes, "Hashish! . . . come to my mouth!"

Martí introduced Ralph Waldo Emerson and Walt Whitman to Latin America, and wrote about Mark Twain, Washington Irving, Louisa May Alcott, and Henry David Thoreau for a Spanish-speaking audience. Shortly after arriving in New York he wrote a friend, "If you could see me struggling to dominate this beautiful but rebellious English; three or four months more and I shall open a way for myself." His syndicated columns covered domestic U.S. politics, which he saw as increasingly corrupt, and U.S. foreign policy, whose frightful expansionism alarmed him. He wrote of women's suffrage, the streets of New York, and the memorial service for Karl Marx. He sympathized with the anarchists hanged for the Haymarket Square labor riot in 1886. "This Republic," he wrote, "has fallen into the injustice and violence of monarchies." His writing was of the sort that might appear in the *New Yorker*—descriptive, and a bit precious. He foretold his own death, chronicled in his poetry and prose. "I am now, every day, in danger of giving my life for my country," the apostle wrote in an unfinished epistle the day before he died. He was a humanist and an optimist whose grief-stricken verse often dealt with nature and love, frequently infused with a subtle sensuality.

One day toward the end of my stay I learned of two youngsters who swore they saw José Martí and Fidel Castro whispering to each other on the streets of Habana Vieja. The kids were half right. The fellow at Fidel's side was Daniel Lugo, a Puerto Rican actor playing Martí in a Venezuelan film production of Martí's life. A front-page picture in *Juventud Rebelde* showed the most influential Cuban of the nineteenth century talking to the most influential Cuban of the twentieth century. What advice should the poet have given the premier?

Two other films have featured Martí. One, *La Rosa Blanca* ("The White Rose," named for a famous Martí poem), was a Mexican production starring a Mexican, written by a Mexican, and filmed partly in Mexico. Despite heavy chauvinistic criticism, the movie is said to be a decent portrayal of Martí. Richard Gray, a Florida professor, saw it at a Cuban theater in 1956 and wrote that it was poorly attended and "subject to ribald comments and laughter." A far worse film was *Santiago*, a 1956 Hollywood movie about the Spanish-Cuban-American War that has Martí alive in 1898, living in opulence in Haiti. When Martí appeared onscreen, the "audience roared with laughter accompanied with good-natured sarcasm," Gray wrote. *Santiago* still provokes venom: thirty-five years after Warner Brothers released it, *Granma* called it "philistine and degrading," and an "appalling neocolonial product made in the pseudorepublic that frustrated Martí's dreams."

One of the first places Martí lived in New York was a rooming house run by a Cuban-Venezuelan woman, Carmen Miyares de Mantilla. His wife—also named Carmen—didn't care for José's exile politics and preferred to live in Cuba under Spanish rule. A few years earlier Martí had written, "Others go to bed with their mistress; I with my ideas," but now, while his wife and their son, Pepito, lived in Havana, José went to bed with both. When Havana Carmen visited her husband in New York she may have noticed that New York Carmen was about to give birth, but she certainly didn't know that the father was her husband. After a trip that confirmed their estrangement, and less than three years following their marriage, Carmen Zayas Bazán de Martí returned to Havana with two-year-old Pepito, and a few days later in New York José became a father again.

Martí showered affection and gifts on María, his new child, but she grew up thinking he was her godfather. María married in 1905, and two years later gave birth to a boy, Cesar. José Martí, revered throughout Latin America for his soft-spoken revolutionary militance, was the grandfather of Cesar Romero, the gallant Hollywood romantic who has appeared in more than one hundred movies, including *The Gay Caballero, Viva Cisco Kid*, and the 1966 *Batman*.

Cesar Romero's mother didn't know who her natural father was until she was in her fifties, the actor told writer José Miguel Oviedo. "All the Cubans in New York in those days knew," he said. "But no one said a word" to María, "not even her mother." The actor told a Cuban journalist, "Undoubtedly Martí was the Man of the Century, and the fact that I am his grandson fills me with great pride." Martí carried a picture of his fourteen-year-old daughter over his heart when he went into his one fateful battle, "to protect against bullets."

A middle-aged Havana music teacher, according to author Richard Gray, said she knew "a socially prominent Cuban woman . . . who was Martí's second illegitimate child by a woman in Cuba. As to this reflecting a defect in Martí's character, she laughed and said that in view of Martí's greatness one could forget anything. He was, after all, 'very gallant with the ladies.' "

The wholesale devotion to Martí can be understood, but it is surprising that no one has written a novel demythologizing his life, à la Gabriel García Márquez's fiction about Simón Bolívar, *The General in His Labyrinth*.

Martí's tender prose lends itself to parody, but Cabrera Infante is the only writer I could find who has spoofed the apostle. In *Three Trapped Tigers* he imagines how Martí might have covered the death of Leon Trotsky (who was killed thirty-five years after Martí died). Scatological versions of his poetry have been schoolyard fare for generations, told and retold by students who, from infancy, are showered with his words and likeness.

More bicycles arrived from China. The shift in transportation patterns was becoming more evident. Whether going to school, work, or the beach, to visit friends across town or relatives across the country, Cubans were changing how they traveled. In the cities some people simply hopped on the backs of trucks. In the countryside, more and more oxen were replacing fewer and fewer tractors. Like the ration system, provisional at its inception in the early 1960s and now a permanent part of the country's culture, the transportation problem was seen as a situation that would never return to its previous condition.

The U.S. blockade was a handy and blameworthy excuse, but it had become part of Cuba's rhetorical soundtrack. In the increasingly fractured final months of Mikhail Gorbachev's rule, Cuba was suffering almost as much as the Soviet republics. Soviet oil tankers were no longer part of the seascape. Beasts of burden had become part of the landscape.

The house where José Martí was raised has been preserved as a museum. It's close to the major train station and not too far from the docks. Why didn't Martí become an engineer or a stevedore or something useful? I started to ponder this sacrilegious thought late one afternoon in Havana's Central Park, where, in 1949 when Harry Truman and Carlos Prío were in power, two drunken U.S. sailors scandalized Cuba by urinating on the statue of Martí, after which one of them climbed up on José's shoulder. A columnist responded, "The offense committed by these devils dressed as sailors is the same as that which is instigated daily against Cuba by the imperialists." Quickly, a stateside car company with a Havana showroom set up a scholarship for Americans to study Martí at the University of Havana summer school, and the U.S. ambassador, and later a delegation of sailors, laid a wreath of flowers at the monument.

I started over to some friends' apartment, and at Neptuno and Industria I waited for traffic to clear while standing on the southeast corner, *la esquina de fraile*—the friar's corner, so called in past generations because as the corner with least direct sunlight it was considered worthy of a friar. A sign plastered on a wall had won my most-ubiquitous-slogan award: THE FUTURE OF OUR COUNTRY IS AN EVERLASTING BARAGUA. Baraguá, a small town in eastern Cuba, has become a buzz word for never-say-die. It was there in 1878 that General Antonio Maceo renounced a treaty between Cuban insurgents and Spanish generals ending the Ten Years War. Maceo, a guerrilla tactician, pledged to fight on for independence rather than agree to anything less. The Protest of Baraguá, as it became known, was a short-term failure—Maceo and his dwindling forces gave up a few months later—but eventually the independence movement regained steam, and today to mention Baraguá is like saying "Remember the Alamo."

I bought a bag of cookies at the hard-currency counter of the Hotel Lido, where I had stayed on arrival the previous summer, and dropped in on my friends. My own etiquette dictated that a foreigner with dollars should always bring along a little something when paying a social call. I had met a foreigner who felt quite the contrary—that to do so reinforced the uncomfortable distinction between Cuban and foreigner. This point of view struck me as ideology colliding with companionship, and while I knew Cubans who respected it, I never met one who agreed with it.

My friends had some rum they had acquired on the black market. "It would have gotten out to the public sooner or later anyway. We just got it ahead of time." They put on a cassette by Los Van Van, the big dance band whose Afro-Cuban rhythms had made them a hit on stages in Latin America and Europe. It reminded me that Avilés had not gotten back in touch about the intramural baseball game against Los Van Van. Further oboe lessons were beginning to seem as unlikely as Gloria Estefan singing Cuba's national anthem in Havana's Latin American Stadium. I repeated for the rum and cookies crowd what I had heard about Los Van Van a few days earlier: Fidel comes back to Cuba a hundred years after he dies and goes up to the first man he sees. "Who was Fidel Castro?" he asks, expectantly. "Fidel Castro? Never heard of him."

Surprised, Fidel goes into a nearby school and asks a student, "Who was Fidel Castro?" The student thinks hard. "Fidel Castro?" she says. "I don't know."

Concerned, Fidel goes into a history class and asks the teacher, "Who was Fidel Castro?" "Mmm—I don't think I've heard the name," the teacher replies. Upset, Fidel marches to the school library and looks himself up in the encyclopedia. CASTRO Ruz, FIDEL, it says. *President of Cuba while Los Van Van were popular.*

The receptionist at my *pensión* handed me a message that Salmerón from the Sports Institute had called. I should report to the ballpark in Matanzas at noon the following Tuesday and Juan Castro, manager of the Pinar del Río Forestales, would be waiting for me. The next morning I thought I glimpsed Wormold's ancient Hillman tooling along the Malecón.

The *Tribuna* ran this announcement for Coppelia one day: "They're out of cocoa and strawberry syrup, but they hope to have them back very soon. They want to produce the flavors that people prefer."

Coppelia was still selling ice cream. Fewer flavors, shorter hours, longer lines, but still Coppelia ice cream. Coppelia, established in 1966 as a showcase of egalitarian cones and sundaes, replaced El Carmelo, a step on the prerevolutionary social staircase. Coppelia now takes in ten million pesos a year from an estimated thirty thousand customers a day throughout the country.

"¿*El último?*" I asked a man carrying an empty plastic bowl. I was already two scoops to the wind and wanted more. The line was stalled, and looked at least a half hour long. The first ice cream line formed in 1810, when Boston sent Cuba its first block ice, but Havana already had an ice machine. By the middle of the nineteenth century Cuba had already developed the art of making and marketing ices. Anthony Trollope wrote in 1859 that most men passed their time "eating ices and playing billiards. The accommodation in Havana for these amusements is on a very large scale." An 1868 *Handbook for Havana* exclaimed, "It is perhaps in the sherbets that the Havana confectioners will be found by visitors from abroad to excel." Federico García Lorca slurped prodigious amounts of ice cream when he visited in 1930. A Party member and a homosexual converse over ice cream at Coppelia in "The Woods, the Wolf, and the New Man," a short story by Senel Paz set in contemporary Havana. The two are sitting at a highly visible table, which somewhat unnerves the Party member. "Although there was chocolate that day," the Communist recalls of his dining companion, "he had ordered strawberry. Perverse."

The man in front of me planned to fill his plastic bowl with ice cream, then hurry home in his car in which his family was parked a block away. He had tried the newest flavor, strawberry bonbon, a few days earlier. Huge cardboard buckets of *rizado de chocolate*, chocolate swirl, arrived on a cart and the line started to move. The plastic bowl man nudged me. "Look. Maybe the wait was worthwhile after all."

Forestales manager Juan Castro stands slightly over six feet. He's a good-looking fellow, almost matinee-idol handsome, with slightly wavy black hair, clear brown eyes, and baseball muscles. When the thirty-seven-year-old retired catcher greeted me at the Matanzas stadium, his team was in the middle of its morning workout, preparing for the opener of a three-game series that night. He wore the Forestales uniform: green cap, tree green jersey with *Forestales* scripted across the front, and white pants. He had been expecting me, which reinforced my notion that INDER, the Sports Institute, was the most efficient government *organismo* in a distressingly muddled bureaucracy. We chatted a bit and he turned me over to the front office crew for the home team Matanzas Henequeneros.

The Henequeneros—literally, those who work with henequen fiber—were national champions. They had beat Havana on the final day of the previous season and now, with the new season under way, they were again leading the league with an 8-2 record. The Forestales, on the other hand, with a 3-9 season, were the doormats of the league. The three Matanzas baseball executives didn't quite phrase it like that, but that was the clear impression they gave. Ramón, the provincial baseball commissioner, and Armando, on the board of directors, left me with Carlos, the Henequeneros' publicist.

I told Carlos about the youngsters playing ball on the beach east of Baracoa. "Let's say one of them is named Julio." I picked the name in honor of Julio Becquer, the Cuban first baseman and pinch hitter for my boyhood Washington Senators. "How could Julio get to play for the Henequeneros or any of the other teams?"

It's a simple process, he said. Julio starts out on community sports fields, and at age ten, if he's got the knack, desire, and parental permission, he begins Sports Initiation School. Julio and the others are picked by playground directors and other sports bureaucrats for this boarding school. Julio goes to classes in the morning and takes physical education in the afternoon. Baseball development at these schools goes in two-year cycles, promoting the ones with aptitude and potential. If Julio is among the best players in the sixteen-to-eighteen-year-old bracket, he's promoted to the provincial squad for play in the eighteen-team, forty-five-game Serie Nacional. Each province plus the city of Havana has a team in the National Series, and two provinces and the city of Havana field two teams each. Those second teams are made up of freshmen playing rookie ball, on-the-job training for developing players. The National Series has a east and west divisions that compete in playoffs after the regular season. When the playoffs are over, if Julio is among the best players in the National Series, he is tapped for one of the eight teams consolidated from the original eighteen to play in the Serie Selectiva. It was the sixty-three-game Selective Series championship that Matanzas had won the previous spring. The best players from the Selective Series represent Cuba in postseason international play such as the Caribbean, Pan American, or Olympic games.

Carlos sat me down in front of a monitor to watch a videotape of the last game of the Selective Series in its entirety. "We won in the final innings. It's very exciting." The first few innings were very unexciting, and I wandered back to Carlos's office behind the upper-deck grandstands.

"Seen enough? All right." He walked over to a closet and picked out a few items. "The Henequeneros would like you to have these as souvenirs of your trip." Carlos weighed me down with heavy medals of José Martí, the Henequeneros, and Vladimir Lenin. I stashed them in the bag with my Rawlings glove.

"Are you sure you want to stay in the dorm?" My request had been approved on the local level. "It's full of dirty clothes. It's sweaty. You'd rather stay there than a hotel?" Carlos's question had an air of disbelief. "There's probably no room, anyway. We expanded the size of the teams this year, and with the trainer and the driver and the others in the dorm, too, well, I doubt they can squeeze you in."

"If I wanted great accommodations I'd stay at Varadero," the sparkling international resort nearby. "But right now I'm interested in baseball, not the beach."

Carlos took me to the stadium's catacombs beneath the grandstands, where my team, the Forestales, was just returning to its locker room cum dormitory. Outside, a grounds crew was smoothing the base paths in Matanzas's 35,000 seat Estadio Victoria a Girón. Yes, Matanzas, a province that includes Playa Girón—the Bay of Pigs—named its stadium for the 1961 Cuban triumph there. "Victory at Girón Stadium" could be translated to We-Whipped-the-Pants-Off-the-Invaders Stadium. Baseball, America's most peaceful and benevolent export, is celebrated in a stadium named for one of its most disastrous and humiliating defeats.

Juan Castro held a team meeting to announce that night's starting line-up, and what they could expect from the Henequeneros. "We're facing Ariel Tapanes. He's got a good fastball." Juan had played on Pinar del Río's A-team for sixteen years. His half-dressed players lounged on bunk beds, some, including manager Castro, puffing on cigarettes. Castro introduced me. "He will be with us for the next few days."

"El Man," as he is called behind his back, asked me to say a few words. "If it's all right with you, and there's room, I'd like to stay in the dorm with you guys. And if there's enough food in the dining rooms, I'd be honored to eat with you as well."

A voice came up from the dominoes game in the back: "If we don't have enough food, well, we'll just each take smaller portions." A murmur of assent came from some two dozen players. They cleared a lower bunk for me against the wall. The dorm had a refrigerator but no booze, and two tables for dominoes, where I refused a friendly invitation to play from pitcher Félix Asqui.

I stayed in the dorm for two hours during which my teammates

listened to my shortwave radio, passed my glove around, and told me
about their favorite movies. Radio reception underneath the stadium
was decidedly limited. Asqui, a southpaw, asked if I would trade my
Rawlings for his Cuban mitt. An outfielder in the bunk next to mine
said, "Henry Fonda is one of my favorites. What is his most recent
movie?"

"*On Golden Pond,*" a shortstop answered.

"Right. *On Golden Pond.* How is he?"

"He died a few years ago."

A chorus of "*¡Noooo!*"'s went through the players faster than a
6-4-3 double play.

Manager Castro pulled a T-shirt out of his bag and held it up
proudly. It said MILLINGTON, TENNESSEE on it. He had played there
on the Cuban all-star team in 1986. Rodolfo Martínez, a certified old-
timer in his sixties known to all as Tata (Gramps), came in with a
big plastic bag of crackers. Everyone stuck his hand in for a fistful.
The lights were dimmed and the Pinar del Río Forestales took their
afternoon nap.

When we woke up, Carlos, the home team publicist, had bad news
for me. He had been in touch with INDER in Havana; I was to stay
in a hotel. "We've arranged a room for you at the Louvre. It's not the
best in the world. All the efforts at hotel improvement in Matanzas
province go to Varadero. The city of Matanzas itself is overlooked."

The Louvre had obviously once been a gem of a hotel. Frosted
windows had etched designs, doors were wide, the lobby grand, the
ceilings high, and the grillwork fancy. It was not, however, one of
those you-should-have-seen-it-before-the-Revolution gems; a friend
who stayed there in the mid-1950s tells me he thought at the time,
gosh, I bet this was once a wonderful hotel. Whatever its history, it
gave the impression that no one had paid much attention to it above
the ground floor. Stuffed chairs surrounded a television at the top of
the stairs to my floor. My room had a tall armoire, a large bureau, a
mirror dimmed by rust that stretched halfway to the twenty-foot-high
ceiling, a mattress spongier than packaged white bread, frayed sheets,
and two tall, narrow doors that opened on to a balcony overlooking a
plaza. The four umpires roomed down the hall.

Back at We-Whipped-the-Pants Stadium, a tall, skinny fellow ner-
vously paced the empty field. He was seventeen-year-old Pedro Luis
Lazo, a pitcher from San Juan y Martínez, the tobacco-growing region.
Lazo was starting for the Forestales in the opener against the Henequeneros. So far that season he had pitched eighteen innings and given up

only one run. It was late afternoon, and the rest of the players passed the time shining shoes, playing dominoes, reading.

The visiting team dining room was on the second level through a few doors and hallways. I passed a sign that said IF DISCIPLINE EXISTS IN YOUR HOME, PRACTICE IT HERE TOO. The Forestales were served generous portions of bean soup, rice, lettuce, tomato, plantains, milk, and yogurt. A sign on the wall said:

If I'm ahead of you, follow me
If I slow down, push me
If I go backward, kill me.

I sat beneath the sign with Tata. We talked about the difference between baseball in the States and Cuba. "You have stronger and superior players. There can be no doubt about that. Our system doesn't allow for that sort of professionalism. But every time we play the U.S. amateur team we win. We beat the professional teams from Mexico and Venezuela."

Tota came from Pinar del Río. "You know, Pedro Ramos came from Pinar del Río."

"I used to take the trolley to Griffith Stadium to see Ramos pitch for the Senators. Now there's no trolley, no Griffith Stadium, no Senators."

"I remember when Ramos went to play for Washington."

"We had a saying, Washington—first in war, first in peace, and last in the American League."

"In those days I played for the Matahambre Mine team in Pinar del Río in the Liga Popular," the People's League. "Nineteen forty-five to 1956. First and third base. We were the champions in 1955. That year I batted .375 and hit thirty-two home runs." Tata had also worked one kilometer below ground level in an open-pit mine.

"Then I joined the Revolution. I was a combatant against the dictator Batista in the Sierra de los Organos." Tata's nom de guerre during the fighting was Iso. We finished our yogurt and left for the locker room.

Pedro Luis Lazo lasted almost three innings before Juan Castro mercifully pulled him out. He had tossed out the first Henequenero on a weak ground ball back to the mound. The second batter hit an easy one-hopper that second baseman Alexis González bobbled. Tata leaned back, pointing his chin toward González. "He's new. He's nervous.

Remember, this is a school team. They're still learning." Jorge Gall-
ardo in center field caught a long fly on the run for the second out.
Right-handed Lázaro Junco stepped up and the crowd of some ten
thousand roared. Junco, hitting .320, took a few practice swings with
his aluminum Emerson bat. His swings were high and level. Lazo
threw a fastball, strike one. Junco fouled off a low pitch, strike two.
Ball one, high and inside. Ball two, low and outside. Chatter from
the dugout, "Strike 'em out, you can do it." "Over easy, over easy."
The windup and the pitch, the swing and the aluminum *clenk*. Lázaro
Junco sent a high fastball to left-center field so hard that the outfielders
never bothered with the obligatory jog toward the wall. Junco's two-
run homer was still on a skyward trajectory when it cleared the fence,
flew over the bleachers, and left We-Whipped-the-Pants Stadium. He
must have hit it halfway to Baraguá. On the Forestales' bench manager
Castro sat with his chin in his palm, a pose he was to grow accustomed
to throughout the season. "That was a gift," batting coach Benietez
whispered to him. "A gift."

The Forestales got one hit in two innings while the Henequeneros
kept piling up runs. In the bottom of the second Matanzas catcher
Jesús Figueroa doubled to right center. Lazo walked a circle around
the mound and faced Carlos Kindelán, batting .340. He walked him.
"The kid is nervous," Tata repeated. Juan Castro trotted out to the
mound. Four infielders and the catcher joined him. Castro nodded.
Lazo nodded. The four infielders and the catcher nodded. Lazo threw
a change-up strike to Julio Fernández, Matanzas's first baseman. On
the next pitch Fernández laid down a bunt that dribbled to the third
base side of the mound. Before Lazo could pick it up and uncork his
long frame the bases were loaded. That's when Juan Castro yanked
him.

By the seventh inning the score was 6–0, Matanzas. The Forestales's
Pedro González provided a good argument against the designated
hitter: he struck out three times. After his second missed swing in his
third at bat Juan Castro yelled from the dugout, "*Muchacho*, control
yourself!" A woman wearing a Minnie Mouse T-shirt that said BOP
TILL YOU DROP leaned over the railing next to the dugout. "Do you
like baseball," a coach asked her, "or baseball players?"

She smiled. "Let's just say I'm a fan."

During the seventh-inning stretch twenty-seven-year-old Rogelio
Saliente ran around the field twice. Rogelio was running from Santiago
to Havana on behalf of the National Workers Federation, carrying the
flag of Cuba the entire way. He had left Santiago almost three weeks

earlier on the anniversary of the landing of the *Granma* at Playa las Colorada. He had run more than eight hundred kilometers so far, and the media had been covering his efforts almost daily. Saliente, in his track clothes, had dropped in on the team dining rooms earlier and maneuvered himself in front of every reporter he could find for an interview. "I hope to arrive in Havana in two days in time for the League of Federated Students Congress. I'm also running in recognition of José Martí, who lives in our hearts. He's not dead, he's alive." When Rogelio ran around the field the crowd cheered, especially when it was announced that he had fought in Angola. Players in both dugouts stared at each other with a who-*is*-this-guy? look on their faces. Saliente had another hundred kilometers to go in his cross-country marathon.

The stadium that Saliente ran in was built in the mid-1970s. It has well-cared-for grass and no prevailing winds to turn pop-ups into home runs. The outfield fence is 325 feet down the foul lines and 400 feet to dead center. Even during the Special Period banks of powerful stadium lights illuminated the field from all angles. The electronic scoreboard did not sing or dance or explode or turn into a television screen or shout *CHARGE!!!* It gave the inning-by-inning score, the batter's name and his up-to-the-minute average, the count, and scores from around the league. The fans were in a good mood, chatty, noisy, quick to respond, slow to boo. Down the left field line a sign said LIVE LONGER, PLAY SPORTS. The right field sign said SMOKING IS BAD FOR YOUR HEALTH.

We-Whipped-the-Pants Stadium is also a civil defense center. An elaborate series of instructions and illustrations lined a huge wall next to the major ramp behind the grandstands. One panel asks, "What is a zone of Defense? A zone of defense is a division of the national territory in parts smaller than cities. It grows in times of peace and activates in time of war. . . . It assures internal order . . . and the continuity of the life of the whole country." Baseball fans walked by the display as if it were a familiar decoration. One panel listed the supplies each defense brigade should have. They include ten kilograms of TNT, twenty-five blasting caps, fuses, a land mine, and concertina wire. Beneath the list was a drawing of a box of grenades. The next poster listed "Favorable Positions for Firing on the Enemy." Drawings showed civilians shooting down unmarked planes and firing on an unidentifiable foe from buildings, trees, bunkers, and foxholes. The Forestales picked up their one and only run with three singles in a row during the time it took to read that far.

A set of instructions told how to prepare food with a minimum of utensils. One method: "Use a reflector to help the fire and hide from observation. If you see parachutes falling, do the following: yell There are parachutists! We must act quickly! Tell everyone we saw some parachutists!" Children have their own special guidelines: "If I'm in school I tell my teacher. If I'm at countryside school, I tell the Pioneer guide. If I'm in my house, a theater, park, or anywhere else, I tell my parents and the CDR." What to look for: "Falling objects, a change in vegetation, helicopters, unusual overflights or nosediving planes, dead or sick animals, fire, and infiltration from the sea." A drawing showed a Cuban throwing a Molotov cocktail at an approaching enemy tank.

A roar went up from the crowd inside the stadium.

"The war of all the people covers strategic planning in case of military aggression against Cuba by the United States Armed Forces. Revolutionaries, all patriotic Cubans, every dignified man or woman will have a task, a place, and a form of repelling and annihilating the enemy. We follow the principles of a prolonged and total armed struggle. All methods of warfare will be used because it's a strong and predatory enemy . . . and the war will be fought in conditions of total blockade, isolated and separated by thousands of kilometers from our allies." When I finally got back to the Forestales' bench, the Henequeneros had scored twice more—doubles and singles. The score was 8–1.

In the bottom of the eighth inning, with one out and home run hitter Lázaro Junco on first—he was four-for-four—the power went out. The stadium was black. The only light came from stars over the Caribbean. Fans reached into their pockets for matches and lighters to hold aloft. Soon the grandstands looked like the end of a Bob Dylan concert. No one knew if this was a stadium outage, a citywide blackout, or foreign invaders. Matches and a lantern lighted the Forestales' dugout. I gave Félix Asqui, the pitcher who coveted my Rawlings glove, my portable radio to tune in the local station for news. Tata produced a thermos of hot coffee and poured *cafecitos* for everyone. The umpires conferred with Matanzas team officials. Instead of finding a local station Asqui tuned in Ramón Rivera's nightly call-in sports talk show broadcast from Havana.

In the dugout, infielders started thumping on their helmets, first quietly, then incrementally louder. Their drumming had a polyrhythmic beat to it. Outfielders and pitchers clenked aluminum bats against each other for the obbligato. Soon a designated hitter began dancing the rumba by himself, quickly joined by a catcher and a coach. Finally more than half of the Pinar del Río Forestales baseball team was jumping and jiving, singing and dancing. Members of the Communist Party shook their bodies alongside players who had no political interest. The home team had an Afro-Cuban jam session, too. Black players began the spontaneous outburst, joined quickly by mulattoes, then whites. A friend who lives across from the Latin American Stadium in Havana told me that at major games the whole place shakes with singing and dancing.

An assistant to the official scorer wandered into the dugout. "This is our way of combating reality," she said, swaying to the beat. I told her that in my country if a stadium's power had gone out during a game the electrical contractor would probably be fined for each minute of waiting time. She thought I was joking.

Lights came back on an hour later, but only a few hundred fans had stayed to see Matanzas mop up the Forestales. After each game both teams have pizza and soft drinks delivered to the dugout. The umpires gave me a lift back to the Hotel Louvre.

Instead of going to the Forestales' workout the next morning I went to see Rafael Bango, a retired pharmacist and president of the local boosters club. The previous evening Bango had invited me to drop by the Peña Deportiva Parque de la Libertad, the Freedom Park Sports Club, which meets at the Sala de Historia de Deportes de la Provincia de Matanzas, the Matanzas Province Sports History Hall. The sports museum had photographs of great athletes in Matanzas's past. It was named for Santiago García, a bygone boxer. One photograph showed José Raúl Capablanca, the chess champion, at age four playing against his father during a trip to Matanzas. Exhibits showed plaques from winning efforts by Matanzas athletes, and often the clothes they wore in competition. Dr. Bango and a few of the other boosters told me about themselves in the meeting room behind the exhibits.

"For a long time we were simply a group of baseball fans who weren't very organized," the sixty-eight-year-old said. "Last year we traveled with the team to Santiago, and while we were there we saw their sports fans get together at Plaza Martí. We said if they can do it so can we. Now we have more than a hundred members." Havana also has a boosters club, which meets at Parque Central. It's called La Esquina Caliente, the Hot Corner.

I liked Bango for his name, but also because he seemed a contented retiree who wants nothing more from life than to cheer his home team to victory. "When we get together we give our opinions on the teams.

Sometimes the players come. When we lose we talk about what went wrong. All members express themselves on any sports subject, but it must be constructive. We have one rule at the *peña*—you can't speak badly about a *compañero*. We also take up problems with the team's management. For example, a lot of people have been complaining about the bus service to the stadium. We brought it up at the *peña* and now the team is working on it.

"We used to meet twice a month, but now in the baseball season we get together every week. We also follow boxing, basketball, soccer, cycling, and gymnastics. And girls' softball! Of course we talk about the competitiveness and the spirit of sports, too. Have you heard of Yaquelín Hernández? She won a silver medal in kayaking at the Caribbean games in Mexico this year. She is from Matanzas." Hanging above Dr. Bango was a poster of Che Guevara with a dead cigar in his right hand.

"We have three sections at the stadium on the home team side for ourselves and our guests. Won't you please join us this evening?" Membership in the *peña* costs fifty centavos a month. Admission to all baseball games for everyone in Cuba is free. Before I left, Bango gave me a copy of the *peña*'s by-laws.

Francisco, a large man who gives the play-by-play for Matanzas on Radio 26, had been at the *peña*, and walked me over to the Tea Room for some iced tea. "This is a cultural center at night. Writers and artists congregate here." We dropped in across the street at the local chess club, where a poster of Che showed him deep in thought over a chessboard. He had white; his opponent was out of the picture. Carlos, the Matanzas flack, had joined us, and noticed me looking at Che. "He wasn't much of a ballplayer," Carlos acknowledged.

Havana 51, Matanzas 9. That's a baseball score, not a mileage sign. The merciless drubbing took place at Palmar de Junco Stadium in Matanzas on December 27, 1874, the first officially recorded baseball game in Cuba. The stadium, built in the Pueblo Nuevo neighborhood, was used for league play for more than a hundred years, and up-and-coming athletes still use its field for learning baseball fundamentals from government coaches. Pueblo Nuevo has become a breeding ground for successful players. Three major-league infielders grew up in the shadows of Palmar de Junco—Bert Campaneris (A's, Rangers, Angels, Yankees, 1964–83), José Valdivielso (Senators, Twins, 1955–61), and Leo Cárdenas (Reds, Twins, Angels, Indians, Rangers,

1960–75). I went over to the Pueblo Nuevo neighborhood for a look at what is said to be the world's oldest baseball stadium still in use.

Palmar de Junco, officially the Matanzas Province High School for Athletes, was named for a grove of palm trees owned by a foreigner named Junco. It hosts dozens of boys in their teens taking endless turns at bat, fielding countless ground balls, shagging innumerable flies. In the late afternoon ten-and eleven-year-olds play, and after that anyone can use the field. Its benches are wood and concrete. In the beginning, the stadium was really just a field that spectators gathered around. Grandstands and dugouts and other additions came slowly, but during World War II Palmar de Junco finally solidified as a decent stadium with lights and an office and locker rooms. A decade later urban renewal plans slated it for destruction, but community protests kept it from the wrecking ball.

How baseball got to Cuba is as easy to explain as how giant tortoises got to the Galápagos Islands. It was "brought by sailors, students, and businessmen from the United States as well as by Cubans who had traveled north" (*Baseball in the Caribbean*); or, U.S. sailors brought it to Matanzas Bay around 1866 (the version according to *Granma*); or, "A student named Nemesio Guillo had attended school in New York and then introduced baseball to Cuba in 1857" (*Baseball: The People's Game*). I like this last version not only because it jibes with a few other historical accounts, but because it goes back so far and it allows a Cuban to bring the game home rather than the United States to send it abroad. Four years after Havana stomped Matanzas at Palmar de Junco Stadium, Emilio Sabourín formed the Professional Baseball League of Cuba. Sabourín donated profits to the independence struggle, which, according to one baseball historian, led the Spanish to ban the sport from parts of the island and to toss Sabourín in prison, where he died a martyr to both the insurrectionist movement and baseball.

Major league teams from the United States played in Cuba from the late 1800s into the 1950s. The New York Giants and the Pittsburgh Pirates each held spring training there once (1937 and 1953, respectively). The Brooklyn Dodgers held three training seasons in Havana (1941, 1942, and 1947), the last time explicitly so that Jackie Robinson, then with their Montreal Royals farm team, would not have to endure racism in the American South just prior to graduating to the majors that spring. (Even so, Robinson was quartered separately from the white Dodgers in Havana, along with fellow black Royals Don Newcombe and Roy Campanella.)

Cuba, or at least its image, played a role in stateside baseball. Eleven years after that first game in Matanzas, the waiters at a hotel on Long Island formed a team called the Cuban Giants. John Holway, in *Blackball Stars*, says, "They talked gibberish on the field, hoping it would be taken for Spanish." For the next few decades different teams formed along the East Coast using Cuba in their name, though they had nothing to do with the country.

Baseball had gripped Cuba from sophisticated Havana to the most humble provincial settlement. Ralph Estep, in his Packard Motor Car journey through Cuba in 1909, saw the Pinks play the Blues on a Sunday in the town of Macagua. "Cuba is baseball crazy. Each country team has dainty cotton-flannel suits, which they put on after the game for the purpose of parading around the town." The same year, after the Detroit Tigers won the American League pennant (and lost the World Series to Pittsburgh in seven games), they traveled to Cuba for an exhibition series against the Havana Reds. Ty Cobb, who had hit .377 in the regular season and led the league with seventy-six stolen bases, played poorly. Said the *Sporting News*: "Detroit has been badly beaten by the Cuban Negroes."

Major league players could pick up quick money by playing exhibition games in Cuba after the regular season was over. In 1920, after Babe Ruth's first season with the Yankees (.376; 54 home runs), the slugger was said to have been paid close to $40,000 for several weeks of touring with the New York Giants in Cuba. He lost most of it on horses, according to biographer Robert W. Creamer, "including $25,000 on a race that was supposedly fixed," and went home no richer than when he left.

Back at my hotel Ricardo Cárdenas Duouense was passing the time in the lobby. He had been the home plate umpire the night before. The other three sat with him, chatting the day away. Like the baseball players, Cárdenas and his fellow umps draw their salaries from full-time jobs elsewhere and are not paid by their teams or the league. When he's not watching the third base foul line, forty-nine-year-old Cárdenas works at a printing plant in Havana. Lázaro Ronald Ramírez Cepeda, twenty-six, is an engineer when he's not calling runners out at first base. Forty-year-old Raúl Machado Pedroso, a sports trainer in the off-season, had just joined us. And José Alvarez Novo, the forty-six-year-old head umpire, rolls cigars at a factory in Sancti Spíritus when he's not calling balls and strikes. I asked them about the differences between umpiring in Cuba and in the States.

"Well," Machado said with some prodding, "we have a bit lower strike zone." Of the four, Cárdenas admitted to getting the most player complaints. "I signed my first umpiring contract in 1958. After the Revolution there was no profit in the game. In all other ways it's the same."

"With no profit motive, why do you umpire?"

"We do it for the love of the game," Ramírez replied, "and to represent Cuba in international play. We like the sport and the activity. We have training seminars. We've had classes in Mexico, and even Italy and Spain."

"What makes a great umpire in Cuba?"

"Years of experience," Ramírez said, "quality of work, respect from the players, a little of everything. Some of us excel in one thing and some of us in another, but him"—he nodded at Alvarez—"he's the best."

I went to my room to get an article from a U.S. newspaper I had clipped the previous week. It said that major league umpires earned between $40,000 and $109,000, and that the men in blue were insisting on more. The four Cubans were keenly interested in the article, of course, and saw it as good news. "The higher their salaries go," Cárdenas said, "the more respect umpires everywhere command."

I shut the door to my room and a small cardboard sign fell to the floor. I had seen it in hotel rooms throughout the country.

DISCOUNTS FOR DEFICIENCIES IN SERVICE

- no running water for up to 16 hours daily 10%
- no running water for more than 16 hours daily 20%
- no running water at all 30%
- no hot water in 3, 4, or 5 Star hotels 10%
- no elevator service above the fifth floor 15%
- a missing or unusable sink, shower, or toilet bowel 10%
  When a complete apartment or house is rented, the discount will be calculated proportionately by the number of bathrooms. For example: for one incomplete bathroom in an apartment or house with three bathrooms, a discount will be awarded of 3⅓% beyond the basic rate; if two bathrooms are incomplete, the discount would rise to 6⅔%.
- air conditioner broken or missing when at least ¾ of the other rooms have functioning units 20%
  The same proportionate discounts apply to broken or missing air conditioners as apply to bathrooms.

- broken or missing refrigerator (applicable only in tourist
  villas or single homes or apartments) 15%
  Note: These discounts should be applied automatically by
  the management without the user asking.

Bango had told me that on each opening day the boosters club lays a wreath at the bust to Martín Dihigo on Martín Dihigo Avenue near the new stadium. Dihigo, born the year the U.S. began its 1906–09 military occupation to keep a rebellion at bay, was one of the best baseball players ever to wear a Cuban uniform. Or a Mexican or Venezuelan one. Or one from the Dominican Republic. But never a major league uniform. "He couldn't play in the majors." Bango tapped his forearm. "His skin. He was black."

The Matanzas-born all-around athlete played in the Negro Leagues in the States off and on throughout his remarkable twenty-five years in professional baseball. His career cross-fertilizing baseball throughout the Americas illuminates the zigzag history of talented, dark-skinned baseball players in the 1920s, 1930s, and 1940s. He was a free agent who signed on with whichever team he wanted. When the season ended in one country he'd pack his cleats and hustle to the next. He crossed national boundaries as easily as he crossed home plate. His teammates were as likely to be blacks from the States as mestizos from Mexico. One year he managed the Águilas of Veracruz, Mexico, while leading the league in pitching (18-2; 0.90 ERA) and hitting (.387). The Águilas were neck and neck for the pennant with the Mexico City Agrarios, whose star pitcher was Satchel Paige. On September 5, 1938, the two greats squared off against each other. "For six innings" recounts John Holway, "they dueled, 0–0, Dihigo going to his fastball, and Paige, with an injured arm, relying on underhand and trick pitches." Paige was taken out in the eighth inning, and Dihigo won the game for himself, hitting a homer off the relief pitcher in the ninth inning. (Later that year he went 14-2 in a Cuban league.) He played his last year of competitive ball the year Jackie Robinson broke the major league color barrier.

Martín Dihigo's Hall of Fame plaque in Cooperstown, New York, says: *Most versatile of Negro League stars. Played in both summer and winter ball most of career. Registered more than 260 victories as pitcher. When not on mound he played outfield and infield, usually batting well over .300. Also, managed during and after playing days.* Dr. Bango said, "We call him 'The Immortal.' "

* * *

"Cuba was the best place in the world to play baseball," Don Hoak reminisced in a 1964 Sport magazine about Havana's 1950–51 baseball season. The sure-handed third baseman was paid a thousand dollars monthly plus more than enough expense money to cover a *casita* on the beach. When he wasn't playing ball he fished, scuba dived, and golfed. That season had an extra attraction: games were routinely interrupted by noisy anti-Batista college students with banners and firecrackers parading around the field. Fulgencio Batista, a rabid baseball fan, would sometimes watch from the stands. "Surrounded by bodyguards he would sit through the commotion with arms folded across his chest and just a trace of a smile at the corner of his lips," Hoak said.

One night in the fifth inning of a game Hoak had just come to bat when some three hundred students poured out of the stands with their anti-Batista accoutrements. A tall, skinny recent law school graduate took the ball and glove from the Marianao pitcher. He wore a *guayabera* and "tight black slacks and black suede shoes with pointed toes," and sported "a funny little beard at the point of his chin that he obviously had taken great care to groom." Hoak watched from the sidelines. The man on the mound "wound up with a great windmill flourish, whirling his pitching arm overhead about six times." Suddenly the pitcher yelled "Batter up!" Don Hoak, a twenty-two-year-old minor-leaguer from Roulette, Pennsylvania, stepped in and squared off against Fidel Castro, an ambitious twenty-four-year-old from Birán in Oriente province.

"Castro gave me the hipper-dipper windup and cut loose with a curve. Actually it was a pretty fair curve. It had a sharp inside break to it and it came within an inch of breaking my head." The umpire called a ball, Castro and the students were upset, and the umpire told Hoak that he better start swinging or he would have to start calling strikes. Hoak fouled off the next two pitches, both inside and very fast. What Fidel Castro lacked in control he made up for in power.

With a 1-2 count, Hoak turned to the umpire and insisted, "Get that idiot out of the game." Whereupon the ump got the police to clear the field of student demonstrators. "A knot of cops moved briskly on pitcher Castro. Briefly, he made a show of standing his ground, but the cops shoved him off the mound. He shuffled meekly toward the third-base grandstands, like an impudent boy who has been cuffed by the teacher and sent to stand in the corner."

Don Hoak may have given the earliest account of Fidel Castro with a baseball in his hands. Castro's ability was such that it provoked minor interest among major scouts, but he was simply a good athlete whose main interests lay elsewhere.

George Beahon, a Rochester sportswriter who saw Fidel pitch that year in an exhibition game to benefit the agrarian reform kitty, recalled fifteen years later that Castro was "flabby," with "a big gut." Beahon said that *el comandante* was "a horseshit pitcher. . . . He had no motion. No speed and no control. He couldn't even find the plate." Castro pitched one inning, struck out two, one of them "with the aid of an umpire," noted the *Sporting News.* "When the arbiter called the batter out on a high inside pitch, Castro dashed to the plate and shook hands with the ump."

Lee Lockwood had a more relaxed opportunity to watch Castro play ball. As a photojournalist profiling the premier in the mid-1960s, Lockwood watched a game Fidel took part in at a military base, as soldiers and their sweeties looked on. "Castro, in gay spirits, pitched and batted and jockeyed raucously from the bench and clowned hugely with players and audience alike," Lockwood wrote. "There isn't much difference between his fastball and his curve. . . . [T]his time, as on every other occasion I have seen him play, he was clobbered unmercifully." After nine innings Fidel Castro's team trailed 11–2.

When he came to power Castro pledged that he would do anything to keep the Havana Sugar Kings in the International League, one of the top minor leagues. The country's tourist commission gave the team money and the army bought ten thousand dollars' worth of tickets for soldiers. Yet the baseball stadium continued to be a strong magnet for intense feelings, and once some counterrevolutionaries set off a bomb that shook the stadium and cut its power. The night that Castro pitched in the exhibition game the stadium was full of celebrants heralding July 26 Day. "Many troops were in the stands, some carrying tommy guns and side arms," according to *Baseball and the Cold War.* In the eleventh inning of a 4–4 game a stray bullet grazed the plastic-lined helmet of Rochester Red Wings third base coach Frank Verdi. (The Havana shortstop got the same treatment.) It was an accident resulting from overactive fans, went the explanation, one which Verdi, the Red Wings, and the International League formally accepted. Before the 1960 season played out, however, International League officials thought Cuba was too volatile, and the Sugar Kings franchise was moved to Jersey City. Cuba's link with the major leagues had been irreparably severed.

* * *

Wilfredo Sánchez lives within view of Palmar de Junco. Sánchez, the retired national batting and stolen base champion, had played for the Matanzas Henequeneros. I had arranged an interview with him at We-Whipped-the-Pants Stadium, but instead of taking a bus or taxi from my hotel, I walked. Most buildings between the Hotel Louvre and the stadium were sturdy, and appeared to have been built in the 1940s. Wooden walls came out to the sidewalk, and window grillwork protruded even farther. Like other provincial towns, lines at stores were not as long and certainly less harried than those in Havana. The side of one house had a thirty-line poem about the fuel and electricity shortages. It encouraged saving, chastised waste, and rhymed as well. Between the verses someone had drawn a radio playing music and flowers being watered, with the caption *Big and Little Consumers*. Other drawings showed a television, a phonograph, a blender, and a faucet with a drop of water just below it. A few blocks beyond the poem I passed Matanzas's main Socialism or Death produce market next to the San Juan River, where customers were lined up for afternoon deliveries, waiting and hoping. Not for nothing is the verb for both, *esperar*, the same in Spanish. The walk to the stadium took forty-five minutes.

Sánchez arrived a few minutes before I did. The man nicknamed *el hombre-hit* was raised in a sugar mill town where his father, a catcher in the pre-Revolution Pedro Betancourt League, fashioned bats from tree branches and baseballs from corncobs for his kids to play with. "In our house baseball was more important than food," he tells interviewers. "The first things I remember seeing in my life was a bat, a glove, and a ball." Four of his six brothers also play ball. His father was evidently a baseball nut—he used to watch one game on television and listen to another on radio. "The old man could forgive anything except a called third strike." During his nineteen years with Matanzas Wilfredo became the country's all-time base hit leader (2,058) and batted .329. He is considered the best hitter in modern Cuban baseball.

El hombre-hit wore street clothes with a Henequeneros workout jacket on top. He has dark skin, a medium Afro, and chooses his words carefully. He had taken time out from his job coaching the next generation of stars at Palmar de Junco Stadium. "I'm also doing research at the Sports Institute of Matanzas. I'm teaching techniques of batting. Whenever the possibility of managing has come up I've said I don't want to. It'd sap all my strength. Of course I'm at the disposal of the provincial sports office, but I prefer research. If I move to the field I'd rather coach third, where I can improve the base runners' skills." Sánchez stole 382 bases in his career.

Cuban baseball seems to have higher-scoring games, I said, more base hits, and pitchers with less control. Sánchez thought about this, then concurred. "Pitching is definitely more highly developed in the big leagues, it's true. The U.S. has the highest level of baseball, but you also have fine playing in Japan, Puerto Rico, and South Korea." Sánchez has traveled with Cuba's national team in Latin America, Holland, the United States, and Japan. He was in his prime when Cuba began using the designated hitter. "When the International Baseball Association adopted the DH, every other team used it to their advantage so we converted, too. No one thought of it as anything but helpful. Now we have different considerations about what to do with pitchers. Do you get rid of him? Keep him in? With the DH the game is more offense than defense. It's true, the pitching is not as good now." And Cuban umpires aren't as good as the ones in other countries, Sánchez acknowledged. It was the only criticism he made of baseball, his family, or his country; the umpiring isn't as good.

Each team travels with aluminum bats only. Sánchez saw this as helpful, too. "We started converting to aluminum from wood in the late '70s, about the same time the DH came into play. There are more technical possibilities with aluminum. Contact is more effective. Also, it simply feels better in your hands. There's more security. It absorbs the impact."

And the other modern innovation, artificial turf?

"All fields in Cuba have natural grass. We played on artificial turf in Japan. It was awkward at first because we weren't used to it. It affects the psychology of the players and it helps the batter. But I think, speaking for myself, that it's the future of baseball in Latin America. I think we'll be using it within ten years if not before."

The biggest event in Sánchez's career came in early 1985 when he started a home game with 1,997 career base hits. His first time up he singled to center field. To block the pressure he locked himself in a room between innings and watched another game on television. His second at bat he hit a 3-0 curveball; another single to center. When Sánchez next came up he stroked an outside fastball between shortstop and third. Fans charged the field, among them two thousand Young Pioneers, and hoisted *el hombre-hit* on their shoulders marching him around the field. The game was delayed for forty-five minutes. "The umpires didn't know what to do!" When he got home his father was roasting a pig and the local Committee for the Defense of the Revolution threw a party.

Sánchez took part in two sugar harvests, 1964 and 1966, and encourages his students to do the same. He studied farm machinery at a technical school in Holguín. When he was told the salary paid to a major-leaguer, he replied, "I wouldn't exchange that for my 218 pesos a month, because he doesn't have the freedom we have here. Now he's somebody's private property. He's sold himself like a piece of merchandise." Sánchez served in a provincial military battalion, and his wife was a lieutenant in the militia. "I'm ready for anything," said *el hombre-hit*. "Even to forget about batting."

What is it about baseball that brings out so much saliva? This universal question cuts through ideology, borders, and ability. Whatever the cause, this is one category in which, phlegm for phlegm, baseball players in Cuba match their big league counterparts.

Twenty-five fans were waiting at the stadium gate when it opened one and a half hours before 8:30 game time for the next game between the Forestales of Pinar del Río and the Matanzas Henequeneros. Most of the early arrivals rushed over to line up at the pizza stand, which wouldn't begin serving for another half hour. The Forestales were finishing a dinner of black beans and rice, *picadillo*, lettuce, tomato, and fresh-squeezed orange juice. Tata poured *cafecitos* for them when they got back to the locker room. Asqui kept eyeing my Rawlings as if it were an untouched Whitman's Sampler. We walked out to the field together and tossed a ball around as the grandstands began to fill. He picked up a bat and I lobbed underhand pitches to him that he hit back as soft grounders. He was half the distance to the mound. When he drifted off for calisthenics, Suárez, the short Forestales trainer nicknamed El Gnomo, picked up the bat and we continued. I fielded three fourths of the grounders cleanly and, with nonchalant finesse, fumbled the rest. The real thrill, however, was fulfilling every child's fantasy of taking the field with thousands of fans looking on. Coach Benietez needed the bat, and El Gnomo and I retired to the bench. The harmony of baseball sang within me.

The Forestales played even worse this game than they had the previous night. Juan Castro might as well have pitched, he spent so much time on the mound. In the second inning the Forestales' starter walked the leadoff batter, threw wild trying to pick him off and the runner made it to third base. Carlos Kindelán came up next. On a 2-0 count Ernesto Pérez beaned him with a change-of-pace. Kindelán's plastic batting helmet absorbed the blow, but he fell to the ground and players from both sides, including Pérez, gathered around in concern. Pérez mumbled an apology and Kindelán took first. Juan Luis Baro walked, filling the bases. After two successive singles Pérez was taking a shower and the next hapless pitcher for the worst team in the league was being pounded by the best team in the league.

At the bottom of the fourth the score was 6–0 and I joined Dr. Bango in the third base stands. He and his buddies were cheery, cheerful, and cheering. The only times I've seen such contentment at a ballpark have been when the Chicago Cubs win in spring training. Bango pointed out his favorite players, and his neighbor recited their batting averages from the previous year. Cuba lacks the paper to print up scorecards for each game, so fans have to rely on their memory and the scoreboard. I saw only one concessionaire in the stands: a man poured coffee from his thermos into little paper cups at ten centavos a shot. When I looked up it was the bottom of the fifth and Matanzas was mauling the new man on the mound as if he was pitching batting practice. One of the Pinar del Río players who stood out was catcher Yosvany Madera, who caught two men stealing and got two base hits. When he strode to the batter's box a third time Juan Castro told him, "Watch for the low ones, and swing level." Madera struck out with a golf stroke on a low pitch, and Castro snuffed out his cigarette.

Routs are boring, and if you're rooting for the routed depressing as well. I wandered about until I got to the official scorer's perch next to the press box. A Matanzas team official told me, "In 1975 we began using computers to keep statistics. After each game both teams get the stats for that game, and the next day the league office in Havana wires the other games' statistics to us. Of course we can't compete with your computers, but ours serve us well."

Osvaldo Daniel Gómez, the official scorer, took over. "In 1971 we developed a new system of annotation. It involves not only a pitch-by-pitch account of the game, but which specific part of the field the ball goes to. We have divided up the field into distinct zones so that we know if a fly to short left center was closer to the shortstop or the left fielder. We record far more details than simply what field. Do they use this system yet in the States?" He showed me an elaborate scorecard with enough room to list what clothes each spectator was wearing. "It's used all over Latin America. I've been doing this for twenty-five years in Matanzas. I began in the old Junco Stadium."

Next to him young José García punched numbers into a pocket calculator to figure up-to-the-minute batting averages, which he flashed on the outfield scoreboard.

The scoreboard said

| FOR. | 000 | 000 | 0 |
| HEN. | 210 | 332 | = |

and everyone packed up. Matanzas had scored a technical knockout. When ten or more runs separate the two teams after seven innings, the game ends. Tata handed out pizza and soft drinks in the dugout but nobody was hungry.

When I followed baseball as a kid, everyone in Washington called the Senators the Nats, short for Nationals, the Washington team's original name from the early 1900s. Part of my morning ritual was to ask my father, who finished the newspaper before the rest of us got up, "How much did the Nats lose by?" I knew better than to ask if they won. For reasons I cannot fathom to this day, I followed a tall outfielder from Havana named Carlos Paula. The Nats brought him up from their Charlotte, North Carolina, farm club after three respectable years with a .314 average. His 1954 Topps baseball card says: "A good extra-base slugger, Carlos figures to find the range and dent that long left field wall in Washington's Griffith Stadium with some solid smashes." *The Baseball Encyclopedia* has refreshed my memory of his career: in three major league years, all with the Nats, Paula hit .271 and got forty extra-base hits. His best year was 1955 when he batted .299 and hit six home runs; the Nats finished last. The next season he hit .183 in thirty-three games and entered oblivion. A few years later a schoolyard rumor circulated: Carlos Paula had been shot to death as a counterrevolutionary by a Castro firing squad. I wasn't entirely sure what a Castro firing squad was—or for that matter, a counterrevolutionary—yet this common assumption weighed heavily on me for years, and even though I had forgotten what he looked like, whenever I thought back to the Nats of that era the fate of Carlos Paula saddened me.

Jorge Luis Paula, the Forestales' third baseman, joined me at a table in the team dining room the next morning. Most of the players were within a couple years of twenty. Jorge Luis was closer to thirty. He was one of three players on the team from Viñales, the small town I had enjoyed so much in Pinar del Río, and he was one of the team's

two solid players. Like catcher Yosvany Madera, he showed hustle and
confidence. He had hit well in the two losing efforts against Matanzas,
and fielded with assurance. Although the season was less than three
weeks old, Paula already had a modest hitting streak at the plate and
had yet to make an error in the field. He was among the top ten
batters in the league. Perhaps he could shed light on the uncertainty
buried deep within me for more than thirty years. I told Jorge Luis
that in the mid-1950s I used to see a Cuban outfielder named Carlos
Paula play in Washington. He nodded recognition at the name. "Could
he," I asked with some trepidation, "have been of your family?"

Jorge Luis laughed. "See?" he said, touching his wrist. "I have light
skin. He had very dark skin. He couldn't have been from my family."

I have since learned that Carlos Paula did not die as a counterrevolutionary before a Castro firing squad. That myth joins the alligators of
the New York sewers and the jackalope of the western plains. Carlos
Paula died in 1983 in Miami of natural causes.

Jorge Luis went back to the dorm and Tata sat down. We had
scrambled eggs, bread, and hot condensed milk for breakfast. Matanzas
serves decent food, most players agreed, but Cienfuegos serves the best
meals in the league. "Ready for the bus ride?" Tata asked. That day's
game against the Henequeneros was to be played in Unión de Reyes,
a small town more than forty kilometers south of Matanzas. As José
Luis Salmerón had told me in Havana, the last game of every three-
game series is played in a *pueblo* some distance from the provincial
capital so all fans get a chance to cheer their team near home.

Tata had already loaded the bats and the other equipment in the
luggage compartment. Luis Marín, known to all as Niño, sat down
for a cup of coffee. He drove the team bus, a 1987 Ikarus from
Hungary. His life revolved around driving, baseball, and women, or
at least talking about them. This morning women were again topic
A. Unlike the ballplayers, he had no curfew. As for the guys on the
team, Tata said, "Women? No, not in season. It would weaken them."
The clock above the Ikarus's windshield had stopped a few weeks
earlier and Niño hadn't been able to replace the dead batteries. The
previous day he had pulled me aside and asked if I'd pick up a pair
at a dollar shop. At the breakfast table I handed him a small pack of
1.5 volt AA batteries for the team bus. The Forestales could again
tell time.

Juan Castro sat across the aisle from me smoking and reading the
paper as we headed south through the fertile Matanzas countryside.
Was *any* part of rural Cuba boring? I had taken more than a dozen

long-distance drives through all parts of the island and had yet to find a bleak stretch. Castro leaned over and pointed to a story in the paper.

The Ministry of Foreign Relations has been informed by the Republic of Checa and Eslovakia that it will no longer represent the diplomatic and consular interests of Cuba before the United States. This action . . . is consistent with present realities. . . . The Cuban government will find other representation to complete this diplomatic function in a sober and responsible manner.

The manager looked at me with an expression that said, things just keep getting worse. Like Cuba, the Forestales kept getting battered, but ya gotta love 'em. Which despite their grievous errors I did, both. Juan Castro was a member of the Communist Party. I thought back to all the catchers I had admired—Yogi Berra, Roy Campanella, Johnny Bench, Carlton Fisk—and not one of them, as far as I knew, was a Communist.

Niño fiddled with the AM-FM dial looking for Radio 26. Sports pennants hung above the windshield, donated by foreign athletes whom Niño had driven since he began in the late 1960s: Tokyo, Rome, Martinique, Moscow, Czechoslovakia, Buenos Aires. A set of badminton birdies was tacked up to the side next to a Ministry of Transportation award for "20 or more years without a traffic accident." Fuzzy red horsehair streamers dangled from both side-view mirrors saying *¡Cuba va!* Cuba on the go!

The seats reclined, which made the drive even more relaxing. We passed through the tiny town of Cidra, then Juan Gualberto Gómez, where wood and cement houses came virtually out to the street. In one town we drove around a plaza and Niño, who had a habit of honking at every pretty woman within a kilometer of the highway, sounded the horn at all the *lindas cubanas* until they smiled and waved back. This bus driver's trait has been immortalized in Eduardo Galeano's *The Book of Embraces* when the *chofer* of a cross-town Havana bus "screeched to a halt at an intersection. There were cries of protest at the tremendous jolt until the passengers saw why the bus driver had jammed on the brakes: a magnificent woman had just crossed the street. *You'll have to forgive me, gentlemen*, said the driver of *guagua* 68, and he got out. All the passengers applauded and wished him luck."

South of Juan Gualberto Gómez we turned off the main road and drove up to El Barcón, a small lakeside inn with rooms for rent, a restaurant, and an outdoor bar. Music played on the bar's speaker system, and the moment they got off the bus three Forestales, in uniform, started dancing. "See those rooms?" said one of the Forestales, nodding toward the rentals. "Couples use them for afternoon assignations." He laughed and laughed. "Know how I know?" He laughed once more.

We walked toward the lake where knots of players chatted while the restaurant crew completed the table settings. As long as we're talking about shady things, I said, "tell me, do Cuban pitchers use the spitball?"

"Well"—he looked hard at me—"yes. Like this." He demonstrated how to pitch a spitter while avoiding detection by the umpires. I mentioned my conversation the previous day with the umpire crew at the hotel, and that I had wished them good luck. He shook his head with a smile. *"La suerte no ayuda al malo."* Evil can't be helped by luck.

We filled seven tables, five to each one, and our plates overflowed with generous helpings of yucca, rice, and sweet potato. Juan Castro sat down next to me. I asked about Pedro Luis Lázaro, the tall young pitcher who had lasted almost three innings a couple of nights earlier. "It'll take a good five years to develop him, but he'll be good. Very good." I was still tickled at the notion of Communist ballplayers— did sportswriters choose an all-Commie team at the end of the season? Castro pointed out the four Party members on the Forestales plus six more members of the Young Communist League.

I raised the subject of umpires. "They're very bad. In Mexico they're even worse. Venezuelans are better. Puerto Rico has the best. Umpires in the Dominican Republic are very good, too." He nodded a tight smile. "Ours are pretty bad."

"Judging from a few calls last night I'd have to agree with you. Why are they so poor?"

"I don't know. But they are bad."

Waiters brought dessert.

"What motivates a Cuban baseball player?"

"The goal of every player I've worked with has been to play on the national team and represent Cuba outside the country. We feel good about that."

Juan Castro gave me a quizzical look when I asked about baseball's meditative qualities. "I don't understand." I tried to explain, but either my Spanish or the whole idea got muddled between my mouth and his ears. Obviously my baseball reading had drifted to too many armchair essays and too few grandstand scorecards. "You need combativeness to win. It's as simple as that." Just as we got back on the Ikarus the Matanzas bus pulled up for the second lunch shift. Their players got off and started dancing to the music from the bar.

* * *

Nobody on the bus shouted out ¡SOCIALISMO! despite a roadside sign urging travelers to do so. With Niño still leaning on the horn each time a pretty *muchacha* came into view, we honked our way down the main street of Unión de Reyes. Small wooden rails separated the sidewalk from front porches. We finally pulled up to April 16 Stadium, a handsome, creaking, small-town ballpark spruced up for its annual show. Men were chopping up huge blocks of ice, small kids gathered round the bus to see real big-leaguers. Juan Castro opened a new pack of Populares. The stands were filling despite the early hour. The atmosphere resembled an exhibition game, except that it counted in the standings. Neither team had a locker room. I tossed a ball around with El Gnomo again, and when game time approached I took a seat on the Forestales bench. Four thousand fans filled every cement bench in the stands. They arrived by motorscooter, bicycle, car, bus, and foot. It was a lovely late December afternoon as fathers sat hand-in-hand with their young daughters and wives with their old husbands.

The Forestales went down in order in the top of the first inning. The Henequeneros attacked the youthful Pinar del Río pitcher, Ríos. The first batter doubled on the first pitch, took third on a wild pitch, followed by a walk to the batter. Lázaro Junco, who had slugged that cannonball home run a couple of days earlier, singled in the first run. Juan Castro, who had been warming up a reliever since the second pitch, took Ríos out and brought in a fellow named Quintana. On his first pitch the Henequeneros tried a double steal, but Madera threw out the lead runner at third. The next pitch got singled to left, and a run scored. Five more Henequeneros crossed the plate that inning.

I made my way through the stands to the press box and asked a reporter what happened April 16 that it should be a stadium's name. This set off an impromptu discussion, with most people of the opinion that on that day in 1961 Castro declared his government to be socialist. An old-timer had a different answer for the stadium name. "A general strike happened on that day in 1955. We didn't go to work. It was a bloody strike. I remember it well." Then the press box crowd tried to recall the name of the Havana department store that the CIA had bombed in April 1961. Pancho, the voice of the Henequeneros, needed to fill time between innings and introduced me on the air. He had mentioned me during previous games, I learned from strangers when they recognized me as the foreign writer following the three-game series. "So how are you enjoying your stay in Matanzas?" Pancho asked me on the air. I stammered some banalities about how pretty the province was and what a strong team it had. Mercifully the fourth inning began before Pancho could continue.

The outfield scoreboard was operated by a fellow who slid numbered slates into the inning slots. So far it said:

FOR   002

HEN   600

The Forestales had scored on a succession of singles. El Gallego— Jorge Luis Paula's nickname—had driven in both runs.

Pedro Luis Robaina stopped me outside the press box. He worked as a metallurgist in a plant that made parts for sugar mills. "Shouldn't you be at work now?" I said. "It's a weekday afternoon." He was still wearing his yellow hard hat and jeans.

"The boss said that if I came to work early I could leave early to go to the game." From the looks of the crowd, bosses all over town must have had the same attitude. Pedro Luis said that most people worked at the factory, or at a nearby sugar mill, or in the railroad switching yards. "We have intramural baseball teams at the factory. I play a bit, but in my free time I prefer to read. I just feel like it helps me more." He was reading a 1962 book by Alejo Carpentier, *El siglo de las luces* (in translation as *Explosion in a Cathedral*). "It's a very good book. Magnificent. It's about history and customs in the Caribbean."

Two more innings, no more runs. The umpiring was awful. A Matanzas runner was called safe when he was clearly out by a long stride. The Forestales yelled at the call, and Juan Castro wore a look of disgust.

The stadium office had a big sign that said ¡LISTO PARA VENCER!— ready to conquer!—the national sports slogan. *Do you fish? Play dominoes? Take part in senior citizens exercise classes? Practice basic gymnastics? Jog? Well, you're LPV! Unión de Reyes will complete its goal!*

Paula was one of the players Juan Castro had pointed out to me at lunch as a Communist Party member. What does that mean to you? I asked the third baseman in the dugout. "To be punctual, a good worker, and to be an example to others. To know your ideology and don't deviate. For me, it's an honor. You have to be a good worker, and note enemy influence when you see it." One of his teammates was not an exemplary worker and grounded out, ending the top half of the seventh.

Pinar del Río picked up another run, but Matanzas scored twice in the bottom of the seventh, once on a bobbled infield pop-up, and again on a dropped routine fly to center field. Paula turned in a spectacular play in which he backhanded a hard-hit grounder to deep third and rifled it across the infield in time for the out. He is the best Communist third baseman I've ever seen. The score was 8–3 when the Forestales returned to the dugout.

Paula drew me a map of Cuba in the dust and pointed out where he had traveled. He works full-time as a physical education instructor in his home province. He receives 246 pesos a month for this, including his time with the Forestales. "At those international games in Edmonton and Seattle, Omar Linares was offered a great deal of money to defect. They don't understand, we play for the love of sports. I've always loved baseball. We're just not accustomed to the money. Our motivation is to represent the country. I feel a sense of nationalistic pride whenever our team plays abroad."

Time out.

I had heard the same sentiment in similar words from others in Cuban baseball. By and large it's true, but its simple uncapitalist innocence evokes derisive responses from outside. Let's assume for a moment that the words genuinely express their feelings. This does not mean that they wouldn't want to play for major league teams. Of *course* they would. They follow, look up to, revere, respect, and imitate major league players. Any one of them, I'm sure, would be thrilled and honored to have his name on a big league roster. For an athlete to have the opportunity to work and learn alongside the best in his calling?—naturally he'd seize it. The conflict arises from factors far beyond the center field wall. Were it otherwise the sport and both countries could benefit.

Resume play.

The Henequeneros won the game and swept the series. Juan Castro was angry. He called a postgame meeting along the first base line. Watching from the dugout fifty feet away I could see but not hear. Niño sat with me. The coaches each had a turn. The Matanzas bus left. Then the players spoke up. Castro flicked a butt into the grass. As the last of the fans left the park, local kids showed up to reclaim it for their own. They played ball for a short while, and they, too, left. The team meeting went on. A man rode by on his bike, his dog leashed to its handlebar. The flag was lowered. The meeting continued. It was not about ideology.

We—the Forestales, that is—had a day off before a doubleheader with the Metropolitanos in the main stadium in Havana. The team bus was to go the next morning; I decided to go to Havana that evening, and went over to the bus station, where the next Havana departure was ninety minutes away. In order to get in line to buy a ticket I had to get in line to get a ticket with a number on it to get in line to buy a ticket. I had been leading the privileged life of a ballplayer for a few days—no petty black marketeers, no sneaker envy—and this line foolishness brought me back to reality. A man waiting for the Santiago bus pointed out the parking lot next to the bus station as a well-known place to wait for private cars going to Havana. "If you stay long enough you will get a ride. I can assure you."

I got in line to get a ticket with a number on it to get in line to buy a ticket, and shoved it in my pocket just in case. The pickup spot for gypsy rides to Havana was barren save for a fellow working on the rear brakes of a '55 Plymouth. "As soon as I'm finished here I'm leaving for Havana." The etiquette was delicate; was I to ask him or he me? I broached the subject. Without answering he took my bag and tossed it in the backseat. Another rider showed up; his bag went in alongside mine. The driver worked in a Matanzas hospital. The other rider worked on the docks in Havana. About halfway home we negotiated a fee.

"Ten," he said.

"Pesos or dollars?"

He looked over his shoulder with incredulity. "How long did you say you've been in this country?" He dropped me off a block from my room.

Part Five

The holiday season was upon us and Christmas decorations could be seen throughout . . . the hotels and restaurants and stores that catered to foreigners. For most people, December 25 was like any other balmy midwinter day, with almost no public acknowledgment that this day was different from all others. People queued up for buses, groceries, and clothing, students went to class, and the baseball schedule continued. The only public Christmas signs I saw were on the front of a Baptist church in the city's southeast section. What a refreshing change for one year not to have Christmas sales, obnoxious advertising, national Christmas trees, obligatory goodwill, and Bing Crosby. The head of the country's Evangelical Council spoke on national radio about peace and love.

Miguel Barnet, my official writers union host, passed me as he drove down the street and stopped to give me a ride. He was among the intelligentsia who could look forward to an invitation for New Year's Eve with either Gabriel García Márquez, who traditionally spends the end of the year in Cuba, or Alicia Alonso, the ballerina. My plans were to join some friends at Marina Hemingway where Los Van Van were playing an outdoor dinner show, then after midnight go to a private party at a residence in Centro Habana. "And then," I told Miguel, "I'll be leaving the country during the first week of January."

Miguel spoke in confidential tones. "If I were you, I'd think about staying another few weeks. I understand that there will be some major announcements made very soon. You just might want to stay for them." One of Barnet's appealing qualities was his ability to wrap intrigue around the mundane. I thanked him for the ride and got out at the Hotelito del M.E.S.

"I sometimes thought that the only way people could tell I was not Cuban was by my shoes," thought José Yglesias in *In the Fist of the Revolution*. "The men sitting on the sidewalk at the bank, waiting for their bus to arrive across the street, often did not look up farther than my ankles." This was depressingly still true for me and my Nikes. The brazen money-changing jive I used to hear only next to the Habana Libre and on the Malecón now filled the five blocks in between. The Socialism or Death bakery and produce and dairy outlets where I used to wait in line were useless to me now; almost all goods were available only with a ration book, the one book I couldn't quote.

But avoiding lines was impossible. Ice cream, buses, forms, coffee, newspapers, prescriptions, documents, permits, pizza, red tape—you could not go through a day without standing in some line for the better part of an hour or more. That Sunday *Juventud Rebelde* ran a piece called "¿Quién Es el Último?" Who is the last in line? The article told of people routinely lining up at five A.M. daily who won't even learn what items might be available until the store opens hours later. Many people simply hire out to stand in line for others. By exploiting the complex system of who may shop for what items in which stores on a particular day, the piece continued, a sort of line organizers' mafia manages to hold the best *turnos*, spots in line, and sell them. A woman said that she wanted to buy a little children's wagon for sixty pesos. "Places in that line had been assigned for days, so I proposed to buy a *turno* for the same price as the wagon. Ultimately it cost me 120 pesos, but at least I got it. That's the way things go these days." Said another: "If you could afford it, wouldn't you buy a *turno* to avoid the tragedy of waiting in line?" The illustration next to the article showed a heavy lady in curlers carrying two handbags walking over the heads of other women standing patiently in line.

Raúl Riesgo, the writer whose articles sniped at the right end of the Cuban exile community, had also written about lines. "The line has become a social experiment equal to the city bus," he wrote. "Waiting in line is one of life's inevitabilities like CDR meetings and wakes. Lines are dictated by the natural order of things; they are the price we pay for the development of modern society. They are part of our folklore." Lines, Riesgo wrote, have their own vocabulary and internal hierarchy, but he failed to mention lines so long they entwine. One day along Calzada Street, mourners were waiting to get into a funeral parlor while visa applicants were lined up at the nearby U.S. Interests Section. By the looks on their faces you couldn't tell who was going where.

Instead of standing in line to get into the Mella Theater for a concert by the National Symphony Orchestra, I waited until halftime and went around the side. I wanted to say good-bye to my oboe teacher and his wife and return some sheet music he had loaned me. I had tried calling their home off and on for a couple of months, left notes at the symphony office, and sent a message through another musician, but I never heard back. Avilés was on the side patio having drinks with Laura and some other musicians, looking at ease in a performance tuxedo. He greeted me warmly, and I joined them in a toast to his forty-third birthday. He had gotten my messages, but their home phone had been out of order. He had taken ill. The symphony phone was not working. She had been sick. The symphony had been out of town. I had to admire the sheer ingenuousness of Jesús's excuses and the smoothness with which he proffered them. Had he been purposely avoiding me, or was I simply the victim of Cuba day-to-day? I never found out, and the question receded.

"So tell me, what have you been up to lately—seeing more of the country?"

"I've been on a road trip with the Forestales."

"¿Los Forestales? They're rookies!" He made a face. "I told you to go with Cienfuegos. Why, the Forestales are terrible! They're in last place."

"Yes, it's true, but I'm used to it. Remember, I grew up following the Washington Senators."

The next day at the Latin American Stadium where the Forestales played the Havana Metropolitanos I thought about Jesús's admonition. I sat on the bench, as usual, and in the third inning I scanned the crowd hoping to find him when all of a sudden the first base umpire noticed someone sitting in the dugout in civilian clothes and twice as old as most of the players. Unlike the umpires in Matanzas, this crew didn't know me. Before a crowd of about almost ten thousand fans, the umpire motioned me out of the dugout. I got up to leave—the umpire was clearly correct, I had no right to be there—when suddenly El Gnomo and a couple of the Forestales who had befriended me protested that I should be allowed to remain. They did this with the forlorn righteousness of protesting a call they knew would not be reversed. That'll show 'em.

That's about all we showed 'em. We lost again, 5–1. The Forestales had lost all four games I'd seen. Was I a bad-luck charm? Our pitching held the Mets hitless until two out in the fourth, but they had scored on a succession of a hit, wild pitches, and errors. Jorge Luis Paula kept his early season streak going with two more hits. By the end of the game the third baseman was batting just under .400, and he had bare-handed a bunt, tossing the runner out at first. Afterward Tata said, "We lost on errors. But," he emphasized, "they were technical errors."

What struck me most about this game and the previous three was Juan Castro in his maiden season at the helm. He will be a good manager. He is restless and demonstrative. He has mastered the trot. When a manager is about to yank a pitcher, about five feet before crossing the baseline to the mound he bows his head fifty degrees, hunches his shoulders, and trots, as if dodging raindrops in a sprinkle. Juan already shows great promise with the *wha'*? That's the posture a manager assumes when an umpire makes a call that defies credibility. The hands are outstretched, palms up, the mouth half open, eyebrows raised—*wha'*? It's best done on the top step of the dugout or a few steps onto the field. When his players blow a play, which is often, Juan Castro wears a pained look. He can appear put-upon or studious, he shows forbearance one moment and agony the next. Is there more to managing in any country than that?

Between games I went out to the main entrance, where a plaque was dedicated "to the baseball players who fought in the war of independence, nineteen in all." The nearest line was not for food but for sports equipment—jogging shorts, sweatpants, a chess set (six pesos), medicine ball (seven pesos), Ping-Pong paddles and net (3.15 pesos), and swim fins (twenty-five pesos).

We won the second game of the doubleheader! The first game's result was reversed. The line score read:

FOR   110   000   102
MET   001   000   000

Paula got two more hits, including a line-drive double off the left-center field wall. The guys were all cheery, dancing, clowning, happy. Victory tastes sweeter to a team accustomed to losing, and for the Forestales this win was raw sugarcane.

It put me in a good mood, too. I had been invited to a party where someone was to be initiated into santería, and instead of taking a crowded bus or finding a quick cab, I decided to walk through the friendly slums of Centro Habana. I was nearing the end of my stay and I valued every moment on the streets.

Alba, a lifelong resident of Havana, had invited me. She was part of what's called "the marginal class," not affiliated with any organization, mass, local, or professional. She lived in a two-bedroom apartment with her brother and two sons, both in the military. She herself was in her initiate year of santería, wearing only white. I was looking forward to the ceremony; from everything I had learned about santería, the ritual would be extraordinary, full of color, music, and warmth. And usually closed to outsiders, especially foreigners. By walking from the ballpark, though, I missed it by an hour.

The initiate was lounging on a soft mat in the corner of the living room when I walked in. He was to stay there for seven full days. ("Some bosses understand and give initiates the week off.") He wore a yellow crown and white clothes. An ever-changing cast of friends and relatives surrounded him. Next to him sat an altar with a collection plate and a bowl of fruit. Women came out of the kitchen with glasses of drinks and plates of food. We drank clear rum and ate white rice, black beans, green lettuce, and dark chicken. The initiate's plate was brought to him, as all his food would be in the coming days. A man handed me a maraca and motioned me to kneel and shake it in front of the altar. I did as he suggested, but he practically pounced on me. He took the rattle from my left hand and put it in my right. The initiate embraced me. Women continued to pour out of the kitchen, this time with trays of pastries.

"This is toned down from what we used to do," a large lady in white told me on her way back to the kitchen. "We get what we can and improvise the rest. It's an initiation, Special Period style." I repeated what I'd been told at the Julius and Ethel Rosenberg Countryside High School, that you can't be a teacher and believe in santería at the same time: "To teach, you must subscribe to the science of dialectical materialism."

"Did they tell you that?" She laughed, and repeated it for a friend. "If that's the case we wouldn't have any teachers!"

I turned and glanced at a photograph on the wall of a man eating dinner with chopsticks. The diner turned out to be Fidel Castro. I had been alerted earlier about the host of the ceremony: "He's very much with Fidel. The family is active in the Committee for the Defense of the Revolution." This was unusual, my guide explained—not that most followers of Afro-Cuban religions were antigovernment; most were simply nonpolitical, having little interest in either furthering or fighting the government. Believers, as a rule, were excluded from Communist Party membership. Earlier that year the government had permitted a convention of *santeros*, and there was talk that the prohibition against Communist believers would be lifted at the Party Congress to be held the following year.

"I met a woman from Spain who was filming a documentary about the mix of Spanish and Cuban cultures," Alba said. "Everywhere she went she had to be escorted by a Party man from Artex," the state agency coordinating the shoot, "even when I asked her into my home for a cup of coffe. She invited me to a show in town, and of course her *mirón"*—her watcher—"was there. He brought a date. I shook hands with her. She was part of the same Afro-Cuban religion I am, and we could tell by the color of the beads on each other's necklaces and bracelets that we both had Ochun for our saint. It was only when he left us alone for a couple of minutes that we embraced. She said, 'Well, you know I didn't want to do this while the *mirón* was here.' "

Alba hoped someday to visit friends in Spain or the States. If she did, her sons would take their meals at a nearby friend's home. "They could fix their own food at home, but they have no idea how to regulate the supplies. With what Fidel gives us for thirty days they'd use up in three."

A few nights later Alba filled a plastic bag with oranges, bananas, and a pineapple, as if she were going on a picnic. We went outside and walked for twenty minutes until we reached the Malecón. On the way I described the dream I had a few months earlier after seeing the Afro-Cuban street mural painted by Salvador González. "That was definitely an Afro-Cuban dream," she said. "It was from Changó, the god of big wars between nations and small battles among men. The battles are going to work and getting supplies for daily life."

She told me about a dream of hers. She was drowning in the sea, and felt a sense of solitude. A man rescued her and brought her to the surface. "He carefully pulled me to safety. I told this to someone who interprets Afro-Cuban dreams. She said that I have grave problems, but I will be saved—not on my own, but by someone else."

"And what stage of the dream are you at in your life now?"

"Underwater."

Waves crashed against the seawall that December night but not quite over it. After silently watching the bay for a while Alba asked if I had any change. I emptied my pocket of eight coins totaling 3.65 pesos. "Give it to me." She tossed the fruit into the bay piece by piece, then the money coin by coin. "The fruit is for Ochun. If it goes out to sea that means she got it. If it comes back in with the tide, she'll never get it."

"And the money?"

"That's also an offering for Ochun. It's like in Catholic churches except that the priest doesn't get his hands on it first.

"Ochun *loves* men. She's the goddess of sensuality, of beauty. She's the queen of rivers and lakes, the symbol of sweetness." We sat on the seawall and watched her fruit, despite a strong onrushing tide, drift out to calmer waters and finally out of sight all the way to Ochun.

Alba lived in Barrio Chino, Chinatown, or what remains of it. Chinese were first brought to Cuba in the middle of the nineteenth century, eventually as many as two hundred thousand of them according to one estimate. Importers received four hundred dollars a head for each Chinese sold at market, says an 1859 account. The buyer paid his new worker four dollars monthly plus food and two suits of clothes a year for eight years of indentured servitude. Chinese from California began arriving in 1860 and set up small businesses. A restaurant, a theater, and a newspaper were established in the 1870s. A visitor in the 1890s wrote of Havana's Chinese, "Despised by the whites and detested by the blacks, they lead a miserable life, and die like flies in the scorching climate." A second wave of Chinese immigrants came between 1913 and 1929, and Chinatown established itself as a self-sustaining community.

"I used to go there with my grandparents," a woman told me of her youth in the late 1950s. "It was more foreign than a little girl could understand. I was scared. There were men with long fingernails that curled under. I clutched my grandfather's hand for dear life. I thought they snatched little girls and destroyed them."

Alba's family moved to Chinatown in the mid-1960s. "At the time the whole street was Chinese. We were the first black family on the block." She introduced me to an elderly man next door who was born in China. "There are very few left, isn't that right?" He nodded and went into his house. "The Chinese Society was on the first floor of that building across the street. Families lived there, too. Most have left for Spain, Canada, or the United States. The eldest in the families usually stayed." She motioned to the doorway of the gentleman we had just spoken with. "Most of them have died. The descendants of the Chinese, the ones who still live here, they're mulatto."

A few Chinese restaurants remain, best known among them El Pacífico, where Castro goes on occasion. Next to El Pacífico a print shop houses the editorial office of *Kwong Wah Po*, a four-page Chinese weekly. A pedestrian mall around the corner has ersatz Chinese design to lend an Oriental ambience to the neighborhood. Not too long ago the Chinese government gave the city some money to pretty up Barrio Chino. The question of how much had been diverted to other projects has become a matter of some discussion in the streets of Chinatown.

* * *

Los Van Van used the enormous stage and terrific sound system at Marina Hemingway to their great advantage at the big outdoor New Year's Eve concert. Big band salsa intoxicated the full house of foreigners and privileged Cubans. Onstage these well-traveled musicians played as tight as their drums. Later that night at another party ushering in 1991, the revelers put on a cassette from Cuba's latest salsa-rock sensation, NG La Banda. The most popular song by NG (for Nueva Generación, New Generation) was "La Expresiva," an upbeat dance number whose lyrics mention a slew of Havana neighborhoods. "Cubans in Miami cry when they hear this song," I was assured by a woman for whom the Malecón was the closest she had ever been to Florida. "It reminds them of their real home. It brings tears to their eyes."

January 1 brought another anniversary of the Revolution's triumph. Most people were too happily hung over to celebrate the beginning of the Revolution's thirty-third year, and on January 2, Cuba resumed its rhythm, its rhetoric, and its small battles going to work and getting supplies for daily life. I left the country the next day, but first I bought a copy of "La Expresiva." I wanted to hear the streets of Havana back home.

Epilogue

"It's a grand place and I'd be sorry not to go there again," wrote photographer Walker Evans after he returned from Cuba just before the fall of Gerardo Machado in 1933. Most visitors to the island have felt that way, whether their stay has coincided with stability or crisis. I saw both during my residence.

Despite Cuba's festering sores, I embraced Walker Evans's sentiments during the year following my return. I corresponded with friends there, sent books and other gifts with people going for short stays, and even managed to get through on the telephone a few times. I devoured news stories in the American press about Cuba, and subscribed to the daily *Granma* and weekly *Bohemia*. The U.S. press was relentlessly depressing and somewhat unreliable, and the Cuban unreasonably optimistic and somewhat unreliable. Cuba's international trade predicament meant more severe adjustments in its streets and kitchens. The Pan American Games during August provided 1991's one sense of national pride. As sportscaster Brent Musburger said when the U.S. lost medal after medal to the host country, "Cuba, still upsetting the U.S."

A couple of weeks later the coup against Gorbachev failed, and Soviet Communism began its final disintegration. Cuba scrambled to find the succor that its former ally had provided. The Cuban Communist Party Congress that October called for foreign investment and allowed religious believers to join the Party. Other than that, it reaffirmed a doctrine fewer and fewer people followed. By the beginning of 1992, dire reports filtered out of the country about its spotty success at self-sufficiency, and its recalcitrance at the top in the face of wide discontent below. Distressed at the news, and looking for an excuse to revisit a country I felt comfortable in, I went back to Cuba for a few weeks to see for myself.

In many ways the Cuba I returned to was the same one I had left more than thirteen months earlier. The Malecón was still the best show in town. The sugar, symphony, and baseball seasons were all in full swing. Salvador González's Afro-Cuban mural still proved popular. José Martí and Karl Marx still shared the same billboards. Nitza Villapol remained the cook in every Cuban's kitchen.

And on television, Fidel was still giving speeches. The last television I watched before I left in January 1991 showed Castro speaking to an auditorium full of university students. When I flipped on a set thirteen months later there was the familiar face telling his people that they may be facing the most difficult year yet. I had tuned in the Fidel Channel.

I brought a passel of letters with me from Cubans outside their homeland to relatives within. One was from Jorge Daubar, the author of *Capablanca*, who had married a Peruvian woman in Lima. Finally out of the country, he wrote me his full story. He had suffered a bullet wound and imprisonment at a very young age fighting the Batista regime in the 1950s. In the opening years of the Revolution he supported the government, but he soon felt Castro had betrayed his people, and joined up with one of the early counterrevolutionary groups. "In that struggle I was again injured by a bullet, which rendered me an invalid, and I was sent to prison. Later they let me complete my sentence at home under house arrest. In 1973, ten years after the first incident, I took part in a second conspiracy that was uncovered. My *compañeros* were sent to prison. I was under arrest for a few days and then let go." From then on, he wrote, he gave the appearance of having reformed. After Daubar married in Peru, he and his new wife moved to Miami, and he linked up with a centrist, nonviolent anti-Castro group. "When you deliver the letter to my mother, tell her that you saw me and that I'm all right. Tell her about the house we're living in, how we're adapting, about the computer, and my friends. Just don't tell her I'm in a political group. I don't want her to worry about me."

I honored Daubar's request. I visited his mother at her home in the Vedado section of Havana. For twenty minutes she quizzed me all about Jorge, and told me how virtually everything in Havana was now rationed. She hoped to prepare a letter for me to carry back. "When you deliver the letter to my son, tell him you saw me and that I'm all right. Just don't tell him what the conditions here are really like. I don't want him to worry about me."

My next delivery came from Humberto, a Cuban who, like Daubar, arrived in the U.S. in 1991. Humberto had been a *balsero*, someone who risks a trip by raft or inner tube through the Straits of Florida to the United States. In Cuba he had been a driver in the film industry, ferrying movies and projectionists around town. He settled in Arizona, where I met him while he was job hunting. The letter was for his son, who was in his late twenties.

When I got to the third-floor Centro Habana tenement the son shared with other relatives, I learned he was not home. It would do no good for me to return the next day, his sister said sadly, or anytime that weekend. "We don't know when he'll be back." She hesitated. "He's in jail."

Humberto's son had been locked up for trading in the black market. Meat. "He's been in for a while, but they get two-for-one with good behavior. We hope he will be home in two more weeks."

With those depressing visits I began my return trip. The streets were darker. Sidewalks I previously associated with gaiety were just as crowded, but now forlorn. Was I simply projecting my two sad meetings onto the city at large? No; where thirteen months earlier I'd see animated conversations on curbside benches and in vest pocket parks, I now saw slow-motion exchanges, as if discussing a cancerous relative undergoing surgery. With less electricity, there were fewer outside nighttime dominoes games. Store window displays were almost barren, although some showed clothes and manufactured goods left over from more prosperous days. Many movie theaters were open only on the weekends. Office workers had adapted to elevators that, to save even more electricity, stopped every three or four floors only; they had to walk the stairs for the rest. Television broadcast for six hours on weekdays, and twelve on Saturdays and Sundays. *Granma* was reduced to six pages a day, and the dailies in the provinces had been cut back to weeklies. Most copies of *Granma* were distributed in workplaces, and the few for sale on the streets were snatched up immediately. The paper was so thin that all its pages could be posted on the windows of glass-enclosed newsstands. A steady stream of readers slowly circled these booths all day. Castro had reaffirmed the Party's grip on the country's media when he told delegates to the Party Congress that "the press is an instrument of the Revolution, and the first duty of the reporter is to support the Revolution."

City buses had been cut back even more than before. I rode a couple; fewer riders than ever bothered to pay the ten-centavo fare. Bicycles outnumbered cars, trucks, and buses by twenty to one. They were healthy, friendly to the environment, and in a country with meager fuel imports, a necessity. *Bicis*, as bikes are called, sold for sixty to one-hundred twenty pesos at workplaces to virtually everyone with a job. They brought ten times that on the black market.

Repair shops and parking lots for the city's seven-hundred-thousand bikes were all over town. Homemade cargo trailers, seats for children, and rear hub extenders for extra passengers were common. To reach Havana every day, the thousands of commuters from East Havana had simply to pedal their *bicis* up a ramp onto a flatbed trailer to carry them through the tunnel to the city. Even ferry boats across the Bay were equipped for bicycles. The bicyclization of Havana was almost complete.

Galiano, in the past a well-trafficked one-way thoroughfare, had become a nighttime gathering place for *bicis*. Due to the paucity of cars, cyclists crisscrossed the street at will, rode against traffic in all lanes, and turned the entire boulevard into one huge, haywire bike path. Handlebar warning bells chirped incessantly. Few *bicis* had rear reflectors and lots of cyclists pretended cars didn't exist; as a result, accidents between bikes and the few motorized vehicles were common, especially at night. The city government offered classes in bicycle safety.

The shortages revealed things I didn't want to see and provoked comments I didn't want to hear. A white fellow told me, "We call the *bicis* zoos because they're made by lambs," people who do whatever they're told, "they're given away by *el caballo*," the horse—Castro's nickname, "they're ridden by turkeys," dumb people, "and they're stolen by monkeys," blacks.

Austerity brought on a new and complex set of regulations regarding salaries, reduced work schedules, layoffs, job transfers, work in the fields, and vocational schools. The government set up a center so people could trade jobs in much the same manner that they traded homes. The goal was for as many people as possible to find work close to home, thereby reducing transportation pressure.

More Cubans than ever before who had permission to travel outside the country simply stayed abroad. Others who didn't have travel papers left anyway by raft, stolen boat, or in a couple of cases, stolen airplane. Many reached foreign shores, some died along the way, and still others were caught leaving and charged with activity "against the integrity and stability of the nation."

The Malecón had become a small battleground in the fight to maintain some social order. Families and lovers and hustlers still lounged there, but the most romantic stretch in town had also become a commercial free-trade zone. The street-level black market, which a year earlier had meant pesos for dollars, and please Mr. Foreigner, take me to the tourist shop, had become as common as the palm trees. A Cuban could order anything from *jineteros*—bicycles, meat, furniture, clothes, cigars, gasoline, sneakers, construction equipment, milk, beer, rice— every item that was rationed, or totally unavailable through the front door, had developed a back-door supply line. Prices fluctuated wildly, day to day, even hour to hour. Occasional police sweeps cleared the Malecón of its black marketeers, but the effect was to scare off its other habitués, too. "There was a sweep just before Pan Am games," a Malecón regular told me. "And another prior to the Communist Party Congress. Afterward it was empty, and then families started coming out, then the rest of us."

A police sweep had taken place not too long before my visit. Small knots of people had begun forming again, and one lovely February Sunday afternoon the wall was once more filled with families, students, workers, and others taking in the best of Havana. Two women sat talking nearby, one with her son in tow, the other with her healthy four-month-old poodle, Cici. Where does Cici get food to eat? I asked. I'd heard of some dog-owners who made informal arrangements for leftovers with restaurants and workplace cafeterias. "Table scraps," her owner said.

Cigarettes were restricted to three packs a month for each adult. I listened to two university students who shared a cigarette. "Our problem is not the Yankees," said one. "Rather, it's the bureaucracy." To which his companion replied, "Fidel will pull us through. He will think of something."

The stroll along the Malecón brought one surprise. I was on the city side of the thoroughfare near its east end, walking with a photographer from New York with three cameras around his neck and an equipment bag over his shoulder. We were passing a large building when a young man stepped out from behind a column. He wore a clean yellow *guayabera* and spoke in a low, direct voice: "Excuse me for interrupting, but are you foreign journalists?" He clutched some papers in his hand. Somewhat startled, we answered yes, we were.

He identified himself by the name of a well-known human rights group, and asked if he could speak with us. I replied that this was neither the right time nor place to talk—the Malecón was notorious for plainclothes security cops—but I'd meet with him at eight the following morning. He seemed pleased by this. I gave him my first name and suggested the public spot where we could rendezvous. He hesitated at first, then nodded and jotted down the information. He had a shy but earnest countenance. He started to describe his group, but I cut him off. "Save it all for tomorrow. I'll listen to everything you have to say." He nodded, and withdrew back into the shadows. The next morning I wanted until nine. He never appeared, and I went on about my day.

Friends in Havana warned me that crime had risen frightfully during the time I'd been gone. "Everybody has been victimized or knows someone who has. Theft. Robberies. Muggings. I've even heard of a holdup. It was never like this, even two years ago." Small gangs of youngsters on bikes were known to converge on hapless innocents, strip them of anything in their hands, and speed away before the victims knew what hit them. A couple of days later I was walking along the Malecón when *wssssssh*, six teenagers, three on either side, swooped right by me, catching me totally unaware. The closest *comemierda* on the left side reached out his right hand, plucked off my sunglasses, and rode off with the pack. He had barely slowed down to grab the shades, and most remarkably, he never touched my head, not a hair, only the glasses. As the hooligans raced off, the last one glanced back from fifteen yards off.

"*¡Ven acá!*" I screamed, fruitlessly trotting after them—"Come back here!"—which, on reflection, seems a silly thing to have yelled, but under the circumstances anything would have been futile. Losing a ten-dollar pair of drugstore sunglasses was a fairly inexpensive and painless lesson for me. In the free-trade zone, I was told, they could be worn—or sold for pesos, possibly dollars, or traded for a pack of cigarettes—maybe two. The cigarettes could be smoked—or sold for pesos, possibly dollars, or traded for food. The food could be eaten— or sold for pesos, possibly dollars, or traded for clothes. The clothes could be worn—or sold for pesos, possibly dollars, or traded for gasoline. The gasoline could be used—or sold for pesos, possibly dollars, ad infinitum.

One evening I dropped in on a friend in Habana Vieja, and as we sat in his living room someone knocked on the door. My host answered it, retrieved a couple of packs of cigarettes, and gave them to the middle-aged man. In return he was handed a few bulbs of garlic.

"Those were our rationed cigarettes," he explained when he sat back down. "We don't smoke, but we do eat."

I took a cab from his place to an address in Vedado where I was to meet a friend. The driver couldn't find the apartment house, and went to the door of a residence to ask about the street number. From the cab I saw him peel a bill off a wad of money and hand it to the man who answered the door. The man inside then handed him a pack of cigarettes. I asked the driver about it when he got back in the taxi. "I paid him ten pesos for this." He held up the unopened pack.

"Did you know him before?"

"No, but he had some unopened packs out in plain view. He sells them."

Everywhere I went, whomever I spoke with, the talk drifted to the underground price of this item or that product. Most of a typical Cuban salary of 175 pesos monthly was spent on items outside the legitimate ration book economy. Twenty-five pesos for a five-pound sack of rice. One hundred pesos for a case of beer. A fattened-up pig at Christmastime, one thousand pesos. I began asking people how many Cubans they guessed used the free-lance market daily, however benign their participation. Most thought around eighty-five percent.

Supply and demand dominated the flow of cash and merchandise. When dollars entered the equation instead of pesos, the numbers went berserk. You could buy as many eggs as you wanted when I arrived in mid-1990. Now with less chickenfeed, fewer chickens were fed, resulting in a ration allotment of three eggs a person weekly, and one medium-sized chicken for each household of five every three or four weeks. In his position as head of the armed forces, Raúl Castro acknowledged the situation in the Special Period: "Now, more than ever, beans are just as important as bullets."

For the second time in thirty years Cuba had lost its major trading partner and, as before, the country was in a tailspin. The underground market was consumer oriented, better stocked, and more efficient than the state economy it had supplanted. Within a week of my return, this became clear: to understand raw capitalism, it is necessary to travel to a Communist country. Adam Smith had muscled in on Karl Marx.

A flier making the rounds invented a national directive on "Sex During the Special Period." Among the mock edicts:

• sexual activity must be limited to once a week
• you may screw only once during each encounter

- screwing should not last more than a half hour and must adhere
  to the following schedule
  —foreplay and smooching, 5 minutes
  —breast-sucking and oral sex by
  both parties, 15 minutes
  —penetration, 10 minutes
  —total: 30 minutes
- given that couples sweat a lot in our climate, use of the bed is
  prohibited to save on soap for sheets and pillowcases, and wear
  and tear on mattresses
- in the heat of the summer, it is authorized to make love on the
  rooftops, stairs, beaches, and deserted bus stops (if there are any)
- erections are only allowed during the sex act (a limp penis doesn't
  waste energy)
- the vagina must remain closed on holidays
- masturbation will be punished with the death penalty for wasting
  milk products

That week the country's Ecumenical Council announced that sev-
enty-thousand copies of the New Testament would be distributed
through Cuba by the end of the year. The news reminded me to drop
in at Adath Israel synagogue to see Abe the kosher butcher. He had
recently returned from his first trip outside the country, a one-month
stay in Miami with a cousin who owns two clothing shops. Electronic
gadgetry astounded him. "The cars sing when you open the door!
Everything is automated there. And the streets are silent at night."
He dropped in on the Cuban synagogue in Miami. "They have the
same problem we do—difficulty getting a minyan." A rabbi from
Guadalajara, Mexico, was visiting the Patronato across town. He was
in Havana for a few days to gauge the needs of Cuban Jews. One of
their needs was temporarily met the previous year. A mohel had come
from Panama, and within two days performed seven circumcisions on
Jews between two and twenty-six.

From the Patronato I went over to the home of Pablo Armando
Fernández, the writer whose house Jacobo Timerman had the audacity
to criticize. He looked literary dapper in loafers, maroon suspenders
holding up designer jeans, a blue-striped shirt, and black tortoiseshell
glasses. And he was as engaging as ever, agonizing over an invitation
to visit Boston, and proud of the most recent issue of *Unión*, the writers
union literary journal that he still edited. I passed on a joke I'd heard
earlier that day: "You know the three great triumphs of the Revolution,
don't you?"

He looked at me quizzically.

"Education. Health. Athletics. And you know the three great failings of the Revolution?" He tilted his head.

"Breakfast. Lunch. Dinner." He grimaced.

Earlier that evening a functionary from the Ministry of Foreign Relations had brought three young researchers from a Washington think tank by Pablo Armando's house. I wrote in my notes, "PAF—still hail fellow, still well met." The IBM clone computer on his living room table was churning out stacks of manuscripts. "The Michelangelo virus is scheduled to strike tomorrow," he explained. "I'm doing this just in case." Pablo Armando Fernández uses Wordstar 6.0.

The fiction best-sellers that week were (4) *Detective Imai's Last Case*, a thriller by a Russian involving U.S. and Japanese spies; (3) *Ismaelillo*, by José Martí, described as "a notebook of poems that marked the birth of literary modernism in the Americas"; (2) *Girls*, a love story copublished by Cuban and Russian houses; and (1) *Golden Oldies*, stories and legends for young readers. The nonfiction list: (4) *Anatomy for Children*; (3) *Interview with History*, by Oriana Fallaci; (2) *Frank País: Between the Sun and the Mountains*, a two-volume biography of a revolutionary well known within Cuba; and (1) *Einstein: Life, Death, and Immortality*, by B. Kuznetsov.

On my way over to visit Nitza Villapol the next day I stopped by the writers union office. A worker said, "Miriam asked me to say hello to you." La Plume de Matanzas! I hadn't thought about her in a long time. "Please send her my good wishes." I carried with me a two-day old *USA Today*. Miriam's messenger asked, "Anything in there about Cuba?" I pointed to a one-paragraph story on the international news page. It said Cuba has a dismal human rights record. "Ah, well. At least it's a small story."

Nitza answered the door. She was feeding her mother. "Times are hard. They were even harder in the first years of the Revolution. A solution? I don't know. No one is starving. Would you like some coffee?" She spooned raw brown sugar and ground coffee into boiling water, and pouring the whole concoction through a cheesecloth filter.

"The *Miami Herald* came and interviewed me. I should be happy: they made me two years younger than I am. They all want to know how we still eat." She poured us each a shot of rum and started to wash the dishes. Her television show had been shuffled over to Saturdays at six P.M. Viewers had been introduced to grapefruit steak: fried grapefruit rind with garlic and lemon. Cuba was becoming a country of vegetarians, and not by choice.

I got together with Salvador González after he returned from Santiago de Cuba, where he had gone for his grandmother's funeral. He had spent three months in Venezuela painting an Afro-Cuban mural on the Caracas Hilton. His work ended up about fifty yards long divided into ten panels, each one seven yards high. The panel with Changó, said one newspaper, portrayed two peacocks holding the deity's symbolic basin, "from whose wings fall the heads of blacks with rainbows springing from their mouths." González calls the mural *Son of the Sun.*

In Caracas, González threw himself into the local art scene. He exhibited at a gallery show and hosted workshops; he spoke at seminars and went to parties. Every experience exhilarated him. Fresh slang, all the art supplies he needed, new landmarks, indigenous music! Four months after his return to Cuba he was still intoxicated by the experience: "It has broadened my perspective. On everything."

The old Hemingway haunt, El Floridita, had reopened. It was the most expensive restaurant in the country, it took credit cards and reservations, and played on the Hemingway connection shamelessly. La Piña de Plata, a restaurant next door, served the same food from the same kitchen at half the price. Alba came with me to El Floridita one evening. From the front door we could see through the bar into the dining room, where seventeen of the twenty tables were vacant. This was at 9:45, prime dinner hour in formal establishments. The uniformed doorman said they were full. "But you only have people at three tables. Can't you seat us?"

"We only seat by reservation. Have you tried La Bodeguita del Medio? It's only a few blocks away."

"Yes, I've eaten there many times. Now surely you can let us have a table, can't you?"

"We have reservations for ten o'clock we must honor, that will fill us up." I got mildly pushy, and he became somewhat obsequious. "Just a moment please," he said, and ducked inside to huddle with the manager. He came back all smiles. "Right this way." He ushered us to a table where a waiter brought us complimentary daiquiris.

Some selections from the menu: "Gulf shrimp cocktail, the way Hemingway liked it," $13; black caviar with Melba toast and herbed butter, $16; Floridita cream soup with seafood, onions, tomato, and leek, cooked with wine and garnished with diced lobster; $4; "the great Hemingway plate: lobster, shrimp, and fish in garlic sauce, with capers and exotic vegetables," $30.

The help wore red jackets and white slacks or skirts. Most of them were middle-aged or older, and looked like wary, veteran New York servers. The table came with fresh flowers, cloth napkins, and an hors d'oeuvre platter. Hardship in the rest of the country served to reinforce the Floridita as a refuge for foreigners. A forty-year-old *Esquire* article that called El Floridita one of the best bars in the world was framed on the wall. A trio roamed the room.

Manuel Trasancos, the manager, seemed indifferent to any questions about his restaurant. "The place was not remodeled. It was restored, to exactly the way it was in Hemingway's day. We even have the same bar"—he rapped the wood—"polished, of course. We've used the same colors and the same furniture. The painting above the bar has been reproduced as close to the original as possible. We charge these prices because we have the highest-quality service. The value of the product is the best in the country. Our prices are far less than the leading restaurants in New York or Mexico City. The barman who worked here when Hemingway came still tends bar. Antonio Melián." A bust of Hemingway sits in a niche against a wall. His stool at the end of the bar has been roped off. On the wall letters spelled out *The Cradle of the Daiquiri*.

Can Cubans come here? I asked. "Yes, of course. They can come as guests of foreigners. Or they can make a reservation." Yet something told me that this possibility, like so many others in Cuba, was only theoretical. Alba laughed at the notion that a Cuban could call up and reserve a dinner table to be paid for in dollars.

Most of the ten o'clock reservations must have been no-shows, because by eleven only three more parties had arrived. A roving photographer charged five dollars a picture. Our waiter brought a humidor with the finest Havanas. Some Parisians at the next table asked the trio to play a cha-cha. "*Ah, los francesitos*," Alba said with condescension; the dear little Frenchmen. The men's bathroom attendant spent his time drying damp towels under the electric hot-air blower. A crisp, new Che Guevara three-peso note rested on top of his tip tray.

I drove over to Pinar del Río to see the Forestales' parent team play a doubleheader. A hitchhiker I picked up on the way tried his broken English: "I love your president, George Bush. He is very pretty. Democracy!" New billboards said, REVOLUTION, I BELIEVE IN YOU and RESIST DIFFICULTIES—WE WILL WIN. The Pinar del Río team adhered to the second of those; they were leading the western division of the Selective League. Their opponents that day were the Serranos, then in first place in the eastern division.

Capitán San Luis Stadium was named for a revolutionary who fought in the Sierra Maestra with the *fidelistas* and in Bolivia alongside Che. I arrived at the revolutionary's stadium in the bottom half of the first inning, just in time to see the Pinar del Río right fielder hit a three-run homer over the left field wall. Juan Castro, the Forestales' manager, was standing behind the dugout. His team had won thirteen of forty-nine games the year I traveled with them, and finished in last place in the National League. This year they were again last, but with a slightly improved record, 14-34. Pedro Luis Lazo, the lanky young pitcher I had seen the previous year, had been promoted from the Forestales to the parent club, where he was 2-0 on the season. "The Havana team has great respect for him," Castro said. Madera, the catcher I admired, also played for the parent club and was batting .333. I asked Castro about Lázaro Junco, the Matanzas slugger whose home run ball may have reached the moon by now. He started the season with 312 career home runs. "He's leading the league in homers already. Eight." And Félix Asqui, the left-handed pitcher who wanted my glove? "He's at home in Viñales recovering from a shoulder injury." Jorge Luis Paula, the third baseman from the Forestales, was also now playing in the Selective League. He was on the bench that day. I ran into El Gnomo, the Forestales' trainer. He asked me about major-leaguers and I asked him about selective-leaguers.

A sign on the left field wall said, TO PLAY SPORTS IS TO THINK OF THE FUTURE. That's what Rene Arocha thought. The previous summer, after the Cuban national baseball team completed a series in the States, pitcher Rene Arocha slipped away from the others and into a waiting car at Miami International Airport. He is the only Cuban baseball player ever to have defected to the United States. "How did players react when Arocha stayed in the U.S.?" I asked El Gnomo.

"We were shocked at first, of course, but if that's what he wants to do, fine. He's a good pitcher, but his fastball isn't very fast. He's a fan of Nolan Ryan's."

Pinar del Río split the doubleheader with the Serranos, but they kept the lead in the western division.

I also dropped by the cigar factory, where Segundo was reading the morning news to the workers. Israel raids Lebanon. The U.S. and Russia establish a territorial waters treaty. Cuba condemns accusations made at a human rights meeting in Switzerland. Rosa María Valdés, the tobacco roller who had befriended me the previous trip, invited me to visit with her, her husband, and parents that evening. They were formal and polite until the underground market was mentioned. Then they spat out price after price and assailed the current state of the economy. "It's out of control. We never know one week to the next what's available."

María Blanca, the librarian who had helped me find the García Márquez column about Graham Greene, had invited me over to her place, too, where she, I, her brother and two sisters, and a few others sipped rum and talked late into the night. They all said they were optimistic about the future of their country. One said, "Fidel will not let us down."

Cienfuegos was my next out-of-town destination. On the way some hitchhikers and I stopped at a roadside stand for oranges—eight for thirty centavos. At a rest area we each bought a hardboiled egg, bread, and a *cafecito*—less than a peso. Billboards with artwork said, WORKING TODAY FOR EFFICIENCY IN THE SUGAR INDUSTRY and BAY OF PIGS EVERY DAY. I first stopped at Cruces to visit with the elderly small-town *santero* I had met before. He poured some wine he had made. "I use equal parts water, sugar, and carrots. Then I let it sit for forty days. Here." He and others in Cruces said that their living conditions are slightly better than in the city. "We're accustomed to having city folk coming out on weekends to trade," a woman told me. "They have the goods and we have the food."

In Cienfuegos I picked up Orlando García at the writers union office, and we drove out to the Botanical Gardens, where his wife worked. Cutbacks had affected some research projects, one of the scientists said, but so far they have been able to continue with the work they'd undertaken before the Special Period. Just as many foreign tourists still visit, but fewer Cubans come out to the grounds.

Fefi, one of the three women from the public relations office at the Hotel Jagua I had met, still worked there. She invited me to her English class, where the teachers monopolized my time. One of them, a thin woman I called La Flaca, joined me for a bite later. She was also the school's administrator.

"My day begins when I drop off my daughters at day-care and primary school. Then I'm at the school all day and sometimes in the evening." La Flaca had been married twice, and had gone to college at Santa Clara. "My mother used to commute weekly to Havana to get her degree. This was before the Revolution. She was the only one in her family who went to college."

La Flaca was tall and looked perpetually hungry. "I hardly eat anything. It's not the scarcity of food, it's just that I'm consumed by my work." She lived without music, singing, lovers, and dancing. She shook her head. "I was in the Party for fourteen years and I could rejoin if I wanted. They would ask for the opinions of my co-workers and send for the records where I used to work. I just didn't fit in there. I criticized. Constructively, but I criticized. They didn't like that. I was a model worker and I got along with my co-workers. Here, I've committed myself to more than I can do. I read in *Granma* last week about a new stress clinic opening in Havana. I want to go to there next week to see a psychologist."

The paella at La Covadonga, across from the Jagua, was as good as I remembered it. Afterward I walked to the end of the street to a small traffic circle that looks out over Cienfuegos Bay. It was a gathering spot for most of the city's youth and, it seemed, all of its *bicis*. One teenager motioned me over. We chatted aimlessly, then he pulled out some money. He had a ten-peso note issued by the Bank of Spain in 1896 for use in Cuba during the War of Independence. The bill was sealed in plastic and looked good as new. "It's worth two thousand dollars," he assured me, "or at least fifteen hundred. My grandfather collected old money from all over the world. He died three years ago." Now his family needed new dollars more than old pesos. I demurred, but he kept pressing. "How much would you pay for it?"

"I just have no idea of its value."

"It's worth one thousand dollars, that I know. Collectors in Madrid or Florida will tell you. You could ask them." When I passed back through Miami on my way home I did just that. A dealer who specialized in historical notes said, "I know the exact bill you're talking about. It's worth five dollars; seven-fifty if it's in excellent condition."

Orlando had hoped to go back to Havana with me, but his child had taken ill and he had to stay in Cienfuegos. Instead I took a doctor that la Flaca had introduced me to. Dr. Smith—his name comes from Jamaican ancestry—worked eleven months of the year in Namibia; he had just completed his one-month home leave and was to fly out the next day from José Martí International Airport. "This isn't part of my national service. I volunteered for it." He had also worked in Bulgaria, Switzerland, Tanzania, and Uganda. "They speak eighteen dialects in Namibia. To communicate with most patients we talk to the nurse in English and then she translates to the patient."

I flew to Santiago de Cuba for my last out-of-town trip and stayed at the Leningrado, which had not changed its name to the St. Petersburg. The next morning I rented a car for the drive to Manuel Tamayo's farmhouse. I had maintained contact with him and his family through correspondence with Dénices, the teacher whose school was behind Manuel's house.

Most of the family was home the rainy Saturday afternoon I arrived. I recognized all of them and forgot the names of most. Despite the fact that we had almost nothing in common, they made me feel at home—comfortable, rather than special. I drifted from son to daughter, in-law to neighbor, chatting about crops and rain and cars and Havana. One of Manuel's sons, an army lieutenant in his twenties, had died in a traffic accident the previous summer. His picture hung on the wall. Another son asked me to drive him on a beer run. We traveled a couple of kilometers east to a large, open-air dispensary with a tin roof, where dozens of men between seventeen and thirty stood in line with empty pails. *"¿El último?"* we asked. The late-afternoon crowd was noisy, not quite boisterous, waiting for its peso-a-liter beer. Finally our turn came and we bought ten pesos' worth.

Manuel and his brother Rafael, whose daughter initiated my contact with the clan when I gave her a ride the previous year, grow bananas, coffee, and oranges on land they own. After their state quota had been filled, they are free to consume the rest or trade it, within reason.

The sound of squealing pigs came from behind Manuel's house. A baseball game was on the radio. Manuel asked what propaganda people in the United States heard about Cuba. "How do they see change there?" He dipped a glass in the pail of beer for me. Then he took the offensive. "How much does it cost to see a doctor in your country? No Cuban has ever died of hunger since the Revolution. No one sleeps in the streets. No one."

Rafael showed up. He was a few years younger than Manuel and smiled more. When the topic of the underground economy rose, Manuel was quick to say, "A revolutionary is never involved in the black market." I asked Rafael why so many people went outside the established system to get food.

"Well," he started, "people are confused. They—"

"No!" Manuel. "They are *not* confused. After thirty-three years, they know what the Revolution is and they have decided they are not part of it!"

"How have things changed here in the last year?"

"There have been no changes. Everything is the same." Manuel's words had a finality that prohibited further discussion.

Dénices arrived. She had just received the telegram I'd sent from Havana alerting the family to my arrival. We chatted as if our last conversation had been fourteen hours earlier instead of fourteen months. Her married daughter was pregnant. "They're already calling me grandma!" she said with a laugh. Her younger daughter had gone to the national Young Pioneers convention where Fidel had spoken. "She wants to go into the sciences and see the world."

We were called to dinner. One of the pigs out back had been slaughtered, skewered, and cooked over an open fire, and we had a big countryside dinner of roast pork, sweet potato, peppers, rice, and beans. "We do this once a month or so," Manuel said. Afterward he and his *compañeros* played dominoes on the front porch. Again, Dénices gave me her room with the mosquito netting.

The next morning before I left she and I talked about the prices people were compelled to pay for goods. "I've seen pullovers for 180 pesos. I've even had to pay thirty pesos for a three-peso item. I don't know how we can go on like this."

"Manuel says nothing has changed. He seems as supportive as ever."

"Yes, of course. You have to keep in mind what the Revolution has meant to him. He owes everything he has to it."

Guantánamo was only a few hours away, and I arrived there in the early afternoon. I went over to visit Rebeca and her husband at home. She was the provincial UNEAC president who had helped me so much the previous year. She had written me a letter asking if I could find any books about contemporary Spanish literature, and I brought what I could. She filled me in on the local writers union activities. Her office had a small budget for parties, and my visit provided the excuse to buy some beer and rum. "There'll be about twenty people there this evening. You may remember some of them."

I did. I was among friends. I sat at a table with four others talking about music, countries, and literature, the conversation zinging like a ball in a pinball machine. Appropriately loosened up, I asked two of them a question I'd heard in Havana. "Do you know the definition of socialism?" They looked at me rather oddly.

"Socialism is the stage between capitalism and capitalism." The two burst out laughing, then one of them repeated it for the others at our table. Dead silence. It wasn't his delivery.

I told Rebeca what I had learned about the song "Guantanamera." She added to the lore: "It seems around 1950 a man named Diablo Wilson saw a beautiful woman here in Guantánamo. Wilson made up what became the chorus to the song we know today. From here he drifted to Palma Soriano," 125 kilometers west of Guantánamo, "and then to Havana where Joseíto Fernández picked it up. A student in Havana who had heard it went to school in the States, and met Pete Seeger and taught it to him. Whenever the song was written about in the 1950s Fernández said he sang it. It wasn't until 'Guantanamera' became popular in the States and came back to Cuba that Fernández identified himself as its writer, but not before. At least that's the way I heard it."

By the time I got back to Havana the young man jailed for black marketeering had been released on good behavior. I gave him the mail from his father.

The subject about which I found near unanimity was the Rapid Action Brigades, a new form of street-level terror the government had instituted. These groups were established to intimidate dissidence by confronting the dissenter at his or her home. These volunteer shock troops were to steer their backsliding neighbors away from counterrevolutionary tendencies. Usually, though, *brigadistas* were from other parts of town, bused in for an action. When they would go door-to-door soliciting reinforcements they were often met with resistance. In the eastern end of the country people I spoke with dismissed the *brigadistas* as little more than paper tigers. In Havana, Party members and officials and everyone else expressed off-the-record embarrassment, agreeing that they were a loathsome addition to a police network already too thick. A mild-mannered music teacher in his fifties snapped when I asked about the brigades. "They're insulting. We have gone backward by instituting them. They are disgusting. Vile. They are pure fascism. They give air to the fire."

One of the best-known and most appalling uses of the brigades took place in the fall of 1991 at the East Havana home of a thirty-seven-year-old poet from Matanzas, María Elena Cruz Varela, whose human rights group, Alternative Criterion, had issued a simple call for a general amnesty for political prisoners and talks on a multiparty political system. She also wrote a letter to Castro condemning his regime. Rowdy *brigadistas* stormed her home and forced her to eat her words. Literally. On paper. In front of her daughter. Then she was dragged down the stairs and arrested for promoting a dissident group. A neighbor across the street witnessed the mob and started to take pictures, only to be noticed by security officers, who went to her home and demanded the film. Cruz Varela soon began serving a two-year prison sentence.

The need for substantial and immediate change in the system was obvious to Cubans at all levels. Lisandro Otero, in contrast to his hard-line days, wrote of "disturbing signs of intolerance." His article, published in a Venezuelan literary review, said, "In the Cuban intellectual environment it is now understood that silence does more damage than disagreement. . . . [T]o open a space for dialogue, discussion, and criticism" would be indispensable. His essay made its way back to Havana and circulated hand-to-hand like a *samizdat*. "It got as much attention as if it had appeared on the front page of *Granma*," a friend said. No Rapid Action Brigade descended on Otero's home, but after he published a further critique in *Le Monde Diplomatique* a few months later, his easy access to foreign travel credentials was revoked. He had to go through conventional channels "as a common citizen," a friend wrote, "and as a common citizen he was treated."

Otero's first polemic was prompted by the state's reaction to the Cuban movie *Alice in Wondertown*, a black parody of the bureaucracy's grotesque excesses. The film proved immediately popular, and long lines formed for every showing. Within four days of its release thugs were sent into the theater shouting "¡Fi-del! ¡Fi-del!" The movie was pulled from circulation until the international film festival, when it had a restricted run.

A few weeks before I arrived back, singer Pedro Luis Ferrer gave a concert at the Mella Theater. Ferrer started his musical career in the 1960s as rhythm guitar player for a rock band called Los Dadas. He subsequently formed his own band and softened his music. He became well known and toured outside the country. In 1988 he told a Peruvian newspaper of his admiration for the music of Celia Cruz, the salsa queen who left Cuba for the United States in the early 1960s, adding that she should be allowed to return to perform if she wanted. When Ferrer got back home, his music was taken off the radio and he was sent into internal exile for a while. In the middle of 1991 his public attitude changed, and by early 1992 he was allowed to perform at the Mella. Word-of-mouth filled the theater.

Pedro Luis Ferrer has a comforting voice well suited for sweet protest music. His songs that February night, alternately impish and poetic, were full of invective against the government. The audience cheered when he sang of their city,

> *Which Havana should I tell you about, compañero?*
> *The one in which Guillén said, "I have equality"?*
> *Or the one that shouts at me loudly,*
> *"You can't come in!"*

One song used irony to address tourism apartheid:

> Cuba is 100 percent Cuban, and my money is 100
>   percent Cuban.
> Tomorrow I'll get a room at the best hotel in Havana,
> Then I'll go to Varadero and reserve a beach house
> With the money I earned cutting cane . . .
> Tomorrow I'll go to Marina Hemingway and rent a
>   yacht,
> I want to spend my afternoon catching lobster and
>   enjoying the plenty of our shoreline.
> My money is as Cuban as the mambís. . . .

A song of tolerance for homosexuals asked, why criticize gays when we should criticize the elite, who even now eat like royalty.

Agents of the interior ministry, whose building is less than a block from the Mella, began to make themselves conspicuous at the theater. They started down the aisles as Ferrer sang about Fidel,

> Even when you know the answer is no, say yes to him.
> To contradict him is worse for you.

The audience repeated the lines. Then, apparently addressing the police, he taunted softly, "Why don't you sing something for us?"

Ferrer's most elaborate ballad rang as clear and patriotic as any in recent generations of protest music in the Americas. Again alluding to Castro—

> My grandfather built this house at great sacrifice . . .
> He built the walls brick by brick.
> His aim was to make a big house
> So that all could live within.
> Now, in order to move even a pebble you have to ask permission.
> If grandfather doesn't agree, no one can change the building . . .
> Have patience with grandfather.
> Don't say anything against him. Remember what he's done . . .
> Don't forget, grandfather has a gun and a knife.
> Unless we take them away, danger will come.

By song's end, cops had pulled the plug on Ferrer's backup band, and only his voice and his acoustic guitar were audible. Finally, plainclothesmen went up to the singer, took him by his arms, and led him offstage. As he went out of view, Ferrer said to the audience, "This will have a second part." His fans erupted in rhythmic clapping. When security forces started to herd them out, they noticed some carried cassette recorders. Women jammed the tapes into their blouses before cops got to them.

Pedro Luis Ferrer was back on the streets quickly, but word of the concert spread throughout Havana and the whole country. I first learned of it in Santiago de Cuba. I asked about it at a friend's place in Havana and another visitor at the same apartment looked up. He had worked for a few years for the interior ministry at the Combinado del Este prison, but now he had a different point of view.

"Would you be interested in hearing a tape of the concert?"

He had a pirate cassette, and made me a copy that afternoon. Handing it over he warned, "Don't even leave it in your room or pack it in your suitcase when you go. Keep it safely in a pocket all the time."

As the country groped for equilibrium, small, spasmodic indicators of discontent became more public. Huge letters stenciled on a few walls around Havana spelled out a simple message: NO. One Saturday afternoon pedestrians in Vedado looked up to see thousands of little pieces of paper floating down from the sky. They read DOWN WITH CASTRO and FREEDOM MAY 20TH.† Someone had tossed the tissue-thin papers from the top of a tall apartment house. Within minutes police arrived to gather them up, but not before passers-by scooped up some themselves. The same messages floated down from two other buildings in the following weeks. A friend happened by one of the paper drops and, startled, reached out to grab some. I had known him for almost two years, during which he had always shown revolutionary support. He went to a hiding place in his house excitedly and produced the little papers. "A couple of times I've seen buses rounding corners, and as they were in the middle of the street someone tossed antigovernment propaganda out a window so it scattered all over the intersection."

---

†The date in 1902 the Cuban republic began. It followed the formal end of more than three years of U.S. military occupation, which in turn succeeded almost four hundred years of Spanish rule.

I asked, "Who will have the temerity to tap Fidel on the shoulder and say, *¿El último?*'"

His face lengthened. "I don't know. Not anyone anytime soon."

From the Malecón I could see an oil freighter out at sea move toward harbor. Storm clouds threatened but hadn't yet materialized. Two giggling three-year-old girls sat facing one another playing patty-cake. A couple of university students concentrated on their chess game. An onlooker spoke pridefully of his wife's work on a two-week volunteer crew picking crops in the countryside. "Stability is just around the corner," he said. "You'll see." Couples lay on the seawall. Families had makeshift picnics. A portable tape deck blared out salsa for a cluster of excited teenagers. An aging angler pulled in a tiny fish. "I fish all the time," he said, "but I've never caught one here. This must be my lucky day."

Acknowledgments

F ive years ago I started with a healthy dose of ignorance about daily life in Cuba. To bring myself up to speed I received help from innumerable people. My best sources about Cuba were in Cuba itself. If this seems a tad self-evident, consider that many people warned me before I left that I would hear only the Party line, that no one would open up to a foreigner, that the sheer weight of the country's complexities would frustrate my efforts. On the contrary: I found Cubans willing—anxious, even—to talk about baseball, Africa, God, and books. And about their own country. After a while I sensed that far from clamming up, they shed inhibitions to talk about everything. Sometimes my only problem was to shut them up.

Most of the Cubans who helped are mentioned in the book. Rather than repeat their names here, I've listed other people whose counsel, libraries, editing skills, translation advice, and lodging have made my job far less formidable, and certainly less solitary. Often their help came with unexpected enthusiasm; always it was received with heartfelt warmth.

The standard acknowledgments page includes a disclaimer to the effect that the counsel was theirs, the opinions and mistakes the author's. True enough, but in the case of a subject of such volatility, even more so. Emotions provoked by the mere mention of Cuba make those who know the country well wary of its exploiters. To state the obvious: the people and institutions below do not necessarily share my perspective on all things Cuban.

First and foremost, my appreciation to the Cuban Writers and Artists Union (la Unión de Escritores y Artistas de Cuba; UNEAC), whose International Relations section and provincial offices hosted me with kindness. In the States, Sandra Levinson and the staff and library of the Center for Cuban Studies in New York became a valuable source of information. Likewise, the reference room at the Radio Martí Program in Washington, D.C., proved most helpful. My gratitude to Laurien Alexandre, Dan Anderson, Bill Brent, Irasema Coronado, Enrique Fernández, Roberto González Echevarría, Felicia Gustin, Martín Hacthoun, Luis Eugenio Hartly Campbell, Pamela Hayes-Bohanan, Robert Houston, Debra Kay Huffman, Milton Jamail, Michael Malone, Jane McManus, Gregory McNamee, Charles Miller, Jim Mullin, Boyd, Laurie, and Sara Nicholl, Dan Okrent, David

Ossman, Louis A. Pérez, Jr., Nancy Postero, Ron Ridenour, Eliana Rivero, Ellen Rosensweig, Sharon Seymour, Martha Sowerwine, Deanne Stillman, Lynn Stoner, Sandy Tolan, Jesús Vega, Mercedes Wangüemert-Peña, Judith Walcott, Mark Weiss, and Alan West. *Saludos* and an *abrazote* to you all.

—TM

Bibliography

Abbot, Rev. Abiel. *Letters Written in the Interior of Cuba, Between the Mountains of Arcana, to the East, and of Cusco, to the West, in the Months of February, March, April, and May, 1828.* Boston: Bowles and Dearborn, 1829.

Alexander, Karl. *Papa and Fidel.* New York: Tom Doherty Associates, 1989.

Araújo, Nara. *Viajeras al Caribe.* Havana: Casa de las Américas, 1983.

Atkins, Edwin F. *Sixty Years in Cuba.* New York: Arno Press, 1980 (originally published: 1926).

Baker, Carlos. *Ernest Hemingway: A Life Story.* New York: Avon, 1980.

Ballagas, Emilio. *Emilio Ballagas.* Havana: Colección Órbita, 1972.

Ballou, Maturin M. *History of Cuba, or, Notes of a Traveller in the Tropics. Being a Political, Historical, and Statistical Account of the Island, from Its First Discovery to the Present Time.* Boston: Phillips, Sampson and Company, 1854.

Barbour, Thomas. *A Naturalist in Cuba.* Boston: Little, Brown, 1945.

Barnet, Miguel. *Autobiography of a Runaway Slave.* New York: Pantheon, 1968.

———. *Rachel's Song.* Translated by W. Nick Hill. Willimantic, Ct.: Curbstone Press, 1991 (originally published: 1969).

Barrera Figueroa, Orlando. *Sancti Spíritus: Sinopsis Histórica.* Santiago de Cuba: Editorial Oriente, 1986.

Beals, Carleton. *The Crime of Cuba.* Philadelphia: J. B. Lippincott, 1933.

Benjamin, Medea, Joseph Collins, and Michael Scott. *No Free Lunch: Food and Revolution in Cuba Today.* San Francisco: Institute for Food and Development Policy, 1984.

Bolívar Aróstegui, Natalia. *Los orishas en Cuba.* Havana: Ediciones Unión, 1991.

Bremer, Frederika. *Homes of the New World; Impressions of America.* Vol. 2. New York: Harper & Brothers, 1853.

Cabrera Infante, G. *Holy Smoke.* London: Faber and Faber, 1985.

———. *Three Trapped Tigers.* Translated by Donald Gardner and Suzanne Jill Levine. New York: Avon, 1985 (originally published: 1965).

———. *View of Dawn in the Tropics.* Translated by Suzanne Jill Levine. London: Faber and Faber, 1988.

Cardenal, Ernesto. *In Cuba.* Translated by Donald D. Walsh. New York: New Directions, 1974.

Carpentier, Alejo. *The Chase.* New York: Noonday Press, 1990 (originally published: 1956).

Dana, Richard Henry, Jr. *To Cuba and Back.* Carbondale: Southern Illinois University Press, 1966 (originally published: 1859).

Davey, Richard. *Cuba, Past and Present.* London: Chapman & Hall, 1898.

Dechamps, R., R. Carrera, A. Hartman, and T. Avella. "La Croix de Christophe Colomb à Baracoa (Cuba): Son Histoire et l'Identification de Son Bois." *PACT—Journal of the European Study Group on Physical, Chemical, Mathematical and Biological Techniques Applied to Archaeology* 22: (6), 389–400.

Desnoes, Edmundo. *Inconsolable Memories.* New York: New American Library, 1967 (Originally published: 1965).

Estep, E. Ralph. *El Toro: A Motor Car Tour of Interior Cuba.* Detroit: Packard Motor Car Company, 1909.

Ferlinghetti, Lawrence. *One Thousand Fearful Words for Fidel Castro.* San Francisco: City Lights, 1961.

Fernández Santalices, Manuel. *Las calles de la Habana intramuros.* Miami: Saeta Ediciones, 1989.

Frank, Waldo. *Cuba: Prophetic Island.* New York: Marzani & Munsell, 1961.

Fuentes, Norberto. *Hemingway in Cuba.* Translated by Consuelo E. Corwin. Secaucus, N.J.: Lyle Stuart, 1984.

Gallenga, A. *The Pearl of the Antilles.* London: Chapman & Hall, 1873.

Gébler, Carlo. *Driving Through Cuba: Rare Encounters in the Land of Sugar Cane and Revolution.* New York: Simon & Schuster, 1988.

Gray, Richard Butler. *José Martí, Cuban Patriot.* Gainesville: University of Florida Press, 1962.

Greene, Graham. *Our Man in Havana.* New York: Penguin, 1971 (originally published: 1958).

Guillén, Nicolás. *The Daily Daily.* Translated by Vera M. Kutzinski. Berkeley: University of California Press, 1989.

———. *¡Patria o Muerte! The Great Zoo and Other Poems.* Translated by Robert Márquez. New York: Monthly Review Press, 1972.

Gurney, Joseph John. *A Winter in the West Indies, Described in Familiar Letters to Henry Clay, of Kentucky.* New York: Negro Universities Press, 1969 (originally published: 1840).

Halperin, Maurice. *The Taming of Fidel Castro.* Berkeley: University of California Press, 1981.

Hazard, Samuel. *Cuba with Pen and Pencil.* Hartford, Ct.: Hartford Publishing, 1871.

Hemingway, Ernest. *The Old Man and the Sea.* New York: Scribner's, 1952.

Humboldt, Alexander. *The Island of Cuba.* New York: Negro Universities Press, 1969 (originally published: 1856).

Hurlbert, William Henry. *Gan-Eden; or, Pictures of Cuba.* Boston: Jewett, 1854.

Instituto Cubano de Geodesia y Cartografía y Centro de Estudios Martianos. *Atlas histórico biográfico José Martí.* Havana: 1983.

James, Ariel. *Banes: Imperialismo y nación en una plantación Azucarera.* Havana: Editorial de Ciencias Sociales, 1976.

Jay, W. M. L. *My Winter in Cuba.* New York: E. P. Dutton, 1871.

Jones, LeRoi. *Home: Social Essays.* New York: Morrow, 1966.

Kozol, Jonathan. *Children of the Revolution.* New York: Delacorte Press, 1978.

Krich, John. *A Totally Free Man.* New York: Fireside, 1988.

Kurlansky, Mark. *A Continent of Islands: Searching for the Caribbean Destiny.* New York: Addison-Wesley, 1992.

Langley, Lester D. *The Cuban Policy of the United States: A Brief History.* New York: John Wiley and Sons, 1968.

Lewis, Barry, and Peter Marshall. *Into Cuba.* New York: Alfred van der Marck Editions, 1985.

Lewis, Oscar, Ruth M. Lewis, Susan M. Rigdon. *Four Men: Living the Revolution, An Oral History of Contemporary Cuba.* Urbana: University of Illinois Press, 1977.

Lezama Lima, José. *Paradiso.* Translated by Gregory Rabassa. New York: Farrar, Straus Giroux, 1968 (Originally published: 1966).

Lizaso, Félix. *Martí: Martyr of Cuban Independence.* Translated by Esther E. Shuler. Albuquerque: University of New Mexico Press, 1953.

Lockwood, Lee. *Castro's Cuba, Cuba's Fidel.* Boulder, Co.: Westview Press, 1990.

Martí, José. *Inside the Monster: Writings on the United States and American Imperialism.* Edited by Philip S. Foner. Translated by Elinor Randall. New York: Monthly Review Press, 1975.

———. *Ismaelillo; Versos Libres; Versos Sencillos.* Madrid: Ediciones Cátreda, 1990.

———. *On Art and Literature.* Translated by Elinor Randall. Edited by Philip S. Foner. New York: Monthly Review Press, 1982.

McManus, Jane. *Getting to Know Cuba: A Travel Guide.* New York: St. Martin's, 1989.

Michener, James A., and John Kings. *Six Days in Havana.* Austin: University of Texas Press, 1989.

Miller, Warren. *90 Miles from Home.* Boston: Little, Brown, 1961.

Montejo, Esteban. *The Autobiography of a Runaway Slave.* Edited by Miguel Barnet. Translated by Jocasta Innes. Newark: Pantheon, 1968.

Moore, Carlos. *Castro, the Blacks, and Africa.* Los Angeles: Center for Afro-American Studies, University of California, 1988.

Mora, Giles. *Walker Evans: Havana, 1933.* New York: Pantheon, 1989.

Murphy, Marion Emerson. *The History of Guantánamo Bay.* Guantánamo Bay, Cuba: U.S. Naval Base, 1953 (revised 1964.)

Ortíz, Fernando. *Cuban Counterpoint: Tobacco and Sugar.* Translated by Harriet de Onís. New York, Alfred A. Knopf, 1947 (Originally published: 1940).

Pérez, Louis A., Jr. *Cuba: Between Reform and Revolution.* New York: Oxford University Press, 1988.

Philalethes, Demoticus. *Yankee Travels Through the Island of Cuba; or, The Men and Government, the Laws and Customs of Cuba, as Seen by American Eyes.* New York: D. Appleton & Co., 1856.

Phillips, R. Hart. *Cuba: Island of Paradox.* New York: McDowell, Obolensky, 1959.

Ridenour, Ron. *Backfire: The CIA's Biggest Burn.* Havana: Editorial José Martí, 1990.

Rosshandler, Felicia. *Passing through Havana.* New York: St. Martin's, 1984.

Salkey, Andrew. *Havana Journal.* Middlesex, England: Penguin, 1971.

Senzel, Howard. *Baseball and the Cold War.* New York: Harcourt Brace Jovanovich, 1977.

Smith, Wayne S. *The Closest of Enemies.* New York: W. W. Norton, 1987.

Stubbs, Jean. *Cuba: The Test of Time.* London: Latin American Bureau, 1989.

Suchlicki, Jaime. *Historical Dictionary of Cuba.* Metuchen, N.J.: Scarecrow Press, 1988.

Szulc, Tad. *Fidel: A Critical Portrait.* New York: William Morrow, 1986.

Thomas, Hugh. *Cuba: The Pursuit of Freedom.* New York: Harper & Row, 1971.

Vázquez Gonzaléz, Modesto. *Domino cubano.* Mexico: Federación de Domino Cubano de Mexico, 1982.

Woodruff, Louisa Mathilda. *My Winter in Cuba.* New York. E. P. Dutton, 1871.

Woon, Basil. *When It's Cocktail Time in Cuba.* New York. Horace Liveright, 1928.

Wurdemann, John G. F. *Notes on Cuba.* New York: Arno Press and The New York Times, 1971 (originally published: 1844).

Yglesias, José. *In the Fist of the Revolution.* New York: Pantheon, 1968.

Index

About the Author

TOM MILLER has been writing about the American Southwest and Latin America for more than twenty-five years. His six books include *The Panama Hat Trail* and *On the Border,* and his articles have appeared in *Life,* the *New York Times, Rolling Stone,* and other publications in the United States and Mexico. He lives in Tucson, Arizona.